The Encyclopedia of TV Pets

The Encyclopedia of TV Pets

A Complete History of Television's Greatest Animal Stars

Ken Beck and Jim Clark

RUTLEDGE HILL PRESS®
Nashville, Tennessee
A Division of Thomas Nelson, Inc.
www.ThomasNelson.com

Published by Rutledge Hill Press, a division of Thomas Nelson, Inc., P.O. Box 141000, Nashville, Tennessee 37214.

Library of Congress Cataloging-in-Publication Data

Beck, Ken, 1951–
The encyclopedia of TV pets : a complete history of television's greatest animal stars / Ken Beck and Jim Clark.
p. cm.
Includes bibliographical references and index.
ISBN 1-55853-981-6 (pbk.)
1. Animals on television. I. Title: Encyclopedia of television pets.
II. Clark, Jim, 1960– III. Title.

PN1992.8 .A58 B43 2002
791 .8—dc21 2001007021

Printed in the United States of America
02 03 04 05 06 — 5 4 3 2 1

Contents

Preface vii
Acknowledgments ix
The Abbott and Costello Show 1
The Adventures of Brisco County, Jr. 2
The Adventures of Rin Tin Tin 4
Alex, the Stroh's Beer Dog 7
ALF 10
The Andy Griffith Show 11
Annie Oakley 14
B. J. and the Bear 15
Bachelor Father / Get Smart 18
Baretta 20
The Beverly Hillbillies 23
The Bionic Woman 26
The Black Stallion 29
Blondie 32
Born Free 34
The Brady Bunch 39
Call of the Wild 41
Caroline in the City 44
The Chimp Channel 46
Circus Boy 47
Coach 52
Columbo 53
Corky and White Shadow (The Mickey Mouse Club serial) 54
Cowboy in Africa 56
Daktari 58
Dave's World 67
Dharma & Greg 69
Down and Out in Beverly Hills 71
The Drew Carey Show 73
Dr. Quinn, Medicine Woman 74
Due South 76
The Dukes of Hazzard 79
Early Edition 83
Empty Nest 86
Flipper / Flipper: The New Adventures 90
Frasier 95
Friends 98
Frontier Circus 100
Full House 101
Fury 103
The Gene Autry Show / The Adventures of Champion 108
General Hospital 113
Gentle Ben 115
The Ghost and Mrs. Muir 118
The Greatest Show on Earth 121
Green Acres 122
Hart to Hart 126
The Hathaways 127
Hee Haw 130
Here's Boomer 136
Honey West 138
Hooperman 139
Hopalong Cassidy 141
I Love Lucy / Dennis the Menace 144
In the Heat of the Night 147
Jungle Jim / Bomba the Jungle Boy 148
Lancelot Link, Secret Chimp 150
Land of the Giants 153
Lassie 156
Life Goes On 166
The Life and Times of Grizzly Adams 167

Little House on the Prairie 171
The Little Rascals (Our Gang films) 173
The Littlest Hobo 174
The Lone Ranger 178
Longstreet 186
Mad About You 188
Magnum, P.I. 191
Married . . . With Children 193
Maya 196
Me and the Chimp 199
Meego 201
Mister Ed 204
Morris the Cat 214
Mr. Smith 216
My Friend Flicka 219
My Three Sons 223
Nanny and the Professor 226
National Velvet 228
The Norm Show 230
Northern Exposure 232
100 Deeds for Eddie McDowd 233
The PATSY Awards 235
The People's Choice 242
Petticoat Junction 244
Please Don't Eat the Daisies / The Doris Day Show 250
Punky Brewster 254
Rin Tin Tin K-9 Cop 256
The Roy Rogers Show 258
Run, Joe, Run 265
Sabrina, The Teenage Witch 267
Salty 271
Sam 273
Sergeant Preston of the Yukon 274
Sheena, Queen of the Jungle 279
Skippy (the Bush Kangaroo) / The New Adventures of Skippy 280
Spin City 283
Spuds MacKenzie 285
Star Trek: The Next Generation 286
Taco Bell Chihuahua 288
Tales of the Gold Monkey 289
Tarzan 291
Tequila & Bonetti 296
Thunder 297
The Today Show 299
Topper 309
The Waltons 312
The Westerner 316
Wishbone 318
Bibliography 323
Index 325

Preface

From the early days of television right on up to the beginning of the twenty-first century, TV producers have always known that the right pet in the right cast can help turn a TV show into a hit.

Not only that, the right animal can make a hit series all by itself.

Most fans of TV are familiar with dogs such as Lassie, Rin Tin Tin, Eddie, Wishbone, and Higgins, the Petticoat Junction dog (who became the movie star Benji); horses such as Mister Ed, Silver, Trigger, and Fury; cats such as Morris and Clarence, the cross-eyed lion; the bears on *Gentle Ben* and *Grizzly Adams;* Tarzan's chimpanzee Cheetah; and Arnold the pig.

When you sit down and think about it, we've been blessed with an amazing heritage of creatures that have entered our homes via the TV set. Cats and dogs, sure. Horses, of course. And certainly plenty of lions and tigers, and bears (oh, my!). But think of all of the wonderful chimpanzees, monkeys, and orangutans—not to mention pelicans and cockatoos, elephants and kangaroos, dolphins and sea lions, moose and pigs, and on and on.

When we first considered compiling a book on TV pets, we figured, "Wouldn't it be fun to write some short stories about all of the wonderful animals and show a few pictures of them? What a neat, little project."

We may have expected it to be "little," but little did we expect the exciting adventure (and yes, occasional pitfalls) that awaited us as the book evolved into a nostalgic safari through the marvelous jungle of TV history. Our amazement grew with each new discovery as we steadfastly tracked down the many facts and fun stories behind TV's most interesting animals. We tried our doggonedest to get to more than one source on every critter. Even so, there were still a few animals that proved especially cagey and elusive.

Likewise, we have found sources on the same subject whose tales don't quite dovetail (mainly from a combination of misty memories and the passing of time). And in a few instances, notably the Lone Ranger's Silver, we talked to more than a dozen people who knew the horses from a little bit to a lot, and we still aren't positive that we see clearly through the resulting cloud of dust. (Maybe the horse is the one who should have worn the mask!)

One thing you learn quickly when you get behind the scenes of acting animals is that for every star animal, there is almost always a double or two or three. And if a TV series runs for more than a couple of seasons, that star pig you loved so well may have actually been six or ten or a dozen pigs. Talk about a pig sty of confusion!

So, while we hate to admit it, we would just about bet there are some (we hope only very few) animal "facts" between these pages that might be debatable. But any discrepancies that might have slipped in from the wild will have done so despite our best efforts at training the facts to work together as best as possible.

In any case, we believe that what you'll find in these pages is a comprehensive history of TV's greatest animal actors as told by their owners and trainers and the stuntmen, stuntwomen, and actors who worked with them. There are stories that have never before been published and even some that have never before been told. And the photographs! Included are bushels of dazzling, delightful, and often rare photographs, including many from the personal collections of trainers and others who have worked closely with these beloved animal stars.

So, we invite you to "Sit" and enjoy the special rewards offered by these all-time favorite TV pets. Happy tails!

Acknowledgments

This incredible journey through the kennel of TV pets and the time tunnel of all of television could not have happened without the kindness and patience of many who shared memories, friendships, and photographs with us. If we were dogs, we'd owe you a lifetime of tail wags, but since we're only human, we will say thank you so very much. This book sits here because of your dedication to your craft and your devotion to animals.

Well over one hundred people contributed their time and memories to help make this book a special tribute to TV animals and the people who worked with them. Several people offered key assistance with our gathering of information and especially in helping us make the connections to tell the stories in this book.

We have special thanks and a warm, friendly bear hug for Doree Sitterly Baylis, Ace Collins, Stephen Cox, Ralph Helfer, Frank Inn, Laurie Jacobson Provost, Peter Kaufman, Loretta Kemsley, Genny Kerns (formerly Gerry Warshauer), Bridget Madison, Karl Lewis Miller, David Rothel, and Hubert Wells.

And we give our sincere appreciation to the following people who played a part in making *TV Pets* a reality. You're the bee's knees, the cat's pajamas, the top dog, the pick of the litter, and just plain good folks: Lee Aaker, Rosemary Addison, Janine Aines, Charlie Aldridge, Bobby Lee (Beverly) Allen, Dayton Allen, Stefan Arngrim, Cathy Baker, Cheryl Rogers Barnett and Larry Barnett, Laura Bates, Lloyd and Ken Beebe, Michelle Bega, Dorothy and James Best, Bob Blair, Rob Bloch, Tony Bonner, Grace Bradley Boyd, Sandy Brokaw, Rand Brooks, Ricou Browning, Victor Buhler, Richard Calkins, Joe Camp, Bruce Campbell, Mary Grace Canfield, Nick Carrado, Bill Casey, Bill Catching, Fernando Celis, Gary Collins, Jesse Collins, Kevin Corcoran, Henry Crowell, Joann Curtis, Lena Jo Davenport and the late Bobby J. Davenport, Mark Dawidziak, Mathilde de Cagny, Jonathan Dees, Robert De Franco, Deborah Dellosso, Bobby Diamond, Moe and Sue Di Sesso, Micky Dolenz, Christian Drake, Bob Dunn, Douglas Earthman, Charles P. Eisenmann, Marilyn Eldrenkamp, Jane V. Ellis, Robert Ellis, Joanne Engle, Peggy Evans, David Field, Joe Fithian, Megan Follows, Mark Forbes, Soleil Moon Frye, Glen Garner, Fred Goodwin, Peter Graves, Dennis Grisco, Bobby Gropp, Ben Gross, Bill Groves, Ted Haggis, Earl Hamner Jr., Melora Hardin, John Hart, Scott Hart, Jimmy Hawkins, Bobby Herron, Dennis Hill, Alice Horton, Joe Hostettler, Clint Howard, Whitey Hughes, and Will Hutchins.

Whew! We need a paws to catch our breath. OK, here are some more big helpers: Cindy James, Steve Jensen, Jackie Martin Kaplan, Tracy Kelly, Mick LaFever, Kenny

Lee, Laura Levy, Sandy Liles, George Lindsey, Betty Linn, Stan Livingston, Sam Lovullo, Boyd Magers, Rona Manash, Tammy Maples, Kevin Marhanka, Robert Martwick, Steve Martin, Brenda McClain, Kevin McCorry, Karen McKlemurray, Maggie McManus, Alvin Mears, Buddy Mennclla and Roy Waldron and Jerry Preis, Cristie Miele, Karl Mitchell, Joan Neidhardt, Ray Nielsen, Jay North, Rick Parker, Barbara Perry, Rex Peterson, Allen Pinson, Cathy Pittman, Jon Provost, Corky Randall, Bryan Renfro, Bill Raymond, David Regan, Bob Riedell, Steven Ritt, Karen Rosa, Wally Ross, Roland Ruffin, Geoff St. Andrews, Denise Sanders, Kim Sandifer, Pat Saukko, Roger Schumacher, Sherwood Schwartz, Henry Shannon, Cheryl Shawver, Dick Simmons, Marlene Smith, Gordon Spencer, Carl Spitz Jr., Vic Sutton, Nancy Swanner, Julian Sylvester, Rockne Tarkington, Ken Taylor, Keith Thibodeaux, Louise Thomas, Frank L. Thompson, Jerry Van Dyke, Jerry Vance, Sandra Vian, Jon Walmsley, Bill Ward, Dick Warlock, Glenda Washam, Johnny Washbrook, Jesse Wayne, Richard Weatherwax, Robert Weatherwax, Johnny Weissmuller Jr., Dan Westfall, Drew White, Rod Wolf, Steve Woodley, Alan Young, and Margo Zinberg.

And to our friends in the publishing world (where it really is a zoo out there), thank you to Larry Stone, Bryan Curtis, Jennifer Greenstein, and Lori Lynch at Rutledge Hill Press, and to D. Michelle Adkerson, Norma Bates, and Denver Sherry.

And for their enduring love, support, and help, we give our heartfelt thanks to Wendy Beck (Ken's wife) and Mary Clark (Jim's wife). They've sure trained us well (though they may not agree with us on that point). We also thank Ken's son, Cole Beck, and daughter, Kylie Beck, for their tremendous assistance.

2002

The Encyclopedia of TV Pets

The Abbott and Costello Show

CBS, 1952–1954, 52 episodes

*Starring **Bingo the Chimp,** Bud Abbott as himself, Lou Costello as himself, Sidney Fields as himself, Hillary Brooke as herself, Gordon Jones as Mike Kelly, Joe Besser as Stinky, and Joe Kirk as Mr. Bacciagalupe.*

The Abbott and Costello Show centers on the slapstick antics of two friends, Bud and Lou, who share a room in a boardinghouse and who are always trying to make a fortune or avoid paying bills.

Jerry Seinfeld, an ardent admirer of the duo, hosted a ten-hour marathon of *The Abbott and Costello Show* on Comedy Central in 1993 and said, "Truly the most bizarre addition to this entire series was the idea of Bingo the Chimp. That these two guys, who literally did not have a quarter for a sandwich, would adopt—not as a pet, but as a son—this chimp."

Joe Besser, who later became one of the Three Stooges, was a cast member, but Bingo took his job.

"I left the series after the first season when Lou decided to revamp the show's format—including the cast," Besser wrote in his 1984 autobiography, *Not Just a Stooge.* "I was replaced by, of all things, a chimpanzee. . . . I never lost out to a chimp before, but I never resented Lou for making this move. He had done plenty for me just by being my friend."

Not many facts about the real-life Bingo abound, but he was a she, a female chimpanzee who dressed like Lou Costello, derby hat and all. Costar Hillary Brooke remarked that she was fond of the chimp, but Bingo first bit cast member Sid Fields, and then, when she nipped star Costello, the cushy role was over. Lou fired her.

Bingo, according to the script, ate watermelon for breakfast and fifty pounds of bananas per week.

Bingo the Chimp and Lou Costello never got along. After Bingo bit Costello, the chimp was history.

The Adventures of Brisco County, Jr.

Fox, 1993–1994, 27 episodes

Starring ***Copper and pals as Comet,*** *Bruce Campbell as Brisco County Jr., Julius Carry as Lord Bowler, Christian Cremenson as Socrates Poole, John Astin as Professor Albert Wickwire, John Pyper-Ferguson as "Slippery" Pete Hutter, Kelly Rutherford as Dixie Cousins, and John Drago as John Bly.*

Brisco is a lawyer turned noble bounty hunter who is on the trail of his father's killers. Brisco's sometime rival and frequent partner is fellow bounty hunter Lord Bowler. But his most steadfast partner and faithful companion is his horse, Comet, who is such a talented horse that it took five actor horses, each with special talents, to successfully capture his full range.

Says Bruce Campbell, who portrayed Brisco, "The main horse I used was Copper. He was about fourteen years old, so he was a bit slow and cranky in the beginning. However, he got in better shape throughout the run of the show because he was used almost every day, and he perked right up. I nicknamed Copper 'Leadbelly' because he was a very calm horse and could be used during a gunfight or for dialogue scenes. He also had to wear makeup because his colorings had to match the main horse, Strip. So this gave us a special bond. Strip had a white stripe down his nose and three white 'socks.' Each of the other horses was made to match with 'clown white' greasepaint or white hair spray on their legs. It was funny to watch them go through the same humiliation I did in that respect."

Trainer Gordon Spencer remembers how Copper and the other horses were selected for *Brisco County.* "When they started the pilot, they didn't have much time, and the producer came out to my barn because they had a black horse that had a lot of 'stuff' on him. He had a liberty rear [the ability to rise upward on hind legs] and a lot of tricks on him, and they didn't want Brisco to be on a black horse. So the producers came out and looked at different horses that were there, and they saw the horse called Strip. I'd done a thing in New York with him, but didn't have very much 'stuff' on him. So Carlton Cuse, one of the producers, asked me if I could get the stuff on him that I needed to do in the script for the pilot, and I said that I thought so. I only had five weeks to go, but we did it. We got enough on him to get the pilot done good, and there was a break in between the pilot and the series, and I started working the horses.

"When you do a thing like that, you always have to have a backup or two in case the horse gets sick or he doesn't want to perform that day or whatever. So that was how the horses came to be. I picked Copper for Bruce to ride because when Bruce started he'd done a couple of things, and this horse was the gentlest horse. The company wanted Bruce to do his own galloping and all that stuff, and this horse that I picked out for him was very smooth to ride and very gentle. They all were gentle, but generally, in a situation like that you don't like to let anybody ride your trick horses, because the more others ride, the less attention the horses pay to the trainer, and also the horses get tired during the events of the day. If the horses are out there for fourteen hours, and you've been riding or using them all day, and at the end of the day somebody decides that they want the horse to do some tricks, he's not going to perform like he would if he was fresh."

Campbell says, "The true show horse was Strip. He was the key trick horse and could do lip wiggles and head nods and hoof scrapes—all the basic stuff, but you wouldn't want to ride him because he was pretty high energy." Adds Spencer, "Strip did all the head work, all the lip-ups and the head shakes for 'yes and no' and the look-arounds and the digs and all of that. That was all Strip, as well as tying the knots and opening the door and going into the rooms and all of that."

"The stunt horse was Boss," says Campbell. "He was a beautiful and powerful horse and was used for tricky riding stuff, so only the stunt guys would deal with him. I nicknamed him 'Widowmaker.'" Says Spencer, "Boss would do most of the long-range shots. And Boss went through the windows in the bars and he did a lot of chases, and we did the train transfers with him."

Two other horses that were regulars in the role of Comet are remembered fondly by Campbell. "Ace was a specialty horse. He did all the rearing and was mainly good for that and other assorted stunt stuff. Sadly, he has since departed. Near the end of the show, we began to break in a new main horse. His name was Comet, so that he would get used to hearing the actual name. He was coming along fine, but the show was canceled before we got any real use out of him."

Spencer recalls Ace's injury. "One night in a stall he rolled where he couldn't get up, and he fractured his pelvis. I had to get another horse ready, and Comet was the one."

The character Comet was smart enough to do things like crack combination safes and play chess, and he could understand English very well. But rather than bothering to learn to speak English, like, say, Mr. Ed, Comet instead trained Brisco to understand

Bruce Campbell rode the wild and often wacky West astride his steed Comet.

the more succinct "horse language." Campbell recalls, "The talking scenes were done with Gordon the wrangler standing close by with a stick that Strip watched. This would signal his activity. The trick was to not have my dialogue overlap Gordon's, since he had to give verbal cues as well. Eventually Gordon would become familiar with the 'dialogue' in the scene, and it worked out pretty well. I also had a special grain pocket sewn in my jacket, so I could reward Strip after each take."

About Spencer, Campbell says, "Gordon was a real no-nonsense guy, and he wouldn't take any crap from anybody—least of all a pansy, actor-boy like me. Gordon and I got along really well because I was willing to take a month to learn how to ride properly and get to know the horses, and I didn't give him any lip. Gordon was really a great guy to work with. His favorite thing to do was come up to me and say, 'You really are a phony b—d, aren't you?' then walk away laughing. That's how you knew he liked you."

Spencer has fond memories of the series and praise for the horses and Campbell. "I was proud of the pilot, when Brisco and Bowler were tied up on the railroad track, and Comet had to come walking up and pull the rope loose and untie them and get them loose. But basically everything that the horses did I was proud of. Working a TV series for a trainer of horses is very tough because you don't have any time to prepare for the next show. It was a good experience. It was a tough show, but I was very proud of the horses because they worked well, they never held the company up, and everything seemed to work fine. Bruce had a good rapport with all of them. Bruce was excellent to work around. He made it a lot easier."

Campbell hopes his old equine coworkers had happy trails in their years after *Brisco County*. "I don't know exactly what Strip is up to these days, but last time I heard, he was living comfortably somewhere in southern California. Ahhh, the life of a horse!"

And Spencer still owns the actor Comet, who has been busy in other films and commercials since *Brisco* ended.

The Adventures of Rin Tin Tin

ABC, 1954–1959, 164 episodes

Starring ***Golden Boy Jr. (aka J. R.) as Rin Tin Tin,*** *Lee Aaker as Rusty, James Brown as Lt. Rip Masters, Joe Sawyer as Sgt. Biff O'Hara, and Rand Brooks as Cpl. Boone.*

The Adventures of Rin Tin Tin is set in the Old West, as an orphaned boy, the survivor of an Indian raid, and his dog are adopted by cavalry soldiers at Fort Apache, Arizona. The duo has various escapades, and Rusty's cry of "Yo Ho, Rinty!" still rings in the memories of the show's legions of fans.

Lee Aaker and Golden Boy Jr. starred as Private Rusty and Rin Tin Tin in *The Adventures of Rin Tin Tin.*

Courtesy of Lee Aaker.

German shepherds' success in movies began long before the television version of Rin Tin Tin. The mighty Rinty's story began in Fleury, France, during the final days of World War I when an American Air Force pilot, Lee Duncan, found a batch of German shepherd pups.

He gave several away but kept two of them, Nenette and Rin Tin Tin (the pair was named after knitted good-luck charms the French carried during the war), and brought them back to the United States. Nenette died, but Duncan trained the boy dog, and in 1923, Warner Bros. introduced Rin Tin Tin in the silent adventure flick *Where the North Begins.*

Rin Tin Tin made a litter of movies for Warner Bros. in a nine-year span and brought the company back from the brink of bankruptcy, thus earning himself the moniker "the dog that saved Hollywood."

The first Rin Tin Tin died on August 10, 1932, and one of his newspaper obituaries read: "Rin Tin Tin, the greatest of the animal motion picture actors, pursued a ghostly villain into a canine happy hunting grounds today. More than eighty years old as comparative human age is measured, his passing was mourned this morning by his owner and friend, Lee Duncan."

Duncan then brought out Rinty's son, Rin Tin Tin Jr. (aka Rinty II), who starred in five movies during the 1930s. After World War II, Duncan trained a third Rinty, a veteran of the K-9 Corps, who had reached the rank of sergeant in the service and won several medals, including a Purple Heart for an injury caused by a Jeep that ran over his leg. Rinty III starred in 1947's *The Return of Rin Tin Tin.*

It was Rinty III that Duncan hoped would be the star of the 1954 television series, but the dog couldn't meet the demands required by a weekly show. So the star of *The Adventures of Rin Tin Tin* became Golden Boy Jr. Trained by Frank Barnes, Golden Boy, who was nicknamed J. R., was the son of another movie star dog, Flame, who starred in his own Rusty series of films during the 1940s.

Actor Rand Brooks, who costarred in what may have been the greatest film ever made, *Gone With the Wind*, recalls his canine costars on *Rin Tin Tin*: "The first dog was nice but not up to the task and shooting

Among the stalwarts of Fort Apache are, clockwise from bottom, Rin Tin Tin, Lee Aaker, James Brown, Rand Brooks, and Joe Sawyer.

schedule of a TV show. He was a little bit slow in moving and didn't have the vitality. I was the fourth wheel to the dog.

"They brought in Golden Boy Jr., son of Flame. He was eleven months old when we started the TV series. He was a big dog. Frank Barnes was the greatest German shepherd trainer ever, and Rinty was the greatest dog that ever lived.

"Frank called the dog 'Jay-Are' [short for 'Junior'], but the 'r' was slurred because of his strong Southern accent. At shows [publicity appearances] youngsters would ask Frank, 'Mister, can I touch that dog?' Barnes would say, 'Boy, are your hands clean?'" recalls Brooks with a laugh.

"J. R. really could do anything," Brooks says. "He was a marvelous dog. J. R. was in every scene, except for one day when he went to New York, and we used a double, Bearheart.

"We had a dog named Hey You that belonged to Lee Duncan, who owned and trained the original Rin Tin Tin, and Hey You did the fights and running with the horses."

"I always liked dogs," says Lee Aaker, who played Rin Tin Tin's best boy, Rusty. "I remember the trainer, Frank Barnes, and going over to his house when I was eight or nine. It was a nice, friendly job. I knew the dog real well. The dog was an actor and part of the troupe. He just did his job like we all did, and it was pretty exciting.

"The dog really never took to anybody but his trainer. I played with the dog every once in a while. The thing that always amazed me was when we went on planes and the dog would sit on a seat like everybody else. And on tour, all the kids were poking at it and pulling at it and wanting to pet it, and it never bit them. He had a great temperament.

"We went on tour for three or four weeks out of every summer, mainly playing state fairs and rodeos. We went to Madison Square Garden, the Boston Gardens. It was usually Jim Brown, Rand Brooks, and myself and the dog. We did some routines, the stuntmen did gunfights and the dog performed little tricks. Our sponsors were the National Biscuit Company, Nabisco, which made shredded wheat and Milk Bone dog biscuits, so Rinty got lots of their biscuits."

Aaker recalls J. R.'s doubles Hey You and Bearheart, but says there was a fourth Rinty on the set: a dummy dog. "We had one stuffed dog that was used during fight scenes. When there was a closeup of a bad guy, then they would shoot a tight shot of the dummy dog flying through the air hitting the bad guy in the head."

The Adventures of Rin Tin Tin was shot at Corriganville and at Big Bear, California.

"When Frank Barnes would go away, he would leave the dog with me at my house in Tarzana," says Brooks. "Frank taught me a lot about training. He was the master, and J. R. was just a wonderful, solid, fun-loving dog. He was only six when we finished the series. He could do anything. You just had to show him once. Look at the pictures, and everything that he did.

"He got cancer in one leg in about 1962 or 1963. They had to put him down. I had a litter through him, though. Frank was so protective of J. R. that he only bred him once. I picked one from his litter, a female, and I bred her back to Bearheart, the double dog. One of those pups went over to Roy Rogers and became one of the last Bullets, one of my dogs."

Alex, the Stroh's Beer Dog

Well before Spuds MacKenzie began partying for Bud Light, Alex was a beer-drinking guy's best friend—a dog who could retrieve an ice-cold Stroh's beer from the fridge.

Trainer Alvin Mears of Alvin Animal Rentals tells about this remarkable dog, who really could open refrigerators and do other dexterous tricks: "Alex was a mixed-breed retriever. I would say golden retriever, Irish setter, and whatever got lucky that night. His real name was Banjo. He stood as tall as a Great Dane. I personally got Banjo out of the animal shelter. We were doing a Disney movie, and we were actually utilizing the facilities of a real animal shelter. So I walked around through there and saw this grungy little skinny dog curled up in the corner. He didn't look to be any bigger than a Labrador retriever, and I got him to stand up, and he was really tall, and I got him out. I went to the people at the shelter and told them to put a hold on this dog for me, and I filled out the paperwork because I knew a couple of the movie people would see him in there and would want to get him also. And they did, and by that night, before we were through shooting, three other people were interested in getting the dog.

"We never put a leash on this dog, never took him out of his kennel. You could just see his disposition and his charisma and the character and the love in his eyes while still in the kennel itself. All you could do was pet him through the wire. I was offered $500 for that dog, and he never even had gotten out of the kennel yet. That's how remarkable he was. Alex was as close to a human character in his eyes, in his demeanor, and in his understanding and willingness to please as any dog I ever worked with.

"He was like a human, and I didn't talk to him like a dog. I'd tell him, 'Alex you've got a half hour here of a line of people, and you're going to be a little tired when you're done with this.' And these were just people taking still photos and just wanting to meet the dog. When Stroh's brewery would do big conventions, the dog was first on their list: first-class everything in transportation, limousines, hotel suites. Every Christmas holiday or wherever Stroh's held their convention, three hundred to four hundred people would be standing in line in their tuxedos to get a picture with this dog. And this was just for the 'in-house' things.

"When he went on tour, they gave him keys to the city, parades, and that kind of thing. They had a Stroh's beer car that would look like a beer can, but it was a car, and he would do parades throughout Michigan. He's got all kinds of good citizen awards because he would do charitable events and raise money for animal shelters and homeless dogs, and he would do a lot for children's events and raise money. He actually campaigned for Vote America. He went on tour to encourage animal lovers to vote in the presidential election. He did *Good Morning America*, and he did the *Today Show*. Every city he went in, he did at least five radio appearances, and we would close the main tavern bars that carried Stroh's beer at two in the morning.

Banjo poses for a publicity shot as Alex, the enormously popular spokesdog for Stroh's beer in the 1980s.

Courtesy of Alvin Mears.

"He had a strenuous work schedule when he was popular. We would start in the morning, we would take six hours off in the middle of the day, and then we'd start back in the evenings. I can't say enough about Alex. People would have tears in their eyes when they got to meet him.

"The very first Stroh's ad he did was a still photo for a print ad with him riding on a motorcycle. I showed him, literally, one time how to get up on this motorcycle. He had to have his paws like they were on the steering wheel, and he had to have his back feet like they were on the brake and on the clutch. It was fixed, but they made it look like it was moving with fans. He had a scarf on his neck like it was blowing in the wind. He literally was shown one time, and then he knew how to get up on this motorcycle and place his feet and hold his paws for fifteen to twenty minutes at a time. That's how human he appeared to be and how willing he was to please you. Very special."

Adds Mears, "He wouldn't fight another dog and wouldn't come up to you too fast if he thought you were a little nervous because he was so tall and so big. He was very gentle with children. They could pull on his ears and tail, and he would never whimper or whine. I never saw him act like, 'I don't feel like working today.' But I could read it in his eyes when he would get tired, and I would just tell whoever we were working with that he needed to take a break. When he took his break, he utilized it. He'd run and play and want to go chase a duck. He was a gentleman and a scholar in every phase, form, and fashion of his lifestyle."

Mears recalls Alex's first work: "Alex came on the scene for Stroh's around 1984, and it ran till at least '89 or '90. Every commercial he did was in the Top Ten commercials while it ran. Then they went with a different advertising agency, and you have different ideas, and so they went with a new campaign. And so they stopped having Alex be the spokesperson and the mascot. That lasted about two years, and they called back and said, 'Alvin, we got rid of that agency, and we want Alex back.' Alex came back, and he ran good for another three years before Stroh's actually was sold. They didn't give up on him; they just changed ownership."

In the meantime, Alex was top dog. "Oh yes, Alex had his own line of cologne and his own shampoos and a hand lotion," says Mears. "He had numerous posters—anything from wearing military hats to Christmas posters with Christmas trees behind him. Just endless stuff with his face on it—toys and all kinds of things."

Mears says that Alex—that is Banjo, but even Mears calls him Alex—died of cancer a few years after the second tenure with the Stroh's campaign ended. But Mears and many TV lovers and beer lovers throughout North America will always remember this special, seemingly human retriever. As Mears sums up simply, "Alex was extraordinary."

ALF

NBC, 1986–1990, 102 episodes, 1 TV movie (1996)

*Starring **Sparks as Lucky**, Paul Fusco as the voice of ALF (aka Gordon Shumway), Max Wright as Willie Tanner, Anne Schedeen as Kate Tanner, Andrea Elson as Lynn Tanner, Benji Gregory as Brian Tanner, Anne Meara as Dorothy Halligan, Liz Sheridan as Raquel Ochmonek, John LaMotta as Trevor Ochmonek, and Josh Blake as Jake Ochmonek.*

ALF (the letters stand for "alien life form") was about a furry little creature from the planet Melmac, who crash-lands his spaceship into a suburban family's garage and winds up hanging around the Tanner household for several years making wisecracks and a general nuisance of himself.

Five or six different cats were used to play Lucky, the Tanner family pet on *ALF*, not because ALF's favorite snack was a cat, but because different strokes are needed for different catty folks.

A brown, male alley cat named Sparks, who was found in the pound, was the number one pick of the kitty litter.

Sam Coulter, who spent twenty-five years working with Cindy James in the animal acting business, was one of several trainers who worked on *ALF* for Frank Inn Animals. "Surviving the puppet was the hardest part," she says of the cat actors. "When you have unnatural things like a puppet, the cats are not really accepting of that." (The ALF character was generally performed by puppeteers working from beneath the stage, while a short person worked in an ALF costume for walking scenes in earlier episodes.)

"ALF was worked from underneath (by the puppeteers), and the cat was always wondering 'what's going on down there?'"

Coulter adds, "The producers wanted an orange cat in the beginning, but that was too close to ALF's color. So they went for brown."

Among the other felines on the team were Gordo, Fat Cat, Electra, and Sparkle.

Sparks, the lead, was the most laid back of the whole team. Coulter says, "He was kind of like Morris—'whatever, yeah, let's go.' But he was not high energy. Electra and Gordo were high energy."

The behaviors for the cat on *ALF* were not too difficult. A lot of Lucky's scenes were simply him running away from ALF so he wouldn't wind up a snack.

"Pretty much they just had the cat hanging out most of the time," says Coulter. "Michu [Meszaros] was the little person who did ALF in costume, and the cat wasn't too sure of himself when ALF was walking around. We'd have to get him used to ALF's moving around. The cat thought, 'This is too weird,' and sometimes we would have to stop and train.

"The biggest problem was if they had a track where ALF worked behind the couch, then there were holes from where the puppeteers were working, and the cat would start looking down instead of working up on top."

The cats were rewarded for good jobs

with baby food. "They would be given their treat off a spoon since it is easy to serve, just one little lick," Coulter says.

Top cat Sparks moved from TV to the big screen when he went on to *Stephen King's Sleepwalkers* in 1992.

"He was the star cat for our compound for a lot of years," says Coulter. "He did a Purina commercial and one for Fresh Step. He was just an all-around kitty."

The Andy Griffith Show

CBS, 1960–1968, 249 episodes

Starring Andy Griffith as Sheriff Andy Taylor, Don Knotts as Deputy Barney Fife, Ronny Howard as Opie Taylor, Frances Bavier as Aunt Bee, Howard McNear as Floyd Lawson, Jim Nabors as Gomer Pyle, and George Lindsey as Goober Pyle.

This show captures the generally pleasant life in the small town of Mayberry, North Carolina, and the imaginations of generations to come with the daily goings-on of a widower sheriff and his family and their highly likable (and often a little zany) friends.

Though there were not any pets or animals who appeared in the same role in more than one episode of *The Andy Griffith Show*, animals were central to the stories of many episodes of the popular show, including "The Loaded Goat" (about a dynamite-eating goat), "The Cow Thief" (in which the thief disguises his crime by putting shoes on his stolen cows), "Big Fish in a Small Town" (about a mythically hard-to-catch fish), "Goodbye Dolly" (about a milk-delivery-cart horse in danger of losing her job to a vehicle with man-made horsepower), and the classic "Opie the Birdman" (in which Opie raises three baby songbirds).

Frank Inn recalls this little dog, seen here with Opie (Ron Howard) in the episode titled "Dogs, Dogs, Dogs." "That dog was also one of *The Beverly Hillbillies* critters. There were actually two of them, a brother and sister. They were kind of Chihuahua and schnauzers. I think Elly May called it Arnie."

Sheriff Andy Taylor (Andy Griffith) and Spot (Pluto) watch as Goober (George Lindsey) does his doggone best to be a convincing canine in "A Man's Best Friend" on *The Andy Griffith Show.*

Courtesy of TAGSRWC Archives.

Legendary trainer Frank Inn provided virtually all of the animals used in Mayberry. "Whenever they had animals on *The Andy Griffith Show*, *The Danny Thomas Show*, or anything Sheldon Leonard had anything to do with, they called me," says Inn. "I worked with Sheldon Leonard when he directed Lassie pictures when I was working with Lassie and training the doubles for Lassie. And then when Sheldon Leonard spread out and began doing *The Andy Griffith Show*, *The Danny Thomas Show*, and *The Dick Van Dyke Show*, he said, 'Hey, you get the animals from Frank Inn.' And that helped me out a lot. He was sure wonderful for me and he respected my animal work."

One of Inn's busiest animal actors played two of the most memorable roles in Mayberry: Blue, the dog in "Barney's Bloodhound," and Spot in "A Man's Best Friend." Around Frank Inn's house and when not acting, the dog was known as Pluto. Inn remembers, "Pluto was a dog I got from the animal shelter. He had mixed Airedale in him. I bred Pluto to a natural Airedale and got three dogs that looked almost like it, and old Pluto outlived all of his sons. His sons lived to be about twelve to fifteen, but Pluto lived to be about eighteen, and so Pluto was only two or three years old when he had the pups, and he outlived every one of them, and they all lived to a good age.

"You'll never realize how many things that Pluto worked in. He worked a little bit in everything. Pluto used to work with about forty other dogs on *The Beverly Hillbillies*. He did a couple of episodes as Andy Clyde's dog on Lassie. And then he did *Happy* with the talking baby, and he was the dog on *Hazel* (named Smiley). His sons would stand in for him. He also was the dog on about three or four adjoining episodes of *Bonanza*. They wanted the dog to lie real still, and so I sold them one of the sons as a double to put to sleep so it would lay still, but Pluto lay so still that they didn't have to put the dog to sleep (but I got paid for the other dog anyway). He just lay that still."

Pluto wasn't always so calm and still. Actor George Lindsey remembers working with Pluto in one of his favorite episodes of *The Andy Griffith Show*, titled "A Man's Best Friend," in which Goober thinks his dog Spot (played by Pluto and named "Spot" because he doesn't have any spots) can talk. "Of course, all the dogs that they use in the movies have trainers just out of camera range," says Lindsey, "and they do whatever the trainer says and not what the actor says, and you have to realize you're working with a non-human and you don't know what this non-human may do because he doesn't understand that you're doing dialogue. So he just decided during this scene to reach up and give me a shot on the cheek. But we just continued with the scene."

But Lindsey and Pluto made up. "At the end of the episode, 'Spot' stood up on his hind feet and begged, paws up in the air. Well, you know that was the trainer doing that. It's funny, but when you're doing a scene with an animal, sometimes I guess you forget that you're not really dealing with another actor."

"That's my cow that he's sitting on. That cow worked in Lassie pictures and several others," says Frank Inn, talking about this scene from "The Rehabilitation of Otis." Actor Hal Smith (Otis) once recalled working with this cow. "It wasn't easy. I'd ridden horses for a long, long time. The shoulders on that cow came right to a point. I sat back as far as I could get and she'd take three steps and stop, and I'd go brrrt . . . right up that backbone. That almost ruined me. It was like riding a xylophone, and if you've ever ridden a xylophone, you know what I'm talking about."
Courtesy of TAGSRWC Archives.

Annie Oakley

ABC, 1954–1957, 81 episodes

*Starring **Target, Pixie, and Forest;** Gail Davis as Annie Oakley; Jimmy Hawkins as Tagg Oakley; and Brad Johnson as Deputy Lofty Craig.*

Annie Oakley is set in the town of Diablo, where sharpshooter and rancher Annie Oakley and her younger brother Tagg help Deputy Lofty Craig keep the peace.

The law-abiding trio in *Annie Oakley* had to have sturdy mounts for all the action and adventure they met on the trail. Annie rode Target, Tagg was aboard Pixie, and Lofty Craig sat tall in the saddle on Forest.

The show was shot at Gene Autry's Melody Ranch in Newhall, California, as well as at Pioneer Town in the high desert outside of Palm Springs, Corriganville, and Vasquez Rocks, outside of Los Angeles.

Actor Jimmy Hawkins doesn't recall a lot about Annie and Lofty's steeds, but he remembers his own very well. In fact, Pixie was his personal property, acquired when Hawkins was a teen. "For the first three years they rented two horses [as Pixie]," says Hawkins. "Then Gene Autry [who owned and produced the TV series] wanted me to go on tour with him. So I got my own horse, an Amigo colt. He had perfect matching spots on both sides, and he had a real target on his rump.

"I got him at an auction in Los Angeles. He had shipping fever. Trainer Mark Smith, who had the horse Wildfire, first saw him and said, 'If this horse lives, it will be a great horse.' Later Monty Montana tried to buy him.

"I took Pixie on tour and used him on the show. He was fabulous at learning tricks and always good with the kids. He was just a good friend, somebody to talk to and ride the trails. A very special friend.

"He could shake his head yes or no, he could say his prayers, smile and bow. He was two years old when I bought him and lived to be twenty-eight. He was just a great horse. He was very good at going into hospitals. He wore special boots made so he could go indoors.

"There was a party I did for Cardinal McEntire in Los Angeles, and Pixie would go up the elevator into the Embassy Room and perform for the kids. Then Gene and I would go on the tours. He and I would fly everyplace in his private plane. Gene would have his big western show with ropers and wire acts and girl dancers. We did lots of state and county fairs."

Hawkins recollects performing with Pixie

at state fairs in Texas, Oregon, California, and Arizona during the heyday of the *Annie Oakley* show's popularity between 1955 and 1959. His and Pixie's grand finale was the hoop of fire where horse and rider plunged through a burning circle. The duo's last great partnership was as grand marshals of the 1960 Rose Parade.

Hawkins says that, in the role of Annie Oakley, star Gail Davis rode two different horses playing Target. They were rental horses from the Ace Hudkins stables. One was a docile animal used for the close-ups, while the other, the friskier of the two, was used for chase scenes.

Jimmy Hawkins and Gail Davis hold Target's bridle during a location shoot for *Annie Oakley*.
Courtesy of Jimmy Hawkins.

B. J. and the Bear

NBC, 1979–1981, 50 episodes

*Starring **Sam as Bear,** Greg Evigan as B. J. McCay, and Claude Akins as Sheriff Lobo. This popular show features the adventures of a young, big-rig truck driver and his trucking buddy chimp as they travel around the country.*

Trainer Julian Sylvester recalls that head trainer Marvin Downey and animal trainer Steve Moss co-owned Sam. Why was he called Bear? "Well, he used to wear this hound's-tooth hat like Bear Bryant, the football coach, wore," says Sylvester.

Sylvester adds, "B. J. [Greg Evigan] is the truck driver on the show, and he apparently found this chimp in Vietnam. I don't know how he got from Vietnam to here, but he was a medevac pilot and he brings this chimp home. Since they're buddies, the chimp, of course, rides around in the front seat.

"In the scenes in the truck cab, I was always behind Greg in the jump seat keeping an eye on the chimp so he didn't hit the jack

Greg Evigan and Sam were true trucking partners in *B.J. and the Bear.*

brake with his bloody foot. It was a real dangerous situation when you think about it. We'd be going down the freeway on the third shot, and the chimp sitting there and you'd see that foot sneaking toward that jack brake, and I'd just gesture, 'Uh-uh, don't even think about it.' There could be eleven people in that cab at one time. There were cameramen, the script and lighting and props people, and others sitting a little behind the driver's seat keeping an eye on the chimp."

Sylvester adds, "Sam was a pretty young chimp. I didn't do the pilot, but I did the first year as a TV show, and he was already hired on that one. I think he was about three years old. He did tend to nip on some people, which was not good. Apparently he bit quite a few people after I left because he was getting older, but he had a very good relationship with Greg Evigan. He didn't like the women too much. He'd grab their shirt and put his head underneath their blouse and have a look, which is very unnerving for the trainers—most of them, that is, but Marvin thought it was very funny."

Sylvester says that Sam wasn't required to do anything out of the ordinary for his role as Bear. "Just basic chimp stuff. He had to stand up, and we taught him to put his hands up against the wheel on the semi so he could be frisked. Every time B. J. got stopped by the cops, the chimp would do the same thing. We taught him to throw beer cans and pour beer out and basically be a little hood and pick up stuff and steal things out of back pockets and shake his head yes and shake his head no and scream and yell and do little chimp things. But basically that's all he had to do to sort of fill in the gaps."

As far as motivations, Sam seemed to have a well-developed sweet tooth. "Oh, he liked his Coke, like most chimps," says Sylvester. "They like Coca-Cola. Any soda pop was pretty good. He was just like a kid—a kid with big teeth."

Sylvester says that Sam didn't really have any "big moments" that jump to mind all these years later. "To tell you the truth, it was pretty uneventful. I do remember that it was very hard working in Vegas. We shot at Circus Circus, I think it was. The chimp was living in my room, which, you know, is a real drag. A lot of time, you're sitting and waiting on the set and security was OK, but it wasn't all that good. They were mostly protecting the actor. You'd sit in the corner and all of a sudden there were fifty or sixty people all wanting to touch the chimp and that could be very dangerous. The people are getting closer and closer. It's just intimidating for me and the chimp."

Sylvester also notes that Sam wasn't the only chimp on the *B. J. and the Bear* set. "He had several doubles, but his stunt chimp, as it were, was a wonderful chimp—probably the best chimp in the business—called Karanja, which is a Swahili name, just like 'Fred,' but it's Karanja. He grew up to be just a huge chimp."

Sylvester says that one of Karanja's best stunts was to ride elephants. "Karanja wasn't afraid of elephants, but Sam was horrified. You couldn't get Sam within twenty feet of an elephant's butt; he'd say no way. I think

Sam the Chimp is all grins with Julian Sylvester, the trainer who partnered with him on *B.J. and the Bear.*
Courtesy of Julian Sylvester.

we got him on once or twice, but basically Karanja loved doing the job for him. Each one just has a different attitude about things, and Karanja just didn't care. He'd just hop on the elephant and sit down."

Sam's other stunt double was a chimp called Oopsie. "I don't know how she got that name," says Sylvester. "She lives with Bob Dunn and she's one of his best breeders. She has babies every year, beautiful babies. She's still around and she's still recognizable. I mean this has been from 1979. I wouldn't dare to go in there. She's as big as I am, bloody scary-looking, ugly as hell. A few chimps get really ugly. But she was a really good chimp, a nice chimp."

Sylvester points out that most chimps that are used as performers on television and in movies are usually fairly young. "They're usually from the age of one to about six or seven, then they tend to get a little tough because they get sexually mature and they want to kick everyone's butt. They're just teenagers, you know, socially aggressive. They want to be in charge, they want to become politicians," he says with a laugh.

Not long after *B. J. and the Bear* wrapped its final season of filming, Sam got liver cancer and died. "He must have been about seven or eight, and it was like a year or year-and-a-half after the show," says Sylvester. "He just keeled over. It might have been longer, but it wasn't much longer than that. He was very young. Everybody gets these kinds of diseases, but it's always a bit of a shock."

But if there's an eighteen-wheel banana truck in heaven, there's no doubt who's driving it.

Bachelor Father / Get Smart

***Bachelor Father:** ABC, 1957–1962, 157 episodes*

*Starring **Tramp and Jasper as Jasper,** John Forsythe as Bentley Gregg, Noreen Corcoran as Kelly Gregg, Sammee Tong as Peter Tong, Jimmy Boyd as Howard Meechim, and Bernadette Winters as Ginger.*

Bachelor Father is the story of a Beverly Hills attorney, a bachelor who must make changes in his lifestyle as he raises his thirteen-year-old niece after her parents are killed in a car accident. He gets much-needed assistance from his Chinese house servant.

***Get Smart:** NBC and CBS, 1965–1970, 138 episodes*

*Starring **Jasper as Fang,** Don Adams as Maxwell Smart (Agent 86), Barbara Feldon as Agent 99, Edward Platt as The Chief, Bernie Kopell as Conrad Siegfried, Robert Karvelas as Larrabee, Victor French as Agent 44, and Dick Gautier as Hymie.*

Get Smart follows the exploits of two spies, the confidently dense Agent 86 and the intelligent Agent 99, as they help the good guys of C.O.N.T.R.O.L. battle the bad guys of K.A.O.S.

The original dog that starred on *Bachelor Father* was named Tramp. He was owned and trained by Rudd Weatherwax, the man behind Lassie.

"Rudd trained Tramp and then my father took over and worked the TV series," says Richard Weatherwax, son of Frank Weatherwax. "Tramp was a very friendly dog. He liked to climb up on you. He thought he was a lap dog. He liked to play."

As *Bachelor Father* continued its five-season run, they realized that Tramp was getting too old to handle the load, so the production company found another dog that they named Jasper and gave him to Frank Weatherwax to train.

Agent K-13, aka Fang, and Maxwell Smart were bumbling but beloved agents for the good guys in *Get Smart.*

The changing of the hounds was not complicated, and Richard Weatherwax believes they even wrote it into the script by showing Tramp getting old and passing away and a younger dog coming into the Gregg home.

"They were always friendly dogs, since they had to work with children and strangers," says Richard Weatherwax, who got to know Jasper cheek to cheek, so to speak. "I recall my father was training him to give a kiss. My dad had me sitting on the floor with my back against the door. Then he would take baby food and smear it on my cheeks and have the dog lick it off."

Richard says that young Jasper was pretty well trained, and that when *Get Smart* came along, he joined the cast as Agent K-13, Fang. "We fought the urge to call him Agent K-9," writer Buck Henry once recalled.

For *Get Smart*, the reins of Jasper were turned over to Bill (aka Mac) Weatherwax, but the folks on the show didn't think the dog was too smart. "We hired a dog who couldn't do anything," said executive producer Leonard Stern. "We unwisely chose him because of his personality rather than his ability to respond to commands."

Star Barbara Feldon also recalled Jasper's problems in one tricky episode, while talking to Donna McCrohan for her book, *The Life and Times of Maxwell Smart*: "I was in a rowboat, and he had to untie my bonds. At first he wouldn't jump into the boat, and he wouldn't do what he was supposed to do with the ropes. Finally, someone had to stand off camera and throw Fang into the boat. But he still wouldn't go for my wrists, not until we put meat between them. This time we couldn't keep Fang off camera long enough. And then, he didn't stop at nibbling the meat from my wrists. He began searching me. He was thinking, 'You never know where else there might be meat.' So I had to fend off Fang."

Leave it to good old Jasper to be the one who has to be different and not look at the camera. His fellow *Bachelor Father* cast members are Sammee Tong as Peter Tong, John Forsythe as Bentley Gregg, and Noreen Corcoran as Kelly Gregg.

Courtesy of Photo History.

Eventually, Stern recalled, they had to extract the undercover canine from the show. That's right—he was written out of C.O.N.T.R.O.L. But who knows—maybe he was secretly a double agent for K.A.O.S.!

Baretta

ABC, 1975–1978, 80 episodes

*Starring **Lala as Fred,** Robert Blake as Tony Baretta, Dana Elcar as Inspector Shiller, Edward Grover as Lt. Hal Brubaker, Tom Ewell as Billy Truman, Michael D. Roberts as Rooster, Sharon Cintron as Mimi Ames, Chino Williams as Fats, and Angelo Rosetti as Little Moe.*

Baretta is about a streetwise, maverick cop with the Fifty-third Precinct who lives in a seedy hotel in New York City with his pet cockatoo. A master of disguise, Baretta generally wears a cap low on his forehead, a T-shirt, and jeans, as he dispenses justice with little respect for standard police procedures.

Tony Baretta's best pal is a bird, a milk-white cockatoo named Fred, who loves nothing better than to lie on his back and sip booze from a bottle. The actor behind Fred was Lala, born in Hong Kong and discovered in 1967 by animal trainer Ray Berwick, whose avian credits included *The Bird Man of Alcatraz, The Birds*, and *Jonathan Livingston Seagull.*

"Lala was smuggled out of Hong Kong and found in a load of chickens," says Karl Mitchell. "That is why he had the rooster sounds and all that." Mitchell, Berwick's protégé for five years, including on *Baretta,* explains, "The bird was rehabilitated over to Ray by U.S. Customs officials."

Berwick first had to teach the cockatoo a second language, English, since he was conversant only in Chinese. Among other tricks, Fred could perform a cartwheel, pedal a bicycle, ride a scooter, wave, imitate dogs and cats, give a kiss, and say "Hello," "I love you," and "Freeze." As for the bottle binging, he was trained on sunflower seeds.

"You have no idea how many of his fans think Fred's a parrot," said Berwick during an interview in 1975. "Fred would be furious if he knew. He thinks he's much more rare and definitely more beautiful."

"Lala, who was blue-eyed, was a great triton, a subspecies of cockatoo, and stood about fourteen inches high and weighed about a thousand grams," Mitchell says. "He got his name because of his irritating habit of rocking back and forth and going la-la-la-la. He had an excellent personality and was the most outgoing little animal to work with, but if you didn't give him his proper respect with seeds on cue, he could become obstinate.

"He was a very sweet bird but was smart enough to know how many seeds he got for each trick, and if he didn't get seeds he would scream or bite."

Another Berwick protégé was his nephew, Bryan Renfro, who also worked with some of the fine-feathered friends on *Baretta.* "When they developed the show, originally they wanted a picture of a mynah bird on the wall that Baretta would refer to," says Renfro. "Then they said, 'Let's make it a stuffed bird,' and then they said, 'Let's make it a real bird,' and they called Ray down there. They wanted a mynah bird, but you couldn't get the behaviors from a mynah. After Robert Blake saw the cockatoo work, he said, 'Hire him.'"

Trainer/owner Ray Berwick has Lala perch on his head while he holds Samantha the goose (*Friendly Persuasion,* 1975) and Baby, a golden eagle who appeared in the TV movie *Adams of Eagle Lake.*

The weekly beat paid Lala one thousand dollars an episode, and he had a look-alike understudy named Harold who handled the dangerous work—the flying stunts.

"Lala was the main bird. He did all that talking on the phone and drinking out of the bottle," Renfro says. "Harold, the bird I trained, did the flying stunts. There was one scene where Robert Blake had gotten into a fight and had a black eye. They wanted the bird to fly over and pick up a handkerchief, fly over to a sink, dip it into water, and fly back to put the handkerchief on his eye. It worked great."

Renfro says Harold died from a liver illness after the first season, but there were more Lala look-alikes waiting in the wings. "There were two birds called Sweetheart. One we used as the flying Sweetheart, and the other one did the sitting since he was a very good sitter. He would sit on Robert Blake's shoulder when he was walking down the street or driving in the car."

But sweethearts or not, Lala was the big bird of *Baretta.*

"Lala communicated yes and no, could speak on cue, and had an unlimited vocabulary," Mitchell says. "His most famous trick was answering the telephone and saying hello into the telephone. The producers of the show originally wanted a raven, and Ray showed ravens and mynah birds, but the cockatoo won them over immediately. He had a mynah named Howard, and Howard was great, but he was no Lala."

For his fine feathered efforts, Fred got tons of fan mail that included proposals of marriage from other birds and lots of letters from children. He also was named the first Grand PATSY Award winner in 1976 and repeated the feat in 1977.

Baretta costar Tom Ewell told David Rothel for his 1980 book *The Great Show Business Animals*: "Animals, in this case cockatoos, are not easy to work with. You have to

Robert Blake acts as a perch for Lala the cockatoo, who played his *Baretta* costar Fred. Fred lived in Baretta's hotel apartment and squawked "Freeze" every time Baretta entered the room. When he was in a good mood, he would kiss Blake on the nose. His repertoire, taught him by trainer Ray Berwick, included barking like a dog, meowing like a cat, and running on a treadmill.

adjust yourself to them and you have to watch them instead of trying to concentrate on your own performance. You have to concentrate on their performance because you can't use the take that you do until they get it right. This can be a very painful, long process. Offstage, they can be very friendly and very wonderful. Fred was very friendly—he only bit occasionally. As a result, I loved to play with him. Working with him—no."

Star Blake also had some problems in working with the cockatoo of the walk. He once joked that he was getting jealous of the bird. "A TV newsman cancelled his interview with me one day after he found out Fred wouldn't be there," Blake said. "He told me the interview would be a lot more visually interesting on a day Fred was there. And he was right."

"The bird liked Blake more than Blake liked the bird," says Mitchell. "Robert Blake became blasé about it because the cockatoo was getting more fan mail than him. There would be days when Blake would forget how many seeds to give the bird, and Lala would chase him around the set, reminding him, 'I am not an animal but a living being. I am not a prop.'"

Mitchell says that while Lala got sunflower seeds as a treat, his diet was a rotation of corn, rice, and other bird feeds.

"Lala went on to live out a long life and, after *Baretta*, performed at the San Diego Wild Animal Park," Mitchell says. "He was full grown when Ray got it and lived to be about seventy. I think it was a male because this bird never laid eggs and was blue eyed, while females tend to have brown eyes. In 1978 *Photoplay* said Lala was the most famous animal star of all time. We had to have amazing security for this bird, but he was such fun to work with."

Mitchell, who went on to work with most of the animals on *Fantasy Island* and the birds in Mel Brooks's *High Anxiety*, today works out of Las Vegas. His company, All Acting Animals, provides tigers, lions, and other animals for films, TV commercials, and rock music videos. He is also executive director of Big Cat Encounters.

He has nothing but the highest praise for the late Berwick, whom he calls "the premier bird trainer of all time." "Berwick created the genre of bird shows. He created the San Diego wild bird show," Mitchell says.

Berwick entered the animal training business back in the 1940s and by the 1960s and 1970s was furnishing most of the animals used by Universal Studios. He worked with dogs, cats, and birds, and had animals that starred in such TV series as *Columbo, Emergency!, Little House on the Prairie,* and *Here's Boomer.* Berwick also wrote several books, including *How to Train Your Pet Like a Television Star* and *Ray Berwick's Complete Guide to Training Your Cat.*

Mitchell was a combat medic who returned from Vietnam and in 1975 saw the Universal Studios tour, which featured performances by Berwick-trained animals. Because he had an easily trainable housecat that rode with him on his motorcycle, Mitchell asked Berwick to help him get his cat into show business. A few months later Berwick offered him a job in his kennel, as well as an opportunity to learn show business with animals, and for the next five years Mitchell learned his craft from one of the best that ever taught an animal to act.

The Beverly Hillbillies

CBS, 1961–1971, 274 episodes, 1 TV movie

Starring ***Stretch and Duke as Duke,*** *Debbie as Cousin Bessie, Buddy Ebsen as Jed Clampett, Irene Ryan as Granny (Daisy Moses), Max Baer as Jethro Bodine, Donna Douglas as Elly May Clampett, Raymond Bailey as Milburn Drysdale, Nancy Kulp as Jane Hathaway, Bea Benaderet as Pearl Bodine, and Harriet MacGibbon as Margaret Drysdale.*

The Beverly Hillbillies is about an Ozark clan of four who strike it rich in oil and move to Beverly Hills. They learn to live with their country ways in the big city.

No television series could ever keep up with *The Beverly Hillbillies* when it comes to total number of critters that pass through the Clampett doors. It seems like there were hundreds. Among them are bears, a bobcat, a buzzard, cats, chickens, chimpanzees, a crow, a dolphin, a goat, a kangaroo, an ostrich, a pigeon, poodles, possums, puppies, raccoons, a rooster, seals, skunks, a squirrel, and a turkey.

Most notable were Jed's bloodhound Duke, and Elly May's pet chimps. She had three: Bessie, Skipper, and Maybelle. Bessie, who was played by Debbie, was quite a trouper, costarring also in *Lost in Space* and *Lancelot Link, Secret Chimp.*

Skipper was Douglas's favorite of the three. "When Bessie, the second chimp, got big like Skipper we had to watch her," Douglas once said. "Because Max accidentally

Dogs, cats, chickens, and skunks are just a few of the pets that Elly May enjoys at her menagerie in the hills of Beverly.

stepped on her foot and when she got big . . . boy, she had her eye on him."

Jed Clampett's hound dog Ol' Duke may have appeared lazy, but he moved around a lot. You see, first he hung out with Tennessee Ernie Ford and then he appeared with Andy Griffith in the film *No Time for Sergeants*, before going to the Ozarks and loading up on the truck for Beverly.

Tennessee Ernie called him Old Ring, and he was Old Blue to Griffith in *Sergeants*, but his real name was Stretch, and for a good reason. "There was a lady that raised bloodhounds, and she had this dog with real loose skin. We called it Stretch after I bought it from her," says Frank Inn. "He would do everything. He was well trained."

He continues, "For *The Tennessee Ernie Ford Show*, Ernie would come out on stage and his dog would come with him, and Ernie would say, 'This is the smartest dog that ever was. He's a hunting dog.' Then Ernie would point and tell the dog, 'Over there. There's something over there behind that bush,' and the dog would just kind of stand there. Then I cued the dog to lay down, and he would lay his head down. Then Ernie would say to the audience, 'You see how smart he is? He knows there ain't anything there.'"

Stretch worked with Tennessee Ernie Ford for five years and then started out as the Clampett dog. After he died at age sixteen, his son, Duke, who had been his stand-in, took over.

"You can see the differences when they're riding in that truck (during the opening credits). I think the first one was laying down in the truck, and the second one was sitting up," says Inn. "But they were very close in appearance. I don't think the skin on Duke was quite as stretchy but it was stretchy enough."

There are probably dozens of animal tales from the set of *The Beverly Hillbillies*, but Frank Inn recalls the funniest. "The show had Elly May riding a hippo as it's swimming in the 'cee-ment' pond. Inn had a four-year-old male hippo named Herman that was in love with a female baby elephant named Lisa. The hippo would not go anywhere without the elephant, since the two had grown up together. To get the hippo into the pool, the elephant had to go in first.

"We practiced this routine to get control. Donna was in her dressing room at the time. We led the elephant and the hippo into the water, and as soon as they hit that water, they gave in to the wants of nature real quick! I mean, they both let go and that water immediately turned the most putrid green that you've ever seen. . . . It was a mess."

He took the creatures from the pool and they skimmed the water, but it was still green. So they added some blue dye and stirred it with boat oars. The results weren't bad.

"We got the hippo in the pool, and it was OK because it was empty by now," continues Inn. "Then they asked Donna to come down and the first thing she remarked was, 'Oh my, what a pretty blue. Why is the water so blue?' I said, 'Well, Donna, the reason is the hippo is supposed to be swimming and in the clear water you could see the bottom of the pool.' She bought it. Next day at lunch, she gave me a heck of a whack across my shoulders. Somebody had told her."

Y'all come back on in now, ya hear?

Well, doggies? Well, no, chimpanzees seem to be more like what Jed Clampett (Buddy Ebsen) is thinking as Granny (Irene Ryan) hugs one of the three chimps that come to stay a spell with the Clampetts.

Frank Inn showered *The Beverly Hillbillies* with more than a hundred of his amazing critters during the long run of the series, much to the delight of Elly May (Donna Douglas).

The Bionic Woman

ABC, NBC, 1976–1978, 58 episodes

*Starring **Bracken as Maximillian,** Lindsey Wagner as Jaime Sommers, Richard Anderson as Oscar Goldman, Martin E. Brooks as Dr. Rudy Wells, Ford Rainey as Jim Elgin, Martha Scott as Helen Elgin, and Lee Majors as Steve Austin.*

The Bionic Woman revolves around the exploits of Col. Steve Austin's girlfriend Jaime Sommers, who is injured in a sky-diving accident. A bionic operation fails, but she is restored to life and given bionic limbs. She now becomes a schoolteacher while working undercover as an agent for the Office of Scientific Intelligence.

"What has four legs, outruns motorcycles, chews up rifle barrels, bends iron bars, and finds heavyweight vans a pushover? Why, Maximillian, the bionic dog. Max, the latest star in the TV bionics craze, will appear in *The Bionic Woman* with Lindsey Wagner where he will do all of the above. At least, Max will. The part will be played by four-year-old Alsatian Bracken, plus three stand-ins. Owner Moe Di Sesso says, 'The work's too difficult for one dog, and they all look alike. . . . The dogs get jealous when they see one is working and they're not. But you can't fool them.'"

Moe Di Sesso's career spans fifty years as a Hollywood animal trainer. One of his most famous creatures was Jimmy the Raven Jr.

So goes a publicity report on Jaime Sommers's canine sidekick from 1977.

There were several German shepherds who filled Max's bionic shoes, but for the most part it was big Bracken, owned and trained by legendary trainer Moe Di Sesso, who has been working professionally for fifty-five years. "He was big," Di Sesso emphasizes. "When he was a puppy, he won first place at a dog show. When he grew up, he couldn't win because he had big feet."

But Di Sesso says Bracken's big size was one of the main reasons he won the job. "They interviewed a bunch of German shepherds, but they were all small. I trained him to do about anything under the sun. He was fantastic. You could make him snarl and look mean and vicious but he was not going to hurt anyone. He was very gentle," Di Sesso says of the dog he purchased as a pup from a breeder. "He was a very smart dog. Bracken could probably outthink a person."

One of Bracken's toughest tricks was to

set off special effects while he was crawling through a forest fire. "I trained him to go on his shoulders because that was where they put the electronics. I don't know of any other dog that was trained to crawl sideways like that. When I go 'Bang!' he falls over and plays dead. He could jump through fire," says Di Sesso.

He describes the hardest set of behaviors that Bracken went through during one episode of *The Bionic Woman.* "There was a little girl in a Volkswagen on top of a hill and the van starts running down the hill. The dog smashes through the window of a car, jumps out, and runs to the rolling van and grabs the bumper to stop it and save the kid's life."

Bracken was a sociable creature on the set also. "He made friends with everybody. He let everyone in," says Di Sesso.

The German shepherd worked in other films and shows, including *Hound of Hell* and *The Hills Have Eyes.* And in the mid-1970s, Bracken became Rin Tin Tin the seventh when Di Sesso became the only trainer legally designated by Mrs. Lee Duncan (who owned the rights to Rin Tin Tin) to work "Rinty."

The job involved performing one new trick per show as actor James Brown introduced old episodes of the 1950s *Rin Tin Tin* series. The "wraparounds" with Bracken as Rin Tin Tin were filmed in color and edited to fit with thirty-six shows.

Bracken, who lived to be about fifteen, had a partner on *The Bionic Woman,* Striker, who did much of the backup work. There were two other doubles, but according to Di Sesso, they were not needed in front of the cameras.

New Jersey native Moe Di Sesso began his career training horses and performing in rodeos in the mid-1940s and dreamed of being a Hollywood stuntman. He became the stunt double of John Garfield and soon saw how dangerous the work was.

In the meantime, he was befriended by Hollywood animal trainer Curly Twiford and became his driver. Twiford supplied the raven in *The Wizard of Oz.* He gave Di Sesso a couple of raven eggs, and Di Sesso put then under a banty chicken and hatched and raised them. Under Twiford's guiding hand, Di Sesso trained Jimmy the Raven (actually Jimmy Jr.), and the bird became a celebrity of the 1950s, appearing on many TV shows and in films, including *The Raven* with Vincent Price.

Di Sesso also trained small exotic animals, such as pigeons, squirrels, owls, and rats. He won his first PATSY with Herman the pigeon in *The Gazebo* in 1959 and really hit the big time with his rats in the early 1970s movies *Willard* and *Ben,* capturing PATSYs for both films.

He has won eleven PATSYs during his

Bracken, who starred as Maximillian the bionic dog on *The Bionic Woman*, soars over trainer Moe Di Sesso's head.

Photos courtesy of Moe Di Sesso.

career and had his animals in such films as *Monte Walsh, My Stepmother Is an Alien, Romancing the Stone*, and *Seven Brides for Seven Brothers*, plus he trained the dog that played Sandy in the *Annie* feature film.

Among his television show credits are *Barney Miller, Batman, Bonanza, Dragnet, Gilligan's Island, Gunsmoke, Little House on the Prairie, The Lucy Show, Mannix, The Waltons*, and *Tucker's Witch* (Hubie the cat).

More recently his animals have appeared on *Murphy Brown, Third Rock from the Sun, Will and Grace* (the harlequin macaw Guapo and the Labrador Klaus von Puppy), and *Seinfeld* (the rooster Little Jerry Seinfeld).

Di Sesso also trained many of the wild animals on *Lassie* during the 1950s. His other PATSY-winning critters include Zorro the raccoon, Ginger the coyote, and Koko the hawk. He worked Frank Inn's Arnold the pig for several seasons of *Green Acres.*

One of the other dogs that portrayed the German shepherd known as Max was Jerry, an American bred from the West Coast, owned and trained by Karl Lewis Miller. "Jerry was over nine months old when I first acquired him," says Miller. "He was two-and-a-half or three when he did the bionic dog. The neat thing about him was he had the personality of the written character of Max.

"When I prepared Cujo for the movie, I went through twenty-four Saint Bernards in training. Out of twenty-four, one had the personality of the lead dog. It was the same thing with this German shepherd. In casting, we try to match the proper dog for the personality of the fictitious character. In this case we had several German shepherds but just one dog literally was the best all-round dog to play the character of Max the bionic dog.

"Jerry had that star quality, and German shepherds have proven to be the most versatile pure-bred dog ever bred. You name it, the German shepherd has been trained for service to man in that category. So I had a head start just because of the breed."

Miller adds, "Everything an animal does on film has to be predictable. It is easier for us to do the most difficult trick than to have a scene that says the dog is there but doesn't do anything." As for Max, Miller recalls that he crashed through brick walls, pulled bars out of jailhouse cellar windows, and rode Ferris wheels. But Miller says those weren't difficult feats—simply "A to B things."

"It's the way they film them that makes them look spectacular," Miller explains. "The dog will be running as fast as he can, but the camera can make it appear to be a hundred and twenty-five miles per hour. The biggest trick for any animal actor is that he has to perform every day the same old trick, but with a new actor in a new environment and a new approach."

While Bracken and Jerry ably appeared to be bionic, neither was immortal. Both died from old age.

The Black Stallion

The Family Channel, 1990–1993, 78 episodes

Starring ***Justin (aka Docs Keeping Time) as the Black Stallion,*** *Richard Ian Cox as Alec Ramsay, Ryan Koch as Jeremy Ramsay, Mickey Rooney as Henry Daley, Virginie Demains as Catherine Varnier, Michele Goodger as Belle Ramsey, Jean-Paul Solal as Pierre Chastel, Marianne Filali as Nicole Berthier, and David Taylor as Nate MacKay.*

The Black Stallion TV series (also known as *The Adventures of the Black Stallion*) was inspired by the great success of the 1979 feature film *The Black Stallion*, which starred Kelly Reno, Mickey Rooney, and Cass Olé, a purebred Arabian who had the title role. Based on the classic children's novel by Walter Farley, the film was about a boy who is shipwrecked on an island with a horse that he later trains to race for the championship. The movie was followed by a sequel, *The Black Stallion Returns*, in 1983.

In 1990, eleven years after the first film, came *The Black Stallion* TV series. For the show a new horse was sought for the lead role. Finding the right steed was no easy chore.

To the rescue came sixteen-year veteran horse trainer Rex Peterson, a Nebraskan who'd schooled under Glenn Randall. Peterson found the right stud on the horse track at Bay Meadows. "I bought a quarter horse straight off the track. Six weeks later we were in Vancouver, Canada, in front of the camera," says Peterson, who cut his teeth working under Randall in a Wild West show in the mid-1970s.

"The horse's name was Docs Keeping Time, but we called him Justin. He was a three-year-old straight off the track, but he wasn't running fast enough for the track. I looked at him said, 'Yes, I'll take him.' We called him Justin because I got him 'just in' time.

Mickey Rooney, whose movie work with horses goes back to *National Velvet* in 1944, reprised his role from *The Black Stallion* feature film to star in the TV series version in 1990.

"He had to work at liberty—meaning with nothing (ropes, bridles, reins) on him. I had a rear [the ability to rise upward on hind legs] on him when I got there. By the end of the season, he could lay down, push, do the camel stretch, sit up, kiss, say yes and no. Justin has an attitude that is out of this world."

The horse had to compete with a couple of Arabians for the lead role of the series. "Mickey Rooney showed up the first day to work," recalls Peterson, "and we had two of these Arabians up on the set, and Mickey comes into the barn and says, 'What's this horse? Throw a saddle on him, son.'

"Mickey jumps on him and rides him about a hundred yards and bails off. I had to get control of them in a big hurry. Mickey said, 'I'm not working with those Arabs.'

"The little quarter horse stud became the best one in the bunch. He had a better attitude. Mickey loved him. He knows a good one from a bad one. 'When you see me, you bring Justin up here or I won't be here,' Mickey said. Here comes Justin straight off the track, and he's the one Mickey liked and the little boy can trust him."

Peterson adds, "That little boy [Richard Cox] was a pretty good boy, but he didn't know how to ride. Him and Justin got along good because we worked at it. On Saturdays and Sundays when we weren't working, I got him to come out and ride as much as he could. I set up little jumps and got him to ride cross-country—a lot of things to get him really comfortable at riding.

"I put Justin in the gates one day. He'd only been off track two-and-a-half months. I put Richard on him, and we popped them gates, and I'm standing right over the top of the camera. They didn't think he would stop, but when he saw me, he stopped right in his tracks.

"Justin just got better and better. The great thing about Justin is he goes just as good as the person on him. My boys started riding him when they were three or four years old," says Peterson. "After nineteen episodes I realized what I had. The studio didn't."

After the first season wound down, Peterson and Justin separated from the TV series and went on to other roles. Peterson's credits include *The Electric Horseman, Centennial,* both *Black Stallion* feature films, *Sgt. Bilko, Runaway Bride, Sylvester, Far and Away, The Horse Whisperer, All the Pretty Horses,* and *Patriot Games.*

Justin, after *The Black Stallion,* went on to star in *Black Beauty,* a 1994 British production. Later, he showed up in the first scene of *The Horse Whisperer* where two horses slide down a hill. And that's not the only shot he did where he gets dirty.

"I did a music video for the band Procol Harum, and I buried Justin alive. There was not one ounce of him visible, and then I called him up out of the ground. It was then when I realized how great a horse he was," says Peterson. "I let the director pick the first horse. He picked Justin because he looked the part. We go and do it once. We ended up doing it nine times, and we did it all nine times with Justin. When the going got tough, he went to work. He's just a pretty good horse."

Peterson says he owes a lot of his success as a trainer to those he learned from. "I was very fortunate in my career to be around Glenn Randall. He was the master, and there will never be another one like him. Glenn spent years and years with Trigger and did stuff nobody else will ever do. It was Glenn who gave the video director my name as a recommendation to do the burial trick. Nobody had ever done it before, and after the video shoot I showed it to Glenn. He told me, 'Well, I taught you enough to figure 'em out.'"

As for the original Black Stallion in the two movies, that horse was trained by Glenn Randall's son, Corky Randall. Corky began working with horses during his high school days in the late 1940s, but he really got his breakthrough in 1960 while working with the steeds in John Wayne's *The Alamo.*

The horse he trained to star in *The Black Stallion* was one Cass Olé out of San Antonio, Texas. Corky recalled those frenzied early days getting ready to make the movie: "They fiddled around and did all the preparation to get things going, and then my brother ran down to San Antone and looked at the horse. What a beautiful animal he was. Did I want to train him? The horse is in Texas and I haven't seen him. My brother said, 'Cork, I'm in bad shape. You got to take the job—it will make you.' I told him OK.

"So I started on *The Black Stallion.* We left with just that horse, the doubles that were my brother's two horses, sorrels, and one other, an Arab the director had bought. He was a nice-looking horse, but he was a nut. We didn't have a second trained horse in case something happened to Cass."

But Cass Olé was so good Randall didn't have to worry about a backup. Randall recalls, "Cass Olé was a horse that enjoyed people and enjoyed performing. When we were in Sardinia, he walked along like the rest of us. We couldn't drive. Kelly wore his little skimpy outfit, and we all walked. Cass Olé just walked along with us and followed, never on a rope or a halter. You could leave him loose around the company. He was as good a horse as any I've been around in my life.

"He was the only horse I ever knew that could make a facial expression. Most horses never change expression—their eyes and ears yes. But Cass was it for my career."

He adds, "Cass absolutely did not like apples, and he is supposed to pick an apple up in the picture. I cut apples up as fine as you could, and he would eat every ounce of his grain, and this little pile of apples would be there.

"My dad couldn't get him to eat an apple either. He would nuzzle the apple and push it off the tombstone. Finally we had to nail the apple down, but the director never got his shot of the horse eating an apple."

Randall notes, "Cass Olé never made any pictures other than two *Black Stallions.*"

Blondie

NBC, 1957, 26 episodes

Starring ***Daisy,*** *Arthur Lake as Dagwood Bumstead, Pamela Britton as Blondie, Florenz Ames as J. C. Dithers, Stuffy Singer as Alexander, Ann Barnes as Cookie, Elvia Allman as Cora Dithers, Hal Peary as Herb Woodley, and Lucien Littlefield as Mr. Beasley the mailman.*

CBS, 1968, 14 episodes

Starring ***Shaggy as Daisy,*** *Will Hutchins as Dagwood Bumstead, Patricia Harty as Blondie, Jim Backus as J. C. Dithers, Peter Robbins as Alexander, Pamelyn Ferdin as Cookie, Henny Backus as Cora Dithers, Bryan O'Byrne as Herb Woodley, and Bobbi Jordan as Tootsie Woodley.*

The two television versions of Blondie became the fourth medium to treat Americans to the life and times of Dagwood Bumstead, a husband, father, and employee, as created by artist Chic Young. Young's antics with Dagwood and Blondie originated as a comic strip in 1930, and then between 1938 and 1950, Columbia Pictures churned out twenty-eight feature films as the hapless Bumstead encountered obstacles at home and work, not to mention the sidewalk and the mailman. A radio show began running in 1939.

The Bumsteads' favorite pet was Daisy, "the purebred mongrel."

And mongrel he was. Larry Weatherwax, son of Frank Weatherwax, recalled that the star canine was just "a mutt dog my dad found in a dog pound. He was a shaggy mixed breed, and Shaggy was his real name. The dog was two years old when we did the *Blondie* series. I worked on the show with my dad. He was a fun-loving dog: real smart and everybody loved him. He was just a dog meant to be with the kids."

As for treats, nope, no Dagwood sandwiches, but dried liver. Yeech! Weatherwax recalls, "I used to boil up some liver and let it dry out, and feed him that during the show. Little pieces of beef liver. He loved that."

Weatherwax said Shaggy died of natural causes at about ten or eleven.

Will Hutchins, who starred as Dagwood in the short-lived 1968 TV series, has a few faint memories of the dog. "Whenever Daisy had some tricks, it would slow things down, but I loved the dog. He was a lovable dog. He never bit me. He didn't have fleas or anything.

"We had to be very patient when the dog had to do some kind of a trick. The trainer would be off camera talking to the dog. It was hard to make the sound come out right, but the dog was fine."

"I used Daisy in a radio show I did recently," adds humorist/punster Hutchins, who occasionally appears at nostalgia shows and acts out skits. "I did a rewrite on one of the *Blondie* TV scripts and added a gag. As I come down the stairs, late to work, I go 'Goodbye honey, goodbye kids, goodbye Sandy'—growl—'goodbye Daisy.'"

"As I recall," continues Hutchins, the world's only living Dagwood, "Daisy was a perfect gentlewoman, or was Daisy a fellow? As Groucho Marx said, 'Ever since they found out Lassie was a boy, the public has believed the worst about Hollywood.' Daisy was a real pro. She/he always showed up on time, knew her/his barks, and did what Mr. Weatherwax told her/him to do. I miss Daisy."

Trainer Frank Inn remembers the days of Daisy during the heyday of the movie series: "Trainer Rennie Renfro owned Daisy, but he was originally trained for Rennie by Rudd Weatherwax for the first Blondie movie. Rennie had found him in an animal shelter and named him Spooks because his personality was so nervous. Weatherwax trained the dog and made him good.

Will Hutchins was Dagwood and Patricia Harty was Blondie in the 1968 TV series *Blondie*. Daisy, the family dog, is at left. Peter Robbins played Alexander, and Pamelyn Ferdin was Cookie.
Courtesy of Will Hutchins.

"When I went to work for Rennie in the late 1930s, he already had Daisy and those pups, and the Weatherwaxes had moved on to having their own business. Rudd also trained the original bunch of pups in the *Blondie* series."

Then an accident claimed the lives of Daisy's pups. "One day, while Daisy was on the set working, Rennie left the pups in a van parked at the studio," recalls Inn. "Somebody backed up a car next to the van and left it running. The carbon monoxide smothered those dogs to death. That's when Rennie wanted me to work for him because he also used those dogs in an act for Ken Murray's *Blackout.* He was desperate.

"In six weeks, I had trained duplicates of Daisy's pups into doing the tricks on the stage, and I trained a double for Daisy. There were about five puppies, one named Elmer and three or four others. They were mixed toy poodles, and they had trimmed them down to look like Daisy and painted them to have the same markings as Daisy, who was just a mutt."

Uhh, better make that "a purebred mongrel."

Trainer Rennie Renfro poses with his dog Spooks, who played Daisy, animal star of Columbia Pictures' *Blondie* series during the 1930s and 1940s. *Courtesy of Bryan Renfro.*

Born Free

NBC, 1974, 13 episodes

Starring ***Arusha, Asali, Lamu, and Whooshi as Elsa the lioness;*** *Gary Collins as George Adamson; Diana Muldaur as Joy Adamson; Hal Frederick as Makedde; Peter Lukoye as Nuru; and Joseph de Graft as Kanini.*

Filmed in East Africa, *Born Free* was inspired by the book and movie of the same title and loosely based on the lives of George Adamson, a game warden in Kenya, his wife Joy, and their lioness Elsa. They meet a variety of adventures as they care for the wildlife and guard the creatures from natural disasters, as well as human foes.

Actor Gary Collins remembers working with the big cats that played Elsa very well. "There were several Elsas," says Collins "We had imported all these lions from the United States. There was no way you could work with an untrained animal. We had a compound with eight lionesses and a couple of male lions, and we had monkeys and all sorts of animals."

The TV show was shot in Naivasha, Kenya, about an hour out of Nairobi. Collins says four different lionesses were used to play Elsa. He recalls, "The lionesses did no tricks. Their deal was to run from point A to point B. It was all for the camera. We would rotate them. If one was having a bad day, we would use another one. You couldn't tell them apart. The show gave us a tremendous respect for these animals in terms of their size and their power. You could not take them for granted. You could not treat them like house pets. There was always the outside chance, even though they didn't have their claws, they sure as hell had those teeth, and one bite could tear your arm off.

"The cubs were a different story. We had an orphanage there with us where women nursed animals that had been left or were in bad health. The funnest little thing to play with was the cheetah. He is the largest cat that purrs. You could sure as hell tell when he was happy."

Collins says the trainers pretty much worked the lions through their paces, and that the actors themselves didn't fraternize too closely with the beasts. "They were extremely strong and, not being a trainer, you couldn't really control them when you were with them one on one. Getting them to do what we needed them to do required a trainer at both ends of the set. They would walk them through, and when we stepped in, they would go from Joy to me."

That was a trick in itself; one that left the actors holding their noses. "We had to put this rank meat in our pockets. We lugged that around in our pockets, and they looked like they loved us. When they nuzzled us, they were looking for that meat," said Collins.

He adds, "We had to be very careful with our daughter, who was six, when she was around the cats. A lot of these animals have been raised domestically and they get too big, so we were very conscious. When the animals would get too rambunctious, the trainers told us to hit them as hard as we could between the eyes. It kind of got their attention."

The male lion Sudan greets Hubert Wells on a Uganda Railway car.
Courtesy of Hubert Wells.

Diana Muldaur and Gary Collins stroll along a jungle path with Elsa in the TV series *Born Free*.

Collins says that besides Hubert Wells, who trained all of the lions, they had a Kenyan herpetologist on the set. Perhaps most interesting of all was getting to know the real-life George and Joy Adamson. The couple had more than a few boisterous arguments and eventually separated.

"Joy lived just down the road from us. We became quite close," says Collins. "The real story of *Born Free* happened in northern Kenya when Joy and George were together. They found Elsa and raised her and then it was Joy who decided to write a book about it. That and the movie made them famous.

"Joy left him to live in Nairobi, while George was still a game warden, but during a madcap argument, they chased each other down the escarpment [in cars] and she had an accident that left her right arm useless. This remarkable woman taught herself to paint with her left hand. She would collect all sorts of animals at her place on the lake and nurse them back to health.

"If she caught you with wild animals, there was hell to pay. She was not at all like the character portrayed by Virginia McKenna in the movie. Joy was very autocratic. Man, you didn't mess with this woman. She was very demanding. Sadly, both of them met violent deaths." (Joy Adamson died in 1980, killed by a servant in a wage dispute, and George Adamson was killed by Somali bandits in 1989.)

Collins remembers that there were other interesting tales involving wildlife around the location where *Born Free* was filmed. "Julian Sylvester, the herpetologist, was keenly aware of Africa's extremely poisonous snakes, such as puff adders, but he was after the horned viper, which is very rare. Word quickly got out that Julian would like for someone to catch him a horned puff adder and that he would pay quite a few shillings for one.

"Before you know it, these ten- and eleven-year-old kids show up with some, and so he paid them. The next morning these snakes were dead. The kids were breaking little thorns off of trees and sticking a straight pin in one end and then sticking the thorn in the snake's head. Julian thought he was getting a find, but these were just regular puff adders with thorns. He found out how enterprising the kids were."

Another not-too-pleasant memory, says Collins, was of a colobus monkey who liked to make it rain. "He would literally thrive on peeing on you. I don't care where you were, if you were near him, he'd let go, and he would laugh and scream and holler."

Among other sights in Kenya was the amazing proliferation of wildlife. "We were near Crater Lake where there was lots of dense foliage," Collins recalls. "There were several big anacondas and animals all over the place. You would see the trail the snakes would leave, and you could see if they had eaten, because it would be deeply or lightly troughed. Several times you could see they had swallowed an impala. It was fascinating to look at. Every morning we went over this bridge, and there were hippos and ostriches and lots of giraffes. It was the most beautiful place I have ever been."

The wild animal trainer on *Born Free* was Hungarian Hubert Wells. He began in the industry in the mid-1950s. After defecting from Hungary in 1956, he came to Hollywood in 1964. He purchased most of the big cats used on the TV series at Lion Country Safari in Orange County, California.

"We had four main characters, and we had some cubs coming up. I had fifteen lions in the series—males, females, young ones, and old ones," says Wells.

The Big Four who all took stints before the camera as Elsa were named Arusha, Asali, Lamu, and Whooshi. They did know several commands for the camera, including cut, stop, stay, lie down, jump, snarl on command, and the motion-picture attack.

Wells explains that the motion-picture attack on command is where the lion jumps on you and knocks you down. Later sound effects are dubbed in so realistically that viewers would swear the lion was killing a person.

Though attacks were made to be as realistic

Jackie Kennedy visits the set of *Born Free* and poses with one of the star Elsas, the lioness Arusha.

Hubert Wells's leopard Lolita attacks his master in this shot from *Born Free.*
Courtesy of Hubert Wells.

as possible, Wells says that the most important trait to him of his actor animals was that "they get along with the actors."

Wells says two of his cats, Arusha and Asali, costarred in the movie *Living Free*, the sequel to *Born Free.* The trainer's cats were also used on the TV series *Bring 'Em Back Alive* and *Peaceable Kingdom.* Their main diet was chicken and beef.

Wells had a few other animals used regularly on *Born Free*, including a leopard named Lolita and an elephant named Tembo. And from time to time he used local animals like hyenas, crocodiles, and monkeys.

The trainer recalls a few precarious times during the filming in the Kenyan jungles and plains. "We were shooting a scene where Elsa meets an elephant, and we used a wild elephant in a national park," says Wells. "We found this young cow in a riverbed, and I turned one of my lions, Asali, loose to encounter it. In cases like this, you don't know what will happen. The lioness was very interested in this big thing. She goes into the riverbed, and the elephant notices her and puts his trunk up and makes a tremendous trumpet blast and goes after the lioness.

"The lion knows only the safety of the transporter, so the lion and the two human beings [Wells and his assistant] jumped into the Land Rover at the same time, and luckily the elephant stopped about fifteen feet from the Land Rover."

Then there was the case of a mistaken identity. "We used Lamu, the dumb blonde of the group, for a shot," Wells recalls. "She was very lovable, but not much in brains. I turned her loose on a big male elephant walking across the savannah, and the elephant was so surprised that she took off. When she realized she was running from a little thing, she turned around and chased Lamu into a clump of bushes.

"I went into the bushes to get Lamu, but my assistant gets some meat and goes up to a lion lying under the shade of a tree and says, 'Come here, Lamu, come here,' and he starts cussing her because she won't come to him. Then the lion stands up, and my assistant notices the noise made by this totally wild young male." Wells, who was, of course, out of harm's way, laughs as he recalls this incident. The assistant fortunately escaped the dangerous circumstance.

The Brady Bunch

ABC, 1969–1974, 117 episodes

Starring Tiger the dog, Tye as Fluffy the cat (pilot episode only), Florence Henderson as Carol Brady, Robert Reed as Mike Brady, Ann B. Davis as Alice Nelson, Maureen McCormick as Marcia Brady, Barry Williams as Greg Brady, Eve Plumb as Jan Brady, Susan Olsen as Cindy Brady, Christopher Knight as Peter Brady, and Michael Lookinland as Bobby Brady.

The Brady Bunch is the story of a widow (a lovely lady) with three daughters and a widower (a man named Brady) with three sons who marry and live the good but chaotic life of raising six kids in suburban Southern California.

Tiger, the shaggy dog pet of the boys and girls named Brady, was portrayed by several different pooches over the course of this family sitcom. "I did the pilot with a dog named Chip, a mixed bearded collie," says Henry Shannon, who worked for Frank Inn. "He was a fantastic dog. He had an outgoing personality. It was almost like he was listening, and he learned fast. Later he did a TV movie of the week with Elizabeth Montgomery, he worked on *Death Valley Days*, and he did a lot of dog food commercials."

But Chip only got to play Tiger one time. "Once the pilot sold and went to series, that was it," says Shannon.

Shannon also worked with the Brady girls' cat, Fluffy, on the pilot. He recalls, "We used three cats for the pilot because there was a lot of running and jumping, so we had one hyper cat and one docile cat for being carried. I remember that two of the cats were named Tye and Bigfoot. Tye was the main cat and was a descendant of the cats in the *Rhubarb* movie."

Among Tye's other credits were *I Dream of Jeannie*, *Bewitched*, and *Mayberry R.F.D.* But enough about cats—let's get back on track with Tiger.

Famed trainer Karl Lewis Miller worked briefly with one of the Tigers on *The Brady Bunch* and relates what he knows about the *Brady* dogs. "What happened was one of the animal-supplying companies did the pilot episode with one dog, but when it came time to make the series, a whole new production came in. Another animal supplier, Lou Schumacher, was their man, and he supplied the next dog to play the part of Tiger.

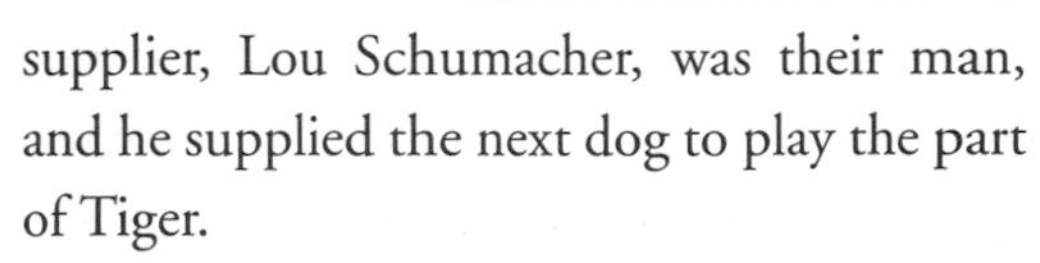

"I was the trainer of the dog for the beginning of the regular series. In the pilot, where they have the big wedding party and the dog chasing the cat, that was another dog that played Tiger."

The dog Miller trained for *The Brady Bunch* was actually named Tiger (Tiger Number 2). After a couple of episodes, Miller had to leave the *Brady* scene to make a movie and had nothing more to do with the *Brady* dog. At this point, Tiger began acting rather strangely.

"We had a Tiger, a very good dog," says *Brady Bunch* creator and executive producer Sherwood Schwartz. "One day, Tiger came in with his trainer, and the dog wouldn't do anything the trainer asked him to do. This was a well-trained dog with whom we'd never had a problem, so we shot another scene and said, 'We'll try again tomorrow.' The next day we tried to do the same scene over again. This was a particularly simple scene. All Tiger had to do was lie on the floor in the boys' room and look up soulfully at them.

"He wouldn't stay on the floor. We had to get on with the shooting. We had a simple solution. We took his leather restrainer (from around his neck) and nailed it to the floor. Now he was upset because his head wouldn't come up from the floor, so he looked balefully around the room, just like we wanted.

"After the scene, we talked to the trainer about it, and he told us the reason. This was a new Tiger. This Tiger didn't understand instructions because he had never been instructed. When Tiger had been taken home the previous week, he got loose from the trainer and ran out on the street and was killed by a car. The only way we could solve the problem was to nail the dog to the floor."

Actor Barry Williams, who starred as Greg, tells much the same tale of *Brady* dog Number 3 in his best-selling book, *Growing Up Brady*. He relates that in July 1969, when they began to film the fourth episode, "Katchoo," where the plot line centers on Jan's possibly being allergic to Tiger, director Lloyd Schwartz noticed that the dog was acting very uncharacteristic and nervous.

When Schwartz questioned the trainer, he responded by saying it was a different dog. He then explained that the original *Brady* dog had gone for a walk the evening before and got run over by a loaded florist's truck.

Williams recalls that the third Tiger wasn't much of an actor and wasn't even any good at sitting still. "In fact," wrote Williams in his book, "the next time you happen across this 'Katchoo' episode, look very closely at the 'Farewell, Tiger' scene. You'll notice that our pseudo-Tiger is actually nailed to the floor! No, we didn't hurt him (c'mon, that wouldn't be Bradylike), but the only way we could get him to hold still through the scene was to have the prop guy nail a dog collar to the floor of the set, and then strap the impostor into it."

Exit Tiger Number 3.

After the disastrous fourth episode, Tiger got the spotlight again in Episode 19, "Tiger, Tiger!" when the pooch disappears, but all is well by the conclusion as the dog is found as the proud father of a batch of newborn pups. This would have been the fourth Tiger.

And one of the *Brady Bunch* Tigers, possibly a fifth dog, who was trained by Joe Hornok, turned up as Blood in the 1975 sci-fi cult classic *A Boy and His Dog*. As Jan might say, "Tiger, Tiger, Tiger, Tiger, Tiger."

Call of the Wild

Animal Planet, 2000–2001,
13 episodes

*Starring **Kavic as Buck,** Shane Meier as Miles Challenger, Nick Mancuso as John Thornton, Rachel Hayward as Adoley Thornton, and Crystal Buble as Emma.*

Call of the Wild is the first TV series to be based on the Jack London novel. There were previously three feature films (one of them silent) and three television movies on the same story. Set in the Yukon of 1898, the adventure follows Buck, a dog stolen from his home in San Francisco and taken to the North Country where he becomes a sled dog in the woolly bully days of the gold rush. The dog winds up in the hands of young Miles Challenger, and the pair encounters a variety of characters and adventures while tangling with human and natural foes.

Shot on the *Bordertown* set in Maple Ridge, thirty miles east of Vancouver, British Columbia, *Call of the Wild* stars Kavic, a five-year-old, 140-pound cross of timber wolf and Alaskan malamute. Owned by Creative Animal Talents and trained by Steve Woodley, Kavic is an impressive animal to behold.

"He's thirty-four inches tall at the shoulders. He's a big, big, big dog," says Woodley. "When he lies down in the living room, it's like having a piece of plywood there. He's very calm in the home, but when you get him outside, he lets go, he likes to run and play.

"He is not like a dog, not like a wolf, but right in between, so you never know what you're gonna get when you get up in the morning. If he's a dog, he's gonna listen well. If he's a wolf, he's gonna make his own rules. For the most part, Kavic is real sweet, real gentle. He won't hurt anything.

"He chases—he loves the hunt and will chase it down but doesn't know what to do when he gets there. He loves kids. My nine-year-old son Dylan can actually ride Kavic. The two of them have spent many hours as a boy and his pony would, out playing in the fields."

Kavic was born in Oregon and became too much of a handful for his owner. He was shipped up to a shelter in Washington where Creative Animal Talent got a phone call about him. Woodley recalls, "He was about a year old when he came to us and all legs and feet. A lot of the TV shows up here, they don't have the budget to pay for a wolf because of

Kavic and Shane Meier take well to the Yukon in *Call of the Wild*, the first television series to be based on the Jack London novel.
Courtesy of Animal Planet.

the training it would take. We have a dog that is half-and-half and who can be portrayed as a wolf. He creeps along the ground and looks all scary.

"He played a wolf for the first couple of years, never any dog work. He has the yellow-flecked eyes, the wolf eyes. The first job he did was on *The Sentinel.* As he emerges from behind the bushes, a tribesman shoots an arrow at him. It hits him and he drops in his tracks and boom, he dies."

The canine had several other TV shows before he got his big gig. He was in *Sleepwalker, Dead Man's Gun, Nothing Too Good for a Cowboy,* and *Stargate.*

Among his many behaviors, Kavic does a great death scene. "I will give him a certain command, and he'll fall to one side and bury his head and shoulder into the grass and flip his rump over on his side, so it looks like he was shot," Woodley says. Another neat stunt is how he takes a horse by the reins and gallops across the field dragging the horse behind him.

"This really was his big break as a dog. In all the other shows, he had played a wolf." Woodley says that when the production company contacted Creative Animal Talent about looking at some of their dogs, they originally had a German shepherd in mind. "But they saw Kavic and his size and his presence, not knowing what he could do. Right there, that was the dog for them."

Kavic stars as Buck in Animal Planet's *Call of the Wild.*
Courtesy of Animal Planet.

Woodley began training Kavic in August 1999 with very little prep time before the shooting schedule started. "It would take a lot of training," says Woodley, "because he was a hybrid, and they are more difficult than a regular dog."

But for one particularly difficult trick, Kavic nailed it on the head. Woodley recalls, "We got the script a day or two before. He had to lead an injured horse by the reins, pull it out of the bush, and take it back into town. We had only a couple of days over the weekend to train, so we just had to hope Kavic would cooperate and help us out. He did his best and pulled it off. That was just him showing his ability to be an amazing animal on any given day."

Woodley adds, "He has no fear of any other animals. In training Kavic, at first some of the things he would do were just insane. He wanted to go around and chase the sheep in the neighbors' fields.

"In the morning when I let him out into his outside pen, which is about an acre and a half, he goes out there and that is his wolf time. He puts his nose in the air, 'scents in' all the animals that have come through our property the evening before, and marks his territory. We call it his private wolf time. He patrols his territory. When I call him, and say, 'Kavic, come on, let's go to work,' he comes running over to me, and he's ready to go."

Woodley trains Kavic with positive and negative reinforcement. And for training, he serves him garlic chicken among other delicacies. "We give him chicken breasts, fried up in garlic and lemon pepper. You put a little water in there, let it boil and simmer. He loves that. He loves tenderloin New York steak, sausages—and we feed him hot dog chicken wieners."

"What's really neat about Kavic," Woodley comments, "is that when we choreograph fight scenes with another dog, he can pretty much take any dog out that he wants to. But his gentleness is what makes him special. When things get out of hand and the other dog gets nasty, Kavic will basically dominate him, mat the dog, and then let him up. He's never hurt another animal."

And occasionally Kavic will make a short but mad dash to get away from the maddening pace of TV production. "Kavic will be working beautifully, like a robot," Woodley observes. "He'll be standing there for just a little too long, and then he starts to get bored after fifteen takes. He decides he's had enough—'what's wrong with you people?'—and then out of the blue he decides to wander over behind the cameras to inquire about the delay. That's the wolf side of him. He'll come back two minutes later like nothing has happened, but sometimes he has to get away to take his wolf break."

Interestingly enough, the toughest trick to teach Kavic was how to bark, something that normally takes Woodley about a day or two to teach a dog. "This animal took six weeks. He was quite pathetic at first. He'd get this groaning kind of whiny sound; out of this big animal, that's never gonna do."

Woodley finally got a wolfy sound from the hybrid: "A wolf sound is different; they don't actually bark. Wolves and malamutes are not great barkers either. They make more of a howl. It's a difficult thing to teach an animal that doesn't normally communicate by barking."

As for Kavic's basic behaviors in film, Woodley says eight of the most important are: (1) sit down, (2) stay, (3) on your feet, (4) back up, (5) lie down, (6) on your side, (7) head down, and (8) lift.

But this big dog does much more. Woodley says, "Kavic knows how to retrieve; he also will jump up. He'll go put his feet up on someone. He'll knock you over. He also knows to bond, which is to come in and look you in the eye. And come easy, which is the slowest pace. He moves up. He drops his head for a look. He digs. He takes someone's sleeve and he bites. He kisses. He nudges."

Kavic and costar Shane Meier took a short time to get to know each other and now they are almost as tight in real life as they seem onscreen. Woodley says, "There are situations where I can't get in the room, like a cabin situation, and I'll have Shane give him a simple command and Kavic listens to him. He likes Shane quite a bit. After thirteen episodes, he's become quite chummy. When he sees Shane, he likes to run to him and greet him, but at first when they began filming, Kavic was very choosy about his friends."

Back home, it's the call of animal camaraderie as Kavic goofs around with a young raccoon named Silverman, a fox named Rico, and a dog. "The raccoon grunts at him, and Kavic runs and spins and jumps," says Woodley. "And he hangs out with the fox and a German shepherd named Primo. They're his buddies."

Caroline in the City

NBC, 1995–1999, 97 episodes

*Starring **Tiki as Salty,** Lea Thompson as Caroline Duffy, Eric Lutes as Del Cassidy, Malcolm Gets as Richard Karinsky, Amy Pietz as Annie Spadaro, Andrew Lauer as Charlie, Tom La Grua as Remo, Sofia Milos as Julia Karinsky, Candy Azzara as Angie Spadaro, and Paul Castree as Chris Duffy.*

Caroline in the City is about a successful Manhattan cartoonist who draws a cartoon strip called *Caroline in the City* that is loosely based on her life and the lives of her friends.

Tiki was one of the least likely feline stars of the 1990s. That's mainly because Tiki was one shy cat who preferred dark, quiet places as opposed to bright lights, cameras, and action.

"She came from a cattery, a place that breeds cats. The owner decided that Tiki couldn't have babies anymore, so they called us," says Tammy Maples, Tiki's owner and trainer and a partner in Jungle Exotics. "They thought she would be good to do commercials because she was so pretty. One of our trainers really liked Himalayas [Tiki's breed], and she said her sister would give her a home.

"We took her, but Tiki was so shy the sister didn't take her home. She lived here on the ranch for three months and stayed under the bed most of the time. We'd put food out, and she'd come out and eat and run back under the bed. She was very shy. She had lived in a cage. We thought she would just become a house cat at the ranch."

Then the producers for the 1993 Disney movie *Homeward Bound: The Incredible Journey* showed up. Jungle Exotics got the job to cast the animals for the film. Maples recalls, "Tiki had just started hanging around in the office and would sit around on the desks. They [the Disney producers] walked in and said, "We don't know the breed for the dogs yet, but that is definitely Sassy.' We thought, 'Oh no,' but she took to training very quickly. We were all surprised. She was the last cat we would have picked to have to work with, but she surpassed all the other cats and ended up being the lead cat."

Later, Tiki won the starring role of Salty for *Caroline in the City.* By this time, her shyness was diminishing but her ego was flourishing. "We always called her the princess. She is a prissy cat, very set in her ways. She would always go where we told her to go, but she wouldn't run. That's just a part of her personality," Maples says. "She thought that a little bit beneath her. And she always hated to be dirty. She always washes it off. On cue she will wash her foot. Tiki pretty much has the personality of Sassy in the *Homeward Bound* movie."

Since the cat will only walk, not run, it also means she is great at standing still. Maples says, "On *Caroline in the City*, for some scenes she would sit in the same place for forty-five minutes at a time without moving."

Maples adds, "She has a total of twenty-five different behaviors. They're all pretty much natural cat behaviors. She waves on cue. She comes to the sound of the buzzer (the cats know they're going to get a good treat when they come), she lies down and stays, she goes to her mark, rubs against people's legs, and she sits up and turns in a circle.

"For the movie *Homeward Bound*, she had to go run with the dogs. She learned to keep up when they acted like they were talking to each other. Their mouths didn't move, but they had to be looking at each other like they were carrying on a conversation."

One minor glitch on *Caroline in the City* was that Tiki did do a lot of talking, well, purring. "She enjoys working, so she does purr," says Maples. "The sound people would come down and say, 'Can you get her to stop purring? We're picking that up.'"

Maples says that Tiki worked well with her TV master Lea Thompson and also liked costar Amy Pietz. "She got along with everybody pretty well. It's kind of funny. When we're sitting at home and she hears Lea doing voice-overs on Chevy truck commercials, she might be on the couch almost asleep, and she'll perk up like, 'Where is she?'"

Tiki had two backup cats on *Caroline*. Remington was the cat best used for carrying around, and Sassy was the running cat.

Maples says that Tiki's taste buds have gotten more particular since she became a star attraction. "Her favorite food started out as white meat chicken. At first it could even be canned. As time went on and *Caroline* went from season to season, she liked broasted chicken. By the end, she wanted broasted chicken from a particular place and it had to be warm. She was getting picky about her treats."

Maples says that Tiki now does occasional guest appearances—little parts—because she is "mainly retired and kind of an older cat. She lives at the house with me and does

Tiki was a very shy feline before owner/trainer Tammy Maples brought out the sunshine in her. Her light soared as Salty on *Caroline in the City*.
Courtesy of Tammy Maples / Jungle Exotics.

normal cat-type things. She gets jealous when she sees the other cats going to work."

Now fourteen, Tiki has two other main credits. She was in Disney's TV movie remake of *The Shaggy Dog*, and the picky eater also worked in a *Lean Cuisine* commercial.

The Chimp Channel

TBS, 1999, 13 episodes

Starring ***Tyler as Timmy Briar and Stan, Chubs as Harry Waller and Bif, Jerri (the sole orangutan) as Murray Price, Tonka as Brock Hammond and Ford Carter, and Maggie as Marina and Candy.*** *Voices supplied by Richard Horvitz as Timmy Briar, Maurice Lemarche as Harry Waller, Eugene Roche as Murray Price, Daran Norris as Brock Hammond, Jennifer Hale as Marina, Richard Doyle as Ford Carter, Dwight Schultz as Stan, and Michael David Donovan as Bif.*

The majority of the simian stars of *The Chimp Channel* were supplied by Bob Dunn's Animal Services. "We had four chimps that were regulars, one orang and some day players," says trainer Denise Sanders. Other chimps came in and played day-player roles. Each show had five to nine chimps plus one orang."

The Chimp Channel was filmed over a period of seven months at a small studio in Burbank. The sole orangutan was Jerri, who has done lots of movies and TV shows, including *Dunston Checks In, Swiss Family Robinson,* and Tang commercials. That's Jerri's picture on all those Tang boxes.

Chimpanzee Tyler starred as Ham, the first chimp sent into space, in the film *Race to Space.* He has been on *Just Shoot Me* and *Third Rock from the Sun*, and in commercials for Mercedes and Toyota Prius.

The chimp Chubs acted in *Ace Ventura II* and was in a German TV series (*Max and Company*) and a French TV series, plus an episode of *Saved by the Bell.*

Tonka, one of the main stars of the Universal animal show at the Universal Studios, was in *George of the Jungle* and *Jungle Book II.* Not surprisingly, Tonka belongs to Universal.

Maggie was in the movie *Buddy* and such TV series as *Caroline in the City, Alex Mack, USA High,* and *Working.*

"Each character seemed like it was written for that chimp, so their personalities shined through," Sanders says. "Maggie is kind of like a diva, so the movie star persona they gave her fit her completely. Chubs's attitude and personality is more laid back, while Tyler is a silly chimp. His main motivation in life is to play.

"We had worked with the writers and directors on previous projects, so they got to know the chimps and their personalities. Of course, they're all chimps, but we had them being as human-like as possible.

"It was nice, because you were only working chimps and didn't have to worry about factoring actors into the scene. We could devote all of our time to the chimps, and it was scheduled so no one chimp was working all day long.

"We were quite busy. Each chimp had wardrobe and wigs, so there was a lot of prep time. We took eight days to do an episode, plus about two prep days, so it took about ten days per episode. We used one trainer per chimp and had one additional trainer to be a runner, so if five chimps were used, we had six trainers working."

The year before *Chimp Channel* went into production, all of the same chimpanzees worked in *Monkey Movies*, spoofs of forty-two different movies for TBS. Among the films from which the chimps satirized scenes were *Titanic*, *In and Out*, and *Dances with Wolves*.

Hey, monkey see, monkey act out.

The chimpanzee stars of *The Chimp Channel* did *Monkey Movies*, among other gigs. Here two of the simian stars spoof *Baywatch*.
Courtesy of Bob Dunn's Animal Services.

Circus Boy

NBC and ABC, 1956–1958, 49 episodes

Starring ***Bimbo the elephant, Nuba the lion, Sultan the tiger, Sinbad the camel, Hasan the horse,*** *Micky Braddock (Micky Dolenz) as Corky, Noah Beery Jr. as Joey the Clown, Robert Lowery as Big Tim Champion, Guinn "Big Boy" Williams as Pete, Leo Gordon as Hank Miller, Billy Barty as Little Tom the midget, and Andy Clyde as Circus Jack.*

Circus Boy follows the adventures of twelve-year-old Corky, an orphan, who serves as water boy to Bimbo the baby elephant in Big Tim Champion's circus as the big top troupe travels the West of the late 1800s.

Almost exactly ten years before he became one of the Monkees, young Micky Dolenz, then acting under the name Micky Braddock, worked with a menagerie of animal actors as he starred as Corky in *Circus Boy*.

His best non-human friend on the set was a peewee pachyderm called Bimbo. "The first day of filming I had to get up and ride it. We actually became pretty good friends,"

Micky Braddock (now Micky Dolenz) rides a coin-operated Bimbo with his chimp during a time-out from his 1950s Saturday morning TV show, *Circus Boy*.

says Dolenz, remembering his days beneath the big top and before the camera.

"We used two Bimbos. The first one got too big, too quickly. I remember being told the first Bimbo had to be put down because it went nuts. Bimbo could do all the typical circus elephant tricks—stand up on its hind legs, lift its foot, turn around, follow the trainer, or just stay.

"I would give it candy bars all the time in the wrapper. At first, I would unwrap them, and then the trainer said, 'Give it to him in the wrapper. He likes them that way.' So Bimbo loved Baby Ruths in the wrapper."

Dolenz recalls that *Circus Boy*, which filmed for two seasons, was originally shot at "Crash" Corrigan's Corriganville. "We set up the tent and filmed there for quite a while until a storm wrecked everything. Then we filmed on the back lot at Columbia, a place surrounded by scrubland and orchards, as well as on the sound stage, and we shot some out in Thousand Oaks. I think there's a mall there now, but it was called the World Jungle Compound. It was sort of like a zoo, but it had shows and an area where people could see the animals perform. It had all the animals from the movies, like the MGM lions. And that's where we got all the exotic animals for *Circus Boy*—llamas, bears, tigers, camels, and the elephants."

Dolenz adds, "Bimbo's trainer was a guy named 'Arkie' Arkansas (Eugene Scott), and he had a voice like a cheese grater. The lion tamer was named Mel Koontz." "Chief" Henry Tyndell, a Choctaw Indian from Oklahoma, worked the chimpanzee on *Circus Boy*.

Besides his elephant friends, the young actor rode the dusty trail with plenty of other exotic animals. He saddled up, minus the saddle, and raced bareback on an ostrich and a camel, and also rode a lion (you don't race lions).

There were a few close shaves for the little shaver. "I remember once a lion or tiger got out of its cage on the set and was wandering around loose," recalls Dolenz. "My mother grabbed me and threw me into one of the trailers.

"The chimp was the only animal that ever hurt me. It didn't intentionally bite me, but once I ran up to it early in the morning, maybe to give it a greeting or a hug, and I think I scared it. It bit me on the hand. It was nothing serious, but I never forgot it."

The young Monkee-in-training began rocking and rolling during his *Circus Boy* summer hiatus when he hit the road with Bimbo. "I was this elephant's opening act on the road for one summer. We did about a dozen dates. My parents were singers, so I sang and was learning to play the guitar. Somebody had the bright idea for promotional purposes to go on the road and do dates at fairs and parks. I rehearsed a few songs: 'Purple People Eater,' 'Gonna Sit Down and Write Myself a Letter,' and 'Witch Doctor.' I had my little guitar, and the local band, in whatever city we were, would back me.

"Then the elephant would come out with his trainer. I would stand there and pretend to be the one training the elephant, and it would do all of its little tricks. I remember Kennywood Park in Pittsburgh was our first show," says Dolenz, who once played the boy who ran away with the circus and loved it.

Home of the Animal Stars

By the 1940s, the World Jungle Compound served as one of Hollywood's most famous home bases for movie animal stars.

Although it went through many name changes during its fifty-year lifespan, the compound/farm first came into being in Thousand Oaks, California, in 1926. It was started by Louis Goebel, who had previously worked at Gay's Lion Farm and at Universal Studios, where he butchered meat to feed the lions and acted as groundskeeper.

The owner first named it Goebel's Lion Farm, since he had purchased six lions from Universal at that time. Many studio animal stars boarded on the 170-acre farm, including a number of elephants, water buffalo, zebras, and MGM's proud lion, Leo.

Goebel opened this business to tourists in 1927. Two years later, many of his creatures were hired to appear in *Tarzan the Ape Man.* His pack of pachyderms was in all the MGM *Tarzan* flicks, and the elephants were also coiffed to appear as woolly mammoths in *One Million B.C.* in 1939.

Louis Roth was the chief animal trainer for Goebel in the 1930s and 1940s. Roth trained not only big cats of the wild, but also humans as he taught his bag of tricks to Clyde Beatty and Mabel Stark, among others.

Goebel sold his place to Trader Horne and Billy Richards in 1946, and they called it Trader Horne's World Jungle Compound. In 1956, Horne and Richards

sold their property to 20th Century Fox, and it was renamed Jungleland. Then, in 1961, Louis Goebel reacquired his old stomping grounds. After trainer Roth retired in the mid-1940s, Melvin Koontz came aboard as chief animal trainer.

Animal handler Bill Raymond, who worked a lot on *Daktari*, grew up in the Los Angeles area and was a young stuntman who wanted to learn how to wrestle the animals when he went to Africa USA (Ralph Helfer and Ivan Tors' company). He discovered they had a training program, and he liked working with animals so much that he became a handler.

As a youth he had made many visits with his parents to Goebel's World Jungle Compound in Thousand Oaks. Raymond was fascinated by Goebel's lion tamer Mel Koontz, who was an inspiration to him. Raymond finally got the chance to work with Koontz, when Koontz was hired by Africa USA to help work the tigers on the movie *Rampage*. "I was the only kid Mel allowed to have his picture taken riding on the back of his tiger Satan," says Raymond.

Raymond continues, "In the thirties, forties, and fifties, about ninety percent of the animals used in films came from Goebel's. There were a few other places, but Goebel's had a corner on the market. Mel did the wrestling with the big cats: the lions, tigers, leopards, and cougars—often appearing in the *Jungle Jim* films.

"In the early sixties, the Goebel family leased their place to Roy Cabot and a partner, Tex Scarborough, and the name was changed to Jungleland. But by the mid-1970s, property taxes were raised several times—forcing Cabot to place the business into bankruptcy and sell off the animals. Some of the trainers and handlers who worked there bought as many of the animals as they could. But the rest went to zoos around the country. Thus, the lights went out on one of the brightest locations in Hollywood history."

One other veteran Raymond recalls at the World Jungle Compound was legendary lion tamer-trainer Mabel Stark. "Mabel worked the tigers," says Raymond. "She wanted to die in the arena with her tigers. When she finally admitted to being eighty-nine years old, the insurance company forced her to retire, and about three weeks later she took her life. She was something. She ruled the roost. Nobody crossed Mabel."

Trainer Bob Riedell recalls that Chief Henry Tyndell worked the cheetahs on many of the Weissmuller *Tarzan* and *Jungle Jim* films. "He had a chimp that could shoot a bow and arrow and hit the target and do tricks," Riedell says.

Wally Ross, who freelanced some at Jungleland, says the "Chief," as everybody called him, was a full-blooded Choctaw from Oklahoma. "He trained just about all the chimps. He started there in the late 1930s or early '40s and was there until the place was auctioned off. He worked with all the chimpanzees there," Ross said, including the chimp on *Circus Boy.*

***

Louis Goebel's widow, Kathleen Goebel, at age ninety-five in the spring of 2001, recounted a brief history of Jungleland through her own eyes:

My husband moved from Buffalo, New York, in 1919 and came to California. He worked at Gay's Lion Farm for several years, until Gay had to move due to the area growing. Louis then went to work at the Universal Studio as a butcher for their small private zoo. When the zoo animals were to be eliminated, Louis bought six of the lions.

He purchased several lots facing what was then called '101 Boulevard' in a place way out in the country called Thousand Oaks. (Now where the farm stood is the City Hall.) He first opened to the public in 1927.

This was the start of Goebel's Lion Farm. In the beginning, there were the six lions and a group of dogs that had been used in a picture as a Canadian Mounted Police dog team. We were married in 1928 and worked hard at improving the farm and as we had added many more animals, we renamed it Goebel's Wild Animal Farm. This was now a working farm. People became animal trainers and animals were trained to work in pictures and circus acts.

Most all the animals that played in the Johnny Weissmuller *Tarzan* pictures came from the Lion Farm. Tony Gentry, I believe, had the chimp that was used mostly in the *Tarzan* pictures.

In the early days many circuses wintered at the Lion Farm. They trained for their new acts and on the weekends performed on our stages for the visitors to the farm along with our own trainers and acts. Clyde Beatty was just one of many of these people who wintered with us.

Any of the studios that needed an animal for their picture knew where we were and kept us quite busy. By 1946 our business had grown so big, we decided to sell the animal farm and keep just the import-export part of the business that supplied the zoos with animals.

We sold the working farm to Trader Horne and Billy Richards in 1946. It became known as the World Jungle Compound. In the mid-1950s, they sold the farm to another group of people who renamed it Jungle Land. Mel Koontz went to work for Horne and Richards, and when they left, so did Mel.

It came back to us in 1960, and in 1962 a corporation was formed, and a few years later was

By the 1940s, the World Jungle Compound served as one of Hollywood's most famous home bases for movie animal stars.

dissolved. [It was now known as Jungleland.] Jungleland again, and for the last time, was resold to a new group of people in 1972. In 1976, due to financial difficulties, Jungleland's doors were closed forever with bankruptcy proceedings, as we did not wish to take it back again.

Coach

ABC, 1987–1997, 200 episodes

*Starring **Isaac as Quincy,** Craig T. Nelson as Coach Hayden Fox, Jerry Van Dyke as assistant coach Luther Van Dam, Shelley Fabares as Christine Armstrong Fox, Clare Carey as Kelly Fox, and Bill Fagerbakke as Dauber Dybinksi.*

The game plan for this sitcom is to follow the on- and off-field world of football coach Fox and his appealing team of coworkers, family, and players.

"It was my idea for me to have a dog on the show," says actor Jerry Van Dyke. "I was after them from the beginning, and finally Luther got a dog. It was my idea to have him ride in the little red wagon, too. The idea was that this dog was so lazy he wouldn't even walk. The whole idea was to have him do nothing. I got the idea from *The Ed Sullivan Show.* There was this dog on there that wouldn't do anything his trainer asked him to do, but the trainer was so proud. He'd ask the audience, 'Did you see him? Did you see that?' He asked the dog to perform some trick. Then he'd go over to pick up the dog, and the dog would be limp like a sack of bones. It was hilarious. I loved that dog. He was great. And I'm an animal lover, anyway. I love all animals."

Van Dyke adds, "The biggest problem with Quincy was getting him to sit still in the little wagon because he wasn't supposed to do anything but sit. Sometimes he'd want to jump out of the wagon. Sometimes the hardest trick for an animal is not to do anything. A lot of times, animals will want to look at their trainer or watch something else. When you have an animal that's supposed to be the family pet, it's better to just to let them behave like a real family pet would."

The dog who played Quincy on *Coach* was named Isaac, and he was perfect for the part. "He was chosen for the part because he was not pretty," said his owner and trainer, Cheryl Shawver. "His role was to lay there and do nothing, not to know a hundred tricks."

Isaac unfortunately died during production of *Coach*. Another basset hound took over the role of Quincy, but it just wasn't quite the same. An episode was then written where the Quincy character dies and there's a service with all of his human and canine pals. Luther was then presented with a new puppy and the show went on.

Columbo

NBC, 1971–1977; ABC, 1989–1993, 68 TV movies

*Starring **Henry as Dog** and Peter Falk as Lt. Columbo.*

Columbo is an unorthodox Los Angeles police detective who smokes a stogie, drives a beat-up Peugeot, wears a rumpled trench coat, and slurs his speech. But his razor-sharp mind and method of lulling his suspects into feelings of superiority lead him to solve the crime every time.

Columbo, one of television's most famous characters without a first name, also had a dog without a name. The detective once said, "He's a dog, so we call him Dog." Ray Berwick, who owned and trained the basset hound, called him Henry.

Actor Falk was not keen on the idea of having a canine copilot, but NBC insisted this character have a partner. Once he saw the pooch, he changed his opinion.

Henry made his first appearance in the second season of the *NBC Mystery Movie* in the TV movie titled *Etude in Black*. Here we see Columbo find his dog at the pound and hear his vet suggest that he name him Fido,

Columbo's favorite pooch was a basset hound named Henry. The dog also played the firehouse canine on *Emergency*.
Courtesy of Ted Kerin collection.

Jet, or Munich. Columbo tries the name Beethoven, but when the dog dislikes the moniker, the detective deduces that he should completely drop the idea of names.

Columbo's dog enjoys ice cream, watching the tube, and swimming in the neighbor's pool. He shows up prominently in the *Columbo* movies *Forgotten Lady*, *Playback*, *Try and Catch Me*, *Now You See Him*, and *Make Me a Perfect Murder*.

"Falk as Columbo did a lot of stuff with Henry—walking him and riding with him in his car," says Berwick protégé Karl

Mitchell. "The biggest thing was to get Henry to stay and sit in the car. Peter Falk would sit with him while having coffee between scenes. He let the dog tie him in to his character. He was in character when he had on the Columbo outfit, and when he was in character that was his dog and he treated it that way."

But being Columbo's favorite mutt was not Henry's first claim to fame. Before that series he played himself, just a good old basset hound named Henry on *Emergency!* "He was the firehouse dog, where Henry's whole big job was to lay on the couch and yawn occasionally. Henry is an honest-to-goodness Cinderella dog," Mitchell says, "because one month he was a nobody and the next month he was a television star. He got the job because he was good at doing nothing."

Berwick found Henry at the Burbank animal pound. After his Hollywood days, Henry went to live with folks who kept him as a pet in the backyard. "In private life, he was a happy-go-lucky fellow," Mitchell says. "He died of old age."

Mitchell relates one funny tale from the *Emergency!* set: "Randolph Mantooth had a problem working with Henry because basset hounds have a particular odor. One day Mantooth refused to work with him, so we took Henry and told the production assistants that we were going to give him a bath and put him under a dryer. The P.A.'s were in a tizzy and kept calling us and asking, 'Is Henry done yet?' We brought him back three hours later, but we hadn't done anything to him at all. We took him on the set, and all of the actors said, 'Oh, he smells so much better.' The dog didn't smell at all, but we didn't do anything to him."

Corky and White Shadow (The Mickey Mouse Club serial)

ABC, 1955–1956

*Starring **White Shadow Crider as White Shadow,** Darlene Gillespie as Corky Brady, Buddy Ebsen as Sheriff Matt Brady, Lloyd Corrigan as Uncle Dan, Buzz Henry as Durango Dude, Richard Powers as Sheriff Martin, and Chuck Courtney as the Nevada Kid.*

Set in a small town in the Midwest, a young girl and her German shepherd try to capture an outlaw, the Durango Dude, unbeknownst to her father, the sheriff.

Dog star White Shadow was seen by gazillions of kids on *The Mickey Mouse Club*, but before he jumped to television, many movie fans saw his father, Harvey, in a series of ten feature films as Chinook, "The Wonder Dog." There is some confusion as to whether Harvey was also the star of the Mouse Club serial, but it appears that White Shadow was played by Harvey's son.

So here goes and hang on.

Harvey, whose formal name was Harvey Brindlesiff Offner, was the pride and joy of actress Dorothy Crider. He was the first in a line of white German shepherds that Crider owned, bred, and trained. Harvey's father was Silver Tips, aka Ace, who was owned by Earl Johnson, the man who trained Bullet for Roy Rogers, and Harvey's mother was Lady of Elsereno.

Harvey was also called Chinook I because of a series of low-budget westerns he starred in. He was not white but was silver with black outlines around his eyes, lips, and nose, says Alice Horton, a friend of Crider who owns some white German shepherds that are the offspring of Harvey/Chinook.

"Dorothy said she named him Harvey because his big white ears reminded her of the white rabbit in the play. Dorothy told me that he was silver in color but photographed white in a black and white film," said Horton.

There were already some white German shepherds in Hollywood before Harvey. Bela Lugosi had several as pets, including one named Bodri. But Crider may have had the first movie star white German shepherd with Harvey, who was born around 1938. The dog was best man at Crider's wedding and several years later, when she divorced, Harvey was part of her settlement from her husband, director Reginald Brown.

Crider operated a kennel, White Shadow Ranch, in Sherman Oaks, California. This was where Harvey lived and began his line of other movie star and TV star dogs.

"The dog on *The Mickey Mouse Club* serial was not Harvey, but his son, the first White Shadow," said Horton. "Harvey was known as Chinook I. Dorothy called White Shadow Crider 'White Shadow I.' And White Shadow was the father of Tango, who was known as White Shadow II. White Shadow II was the father of White Shadow Chinookie, aka Chinook II."

Got it? OK.

Crider's four white German shepherds appeared in approximately two hundred films, TV shows, and commercials over the years. Her dogs also worked on stage and at state fairs and USO shows. The dogs won several PATSY awards, and Crider said that White Shadow II entertained with Roy Rogers and Trigger in public appearances in the guise of Roy's dog Bullet.

Harvey's biggest role was in ten films as Chinook. Chinook's human partner in the movies was Kirby Grant, who portrayed a Mountie of the Canadian Northwest. Between 1949 and 1954, the duo made seven Monogram films: *Trail of the Yukon*, *The Wolf Hunters*, *Snow Dog*, *Call of the Klondike*,

Dorothy Crider poses with one of the four white German shepherds she used in movies, TV shows, and commercials.

Yukon Manhunt, Northwest Territory, and *Yukon Gold,* plus three for Allied Artists: *Fangs of the Arctic, Northern Patrol,* and *Yukon Vengeance.*

The late Grant, whom many remember for his Saturday morning TV series *Sky King,* used to get a chuckle out of his movie star dog's onscreen name. Chinook means a warm wind, but Grant said that the dog's personality was quite the opposite.

"He had the conformation of a police dog. He bit almost everybody on the set at one time or another with the exception of myself. He and I got along very well. He was not vicious, just very temperamental," Grant told author David Rothel.

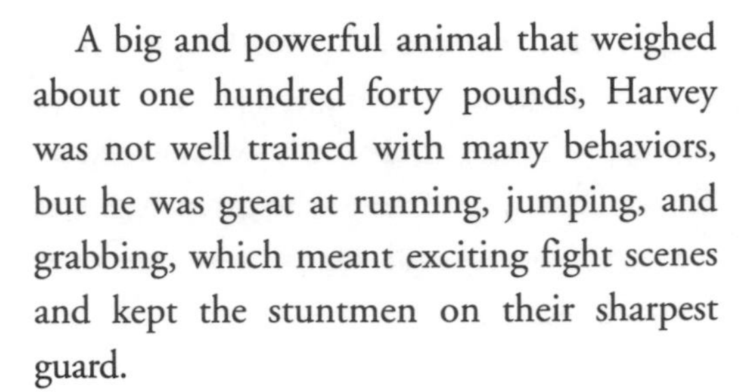

A big and powerful animal that weighed about one hundred forty pounds, Harvey was not well trained with many behaviors, but he was great at running, jumping, and grabbing, which meant exciting fight scenes and kept the stuntmen on their sharpest guard.

Mouseketeer-turned-cowgirl Darlene Gillespie has memories that are not quite as positive as Grant's. Years later she said about her doggy star, "He was an idiot. He was always fouling up takes. I bet you, somewhere in the Disney Studios, there's a million feet of sound film of his trainer yelling, 'Harvey! %*#@%% it! Come back here, Harvey!'"

Cowboy in Africa

ABC, 1967–1968, 26 episodes

*Starring **Pajama Tops as Pajama Tops the zebra,** Chuck Connors as Jim Sinclair, Tom Nardini as John Henry, Ronald Howard as Commander Howard Hayes, and Gerald Edwards as Samson.*

Cowboy in Africa, a spin-off of the 1967 Hugh O'Brian film *Africa——Texas Style!,* is an African western about a world champion rodeo cowboy who goes to work on an African game ranch. He is assisted by a Navajo blood brother and "adopted" by a ten-year-old native boy.

While some second-unit shots were filmed in Africa, the majority of *Cowboy in Africa* was filmed at Africa USA, the same site where most of *Daktari* was shot. Many exotic animals were used throughout the twenty-six episodes, but the main animal star was a zebra named Pajama Tops.

"She was a Grant's zebra, an excellent one, just really sweet. You could ride her," says Ralph Helfer. "Zebras can be really difficult. They have quite a bite and a kick. Everybody was saying, get a white horse and paint black stripes on it. We went to work on her in our gentle way, and she turned out to be just terrific. With us, the trust of the animal was what was important, and whether we worked her with a lion or a python, she trusted us.

"She was one terrific animal. We didn't even put her in a cage or a pen. She was so good we just let her walk around and do her own thing. She always wanted attention. She would line up during lunch break. She knew if she lined up, everybody would give her some goodies. She got along great with Judy the chimp because Judy would ride her."

Bill Raymond, who was an animal handler and sometimes a stuntman at Africa USA, recalls the striped star: "PJ was a good zebra. She was quite workable."

There were other animal semi-regulars, including a simian named Peeli Peeli and two dogs named Get Off the Couch and You Too. Raymond believes that a young baboon trained by Ralph Perry played Peeli Peeli. "Perry would carry that baboon with him everywhere," recalls Raymond. "It had its own security blanket, a little red shop rag. It would take it and put it over its head and wear it like a bonnet."

Another of Hollywood's great animal trainers, Steve Martin, learned the ropes of the business on shows like *Cowboy in Africa* and *Daktari*. "We had a lot of lions and did a lot of big cat work on *Cowboy in Africa*. We used cape buffalo, ostriches, wildebeest, and I remember a baboon named Ridge Rod. Mickey Gilbert, a wrangler and Chuck Connor's stunt double, was a heck of a stuntman. He roped lions, cape buffalo, wildebeest, zebras, and rhinos," says Martin, who worked with elephants, tigers, and bears on *Daktari*.

One of Martin's early jobs in the business was touring the United States with one of the bears from *Gentle Ben*. "He was one of the doubles, Drum, a real nice bear," recalls Martin. "He was a better working animal than Bruno, but Bruno was very good with kids. We put on a regular show and had an emcee and a girl from Hawaii that juggled knives and sticks on fire. We did a whole skit with the bear and her and myself, and Ron Oxley, another trainer."

Cowboy in Africa star Chuck Connors moseys about with four of his costars, a giraffe, a lion, an elephant, and a leopard.

Martin also supplied one bear and all of the animals for the first year of *The Life and Times of Grizzly Adams*, except for the star bear Bozo. "I had one grizzly who did the back-up stuff. His name is Grizz, and I still have him. He's twenty-seven years old," says Martin.

Chuck Connors, star of the TV westerns *The Rifleman* and *Branded,* is ready with a rope in *Cowboy in Africa.*

In addition, Martin provided many of the animals for a Canadian TV series, *Search and Rescue.* Shot in Toronto, the series featured such critters as black bears, African lions, cougars, raccoons, red-tailed hawks, river otters, and a horned owl.

Martin began working while in high school at Ralph Helfer's Nature's Haven in Soledad Canyon in the mid-1960s. After graduating from high school, he went through Helfer's training school and began working in the animal nursery with baby lions, tigers, and elephants. He spent a year getting to know various animals and then left to work with larger animals, especially large cats.

He opened his own ranch, Working Wildlife, in 1974, and has since supplied animals for hundreds of productions, including films such as *The Deerhunter, Babe: Pig in the City, Dances with Wolves, The Santa Clause, Ernest Saves Christmas, The Jungle Book, Cat People, The Great Outdoors, Ace Ventura Pet Detective II, Pee-wee's Big Adventure,* and *Clan of the Cave Bear,* as well as TV shows such as *Northern Exposure, Nash Bridges, Home Improvement, Fantasy Island, All My Children,* and *Hill Street Blues.* Today his menagerie of 150 animals includes bears, cougar, deer, all types of cats, zebra, chimps, alligators, and birds of prey.

Daktari

CBS, 1966–1969, 89 episodes

Starring ***Clarence as Clarence the cross-eyed lion, Judy as Judy the chimp,*** *Marshall Thompson as Dr. Marsh Tracy, Cheryl Miller as Paula Tracy, Yale Summers as zoologist Jack Dane, Hedley Mattingly as game warden Hedley, Hari Rhodes as zoologist Mike Makula, Ross Hagen as game-hunter-turned-photo-safari-guide Bart Jason, and Erin Moran as Jenny Jones.*

Shot for the most part at Ralph Helfer's wild-animal park Africa USA (in Soledad Canyon in Newhall, north of Los Angeles), *Daktari* is the tale of an American veterinarian ("Daktari" is Swahili for doctor) in Africa who operates the Wameru Game Preserve and Research Center with his daughter and other friends. They deal with game wardens, hunters, and guides and are constantly assisted and amused by their two favorite pets, Clarence and Judy, as they try to protect wildlife in the area.

When it comes to films and TV, Ralph Helfer is one of the giants of animal trainers and owners in the second half of the 20th century. Two of his biggest stars were Clarence, a cross-eyed lion, and Judy the chimp. But at one time, Helfer had more than a thousand animals and employed more than fifty trainers in his animal kingdom.

Helfer was the instigator of what he termed "affection training." Clarence and Judy were two of his star graduates of the system. "Instead of dealing with my animals physically, I deal with them emotionally," Helfer wrote in his 1990 book *The Beauty of the Beasts.* "I use love, patience, understanding, and respect to get my animals to perform."

"It was a very unique program," Helfer says of the affection training. "We were generating a tremendous output of performances on the networks and in the movies, so we devised a gentle obstacle course that all the animals went through."

The television series came to be after the success of the feature film, *Clarence, the Cross-Eyed Lion.* It was based on an original story written by Marshall Thompson, the late actor who also starred in the film and *Daktari.*

Thompson had worked in several productions for executive producer Ivan Tors, and

Clarence, the cross-eyed lion, sees the world upside down while playing with Marshall Thompson on *Daktari.*

Tors had been impressed by Thompson's coolness under fire while making the film *A Yank in Vietnam* on location in Saigon in 1964. Tors signed Thompson to his production staff.

At the time, Thompson said, "Tors suggested I try developing a television format which could utilize some of the hundreds of wild animals on his ranch [owned by Tors and his partner Helfer], Africa USA. I had spent seven months in Africa (Kenya, Tanganyika, and the Congo) making the picture *East of Kilimanjaro,*" which is where Thompson learned Swahili.

Cheryl Miller, Marshall Thompson, and Yale Summers go ape with Judy the chimp and little Toto.

"I'd been in veterinarian work on wild animals. So I was fascinated with Tors's trained beasts. I discovered how they were trained through kindness and got pretty good at it myself," Thompson said in a press release in about 1967. "Then I ran into a cross-eyed lion, and I developed an idea about such an animal. I wrote the story, and Tors bought it, gave me the starring role, and the film prompted the *Daktari* series." Thompson spent more than ten months working with lions, tigers, leopards, and other wildlife to prep for his film *Clarence, the Cross-Eyed Lion.*

The late producer Ivan Tors wrote of Clarence with great affection in his autobiography *My Life in the Wild.* "Clarence was an unusual creature without any instinct of aggression. He was a lover, not a fighter. As he grew up, we lavished affection on him, and eventually he became one of the most beautiful full-maned lions I had ever set eyes on. . . . His temperament was even and friendly. He was one of the few lions that tolerated children. Nor did he mind Judy, the chimp, sitting on his back or pulling his tail. He was the Shirley Temple of the lion world."

Stuntman and occasional animal handler Bill Raymond worked for trainer Ralph Helfer on *Daktari* and *Cowboy in Africa.* He vividly remembers working with the cross-eyed lion and his pals: "Clarence's real name was Freddie the Freeloader. Ted Derby, the head trainer, bought him for Africa USA. He paid a dollar for him from a guy in the San Fernando Valley who had raised the lion from a cub in his apartment. This was in the mid-1960s. They had him about a year when producer Ivan Tors [producer of *Gentle Ben* and *Flipper*] decided to use him for his movie *Clarence, the Cross-Eyed Lion.* Tors was a kind of a partner with Helfer in Africa USA.

"When you see pictures of Clarence, there's a dark spot in the middle of his forehead. That's actually a scar. If you watch the *Clarence* movie, you'll see that we had some zebra-striped trucks that had camper shells on top. Whenever we would jump Clarence into the back of the truck, he would bang his head on the lock at the top of that camper shell every time. He really was very cross-eyed and didn't see well. Being as cross-eyed as he was, Clarence spooked very easily when it came to moving vehicles. In scenes when vehicles would ride up, we usually used another cat."

Helfer concurs on Clarence's vision problems: "When Clarence was small, he would jump in back of the station wagon and miss. It took him a while to get used to that. We had an eye doctor see if he could do anything for Clarence, but eventually his eyesight adjusted on its own and he did fine."

Thompson even remembered that Helfer and Tors tried corrective glasses to cure the big cat's cross-eyedness.

Clarence had about four different lions that doubled for him. Among them were Zamba Junior, Samson, and Major. Raymond recalls the lions and their training: "Zamba Junior was the best cat we had on the place as far as lions go. He's the one you see a lot with the chimps and the goats and other animals.

"None of the cats really did tricks. For the most part, we would jerry-rig things one way or another to get them to do the behaviors we wanted. Each individual animal has certain things that they enjoy doing. Some like to jump. Some like to wrestle with their handlers. Some make a game of snarling and snapping, making themselves look mean and vicious. I've known cougars who would give out the meanest-looking snarl you ever saw, while still purring contentedly. We called these things they did naturally 'behaviors.'

"Through observation of the animals, we would discover which animal liked to do what behavior. When we needed a certain behavior in a scene for a film, we would use the animal that did that behavior best in that scene. It wasn't always Clarence you saw on *Daktari.* Just like the human actors, he also had doubles. (Many of the viewers of *Daktari* spotted each time we used them. Viewers got to know the animals so well, that we got many letters every week telling us that it wasn't Clarence or Judy in certain scenes. It really surprised us that viewers were so observant.)

"For some things we needed the cats to do, such as move from one place to another, we had various tricks that we would use. One was particularly low-tech. We would simply place the cat in the scene and tell it to stay; then a trainer, hidden in the area the cat was to go to, would call it over. In the old days, to get a cat to run through a scene, they would tie a chicken to a rope, drag it through the scene and turn the cat loose to chase it. For humanitarian reasons, this practice was stopped a long time ago.

"We at Africa USA had a technique that we used that proved to be very effective—carbon dioxide fire extinguishers. The slow release of air from them caused a hissing sound that made the cats pace nervously. Some of them would snarl and snap at the sound. Quickly pushing and releasing the handle would cause a sharp whooshing sound that would cause the cat to run away from the sound.

"Trainers were placed in the area the animal would run to. They would call the animal, and most often the animal would go to them, usually looking for protection and reassurance. Sometimes, however, the cat would not go to the handler. They would bolt off of the set and run off into the countryside with trainers and handlers in hot pursuit. Thus would start a game that was solely of the cat's own invention.

"They would run off a hundred yards or so and then sit down and wait for the handlers to catch up to them. As soon as we were almost within range of catching them, they would jump up and run off another hundred yards and sit down and wait again. This little game of catch-me-if-you-can would go on until they grew tired of it, at which time they would allow us to catch them and take them back to the set.

"Most of the cats seemed to like to play this game from time to time. It was least appreciated by us humans involved when the temperatures were in the nineties or hundreds. Even though the fire extinguisher technique worked so well, we were never fully satisfied with it, as we didn't like the idea of scaring the animals to get them to do what we wanted. But it was the best we could come up with at the time."

Raymond adds, "Marshall Thompson was almost as good as most of the trainers with the animals, although there was a scene in the movie *Clarence, the Cross-Eyed Lion* (1965) where he really did get his arm bitten by a leopard named Nero."

It was Thompson who renamed Freddie "Clarence" when he wrote his movie script. The man and the beast got along great. Thompson said of Clarence at the time, "He's one of my best friends, but sometimes he's impossible to work with. Sleeping and eating are his favorite activities. He's also a good supervisor and contemplator. But, unfortunately, he is one of TV's few stars who doesn't give a hoot about acting. And when you do get him before the camera, he never looks you straight in the eye."

Thompson added, "When I say Clarence is sometimes difficult to work with, I don't mean he's dangerous. We don't think of him as King of the Jungle. He's more like a toy teddy bear who got too much stuffing. He can take directions very well, when he wants to. But he sees double and so he's frequently not where you expect him to be in a scene. I've seen him jump for a truck and miss completely."

His eyesight didn't keep the lion from giving award-winning performances, but he was never into the Hollywood party animal scene. "Clarence didn't care about winning," Thompson said after the big cat lost out on a PATSY Award to Judy. "He earlier won a PATSY for the motion picture *Clarence the Cross-Eyed Lion*. . . . He was totally unimpressed by the honor. He's not the run-of-the-mill status-seeking Hollywood star.

"Sometimes he just looks at cast, crew, and animals as though he wished we'd go someplace else and let him get a little shuteye. When a *Daktari* director calls him before the cameras, and he's not inclined to act, he has a series of expressions ranging from 'later' to 'you've got to be kidding.'"

Cheryl Miller, like Thompson, got along decently with Clarence and other animals on the show. "Cheryl Miller was fantastic with the animals. She had a rapport with all of them that came across very clearly throughout the series," Raymond says.

Miller was a teen in 1966 when *Daktari* became a vehicle for her acting career. Little did she know that a lion would also become her vehicle. "The first year I had to ride Clarence for the show's opening scenes. I was a little nervous about riding him; he may not have liked the idea," Miller said in CBS promotional material. "The danger in working with animals in scenes comes from the unexpected. Clarence had been ridden by his trainer Ted Derby, but never by anyone else.

Daktari star Cheryl Miller mixes well with the "mane event," Clarence, the cross-eyed lion.

"He shook off three different trainers before it was my turn. The head trainer assured me Clarence would be different with me but, as you can imagine, I had my doubts. Six trainers lined up on either side of the road, just in case Clarence decided to bolt. Then I very cautiously got aboard and the camera started to roll.

"I had to look as though I rode a lion every day of my life, while trying to adjust to Clarence's very strange, sliding motion. Luckily we got the scene the first time. I'm not sure how long Clarence's patience—or my nerve—would have lasted.

"I was so proud of what I'd done, I didn't even change my costume before driving back to town. I went shopping at a very swanky store, and it wasn't until I got there that I realized I was still wearing my pants and shirt covered with lion hair."

Miller also recalled being the first girl to ride a rhinoceros, and there was a little face licking she took from a tiger. "I was quartered for the night with a tiger. I had to lie down under a blanket with the tiger at my side. He was so pleased to have company, he suddenly leaned over and gave me a tremendous swipe on the face with his tongue. It was like being rubbed with a rough grade of sandpaper," Miller said.

But the animals rarely received such sweet treats for their work. What they did receive was affection in the way of encouraging words and petting, and an occasional bite of something good to eat.

"We rewarded the lions with affection most of the time," Raymond says. "Sometimes we would use a small cube of meat as a reward, but we preferred not to. Ralph felt that rewarding them would cause them to get to where they would expect it and start looking for it. So this was really a special treat for them. For the most part, we rewarded them with affection and petted them and talked to them."

As for regular diet, Helfer experimented with his own special menu for his big cats.

"We developed what you might call lion cake. We don't like to interfere with nature, so we had a veterinarian and a nutritionist and myself develop a cake with lots of heavy proteins—eggs and cheeses," Helfer says. "We added meat to it and over three weeks we lessened the meat to no meat. The lions loved it and had no problems with their diet. It also made them cleaner, more docile animals and they had no halitosis."

Helfer recalls that Clarence was mostly famous for his personality and doing the impossible in a gentle way. "He was brought up from a cub with extreme amounts of gentleness. Clarence, as he grew, became extremely heavy and large—550 pounds. He became kind of a clown lion, clown in that he loved everybody, and he would carry rides on his back."

It was a sad day for friends and fans alike when the big, friendly cat died from pneumonia and gastric disorders at seven-and-a-half years of age, just before a scheduled appearance at the Heart of Illinois Fair in Peoria in mid-July of 1969.

Helfer recalls a tense few minutes one day on the set of *Daktari*. "We were doing one scene, and I sent my trainers to get Clarence. They came back with a lion that wasn't Clarence. It was Leo, a very dangerous lion, and they said, 'Here he is,' and I didn't want to alert anybody, so I said, 'We're not going to do that scene right now after all,' and I sent them back with this tough lion. Afterwards, I told the men that they had gotten the wrong lion, and they went back to see Leo, and he charged them."

Raymond recalls another scary moment with another lion, Zamba Junior. "I think this was during the second season. Anyway, the film crew was getting real casual about working with the animals. So much so, that when one of the cats would get loose (which, since we were working them loose, happened often), many of them felt perfectly at ease grabbing hold of the cat and taking it back to the handlers. (Even though we gave specific orders to the film crew every day we worked the animals, that when an animal was loose, the crew members were to stand perfectly still until the handlers had gained control of the animal.)

"We were doing an episode with some milk cows, and we had the cows tied up to some trees. Then came a scene in which we would

Cheryl Miller was in the movie *The Monkey's Uncle*, but most fans remember her as Paula Tracy on *Daktari*.

be working Junior. Now Junior was one of the most gentle cats we had. You just hardly ever expected any trouble with him. His cage was a couple of hundred yards from the film set. We walked Junior up to the set to do his scene. Because we were working several other animals that day, we had quite a few trainers and handlers working, and about six were walking along with Junior. As we walked by the cows, we could see Junior give them a once-over.

"Junior did his scene and we walked him back, and we came by the cows and he gave them a once-over again. When we got back to his cage, he got halfway in and decided to heck with it, and out he came. He took off at a full run with the smallest guy in the place, Ralph Perry, holding onto the chain, sailing along behind Junior. He looked like a pennant on a flagpole.

"Junior jumps astraddle one of the cows, and you should have heard the noise down in that canyon with him roaring and the cow bawling and kicking around. Even though it could have been quite tragic, the whole thing turned out to be almost comical. Because Junior had been declawed, he was unable to hold on to the cow. So it kept throwing him off.

"He would hit the ground, roar, and jump right back astride of the cow. The cow would bawl and throw him off again. This continued until enough handlers got hold of Junior's chain, and by sheer weight of numbers, pulled him away from the cow.

"As I said before, the noise was horrendous, and the scene must have been terrifying, what with the cat trying to get the cow, the cow trying to get away, and the handlers trying to wrestle the cat under control, all in a huge cloud of dust and noise. It sure scared the film crew, who scattered in all directions—in trucks, on tops of trucks, and everywhere else they thought they might be safe.

Daktari human star Marshall Thompson goes over a script with simian star Judy the chimp.

"It was a long time before they felt casual with the animals again. They finally learned that even the best-behaved ones were still wild animals. Actually, it was a good lesson to the trainers and handlers too. We were a lot more alert after that. (By the way, the cow only ended up with three small scratches on her back that were healed up in a couple of days. I think we lucked out that day.)"

As for Clarence's unlikely costar, Judy the chimp was a practical joker, according to Helfer. "She would pull Clarence's tail when he was sleeping or jump up and down on his back."

When she was younger, Judy sometimes stayed in the Helfer house and slept in their bed and even wore their child's pajamas.

Thompson said at the time that there was no rivalry between Clarence and Judy: "They're two entirely, diametrically opposed personalities. Judy's a smarty-pants professional who gloats in doing everything perfectly. She's a career girl determined to go on to bigger and better things. Clarence's only worry is about going on to his next meal and a good nap in the shade."

Associate producer Helfer and Thompson took Judy with them on the first filming safari to Africa ever for a television series in 1967. They went to Mozambique and filmed with the Zulu tribes of South Africa. They became the first TV show to film in the Gonarezhou National Park and later worked in the private game reserve of Mala Mala. The trip yielded film footage of a bull elephant charging at thirty miles an hour and a two-mile chase after a nineteen-foot giraffe. And they found an abandoned village that had become home for a pride of lions. All in all, the five-week safari harvested 50,000 feet of color film.

And Judy saw it all. "Judy was great," says Raymond. "Frank Lamping was her main trainer. She was pretty much what you see—very smart, very clever. One of the things she loved to do was get into mistletoe. She loved to get up in a tree and rip and tear it out of a tree and throw it to the ground. We'd let her do that, and we'd sell it over Christmas.

"Judy would do whatever you told her to do. We would take her and walk her through a scene, tell her to stop here and do this, then walk over to here and do this, and we would turn her loose and that was exactly what she would do. It was just amazing the things she would do: tie ropes, untie ropes, almost anything. We joked with the actors that we almost got more one-takes with the animals than we did with the actors."

Raymond adds, "One food Judy did like was coffee and a doughnut. She got to a point where she wouldn't go to work without her coffee and doughnut. She got real stubborn about it. Everybody else had 'em, and by golly, she was going to have hers. She would flat refuse to go to work without it."

And television wasn't Judy's only domain. In 1965 she starred with Annette Funicello and Tommy Kirk in the Disney feature *The Monkey's Uncle* and played Tony Randall's lab assistant in *Fluffy*. "That is Judy on the stage with the Beach Boys in the opening scene playing the tambourine," says Bob Riedell, who was training the chimp on the set of *The Monkey's Uncle* for Helfer at the time.

"Judy used to sit in Walt Disney's lap all the time. Walt would be at the studio every morning, sitting in one of those director chairs. Judy would get her coffee and doughnut before she went to work. She would get in line with everybody else, get her own sugar, take it over to Disney, sit on his lap, and never get a crumb on him and never spill a drop."

Judy, by the way, was discovered in the jungles of Kenya and came to the United States at one month of age.

Riedell said of the Disney star at the time of filming *The Monkey's Uncle*, "Maybe Judy is a bit temperamental, but so were Greta Garbo and Marilyn Monroe. She is one of the most natural little actresses I have ever worked with. Her gregarious personality and innate sense of humor make Judy an outstanding member of the Animal Actor's Guild."

Disney publicity reports hinted that Judy had a crush on her *Uncle* costar Kirk and was jealous of Annette.

In addition to Judy the chimp and Clarence the cross-eyed lion, *Daktari* star Thompson worked with many other creatures on the show. In the first episode that he directed, the featured beast was a rare white rhino, which Thompson had to ride. He also had some extra animals written into the script: Ethel, a baby hippo (1,000 pounds); Foghorn, a water buffalo (700 pounds); and Margie, an elephant (2,000 pounds).

"The more, the better" was Thompson's motto as director. "That's what people like to see. For sequences that originally had actors talking, we'd have them lead animals into the scene."

As for riding the rhino, Thompson said, "No problem. I worked with the trainer who first got the rhino (named Lunya) accustomed to humans. Then it was a simple matter of taking his place on board.

"Of course, we made sure her mate couldn't see what we were doing. We locked him up because we didn't want to get him sore at us. Have you ever seen a wrathful rhino?"

And Thompson was a firm believer in the way Helfer and company trained their creatures. "People think we use tranquilizers but we don't. Their use would be like getting someone drunk. You wouldn't know what was going to happen. All we use is kindness and it has paid off."

Dave's World

CBS, 1993–1997, 98 episodes

*Starring **Samantha and Scarlet as Ernest**, Harry Anderson as Dave Barry, DeLane Matthews as Beth Barry, Meshach Taylor as Sheldon Baylor, Shadoe Stevens as Kenny Beckett, J. C. Wendel as Mia, Zane Carney as Tommy Barry, Andrew Ducote as Willie Barry, Patrick Warburton as Eric, Shannon Sharp and Angell Conwell as Carly Baylor, and Tammy Lauren as Julie.*

Loosely based on the columns of newspaperman Dave Barry, *Dave's World* is about a syndicated newspaper columnist in Miami, sort of an overgrown kid, who works out of his home as he reacts to life and relationships.

Dave's dog, Ernest the bloodhound, on *Dave's World* was owned and trained by Joe Camp of Jungle Exotics. The dog was played by two different bloodhounds, Samantha and Scarlet.

Samantha, an older dog, took on the role for the first season, while young Scarlet was learning new tricks. Both hounds came to Camp via the Bloodhound Rescue Service.

"Samantha was the first dog hired. I just used her until I got things in order," says Camp. "Sam did the show about a year. She actually came out of retirement to hold the fort until we got a younger dog ready. She was very old at the time and liked to sleep a lot.

"When *Dave's World* called, they said they wanted a bloodhound. We turned to the rescue service looking for new bloodhounds because Sam didn't get along with children. She was somewhat aggressive, so I was skeptical about her going on to *Dave's World* as a companion dog for the children, but she had mellowed and she came to me well trained. She had a lot of obedience training on her.

"Sam did a lot of different things. She sat, spoke, would lie down on command, cover her face, shake on command, scratch on command, and could do simulated tracking.

"Any food was her favorite. Sam ate like a champ. She was more like a male bloodhound, little bit bigger, very outgoing, heavily wrinkled. She was in the TV series *Hunter*, did a pilot called *Sniff* about bloodhounds, and was in commercials for Chevy trucks and Budweiser. She died about a year or so after Scarlet took over, six or seven years ago.

"Scarlet has been the dog that carried most of the load on *Dave's World*. She's done about every show that has a bloodhound in it in recent years. We got her after her owners were leaving California and didn't want to take her with them. I have a standing order for good-looking red bloodhounds.

"She's now about seven or eight. We got her at age one and she was something special. We knew right away she was going to work out. She's one of the prettier bloodhounds. She is very intelligent. No matter what you ask her to do, she kind of figures it out, which is very unusual for a bloodhound.

"I can ask her to do the same things we ask of German shepherds. She can do just about any behavior we need her to do: go to a mark, lie down, roll over, scratch, talk, back up, go with. As far as a studio dog, she has a full repertoire. She has a great personality. Scarlet is one of those dogs who is always very willing. Getting a bloodhound to retrieve is a tough thing.

"She comes up to the house and spends time and likes everybody. She gets along with other dogs. I couldn't ask for a better bloodhound."

Camp says the children on *Dave's World*

Scarlet was the bloodhound that spent most of the time in Dave Barry's house in *Dave's World*.
Courtesy of Joe Camp / Jungle Exotics.

really took to the dog. "She kind of bonded more with the children, and she got along with the female lead quite a bit. She was kind of the family pet, who just lay around the house. She was there but never got involved, but she might be doing little things, like sitting next to Dave while he ate popcorn and watched television. She was always digging up things in the yard. In one episode, the little boy's hamster died, and Dave buried it. She dug it up and brought it home."

Sam and Scarlet were called Ernest on *Dave's World*, and in one episode they had a sequence where the previous owner of the hound attempted to reclaim her. In the process, the family discovered that Ernest was actually a girl dog, so maybe Ernest was short for Ernestine.

There were a number of sight gags that the writers cooked up for the hound. In one episode, after an earthquake that caused the upstairs toilet to fall through the ceiling, they had Ernest lapping drinks from the fallen toilet.

One of Ernest's running gags throughout the series occurred at the conclusion of many episodes. As Dave and Beth got in bed and snuggled, they thought their mate was using his or her feet to caress the other's feet. A few seconds later, they would realize it was Ernest, so they would lift the covers and say "get out of here, Ernest!"

Scarlet has quite a number of tricks up her sleeve but most important, she enjoys hanging around humans. "Her main thing is she likes to be around people and do things. The more she's around people, the happier she is. She is always wanting to get involved and has got her nose in everything," says Camp, who has been training acting animals for a quarter of a century.

Camp adds, "About every bloodhound job done over the last five years in Hollywood, she has been involved in. Scarlet rolls out and goes to work. Now she's kind of in semi-retirement. She has gotten up past seven years. She was in some Bud Light commercials recently. And she is working in *Bloodhounds Inc.*, a new TV series on one of the Christian networks. It's about kids and their bloodhound. Scarlet is a companion to a couple of kids whose father is a radio newscaster. The kids form a detective agency, and Scarlet is their trusty dog who goes wherever they go. She is helping solve crimes because she is a bloodhound."

Dharma & Greg

ABC, 1997–present (still in production)

*Starring **Bub and Twiggy as Nunzio, Chewy and Tramp as Stinky,** Jenna Elfman as Dharma Finkelstein, Thomas Gibson as Greg Montgomery, Alan Rachins as Larry Finkelstein, Mimi Kennedy as Abby O'Neil, Mitchell Ryan as Edward Montgomery, and Susan Sullivan as Kitty Montgomery.*

This is the story of newlywed give-and-take

between yoga-teaching Dharma (the daughter of hippie parents) and her lawyer husband Greg Montgomery (the scion of rich and stuffy parents).

Nunzio and Stinky, the lovable canines of Dharma Finkelstein and Greg Montgomery, are the modern-day odd couple of dogs in the sitcom world. Since Nunzio is the apparent leader of the two (despite the fact that he was a bar mitzvah present for Stinky), here's his story—wait, make that her story—as told by trainer Tracy Kelly: "Her real name is Twiggy, and she's actually a female who plays a male character, which is no problem for her. She's pretty tough. She was born on December 11, 1997, in Farmersville, Texas. She moved to L.A. at about nine months to come and live with me at Boone's Animals for Hollywood. She's a Cardigan Welsh corgi. There are two types of corgis. One's a Pembroke, and one's a Cardigan. She has a tail, so she's a Cardigan.

Trainer Tracy Kelly enjoys the great outdoors with Twiggy.
Courtesy of Tracy Kelly.

"When I got her at nine months, I trained her for about four months and then began her on *Dharma & Greg.* She picked up everything right away. She's completely an intellectual, very intellectual, and so that's why the training only went for four months. Usually it's a lot longer for a four-camera show. And other than *Dharma & Greg,* she's done two commercials, an Animal Planet commercial and a dog food commercial.

"Her biggest motivation is any kind of meat. She's totally into food, and so that's pretty much what she works for, but she also works out of respect for me. We have a great relationship. We're like sisters, and so I could work her without food just as well. Her favorite food is hot dogs, and she does a bunch of special tricks. She does all her basics: sit, stay, all of that stuff. She also rolls over, she loves to beg up for food, she can hold that position for a really long time, which is awkward for a corgi to do because they're so long. She also has a 'watch it,' which I can point to any person—usually of course an actor—point to Jenna Elfman or Thomas Gibson and say 'watch them' and she'll stare at them for an indefinite amount of time, which is perfect for a four-camera show because you never want them staring at the trainer.

"She does circles to show she's happy, and she can go to the bathroom on cue. That just helps out when you're in the middle of a scene and you know they have to go. You run outside and say, 'take a break,' and they go right away.

"When I first started her on the show, Twiggy was still pretty much a puppy, so she was just on 'down, stay on the chair.' All the actors were around the chair having a conversation, and all of a sudden she got up and decided that she needed to scratch her neck and rub it against the chair. She was doing little flips and twists in the chair, while the actors are trying to have this conversation, and I was just sitting behind the camera thinking, 'Oh my gosh, I hope she stops,' and I couldn't say anything because then I would step on the actors' lines. I could just see all the actors faces start to smile because they could see her messing around out of the corner of their eyes. But normally she's great.

"On another occasion she had to dig up a skeleton in the backyard of Dharma's parents' house, and so I sent her in there to go dig. She has that on cue, and I thought she would just dig kind of normally and easily, but she had a heyday with it. She thought it was the greatest thing in the world, so dirt was flying everywhere, and all of the white fur on her coat was completely brown. I just kind of had to wash her off with some baby wipes for the next scene. But she's just a character because she really gets into her acting, and she loves to be a showoff and show people that she can really do something vigorously."

Nunzio was originally played by Bub, but Twiggy took over the role at the beginning of the 2000–2001 season. Likewise, Stinky was originally played only by Chewy, but during the 2000–2001 season, Tramp began phasing in as Stinky because Chewy was getting older. Though April Melcher once handled training for the original actors for both Nunzio and Stinky, Kelly and Susan Benedon for the most part handled the actor animals separately beginning in 2000.

No matter the dog or the trainer, Nunzio and Stinky always create good "Dharma."

Down and Out in Beverly Hills

Fox, 1987, 13 episodes

*Starring **Mike the Dog as Matisse,** Hector Elizondo as Dave Whiteman, Anita Morris as Barbara Whiteman, Tim Thomerson as Jerry Baskin, Evan Richards as Max Whiteman, Eileen Seeley as Jenny Whiteman, and April Ortiz as Carmen.*

Down and Out in Beverly Hills was based on the 1985 movie of the same title and is about a successful businessman whose wife and kids are living a mixed-up life. A bum moves in their house and dispenses philosophical lessons.

The only star of the feature film *Down and Out in Beverly Hills* to stick around for the TV series was a talented, forty-two-pound, black-and-white Scottish border collie named Mike the Dog, who had one straight ear and one floppy ear.

Mike's Matisse could be a nasty piece of work, but the real Mike was a pretty nice guy although a bit shy. When Mike was several months old, his future owner and trainer Clint Rowe found him chained to a doghouse at a ranch in Northern California.

"He has one blue eye, and at the time everyone told me there is no way a blue-eyed dog is gonna work," Rowe recalls.

Then Mike got kicked by a horse and spent seven weeks with his leg in a cast. Things were not looking so good, but Rowe trained him to do more than one hundred tricks, and soon the dog was showing up in commercials for Toyota and Doublemint chewing gum.

He had to audition for the *Down and Out* feature film. Says the film's director Paul Mazursky, "Originally I was looking for a smaller dog, but the first thing that hooked me was those eyes. Then he did the most amazing tricks. He actually climbed a rope ladder with a pail in his mouth!"

Hector Elizondo starred as millionaire Dave Whiteman and Mike the Dog reprised his feature film role as the antisocial pet Matisse when *Down and Out in Beverly Hills* became a TV series in 1987.

Mike, who played a pampered, neurotic pet to a neurotic couple in the *Down and Out* movie, did some amazing feats in the film, like leaping off a diving board, rolling his eyes, and walking on hot coals.

The *New York Times* called his acting "Oscar-caliber work."

"He's just so good. He responds to your emotions," Rowe says. "If you're cheering him, he puts more into it."

The attention the dog received from the movie led to appearances on *Saturday Night Live*, *Late Night With David Letterman*, *Entertainment Tonight*, and *Good Morning America* (Nick Nolte, another star of *Down and Out*, said he wouldn't go on *Good Morning* without Mike by his side). Stories about Mike also ran in *People*, *Newsweek*, *Time*, and *USA Today*.

The hot dog of the town even got his own party at the Hard Rock Cafe in New York, courtesy of the Disney public relations machine. But one of his neatest perks came in February 1986 when Mike became the first dog actor to have his paws put in cement at the Tail O' the Pup, a Hollywood restaurant shaped like an eighteen-foot-long hot dog. However, Mike's favorite munchy, and often his reward for a job well done, was broiled chicken breast.

Another byproduct of his movie fame was an appearance in Little Richard's music video of "Great Gosh a' Mighty, It's a Matter of Time."

Mike made other commercials, including ones for dog food and soft drinks, and his fame and acclaim nabbed him the choice cohost spot for the 1986 PATSY Awards show. In 1987 Mike made his network TV debut as a canine criminal who tries to go straight in the TV movie *Spot Marks the X.*

Rowe kept Mike down on the farm near Acton, California, where he lived with his best friend, Davey, who was his *Down and Out* stunt double. Mike's daily schedule included a three-mile run in the morning and training in the afternoon. His favorite pastime was catching Frisbees. Mike the Dog has since passed away.

The Drew Carey Show

ABC, 1995–present (still in production)

*Starring **Ajax as Speedy,** Drew Carey as Drew Carey, Christa Miller as Kate O'Brien, Diedrich Bader as Oswald Harvey, Ryan Stiles as Lewis Kiniski, Kathy Kinney as Mimi Boebeck Carey, Craig Ferguson as Nigel Wick, Ian Gomez as Larry Almada, John Carroll Lynch as Steve Carey, and Nan Martin as Mrs. Dotty Louder.*

The Drew Carey Show is about the life of an assistant director of personnel at a Cleveland department store who fights with his coworker Mimi, drinks beer with his pals, and runs a micro-brewery with his best friends out of his garage.

In the beginning, Ajax the golden retriever had a most unusual assignment as he played Drew Carey's pet Speedy. He began the role as television's only wheelchair-bound canine.

"He started off the show in a wheelchair built for dogs. He had to have it fit for him, and we had to train him how to walk in the wheelchair," says one of Ajax's trainers, Janine Aines of Animal Actors of Hollywood. (Joy Green is the dog's original trainer, and she also continues to train him.) "He would bump into actors and furniture because he couldn't steer too well.

"Somewhere along the way, Drew decided to have the dog have surgery, and it was a miracle and he could walk." These days on the show, Ajax ambles around on all four legs.

Aines got one of her star pupils from a family that was moving away and decided to leave their dog behind. "He came from a private home," Aines says. "The family decided they couldn't take him with them, and we were looking for a backup for Comet on *Full House.* We saw the ad and went and checked out the dog and saw right away the potential this dog had. We were shaking in our shoes."

Now about nine years old, Ajax is an "attention hound" according to his owner. "He is always happy, and he wants to say hi to everyone," says Aines. "Sometimes that's hard on the set, but he is an incredible dog, kind of brilliant. If he were a person, he would be a genius. He has a big heart and can do some really hard stuff."

From left, Solar, Ajax, and Cosmos work a lot of jobs as a team, but Ajax is top dog on *The Drew Carey Show.*

Courtesy of Animal Actors of Hollywood.

Among his tricks are faking a broken leg, howling on cue, covering his eyes with his paws, shaking up a snake, and raising his hind leg on cue.

Aines says, "He gets along incredibly well with the actors, but Drew wants to play rough with him. We let him say hi, but then we have to get him back to the job and thinking."

There are two doubles who pitch in for Ajax on occasion, Solar and Cosmos. "The only time we haven't used Ajax is if he is booked on something else," says Aines of her star. All three appeared on episodes of *Full House* and *Touched by an Angel,* and Ajax starred in *Fluke* and *The Trial of Old Drum.* Cosmos and Solar appeared in both movies also, and all three were in the movies *Ghost Dog, Watchers IV,* and *Love Stinks.*

Ajax likes rawhide bones and is "ball crazy," Aines says, but his favorite toy is a chewy fuzzy sheep. "He squeezes that and dunks it in his water bowl and absolutely goes crazy over it."

Dr. Quinn, Medicine Woman

CBS, 1993–1998, 147 episodes, 1 TV movie

Starring ***Cody as Wolf,*** *Jane Seymour as Dr. Michaela Quinn, Joe Lando as Byron Sully, Orson Bean as Loren Bray, Chad Allen as Matthew Cooper, Erika Flores and Jessica Bowman as Colleen Cooper, and Shawn Toovey as Brian Cooper.*

This series captures the saga of a women doctor who is pioneering the frontier and saving lives in the Old West.

Cody, the malamute who played Wolf, the loyal companion of Joe Lando's Byron Sully on *Dr. Quinn,* was acquired by trainer Dennis Grisco of Grisco's Animals when Cody was about two years old. Grisco got another malamute, Mika, at the same time. Mika sometimes served as Cody's double.

Grisco recalls, "I got them from another trainer, Karl Lewis Miller. A couple was getting a divorce and gave them to Karl, and he really didn't have a need for them. He just took them rather than see them placed elsewhere and offered them to me, and I took them, and shortly after that I had a script to do a feature called *Lost Boys.* That was Cody's first film."

Before *Dr. Quinn,* Grisco says, "Cody had done numerous TV things, most of the time playing a wolf. I forget the number of years, but it was for a good bit of time before *Quinn.*"

By the time Cody landed the role of Wolf, he was already flying high with a strong repertoire of movie stunt skills. Grisco says, "One of his favorites was to run and hit a ramp and leap off the ramp about ten or twelve feet and then you catch him in your arms, which is quite a feat being that he weighed about eighty pounds. He could do that to simulate an attack. That's what we used it for. It was really a game with him. He loved doing it."

Grisco adds, "Mika's forte was snarling. Cody was so friendly he didn't have a mean bone in his body, and he wouldn't snarl, and Mika would let you tie the bone down and pretend you're going to take his bone, and he'd show all of his teeth. Cody didn't care. You could have the bone."

One of both Cody's and Mika's special tricks was what they could do with their tails. Each was trained to put his tail either down to be like a wolf or up like a dog on command.

Says Grisco, "I'd give Cody a cue, and his tail would still be up. I'd just tell him, 'Put your tail down.' His tail was normally curled over the back. Mika could do this, too."

Cody and Mika may have played a wolf of the wild, but their motivating treat often was more domesticated. "Most of the time I used a commercial treat like Special Cuts," says Grisco. "I also used a little piece of a hot dog. I'd mix it up. I'd use a little bit of chicken at times; I'd use a piece of bacon once in a while."

In order to maintain a certain wolf "awoofness," Cody wasn't allowed to interact with the actors much, either on or off camera. "The producers mainly just wanted him there," says Grisco, "just being in view whenever feasible. They didn't want him to be the happy family pet. They didn't want him to be a dog, but they just sort of wanted him to be Joe Lando's buddy. He just went wherever he went, but not to be a Lassie type. They wanted him to just be there and have his presence known."

When Cody passed on in 1997, another of Grisco's malamutes, Chaz, who had been one of Cody's stand-ins, took over as Wolf for the last couple of seasons of *Dr. Quinn.* (Other stand-ins included Grisco's King and Indy.)

If ever an animal actor was good at being low-key and natural and blending beautifully into any scene and a setting, it was Old West's canine Cody.

Due South

CBS/CTV Network and syndicated, 1994–1998, 66 episodes

*Starring **Lincoln and Draco as Diefenbaker,** Paul Gross as Constable Benton Fraser, David Marciano as Ray Vecchio, Callum Keith Rennie as Stanley Raymond Kowalski/Ray Vecchio, Beau Starr as Harding Welsh, Catherine Bruhier as Elaine Besbriss, Daniel Kash as Louis Guardino, Tony Craig as Jack Huey, Camilla Scott as Margaret Thatcher, Tom Melissis as Thomas E. Dewey, Ramona Milano as Francesca Vecchio, Anne Marie Loder as Stella Kowalski, and Gordon Pinsent as Robert Fraser.*

Due South, whose Canadian French title is *Direction: Sud,* is about the most polite Canadian Mountie of them all, one Benton Fraser, who is assigned to work the Canadian consulate in Chicago. In the Windy City, he teams with a streetwise Chicago cop and uses his own peculiar but effective methods of tracking criminals and solving crime. Fraser lives in a dumpy apartment building with his right-hand dog, a deaf, lip-reading wolf named Diefenbaker.

Once *Due South* went into series production, the main animal star was played by a Siberian husky named Lincoln. He was owned and trained by Ted Haggis, the father of Paul Haggis, the creator and producer of the show.

Ted, a dog trainer for many years, found Lincoln at a registered kennel near Stratford, Ontario. He says, "I saw this ad in the paper for an eight-month-old puppy. I bought him and started training him. He was very headstrong. They only know one thing—to pull.

"We took this dog into episode one, and he did an acceptable job. My daughter [Joey Francis] helped through the first forty-two episodes or so. I've had a lot of dogs in my lifetime, but he's one in a million. Once he got onto the set and working, he loved it.

"He'd do anything you ask him to do three or four times, but don't ask him ten times. He's a nice dog, stubborn in some ways, but a very pretty dog.

"Most of the time he was asked to be near the Mountie and look at him occasionally and ride in the car with him. He could climb a ladder. He had to do a lot of chase scenes, where he had to chase after the car. We would put my daughter in the car, and he would chase after her."

Ted Haggis says Lincoln dines on Iams dog food and that he has guest-starred on one other show since *Due South—The Zack Files,* a children's series.

"I still have the dog," says Haggis. "He's eight or nine and we have retired him. I bring him in the house at night."

The second star dog of *Due South* was named after Draco the Dragonheart. Siberian husky Draco took over the role of Diefenbaker in February 1997 when he was seven months old. Owned and trained by Rick and Gail Parker, Draco is a bit smaller than the first Diefenbaker, Lincoln, and proved a quick study as Benton Fraser's best friend.

Rick Parker looked at about three hundred dogs before he found two near Peterboro, Ontario, that he believed were capable of handling the chores demanded by the high quality of *Due South*, a show that had aired in more than one hundred countries by the time it closed shop in 1998.

"I brought the dogs in and showed them to Paul Gross and the producer. They didn't look exactly the same as the original dog. After a couple of weeks, I went down to show what the dog could do after two weeks of training," says Parker, who operates Canadian Wrangler Motion Picture Animals Limited.

The Mountie and producer liked what they saw. Draco was hired and then he and Parker really went to work. They had two months to learn Draco's "lines" and tricks before filming resumed. Then Draco decided to snoop in a place where he was not welcome.

"Draco stuck his paws in a jaguar's cage and the jaguar bit him, requiring twenty-six stitches," Parker says. "I told the production people, 'Well, the good news is he knows how to limp. The bad news is the limp is for real.'"

Draco performed in the last two seasons and final twenty-six episodes of *Due South*; it was therefore important for him to gel with the cast and crew. "We took our dog down to the set, and for the first month or two we let everybody greet him," says Parker. "He talks and has his own way of coming in to say hi to everybody and he has his own way of telling me, 'I'm not ready to perform yet. I want to greet everybody.'"

Paul Gross's Canadian Mountie Benton Fraser, his canine sidekick Diefenbaker, and David Marciano's Ray Vecchio made a formidable trio of sleuthhounds in *Due South*.

Parker adds, "I picked a good dog. His sister is a good dog, but she doesn't have quite the same personality. He has more personality than Rodney Dangerfield. He's very gregarious, very trusting, and he's very forward. If he feels comfortable about the situation, he has no problem about carrying on. He understands. I only have to show him how to do it once, and then he can go in and improvise his own parts."

He gives an example: "The dog is walking beside Paul Gross coming out of a room, walking along a hallway, and going in through another door. We do a rehearsal and now we do it with the extras, and there is no room for him to walk beside Paul because of so many people. The dog takes two steps and jumps up on the bench, walks along the bench, and gets back down."

Parker notes, "The best thing about this dog is that when I tell him things, he can reason. He actually does reason with each scene. When we go to a new place, I never walk him through. I can stand in one spot and tell him where to go and what to do."

Parker says that *Due South* was Draco's first job as an actor. He shared the bill with his sister Cinder, who performed some of the stunts and did most of the scenes inside the cars.

The last two months of *Due South* were a bit uneasy for Draco because of vision problems. "He didn't like night work or heights because of juvenile cataracts. I took him to the University of Ohio where they removed the cataracts and put new lenses in his eyes. Since then, he's been great," Parker says.

The trainer has always loved animals. His family moved near a riding stable when he was young, and he began working with horses. That led to two vocations: Parker competed in bull riding, steer wrestling, and calf roping as a rodeo cowboy, and he began working with other types of creatures when he met someone who supplied exotic animals. Parker worked at a few private zoos and eventually wound up caring for horses on the set of the Richard Burton film *Equus* in 1977. He later worked for veteran Hollywood trainer Steve Martin handling animals on the television series *Search and Rescue.*

Today his company trains everything from dogs, cats, and rats to snakes, birds, horses, and reindeer. They have supplied an elk for the film *Tommy Boy*, rats for *Storm of the Century*, mice for *Flowers for Algernon*, a cat for *All That Glitters*, a horse for *Bo Jangles*, and pigeons for *Cletis Tout.*

Meanwhile, since *Due South* wound down, Draco performed in *Real Kids, Real Adventures* as a dog that rescues a family from a forest fire.

Today, Draco lives the life of a country dog on the Parker family's ten-acre farm outside of Toronto. Parker says that Draco weighs about sixty pounds and "most of that's hair." For extra good work, the dog gets cheese bits and slices of a hot dog as a token of appreciation.

"He loves horses and likes to run alongside them. He will go over jumps while I am jumping on horseback. He comes up to the barn while we do chores and likes to play with one of the barn cats. He loves to chase pigeons, but his most favorite thing," says Parker, "is to run outside and get real hot and jump in the horses' water trough and splash around. Then he'll come out, and if my son is on the trampoline, he'll get up and jump around."

As for other canine actors who have played the part of Diefenbaker, there are the following: a Siberian husky named Newman starred in the two-hour pilot (the dog has since become the double on the series *100 Deeds for Eddie McDowd*); Lincoln's stunt doubles, Chinook, a mixed breed, and Kaery-Ann, who also acted and served as Lincoln's photo double; MacKenzie King, daughter of Kaery-Ann, who played Diefenbaker in a few scenes; and Kristy, a gray-and-white pup who played Dief as a pup during a nightmare sequence in the episode "The Edge." The last three dogs were purebred Siberian Huskies supplied by the KeeKaWa Kennels.

And last, and least, a dummy dog named Stiffy was used in all four seasons for stunts that would have been too dangerous for real dogs.

The Dukes of Hazzard

CBS 1979–1985, 147 episodes, 2 TV movies

*Starring **Sandy as Flash,** Tom Wopat as Luke Duke, John Schneider as Bo Duke, Catherine Bach as Daisy Duke, Denver Pyle as Uncle Jesse Duke, James Best as Rosco P. Coltrane, Sorrell Booke as Boss Hogg, and Sonny Shroyer as Deputy Enos Strater. Narrated by Waylon Jennings.*

This show chronicles the rollicking adventures of "those Duke boys" as they race around the countryside in their Dodge Charger, christened the General Lee. Sheriff Coltrane and his force, including Flash, try to maintain some semblance of order, if not law, as the world of the Dukes frequently crashes into the plans of the ever-scheming Boss Hogg.

James Best talks about working with the lovable Sandy, who was the primary dog that played Flash, the basset hound on the getaway hit *The Dukes of Hazzard.* "Flash belonged to James Best and Alvin Mears. Alvin was the trainer. I had quit the show for about five shows because they were scuffing me. When I came back, I said, 'What I'd like to have with me is a dog' because on the show I didn't have girlfriends. I didn't have anybody except my little fat buddy [Boss Hogg], and so I said I'd like to have a dog on the show. And they said, 'No, we don't want

Trainer Alvin Mears prepares to put Flash (played by Sandy) into a washtub as James Best (Rosco P. Coltrane) stands by in an episode of *The Dukes of Hazzard.*

Courtesy of Alvin Mears.

Sheriff Rosco P. Coltrane (James Best) is set to rocket down the highway with Flash, played by Sandy, on the trail of hilarious trouble in *The Dukes of Hazzard.*

to pay five hundred dollars for a trainer and a dog on the show.' And I said, 'Well, then you don't want Rosco P. Coltrane. I'll just stay in Florida.' So they changed their mind on that pretty quick."

Trainer Alvin Mears, owner of Alvin Animal Rentals, adds, "Sandy looked to be about six years of age when she started. I had several Flashes throughout the years because they were older dogs. I replaced the original one that was on the first season with Sandy. I had acquired Sandy out of an animal shelter. What ended up happening was there was a trainer that used to do the goats and the chickens on the *Dukes* show, and she knew that I was trying to find a duplicate or a look-alike of the original Flash. She went to the animal shelter and she found her, and she called me up and asked me should she get her out of the shelter because this dog was just like Flash. I told her sure she should. I met with her, and she gave me the dog and said, 'Now you just continue on with Flash. Now you've got a double.' And that's how I ended up with Sandy to do Flash over the years. I later ended up finding a breeder that had some dogs that looked like her, and so I had some doubles. I ended up with about three Flashes throughout the last two seasons. I had one named Pearl and one named Angel."

Best recalls, "Alvin went to the dog pound and got Flash who, God love her, was not going to be adopted—she was sixty pounds of wrinkles. And so 'Velvet Ears' was adopted by Alvin, and he brought her on to the show, and naturally I fell in love with Flash from the very beginning. The only thing is that she weighed about sixty pounds, and I'm still suffering from back strain from carrying her little tush around."

Trainer Mears adds, "A basset hound is every bit of a bloodhound—just no legs. She was dead weight." Adding to her weight was a certain secret prosthesis. "Sandy actually had a little scar on her back from before the show," explains Mears. "And this patch on her back didn't have any hair. It looked like a surgical area—about two inches wide and two inches long. The hairdresser made a little hairpiece for her. You could never tell that she didn't have hair in that spot. It was like a little toupee on the back side of her."

"Alvin was such a fantastic trainer that he could get Flash to do anything he wanted," recalls Best. "He would train her the night before. For instance, let's say Boss Hogg had lost his wallet or something. Flash would go and dig the wallet up and pick it up in her mouth and everything. She was that smart."

Best says he did his best to look out for Flash. "I would find out when she was to be riding with me and I'd say, 'Well, you know, that's dangerous. I don't want to jeopardize Flash's life. So they had a dummy Flash made up that we called Flush. Flush would ride with me, and Flash would be in her dressing room, which I had made up, and it was a little dressing room with a Rebel flag on the top and on rollers, and she'd be on the soundstage and she'd take a snooze until we were ready to shoot, and we'd say, 'OK, Flash, time to go to work,' and she'd come out there really happy and she'd shake a few times, and then Alvin would wipe the slobber off of her little jowls."

Best adds, "She drooled a lot, and she'd come and she'd get in the car with me, and a lot of time we're shooting the process (that's where the car is still and there's a movie screen in the background). We'd want Flash to be looking out the front like I was chasing the Duke boys, and so I'd take a piece of wiener, and I'd put it up above the visor, and, of course, Flash would rivet her eyes on that, and it looked like she was looking forward at the Dukes. As soon as they'd say, 'Cut,' she knew she was going to get that piece of weenie. So I'd give her the weenie, and we'd say, 'OK, Flash, that's it,' and then they'd say, 'Cut' and she'd run back to her little dressing room, and she'd crawl in there and take a snooze."

Mears echoes that memory: "Wherever you placed that weenie, it had her attention. She'd sit there and drool and stare at it until you let her go get it or when you handed it to her. Jim [Best] used to have them on him all the time, and he'd talk to her and she'd bark back at him. They had an excellent relationship."

Adds Mears, "Believe it or not, the hardest thing in the world to do is to get a dog to do nothing with all kinds of commotion around while riding in the car. Rosco always had a great big plate of chicken wings or something that my dog had to ignore—literally ignore everything going on around her or she was out of character.

"Her best trick would be to allow you to lay her down and then she'd lay her head down, and then you could literally manipulate her ears and her jowls and the wrinkles around her eyes and on her back and on the top of her head, and you could make her look just as pitiful as you could by manipulating all this skin to make her look sad. I would say that was probably one of her best qualities. That is, other than when they'd say, 'Cut,' and I'd let her jump up and move around. Obviously, she wanted some of that old Rosco chicken since she had to ignore it for a whole hour."

Best adds, "After about a year or so, Flash became one of the biggest stars on the show, and they made an awful lot of commodities that looked like Flash and she became very popular. But what was happening was the studio was not giving Alvin billing on the screen, and they weren't paying him what they really should've, and so that upset me. Alvin wanted to earn enough money to get a little farm where he could train other animals for motion pictures. That's what he wanted to do, and he was very good at it.

"So I said to Alvin one time, 'Go in and ask them to double your salary and get your money for Flash.' And he said, 'Well, Mr. Best, they will fire me.' And I said, 'No, if they fire you, I will pay the difference for the rest of the series. So you've got a win-win situation here.' And so Alvin went in and sure enough they threatened to fire him. I said to the studio, 'Do you want to fire Alvin and replace the dog?' They said, 'Well, that's what we'll do.' I said, 'Well, then you'll replace Rosco P. Coltrane because if you fire either one of them, I'm gone.' Well, Alvin got the screen credit, he got more money, and he got his little farm."

And Best also worked another angle in looking out for the best interests of Alvin and Flash. "I told Warner Bros. that I owned half of Flash, which I did," Best recalls. "I'd given Alvin a dollar and I said, 'Now I own half of Flash and can legally say that I own Flash and then we can really negotiate.' I said, 'I'll never take a dime that you ever make with Flash,' and it worked out very well. But Warner Bros. still nearly had a stroke because they had eight attorneys on retainer just waiting for some sort of lawsuit when my business manager went in and said, 'Well, where's the commodity money for Flash, because you put out all these commodities on her, and Mr. Best owns the dog?' They nearly had a coronary. I'm sure there were a few lawyers who lost their jobs on that."

Mears says about James Best, "Jim would stick right by me through everything. He has a very kind heart. He was very inspirational for me on the show. I can say nothing but positive things about the relationship with him and the dog and myself."

Mears adds, "I think when the last season ended Sandy probably was about nine or ten years of age. She lived a good four more years after that. So she was probably about fourteen when she passed. Her doubles all have passed since then, too, but all from just old age."

"Flash was six or seven years old when we put her on the show," Best remembers, "and, of course, we were on the air for a long time. We'd been off for quite a few years when she went to doggie heaven. She's got a lot of doggie num-nums now. I'm sure she is taken very good care of. She was nominated for a PATSY. I believe Benji beat her slightly, but I think it was fixed." He laughs. "Anyway she's famous now, and she'll be famous for the rest of time, I guess. As long as *The Dukes of Hazzard* is ever on, Flash will be right up there among the stars. And that's where she is right now."

Early Edition

CBS, 1996–2000, 88 episodes

Starring ***Panther as Carl the Cat, Trucker as Spike the seeing-eye dog, Riley as the second seeing-eye dog,*** *Kyle Chandler as Gary Hobson, Shanesia Davis-Williams as Marissa Clark, Fisher Stevens as Chuck Fishman, and Ron Dean as Detective Marion Crumb.*

This series follows the experiences of Gary Hobson, whose cat's meow signals the delivery each morning of the next day's *Chicago Sun-Times.* Hobson then has to find the correct items of bad news in the paper and race against very real deadlines as he tries to stop the various misfortunes and disasters before they happen.

Trainer Bill Casey talks about Panther, the orange tabby who played the feline star of *Early Edition.* "Panther was a shelter cat, as so many cats like that are. He was actually a very sick shelter cat. I used to go to the shelter to look for other cats, and an orange tabby was so ordinary that I was really not focusing a lot of attention on him. Upon my return to the shelter, he was always there. He seemed to appear a bit sicker each time, but he was very, very affectionate. He would follow me wherever I went and be looking at me when I'd be looking at other cats and was virtually ignoring him. But as I continued to return and he continued to be sicker, he began to kind of tug on my heartstrings as an animal lover. I initially took him not to keep him but to give him a better chance by nursing him back to health. To make a long story short, I took him and I spent thousands of dollars taking him to veterinarian medical schools to try to get this thing cured. After it took me darn near a year to get him back on his feet, the shelter owner said, basically, 'Take him, he's yours.' He also did very much endear himself to me and my family.

"He hardly ever worked initially and I had him more to cure him than to use him, but of course, once I had had him around and had gotten to know him and got to know what a great personality he had, I then did begin messing with him with various film-related training issues. And he did go on then to get various little Purina Cat Chow ads and Sears commercials and all sorts of little things. Many of them were rather bit-type parts.

"And then along many years later comes the director who's looking for a cat to be on *Early Edition.* He had expressed interest in Panther because of the fact that he had an orange cat that wandered around his offices out in L.A. He had taken a liking to that cat, and consequently he basically had given me some explanations as to what a cat would need to do. I said that Panther really would be probably the best choice because he knows a bunch of these odds and ends already. At this point Panther was like a nine-year-old cat, so he was actually becoming an old cat.

"Anyway, we did the pilot back when Panther would have been probably about eightish and then, of course, were not signed on. The pilot was done in March or April, and the show wasn't signed on until July of that year. By that point, Panther was probably pretty close to nine, but he did such a wonderful job with the pilot, which was a real test of his ability to endure the bizarreness of the film business on a grand scale. He did continue on with the show in spite of the fact that upon completion of the first season, he became deathly ill, and there were some issues that the veterinarian believes basically were with him from many, many years back in that he had developed some sort of an infection virtually in the bone around his eye.

"We had him actually skip the final show of the first season to go in for this major surgery that basically involved splitting his face completely open. It was kind of a crapshoot as to whether he would ever go on to do the second season. There were even some articles in the New York papers as to his dilemma about being in major surgery and the fact that we'd actually had a plastic surgeon sew his face back together. He looked literally like Frankenstein. But he had time for recuperation during our hiatus, which gave him a good three months to recuperate, and he was ready and raring to roll and as good as new come season two, and he did continue to go successfully through the final episode of the final season."

Casey says one of the things that kept Panther going was favorite treats. "He was very motivated by Fancy Feast. A lot of things he was conditioned to do—coming here, running there, looking this-a-way or that-a-way—were all related to his kind of spoon-fed reward of Fancy Feast. That was just his favorite."

He adds, "One of the things is that he had personality. He had some wonderful qualities that actually helped us kind of fall into some of those things we did on the show. He would stay, when he was told to stay, but if we made him stay for too long, his reaction was not to get up or to go down. His reaction was to actually meow. So, to be honest, it was kind of a coincidence that he meowed while standing on the newspaper. It wasn't, you know, great animal training. It was just something that was kind of a by-product of some training. That was his way of vocalizing, and it wasn't something that we had to torture him through any great length. If he was just left to sit there for any piece of time, he was meowing and it worked out wonderfully in a lot of situations.

"It's funny how things work out. The cat was supposed to be a bit more of a blip, and then the cat became more of a piece of the show. I did get kind of an understudy for Panther, and I taught it different things to take some of the load off Panther, both because he was an aging cat and because I didn't really think it was fair to him to have to be training him to do new things at ten or eleven years of age. It also helped spare Panther some situations, such as some street settings and some harsher winter situations in Chicago.

"The understudy's name was Carl, and that actually is the name of the cat in the show, and we had just named him that specifically because we got him after the show began, and we thought how nice it would be to have a cat that would actually be called the same thing as he is on the show, because so many times these animals have already been named by us prior to their part. Of course, the nice thing about the *Early Edition* assignment was the fact that the cat was almost somewhat of a mythical, mystical type of a figure, so it was never really identified in the show other than pretty much 'the cat,' yet all of our scripts had him clearly named Carl."

Panther always made headlines in his daily prowls on *Early Edition*.
Courtesy of Bill Casey.

Since *Early Edition* ended production in early 2000, Panther has been taking it easy. Says Casey, "He's about fourteen or fifteen. I have kind of left him to retire. I just feel that he deserves it with everything he's been through and with everything that he's done for me. He was always a favorite pet of mine, even when he was not a working animal. He always comes up and lies on my bed if I'm watching TV or whatever. He'll lie next to me every single night, and he's incredibly good with my dogs, and he's very confident. He'll sleep in the middle of the dogs. He tends, in some respects, to kind of rule the roost. He's not an aggressive animal in any way, but he's got a lot of really special qualities."

Casey also handled Trucker, a German shepherd who played Spike, Marissa's first seeing-eye dog on *Early Edition*. Says Casey, "Trucker actually worked the first three seasons of the show, and then was switched to Riley, who was a golden retriever, for the fourth season. Trucker is actually owned privately by a friend of mine who lives in the Chicago area. We didn't really know how much of a part it was going to be. The focus was really more on the part of the cat.

"The dog part took on a lot of levels depending upon the season. Some years the dog was key and others the dog would sometimes go weeks and never even be seen. It worked its heaviest the first season. Basically what the producers had kind of come down to was the fact that most of the time the dog was walking around her side, and the viewers were not even seeing him because his head was below a lot of the action.

"At the same time Trucker had a career as a search and rescue dog and has been immensely successful at searching for lost people. There was somewhat of an interference and impact on his usage because his searching was a really important quality of his. He's actually good at search and rescue. That is what he has continued on with. To this very day, he is very heavily into a lot of search and rescue cases in the Midwest."

Casey explains further, "Another reason that also helped somewhat to motivate us onto a different dog was that, as the seasons had gone on, different directors and producers had come and gone. The original director, who had picked Panther, was the one who was insistent upon the fact that the dog must be a German shepherd. I was basically explaining to him that German shepherds, as seeing-eye dogs, had really lost popularity. They were definitely *the* dog of maybe the '60s and '70s, but a lot of the retrieving breeds had become far more popular as seeing-eye dogs. I was trying to make that point to him back then, and yet, you know, he is the producer/director, and so whatever his vision is, is what's going to happen. But I continued to re-express my opinions as each season went on, and finally, about the third season, the producing team at that point had kind of seen the light and agreed with me that it seemed like a more logical choice, and that's when I sought out Riley who was only about a year old.

"Riley was actually a very young dog, but I had used him for a variety of projects, and he had done quite well with them. I encouraged his use for the fourth and final season of *Early Edition.* It was definitely a great part, and you never know how those things are going to work out."

And, well, that's it for this *Edition.*

Empty Nest

NBC, 1988–1995, 170 episodes

Starring ***Bear as Dreyfuss,*** *Richard Mulligan as Dr. Harry Weston, Kristy McNichol as Barbara Weston, Dinah Manoff as Carol Weston, Park Overall as LaVerne Todd, and David Leisure as Charley Dietz.*

Empty Nest is about a widowed pediatrician in Miami who frets over his two grown-up daughters, who also live in his house, while mature women are attracted to him. The doctor's best friend and most sympathetic listener is his big dog, Dreyfuss.

"Bear was born into the business," says trainer Mark Forbes of the dog who played Dreyfuss. "His father was Boomer from the *Father Murphy* TV series. Boomer was a St. Bernard/golden retriever mix-breed dog that was rescued from an animal shelter by his trainer and the owner of our company [Birds & Animals Unlimited], Gary Gero. Boomer had a short relationship with a local St. Bernard, and one of the results was Bear.

"Boomer turned out to be one of those one-in-a-million dogs who had both great personality and intelligence, as well as spirit. These traits showed up in his puppies as well and especially in Bear. Besides that, I think the two things that I remember most about Bear was his fearlessness and his love of work. I don't know that I have ever been around a dog who loved to train and work as much as he did.

"Bear had so many behaviors that it's hard to think of what his best ones were, but I guess the most memorable one would be the ones where he would place his head down and then lift his eyebrows up, independently, one at a time. This worked great for a scene at the end of one of the shows where he was watching a tennis match on TV.

"Bear was originally trained by Roger Schumacher. After he got cast as the family dog in the TV series *Empty Nest*, he lived and worked with Joe Silverman for the first four seasons of the series. I started working with Bear before the fifth season and carried on with him throughout the rest of his life. Bear was cast in *Empty Nest* when he was about a year-and-a-half old and worked on the show until he was almost nine."

Schumacher, who worked the dog on the *Empty Nest* pilot, says, "Bear was great, a big clown with a loving personality. One thing he did on his own, and they ended up using—he moved his eyebrows a lot." Occasionally, Bear's brother, Julio, stepped into his shoes, but for the most part it was Bear in the *Nest*.

As for other family credits, father Boomer was in the feature film *Summer Rental*, and brother Bodie shared screen moments with Shirley MacLaine in *Steel Magnolias* and was in *The Bodyguard*. His sons, Bart and Billy and Bogus, have starred in many films such as *Homeward Bound II*, *A Simple Plan*, and *What Lies Beneath*. Bear fathered twelve pups, but the mother sat on six of them and killed them. Three of the survivors shared the role of Rumbo in the film *Fluke*.

Bear was in the film *The Witching Hour* and appeared in a Hollywood dog training video with his former trainer Joel Silverman. One of his most challenging feats on *Empty Nest* was to perform his trademark move: retreating into a kitchen cabinet when he needed privacy. Silverman says it was a difficult chore since the move was a series of twenty-five learned behaviors.

Because of his popularity on *Empty Nest*, his first regular series, Bear appeared on several *TV Guide* covers. In one episode, "Dreyfuss, Got a Minute?" he filled the role of psychiatrist as the Westons shared their feelings with the member of the family most willing to listen.

In 1993 Bear granted an interview to Kitty Kat (an NBC feline publicist), where he spoke candidly for the first time about life on the set of a hit series. "Somehow I always knew I would follow in my father, Boomer's, paw prints," said Bear.

To what does the Hollywood hound owe his success? "Never let 'em see you fetch," he said. "The real secret of working with a trainer is to let him think he's doing all the work. My trainer and I have an understanding, I reward him by following his commands."

For the first four seasons of *Empty Nest*, Bear lived and worked with Silverman. "Working with Joel was an incredibly rewarding experience. He was more than a master, he was a best friend and I miss him dearly," Bear was quoted at the time.

Beginning with season five, Bear began breaking in trainer Forbes, who, like Silverman, worked with Ray Berwick before joining Gary Gero's team of trainers at Birds & Animals Unlimited.

"A typical day in my life is not so different from my human colleagues on the show. Our long day starts at 10 A.M. sharp," Bear was quoted in the NBC publicity material. "Sometimes I get a chance to play between takes or retreat to my kennel for a cat nap, no pun intended.

"To some, entertainment is a dog-eat-dog business, but I was fortunate enough to go straight from the doghouse to the penthouse, rising to international fame almost overnight. The only downside is that I am constantly besieged by fans for souvenir paw prints. I haven't got the ink off my paws in two years.

"I love to travel, but when we stay in big cities I can never leave the hotel without some sort of disguise, usually dark sunglasses and a floppy hat. And that hotel food always tastes like it came out of a can!

"I love the interaction with a live audience and, when there's time, I enjoy meeting some of my fans after the show. In comedy, however, there's always a lot of pressure to be 'on.' Some days I feel melon-collie, I just want to roll over and play dead.

"I'm a huge fan of country music and last season I had the opportunity to howl with one of country's living legends, Garth Brooks."

As for romance, Bear said, "The press has really hounded me for the scoop on my personal life. I have received a few proposals and have a couple of litters of pups running round out there, but I'm hardly ready to settle down to a family life."

Bear added, "I've really been lucky, but sometimes I miss the old days when all I had to do was sit, roll over, and fetch the occasional newspaper. Deep down, I'm just like any other dog. I still enjoy life's simple pleasures."

Life on the set was a pleasure for Bear, and Forbes says that the dog got along with all the cast and crew of *Empty Nest*, but he loved Richard Mulligan the best. "Every morning when we walked on the stage, Richard would be there early working on his script in the dining room of the set. Bear would run over to him, and Richard would stop working, give Bear a pat and ask him how he was doing this morning, then give him a treat and send him on his way. I think that relationship that Richard and Bear had off camera went a long way toward making their relationship on camera believable."

The trainer remembers one hilarious accident on the set: "There was a scene that we were shooting for the end of one of the shows, and Bear was supposed to run down the stairs and out the front door carrying a bra. Almost halfway down the stairs, he got his foot caught in the bra strap. Instead of letting go of the bra, he proceeded to sort of hop along the living room with the bra in his mouth and stuck on his foot. You had to be there."

As for treats, edible or simply playthings, Forbes says, "Bear liked just about any and all foods in as big a portion as he could get them, but I guess his favorite was Bil-Jack liver treats. He would do anything for them. He didn't really have a favorite toy, but he loved chew toys and spent many a long hour lying in the back yard cleaning his teeth on his chews."

Forbes adds, "Bear lived with me during his work on *Empty Nest*. He was a great dog to have around the house. When Bear finished *Empty Nest*, he was almost nine years old, and he retired to my house in the San Fernando Valley. He spent the next three-and-a-half years living the good life of long walks, plenty of chew toys, and lots of love. Bear passed away at the ripe old age of twelve-and-a-half."

Joel Silverman, a Hollywood native, began his animal training career at Sea World in San Diego where he trained killer whales. He worked for Ray Berwick at Universal Studios and then enlisted with Gary Gero of Birds & Animals Unlimited at the time *Empty Nest* was hatching.

Mark Forbes, a native of Grants Pass, Oregon, worked with Bear on the last four seasons of *Empty Nest*. A graduate of Moorpark College, he has worked with all types of birds, dogs, cats, chimpanzees, and orangutans. He has trained animals for theme parks and for feature films and TV, including the cats and penguins in *Batman Returns*, the Doberman in *Death Becomes Her*, Einstein the dog in *Back to the Future II* and *III*, the birds in *The Crow*, and several birds for an episode of *Cheers*. More recently, he has worked with animal actors on the films *101 Dalmatians*, *102 Dalmatians*, *Dr. Doolittle*, *Dr. Doolittle II*, *Homeward Bound II*, *Wonderboys*, *Dante's Peak*, and *Resident Evil*.

As Dreyfuss, Bear was a big member of the cast of *Empty Nest*. He's a happy dog here with human pals, clockwise from bottom, Richard Mulligan, Kristy McNichol, David Leisure, Park Overall, and Dinah Manoff.

Flipper / Flipper: The New Adventures

Flipper: NBC, 1964–1968, 88 episodes

Starring ***Suzy and Cathy as Flipper,*** *Brian Kelly as Porter Ricks, Luke Halpin as Sandy Ricks, Tommy Norden as Bud Ricks, Andy Devine as Hap Gorman, and Ulla Stromstedt as Ulla Norstrand.*

Flipper follows the fascinating aquatic tales of friendly dolphin Flipper and the Ricks family around Coral Key Park in Florida.

Flipper: The New Adventures: Syndicated (1995–1997) and on the Pax Network (1998–2000)

This updated version of *Flipper,* filmed in Australia, is again set in Florida and initially follows the adventures of a grown-up Bud Ricks (who is now Dr. Keith Ricks, played by Brian Wimmer). Inspired by Keith's stories about the legend of the original Flipper, a new dolphin that regularly visits the area is given the same name. Adventures ensue with an ever-changing cast of humans.

Flipper creator/trainer/director Ricou Browning (who, by the way, made his first splash into films as the *Creature of the Black Lagoon*) describes how he came up with the concept for the *Flipper* series and then found and trained his finned stars: "We went over to Marineland Studios to put on a fashion show underwater, and they had girls with costumes of different natures and new bathing suits and whatever. Anyway, while we were there I saw a dolphin show that they had, and I didn't think much more of it other than it was great. Then some years later I was working at Silver Springs in public relations, and I'd remembered in school that they had freshwater dolphins in the Amazon River and in the Yangtze River, and I got the idea as a publicity stunt that we'd capture some freshwater dolphins and bring them back to Silver Springs. We caught some in the Amazon and got them back to Silver Springs. We never did a show. We never did anything with them other than feed them. They became pets.

"Anyway, we had them for several years, and they finally all passed away, and then some years later, while I was still working at Silver Springs, I went home and the kids were watching *Lassie,* and sitting there with them watching it, I thought, 'Wouldn't it be interesting to do the old Greek legend of a boy and a dolphin?' And I thought about it for quite some time and then started trying to come up with a story idea.

"At that time, my brother-in-law was a radio announcer in Ocala, Florida, and he and I were talking one day and I said, 'Hey Jack, you know how to write pretty good. Let's write a book about this dolphin and a boy.' So we spent a weekend in a friend of mine's cottage on a lake and wrote the story of Flipper. I couldn't do much with it, and it was just a short story. But I decided to go to New York and see if I could sell it as a book. So I went to New York and spent a week there trying to peddle it as a book at different bookstores and shops.

"I had a friend, Hugh Downs, who had a dolphin at one time, and I was talking with him, and he made me an appointment at Random House. So I went there, but it didn't work out. So I went to another place and they were interested.

"I'd had some artwork done with a boy kneeling over a dolphin with a Band-Aid on him in the water and some other artwork to go with the story, and these people were interested. But I ran out of money; so I went back home. And then, while I was at home and hadn't heard from the publishers after several weeks or months, I got the bright idea.

"I had done some underwater work with Ivan Tors on the TV series *Sea Hunt.* We'd finished shooting, and so I called Ivan and I said, 'Ivan, I've got an idea for a show, and I'd like you to say that you'd consider it as a movie because I'm trying to sell it as a book.' He said, 'Well, OK, I'll say that but send me a copy.' So I mailed him a copy and I didn't think any more of it. Then about two or three weeks later, I get a phone call from Ivan and he says, 'You know what? Let's make a movie.' So we made the first feature of *Flipper.* That's how it

Flipper checks out his landlubber pals, played by, from left, Luke Halpin, Brian Kelly, and Tommy Norden.

started." (The 1963 film *Flipper* starred Chuck Connors and Luke Halpin, who continued his role when the movie went to TV.)

Browning continues, "When we started to actually get serious about making the film, we had to find an animal. So we went to all the aquariums—Miami Seaquarium, Marineland, etc. And at that time trainers would only have the dolphins jump out of the water or take fish from their hand or do some kind of tricks in the water, but no person was with the animal. It was just a kind of distant relationship. We couldn't find any animal that was friendly to a person, and we were going to shoot pretty soon, like six months down the line. So we were traveling in the Keys, and we went to a place and one of the trainers there said, 'You know, there's a guy that has a dolphin in a little lake next to his house, he captures dolphins for aquariums, and he's got one there now.'

"So we stopped by over there. His name was Milton Santini, and I said, 'Can we see your dolphin?' So we went over there, and I got down in the water, and the animal swam up and swam right up under my arm. I was standing in the water, and I rubbed it and petted it, and it went away and came back and was very friendly. So I looked up at Ivan, and Ivan looked at me and I said, 'I think we've got Flipper.'" Her name was Mitzi. (That's right. Perhaps making up for Lassie's really being a boy, the supposedly male Flipper was actually a girl.)

Browning recalls, "I spent three months down there with my son, Ricky, who was nine at the time [and who would go on to become a stunt double for Luke Halpin in the movie and series]. We trained the animal

Luke Halpin and Tommy Norden enjoy a little finny fellowship with Flipper the dolphin.

for the show because the way the trainers trained the animals in aquariums, they feed them in the same spot all the time, and the animal expects to go to the same place. In other words, you can't get them out of their routine. So we tried to break the routine of the animal doing everything in one spot. We'd go all the way around the lake training it.

"In our show, the boy had to ride the dolphin like a horse. I couldn't figure out how we were going to do that, but one afternoon I was throwing a ball for Mitzi to retrieve. She'd pick it up and bring it back. I got the bright idea of, 'Well, why couldn't she retrieve a boy?' So I told Ricky to run down the dock, and I threw him in the water, and I gave Mitzi the signal to retrieve, so she went over there where he was, and she was trying to grab him. He wore a pair of cutoff blue jeans, and she was trying to grab a belt loop and pull him, and she would pull him a little ways and stop and then she'd come back to me, and I'd send her back again, and she would pull him a little ways and stop. Then Ricky reached up and grabbed her fin, and she towed him right to me immediately; I gave her a fish.

"I said, 'Let's do it again.' So Ricky jumped off the dock, she went over there, he held her fin, and she brought him right back. So I sent him across the lake and did the same thing. I threw a ball over his head so that it didn't hit the water. He jumps in, and she gives him a ride all the way to me. So immediately I knew we had the animal. Our training progressed from there."

As further evidence of Mitzi's "faster than lightning" learning curve and quick problem solving, Browning gives a specific example. "I threw two balls, a big one and a little one, and she would pick up the big one, and she couldn't get the little one. So she would drop the big one and pick up the little one, and then after a few seconds or maybe minutes, she picked up the big ball and then scooped the little one up behind it in her mouth and brought both of them. Later, the dolphins would figure out ways where they'd bring, say, two balls, and if you threw a towel, they would put it under their fin. In other words, they'd figure out ways of accomplishing the task you wanted them to do and they're quite special. They're really some kind of animal."

After the two feature films (*Flipper* in 1963 and *Flipper's New Adventure* in 1964), the time was ripe for a TV series. But first Browning had to find a new dolphin. He explains why. "Too expensive. They decided she was worth a million dollars or so, and we said no thank you. So we got new dolphins at the Miami Seaquarium, which they gave to us to use, and we trained them, and we basically used two out of the five we had over the period of four years."

All five dolphins were female. "The reason we used the female," says Browning, "is because I had heard females were easier to train in the large animal category in general, not necessarily just dolphins."

Suzy was the primary dolphin used initially. Cathy eventually replaced Suzy as the main Flipper, and Scotty got some on-camera work, too. Suzy was an outstanding performer, but Browning says that in some ways her ability to think ahead allowed her to get too far ahead of her training and into inadvertent trouble.

"I can give you an example of what happened," Browning explains. "We trained the animal to retrieve a boy. . . . Well, in the show, say we'll have a scene where the young boy Tommy would ride the dolphin, but his job, let's say, is to look down and see a treasure chest on the bottom. So he lets go of the dolphin and he swims down to the treasure chest, but the dolphin knows one thing: I've got to take that boy over there to get my fish. So she'll follow him down to the treasure chest and that looks great, and then she still wants him to hold on and go over to where she gets her reward.

"Well, after doing this like, say, twenty or thirty times—not necessarily going for treasure chests but doing different things underwater where the boy has to ride the dolphin, let go, and then do something else—the dolphin nudged him, like, 'Hey, hold on to me.' And she nudged him quite hard, so he held on and

Tommy Norden puts Flipper through his paces.

rode her. Now she knows if she nudges the boy hard, he'll hold on. This happened with both Tommy [Norden] and Luke [Halpin] over a period of a month or so. It progressed to eventually she got to where she nudged a little too hard, and one of the trainers threw a fish to get her away from the boy. Now she knows if she hits him hard, she will get a fish. You can see how complicated it's getting. We were creating a problem. The dolphin didn't. We did. Anyway, to break that was very difficult. So rather than taking the time to break those kinds of habits, we just switched animals and then started retraining Suzy. We used Cathy until Suzy was better, and then we switched off a little using both of them."

The one thing that all dolphins have in common is that they are very much motivated by food. "It's like money is for people," Browning laughs. "You know, if you quit paying people, they quit working."

During the series, which was filmed in the Miami area and in the Bahamas (for most of the underwater scenes), Browning used a team of four or five trainers. As Browning graduated more into directing, Ric O'Feldman became the head trainer for *Flipper*. After the *Flipper* series, all of the dolphins went back to the Miami Seaquarium. "They were owned by the Miami Seaquarium," says Browning, "and after the show I'm not sure what happened to all of the animals. I know that Cathy died, and I think the Seaquarium used most of them in their dolphin show there for a while."

As for the *Flipper* feature film and TV series that splashed forth in the 1990s, Browning says that he is not really involved with them. "All we get mostly out of it nowadays is just a credit."

But Browning can also take satisfaction in knowing that he pioneered a whole new frontier in animal training and in work with dolphins. "I think they've really only scratched the surface so far with dolphins as far as what they can do," Browning says. "They're so intelligent."

And what's more, Browning has played a pivotal role in creating a whole new awareness and appreciation for dolphins by many of their fellow mammals—even diehard landlubbers.

Browning and the entire *Flipper* team (finned and unfinned) deserve more than the reward of a fish or two for their efforts. Generations of pleased viewers around the world owe them their heartfelt thanks.

One person greatly responsible for various TV series that featured animal stars was the late Ivan Tors. At one time he and Ralph Helfer were partners in Africa USA, home to more than five hundred animals. Helfer and Tors teamed for such series as *Daktari*, *Gentle Ben*, and *Cowboy in Africa*. And Tors had his own studio in North Miami, Florida, as well as underwater facilities in the Bahamas, where much of *Flipper* was filmed.

The Hungarian native also produced the TV series *Ripcord* and *Sea Hunt*, and he produced the feature films *Gentle Giant*, *Africa—Texas Style*, *Namu the Killer Whale*, *Clarence the Cross-Eyed Lion*, *Zebra in the Kitchen*, *Flipper*, and *Flipper's New Adventure*—several of which led to popular TV series, including, of course, *Flipper*.

Frasier

NBC, 1993–present
(still in production)

*Starring **Moose as Eddie,** Kelsey Grammer as Dr. Frasier Crane, David Hyde Pierce as Dr. Niles Crane, John Mahoney as Martin Crane, Jane Leeves as Daphne Moon, and Peri Gilpin as Roz Doyle.*

This sitcom follows the life of bombastic psychiatrist Frasier Crane and his family and coworkers at a talk radio station in Seattle.

"Moose was a family-owned dog that was born on a farm with lovely people and started to be mischievous from day one," says trainer Mathilde de Cagny. "He was difficult to keep for the family because he kept escaping and chasing cats and chasing horses and having problems with the neighbors and chewing stuff, and the list is endless of mischievous behaviors. So this lady decided to find a new home for him. She gave him to one of the neighbors, but he got returned very shortly after that for the same misbehavior problems, so then she was desperate. She didn't know what to do with him. Her husband had threatened to divorce her if the dog was staying.

"The company that I work for, Birds & Animals Unlimited, has a veterinarian that the lady used to work for, so she thought that maybe one of the trainers from our company would take Moose. Kathy Morrison came in to do a checkup on a dog, and the lady literally gave the veterinarian the dog and said, 'Please take him,' and ran away from him. And that's how he landed with Birds & Animals Unlimited. He then got to travel to California, and I was the lucky one in charge of taking care of him and training him, which was before he got his spot for *Frasier.*

"He was a really, really difficult little dog to be around. He's the kind of dog that you always need to keep your eyes open with because you know something bad's going to happen. You have to anticipate what he's going to come up with, and he always comes up with different misbehaviors.

"This is a dog who is really independent, yet very nice. He doesn't have a mean bone in him. He's just careless and he just minds his own business. He is a dog that's really all about himself. Most dogs are very needy. They need their owner, they need their home family, and that's just how dogs are. They live in packs, and we humans have become their pack and their leaders, and that's what they look up to.

"But Moose is nothing like that. He is his own pack. He likes to be his own chief and have the run of the house. So in that perspective, he doesn't really need anybody, and he was always negligent of my love and my interest toward him, and I'm somebody that's very loving and caring toward my animals. I was frustrated not to see the dog loving me back and pretty much ignoring me as much as he could.

"So I just decided to let him be, because you can't force anybody to be a certain way. But anytime he would come by, and I would

Moose was one of the top TV dogs of the 1990s and his popularity continues into the new century. He's seen here with trainer Mathilde de Cagny.
Courtesy of Mathilde de Cagny; photo by Michelle Miller.

be able to have my hands on him, I would only massage him—deep tissue. I did a type of massage that's called the Tellington Touch that opens up cells, and it's really neat because every massage that you learn has a specific purpose of opening different cells. So anytime he would come by, I would never pet him, I would never kiss him, but I would literally start getting into the shoulder and the neck and this and that, and he really enjoyed that because he was getting something out of it instead of just petting.

"Then he started slowly but surely to come to me hoping that he would get a massage, and I did that for a long time, and it changed him. He now is very appreciative of the hands, and he's always looking forward to it. But it really helped him turn around and be more part of a human being's life than what he was before. I don't think anything else would have worked for him."

De Cagny says that Moose now even responds well to treats. "Oh, he's very treat-oriented. They're not necessarily all that way, and it's not necessarily the way I train everything, but all dogs have their own personalities and their own loving thing that they will work better for, and I always respect what they're about. For instance, Moose's son, Enzo, is ball crazy, and he will work better for a tennis ball than food. Moose is a food-oriented type of dog, and so I do work him for treats quite a bit just because that's what he loves. He likes everything. He eats liver treats, but he's not that particular."

Perhaps the best known trick in Moose's repertoire is his "stare." Says de Cagny, "What I had to do is get him used to watching me, no matter what was going on in the audience or with the cameras and all that stuff. Hard concentration is a real trick for him especially because he was a dog that was really hyper and he wouldn't stay still. Just a simple stare was kind of a problematic behavior for him."

She explains further, "I had to teach him just to really watch me intensely, no matter what was going on. It is something that I built up slowly from a couple of seconds to where you then have people walking by and this and that. You don't let him get bored with it, but basically he's just really watching me. I have one of my fingers up in the air, and he knows that's the stare cue. And sometimes I use a little toy that he really wants or something that may make him look even more intense. Basically, what it is, is that you have the dog and the actor, and I'm in the eye line of the actor."

Moose himself talked about his stare in his memoir, *My Life as a Dog,* which was translated into English by de Cagny and Brian Hargrove and published in 2000. "My stare was funny," Moose comments, "but I couldn't milk it forever. And there was an uprising across America, because people wanted to see me do more. You got to give the people what they want. So the producers started putting in other things for me to do. I, of course, rose to the occasion. And, voila! More history."

Moose added, "My main role in the show is the little irritant that will never go away. When the writers deviate too much from my mission, I have to remind them of what I'm all about, so I politely suggest that they have me stare Frasier down again. They must always remember that I am the Jack Benny of the show and Frasier is my Rochester."

Says de Cagny, "Four-camera shows in general are very, very hard for animal trainers to get the looks right. And especially on *Frasier*—they hardly ever do pickups, so everything has to be in the wide, and it's got to be right and then cameras are in the way, and everybody wants the same spot. So the trainers have no place to be. We've got to be on the outside of the floor toward the audience, which is really exactly the place you don't want the dog to be looking. So it's really hard—especially with a dog like Moose. Moose is very, very complex." (That's why he wrote a book.)

She adds, "He's not the average-trained dog

Moose reigns supreme over the high and mighty as Eddie on *Frasier.*

that you will find that's a hard, good-working dog. He's much, much trickier than that. You always have to try to anticipate what he's going to come up with and what he's going to do. Another thing is that he's not a relaxing kind of dog. He's not the kind of dog where you say, 'Well, we've worked so many years together that we're a good team by now,' which is something I have with all my other dogs. Moose always has something up his sleeve."

Just as is the case in his role as Eddie, de Cagny explains, Moose seems to be constantly thinking. "He's got his own little life going there. It's very, very hard to be able to be part of what's going on or to have the perspective about what's going on. But that's what I have to try to do. That's how I work my dogs. It's all psychological and knowing them and getting into their minds basically, but with Moose, boy, it's been difficult."

She continues, "But I think the getting through is the number one reward. I have to tell you, this dog has taught me so much in training and in life in general because I had to change, I had to adjust to his personality, and I did. That's the only way that got me through a lot of things, and in that respect I ended up learning a lot about training and about adjusting and paying attention to an animal's feelings and being able to think fast if I see something's not going to go right or if I see that he's not focused. I have to have all kinds of little things ready in my mind and in my bait bag to come up with something quick. We have been very, very fortunate to have the success we've been having and for it to keep on going."

That's de Cagny's perspective. But in his memoir, Moose told it differently, "I'm still training Mathilde. But she's worth it." He added, "Different techniques work for different people. Keep at it and you will find a way. And remember: If a person is well trained, you can take her anywhere. She will become a loyal and loving companion for life."

De Cagny is still amazed at how Moose continues to captivate the public's attention, even after several years. "Normally, the first year the dog gets discovered, and people are all over them, and then it fades the second year or the third year, and people usually move on to other shows or whatever. But in his case, his fame has grown tremendously through the years. I mean, every year he gets more contracts, more deals, more invitations. We also do a lot of charities, now even more than ever. I've been a trainer for eighteen years, and I've never seen anything quite like it. Of course, there's Lassie. Lassie's unbeatable, and rightfully so because it's such a classic, but you know, I don't know dogs that have been such a hit for so long with one dog in the role."

De Cagny began her career with Gary and Barbara Gero at Birds & Animals Unlimited. "They took me to their company when I was volunteering, and I've been with them ever since. I have about seven to eight dogs at home at all times. They still belong to Gary and Barbara Gero and the company, but they live with me. They're all rescue dogs except for Enzo, Moose's son. You know, it looks like a long career going on for those two young fellas. It's nice."

Friends

NBC, 1994–present (still in production)

*Starring **Katie and Monkey as Marcel,** Courteney Cox as Monica Geller, Jennifer Aniston as Rachel Green, David Schwimmer as Ross Geller, Matthew Perry as Chandler Bing, Matt LeBlanc as Joey Tribbiani, and Lisa Kudrow as Phoebe Buffay.*

Friends follows the daily goings-on of six twenty- and thirty-something New Yorkers as they hang out together in their apartments or the Central Perk coffeehouse and talk about their lives, their loves, and their views of the world.

Two female, white-throated capuchin monkeys, Katie and Monkey, shared star billing as Ross's pet monkey Marcel. "Most people recognize the breed as organ-grinder monkeys," says Denise Sanders, a trainer who has worked with Bob Dunn's Animal Services since 1993. Dunn, who has trained simians of all types (including Michael Jackson's Bubbles) for about thirty years, is the owner of the *Friends* monkeys.

Katie, born in 1993, came to Dunn from Parrot Jungle in Florida, while Monkey, born in 1988, hails from Pennsylvania.

Sanders says, "Katie and Monkey work all the time. Katie is more active, and we use her for the more action-oriented themes. Monkey (who weighs five pounds and is twenty-two inches tall) is a little more mellow, so she is used more for sitting on the shoulder or sitting down.

"We'll look at a scene and see who would be the best candidate. We rehearse them both and then use the one who is best. Katie does a cute little can-can dance. She covers her eyes, jumps up and down, and picks up objects and puts them where you want. She'll circle, hold your hand, or sit down and put her feet out and hold her hands.

Katie (or is that Monkey?) thought that playing Marcel on *Friends* was a barrel of monkeys. They took a monkeyshine to Matt LeBlanc.
Courtesy of Bob Dunn's Animal Services.

"Monkey is a lot more mellow and doesn't pay as much attention to actors as Katie does. Katie is a better people person. They're both great workers, but if it's something where you need a vibrant monkey, we use Katie."

According to Sanders, the two have about a twenty-word vocabulary. When they are on the set, the monkeys each have a crate that is like their own trailer and a place to rest and sleep.

"We don't let them do too much socializing on the set, but the monkeys really took a liking to Matt LeBlanc, even though it wasn't his character who owned the monkey. And Matt fell in love with these guys, so we let him spend time with them when appropriate," Sanders says.

The Super Bowl episode of *Friends* in 1996 provided perhaps Marcel's (and therefore Katie and Monkey's) best scenes to show off, because it featured Marcel's new-found career as a national celebrity and star of commercials and films.

As for Katie and Monkey's favorite edibles, Sanders says, "They love mealworms and pistachio nuts. We offer them a variety of fruit and vegetables morning and evening. When they are working on the set, the treats are varied."

Monkey and Katie's two main trainers are Merissa Politzer and Mike Morris. The

simian duo's astounding list of credits includes the films *Outbreak*, *Ace Ventura II*, *George of the Jungle*, *Instinct*, *Flintstones II*, and *Addicted to Love*. They have guested on the TV shows *The Steve Harvey Show*, *Coach*, and *Dharma & Greg*, and they appeared in *The Jungle Book* series. Commercial credits include Yahoo, McDonald's, Doritos, Pepsi, Sony, and Bud Light, plus a Diet Coke commercial with the *Friends* cast. And they have also been seen on *The Tonight Show With Jay Leno* and on Animal Planet.

In the summer of 2000, the two had a ball as "the rally monkey" for the Anaheim Angels baseball team. "The Angels made up toy mascots and they sold out, so they brought in a live monkey to certain Angels games and it proved a big hit. We went down to some of the games, and the monkey once handed the baseball to the pitcher for the first pitch of the game," Sanders says.

When not working, Katie and Monkey live the good life on a ranch in the San Fernando Valley, where, according to Sanders, "they do whatever they want, play or rest, in cages filled with tires and ropes." They share their space with a friend, a third monkey named Freddy. After all, that's what good friends are supposed to do.

Frontier Circus

CBS, 1961–1962, 26 episodes

Starring ***Modoc the elephant, a wide variety of other exotic animals,*** *Chill Wills as Col. Casey Thompson, John Derek as Ben Travis, and Richard Jaeckel as Tony Gentry.*

Frontier Circus is a frontier drama set in the 1880s, as the one-ring T and T (Thompson and Travis) Combined Circus tries to survive amid the dangers of the American frontier.

"*Frontier Circus* was filmed all over Southern California," says Ralph Helfer, the man behind the animals in many of the 1960s shows that featured exotic animals. "That was when we first got Modoc [Helfer's prized performing pachyderm, which he found in Vermont for one thousand dollars]. I remember trying to get the camels and the horses to work with the elephants. We spent a long time getting them familiar with the elephants and where they would eat and drink from the same trough.

"Our horses weren't afraid of the elephants, but the local horsemen used their own horses. We furnished all the exotics. We had lions and tigers, and there was always the stunt of a leopard getting loose in the western town. Each episode had its own thrills involved.

"John Derek [who played the circus boss] was fine with the animals. This was quite early in his career, and he was great with the animals. Everybody on the set took to the animals as their own and treated them royally.

"I remember we had a scene with Modoc, and the elephant had to run into a barn. She was so big that she ran into the barn and took the roof off because she was too big. She came out the other end carrying a bit of the barn with her."

Animal handler Bill Raymond also recalls working with Modoc later in the 1960s. "Modoc had a reasonably placid personality. She was one of the elephants we used the most on *Daktari* [and also on *The Greatest Show on Earth*]. Modoc was blind in one eye, and she was a runner—she would run away from us. I remember we did *The Steve Allen Show* one time, and we were moving her out of a truck and into the backstage area, and she decided to take off and run. She took off up this alley, and a little sports car came around the corner. I never saw anybody shift into reverse as fast in my life."

Richard Jaeckel played trail scout Tony Gentry in *Frontier Circus,* a western with a twist—the big top and all its creatures roamed the West.

Modoc, who learned a few tricks from the cowboys, decided to pass on heading him off at the pass.

Full House

ABC, 1987–1994, 192 episodes

Starring ***Comet,*** *Bob Saget as Danny Tanner, John Stamos as Uncle Jesse Cochran/Katsopolis, David Coulier as Joey Gladstone, Candace Cameron as D. J. Tanner, Jodie Sweetin as Stephanie Tanner, Mary Kate and Ashley Fuller Olsen as Michelle Tanner, Andrea Barber as Kimmy Gibler, and Lori Loughlin as Rebecca Donaldson.*

Set in San Francisco, *Full House* is a sitcom about a widower who raises his three young daughters with the assistance of his brother-in-law and a good friend.

When the producers of *Full House* came up with a story line about a dog expecting to give birth to pups, in came canine star Comet. The male dog not only played the part of the mama dog, but he also came back a year later to play one of her pups, named Comet because the producers liked his original name so much.

Comet the golden retriever made the Tanner family complete on *Full House*.
Courtesy of Animal Actors of Hollywood.

Owned by Animal Actors of Hollywood, Comet was trained and is still cared for by Cristie Miele. She got Comet through Golden Retriever Rescue, an organization that helps match dogs with the right masters, when he was one-and-a-half years old. Born in 1987, Comet is enjoying his golden years of retirement.

Miele recalls how her dog came to TV fame. "They had written a script where they found a dog that ended up having puppies. We pushed for a purebred, so we could get puppies [that resembled the star dog]. We just showed a bunch of different dogs that were trained." The producers picked Comet, a true star with a tail.

"Comet is a kind of an all-American dog for an all-American kind of family," says her owner. "He played the female dog that they found in the original script. That dog had puppies, so we got a couple of golden retriever puppies, and after the first year, Comet starred on the show for the rest of its run.

"Comet is a very happy-go-lucky, highly motivated sort of dog. He wants to please. I'm assuming he wasn't doing well as a pet because he was a dog that had been left alone in the backyard. He dug and destroyed things because he was bored. He had a lot of energy that needed to be channeled into working.

"He was trained to do all the movie dog basics, trained to do about everything a dog can do. He could limp on command, he could crawl, he could even attack like a German shepherd, and then act as sweet as pie."

As for Comet's *Full House* mates, Miele says that he "got along fine with the cast. I think they all thought of him as one of the gang."

Of course, Comet could switch with ease to feature film work as he did in *Flute*. "That was Comet as the adult Flute. He was collared and clipped to look like a mixed breed. His specialty was looking natural, especially on *Flute*. He has a very expressive face. I could make him look very sad and then all of a sudden all happy. He would show emotions that would make a dog appear more human," says Miele.

He's done plenty of other jobs, running between commercials, films, TV movies, and TV series. He's got a spot in *The X-Files* to his credit, a segment about a wolf dog, and he made the TV movie *Blue Rodeo*. His double, Ajax, has gone on to star in *The Drew Carey Show*, and Comet has done a bit of subbing for Ajax in that series.

Miele continues to shower special attention on one of her favorite pets. "I always try and give him healthy things. I would cook chicken and turkey, and he certainly loves beef and liver. I cook fresh instead of using processed meats," she says.

These days Comet takes it pretty easy. "He enjoys sleeping in the sun," says Miele. "He still loves to play and go to the beach. We have a nice area where he can walk along, and he still likes to swim. Comet has started to lose his hearing. He still wants to work, but he's not physically able."

And that's the tale of this bright Comet.

Fury

NBC, 1955–1960, 116 episodes

Starring ***Beauty (aka Highland Dale) as Fury,*** *Peter Graves as Jim Newton, Bobby Diamond as Joey Newton, William Fawcett as Pete, Ann Robinson as Helen Watkins, Jimmy Baird as Pee Wee Jenkins, Roger Mobley as Packey Lambert, Nan Leslie as Harriet Newton, and James Seay as the sheriff.*

Set on the Broken Wheel Ranch near Capitol City, *Fury* is an action-packed adventure series in the modern West. On Saturday mornings in the late 1950s, about eighteen percent of all television sets were tuned in to watch "the story of a horse and the boy who loved him."

The series opened with orphan Joey, an innocent boy with a reputation for being a troublemaker, being accused of breaking a window during a baseball game. Rancher Jim Newton takes up the lad's cause, clears his name, and takes him to stay at the ranch, where he eventually adopts him. Pete is the friendly old-timer who serves as Jim's right hand on the ranch where they break and train horses. Joey has two pals, Packey and Pee Wee, who enjoy riding horses. Packey's mount is Lucky, while Pee Wee rides Pokey. The TV series was retitled *Brave Stallion* for syndication in 1959.

Beauty, who starred as Fury, was a beautiful American saddle horse (American Register Saddle-Bred Stallion), born in Missouri on March 4, 1943. Owned and trained by Ralph McCutcheon, Highland Dale made his debut in the 1946 film *Black Beauty*, where he picked up the nickname of Beauty or Beaut, which he was called for the rest of his career.

The coal-black stallion stood fifteen hands high and weighed about one thousand pounds. Beaut chowed down on thirty pounds of mixed feed daily, but his favorite treat for a job well done was carrots. He starred in other films, including *Gypsy Colt*, *Wild Is the Wind*, *Outlaw Stallion*, and *King of the Wild Stallions*, and was ridden by Elizabeth Taylor in *Giant*, by Joan Crawford in *Johnny Guitar*, and by Clark Gable in *Lone Star*.

Stuntwoman Donna Hall recalls that Beaut even did one great stunt for McCutcheon in the musical film classic *Oklahoma*. "In one scene, as the train is rolling down the tracks, Ralph calls for Beauty to come alongside the train, and he makes the transfer from the train to horseback. You see stuntmen go from horseback onto the train but rarely see it the other way. That was how much Beaut trusted Ralph."

The year 1955 saw both the release of *Oklahoma* and the debut of the series that made Beauty famous.

Peter Graves says that the horse and his owner worked incredibly well together on *Fury*. "Beauty was owned, trained, loved, and cared for by Ralph, and was a pal of Ralph's. I don't think I've ever come close to knowing anyone like Ralph. He talked to animals. Every animal in the world was his friend. He was something, and most of the credit for the success of that show should be given to him. He's the guy who never appeared on the screen but who pulled all the strings." Graves says that he never rode Beauty on *Fury*; he did get "up on him once or twice, but he was a pretty valuable piece of property."

Bobby Diamond starred in *Fury*, "the story of a horse and the boy who loved him." Beauty played Fury.

Courtesy of Bobby Diamond.

Fury was shot at the Iverson Ranch in Chatsworth, California. For his part, the horse earned $1,500 week and eventually got a raise to $5,000 per week. Bobby Diamond, who starred as Fury's best friend, Joey, recalled the horse as the smartest animal he ever knew. "He was amazing. I saw Beauty all the time, and I could make him do tricks, but Ralph was his only master," says Diamond. "Whenever Ralph came around, his head perked up. We worked completely in the open, and Ralph would tell him to run away, and Beauty would turn around and run away, and then Ralph would say 'come back,' and he would turn back. Other horses, if you let them loose, they would run away but not come back."

Diamond adds, "McCutcheon was just a great trainer, super with animals. Fury was a trippy number. McCutcheon could teach him things on the spot. He could say yes and no. He could lay down on his back. Ralph could say 'get back on your mark' and he obeyed."

McCutcheon worked his spell wondrously on Beauty and he taught the handsome animal to recognize about ten different words. However, the trainer always claimed this was not a trick horse. "He was a trained horse. There is a big difference," McCutcheon told one interviewer. "A trick horse will perform stunts as if he memorized them. But a trained horse seems to understand the things he's taught. Writers were constantly putting new things into scripts. I just sort of explained the stunt to Fury right on the set, gave him a rehearsal or two, and then he did it."

McCutcheon was so proud of his great horse that he couldn't resist showing him off at times when lots of people were present. Graves recalls one such occasion: "He used to bring Beauty into cocktail parties at his ranch. People would be dressed up, and, after a few drinks, Ralph would go out to the barn and bring him in—no halter or anything. The horse would follow Ralph into the house and tread through the guests and nod and whinny a little bit, and walk on out again, having touched nothing."

Diamond spotted a closer relationship between horse and trainer than was seen in most western or outdoor shows of the era. "Beauty was kind of like a dog. He walked around with the trainer. McCutcheon had a lot of horses, seventy to one hundred. A number of them were pretty well trained. Beauty just wandered around with him. He kept him at his house, and Beauty walked around in the backyard or he would get into the family swimming pool.

"He just hung out with Ralph, but Ralph was always teaching him things. Ralph would read the script ahead of time and teach him something new for that episode. The main thing was that he would learn things on the spot. If he had to untie a rope, Ralph would say, 'pick it up,' and he would do it. Beauty would walk around and pause and look to the right and look to the left."

Graves recollects that there were times when Beauty didn't quite feel like coming to work, so McCutcheon had to work his wiles on him. "The communication between them was really something. We'd come to work in the early morning, and Beauty would be in the first scene having to do something. Ralph would get out there with him and say, 'Hey, Beauty, do this, do that,' and the horse sometimes wouldn't feel like doing anything, and Ralph would go through this dance of coaxing him and seducing him, and the horse would still refuse, and Ralph would put on the anger act. He'd call him all sorts of names, and say, 'If you don't do that, I'm gonna get you.' Finally the horse would cower, and Ralph would chase him, and Ralph would say to us, 'Sit down, boys, relax. Forget the work for a moment. I'm gonna get the horse to do this.' It might take him fifteen minutes, but finally he would get the horse to do what was necessary. It was a beautiful thing to behold, because the horse knew exactly what Ralph was talking about."

Diamond, too, remembers when Beauty came to work with a bad attitude. "Sometimes he would throw a little temper tantrum. He got a little snotty at times, so you had to be careful when he got in a bad mood. When he pushed you, he would open up his mouth and he would grab you. One time with Roger Mobley, Beauty pushed him and grabbed him and caught his pants in his teeth and ripped his pants right off."

During the course of the series, four doubles were used, most of the time for "run bys" where Fury just ran past the cameras or for scenes of Fury galloping in the distance. Diamond remembers that one of the doubles was a black Morgan named Donroe, whose specialty was kicking open doors.

Oddly enough, the juvenile actor had little experience horseback riding when he got the job. "When I got the role, I was asked if I could ride. My mom had told me just to tell them I could do it whenever they asked me a question, but I had never ridden," says *Fury*'s favorite rider.

Graves says the boy and horse were a near-perfect match. "They got along wonderfully. Here was this little kid, nine when we started, and I don't think he had ever been near a horse before. He started out the way you think he would—not knowing which way was up. He got a lot of help from Ralph and all the wranglers, who taught him to ride, and he became a terrific rider, and he and the horse got along beautifully."

Graves reflects on one exciting incident that occurred while filming. "They had rewritten the story of Androcles and the Lion, so Bobby is out in the boondocks somewhere in the hills riding, and he comes across this lion that has escaped from a circus. The studio did an elaborate setup of having the lion in a sort of 'V' of rocks at his back, so he had no way to go back. Then they put a big heavy glass across the front forming a triangle. It was very clean and clear so they could photograph through it, so they could have Bobby on the outside of the glass and the lion on the inside, for safety of course.

"The lion had a thorn in its paw, which Bobby removed. The only trouble was, one day the lion didn't know the glass was there, and he walked right through it. There were about eighty people there with nothing between them and the lion. You've never seen eighty people move so fast—down paths, up trees, over mountains. And the lion kind of ambled through the whole thing, while people were going nuts, and went off in another corner of the hills by himself.

"His owners got his cage and approached him, and they opened the door to his cage and walked away. They told everybody to get away and just be quiet. Sure enough, the lion walked out of the little canyon into his cage, and they closed the door."

And Diamond also recalls one scary accident that had nothing to do with Beauty. "I was racing one of the doubles down a hill. I lost my balance and kicked the horse in the flanks, and he started bucking. I went head over heels and was knocked out cold."

Stuntman Whitey Hughes, who doubled Diamond on *Fury*, also remembers working and playing with Beauty. "When Ralph would be out of sight, I could mimic his voice and say things like 'Come on, Beauty.' I could work the horse almost as well as he could. He was just a real good-mannered horse. You didn't find many like him. You could work him anywhere, any place, any time," says Hughes, who later doubled Johnny Crawford on *The Rifleman.*

"At first a girl doubled Bobby, Steffi Epper, until she started blossoming," Hughes says. Because he was close to the size of Diamond, Hughes then got the stunt work—a role he filled on the show for four seasons.

"We did only bareback riding," recalls Hughes. "We hardly ever used a saddle. We used a midget, Harry Monty, to double Pee Wee [actor Roger Mobley]. One day we did a scene where a kid in a hot rod car comes busting by and narrowly misses the horse. Harry was riding on behind me, and I told him to put his fingers in my belt and hold on. The kid went by, really smoking, pop, pop, pop, and the horse jumped and unseated old Harry, but he kept holding onto the back of my belt or he would been down under that horse.

"We had several doubles. One double, not quite as black as Beauty, we used for chases. Beauty was just worked for close-ups. But there was one double horse, Diablo, you couldn't send him too far away and keep control.

"We didn't have to worry about Beauty getting off. He was so docile, a very intelligent horse. I had him opening doors. It was fun working him. Ralph had a little treat he'd give him for working, little apples, but he didn't mess around too much with feeding any particular treats. He had all his horses on good rations."

Another stuntman-wrangler who worked Beauty was Bill Catching, famous as the stunt double of Roy Rogers. Prior to working before the cameras, he was employed by trainer McCutcheon. Catching recalls, "I used to help Ralph before *Fury* started. Ralph was the greatest horse trainer in Hollywood. He would turn Beauty out in the corral, and the horse wouldn't come to you. Ralph would say, 'Here, Beau. Beauter, come here.'

"Clark Gable rode him in *Lone Star*, and then he was with Bill Holden in *Escape From Fort Bravo.* When that horse comes walking down the gulch with a message, that was old Beauter. He could do anything. They had to put three latches on his gate because he was taught so many things that he could get loose. That rascal, he wasn't very big, but he was beautiful."

Graves says that "Beauty developed emphysema problems in later years of the show and they couldn't use him in the stunts. Ralph kept him and he died at a fairly old age. Seems to me, I heard he was about twenty-nine years old."

Beauty's trainer and owner, Ralph McCutcheon, was a forest ranger in Colorado before he came to Hollywood in the early 1930s. He first made his mark with Dice, a pinto stallion that became a star. McCutcheon's success with Dice allowed him to build a large stable of horses for film work, including King Cotton and Domino.

The Gene Autry Show / The Adventures of Champion

Gene Autry Show: CBS, 1950–1956, 91 episodes

*Starring **Champ and Willie as Champion,** Gene Autry as Gene Autry, and Pat Buttram as Pat Buttram.*

Singing cowboy Gene Autry, his horse Champion, and sidekick Pat Buttram keep the law in the Southwest.

The Adventures of Champion: CBS, 1955–1956, 26 episodes

*Starring **Champ and Willie as Champion,** J. R. as Rebel, Barry Curtis as Ricky North, Jim Bannon as Sandy North, Francis McDonald as Will Calhoun, and Ewing Mitchell as Sheriff Powers.*

A twelve-year-old boy and his stallion Champion and German shepherd Rebel find adventure in the American Southwest of the 1880s.

Nicknamed "the World's Wonder Horse," Champion was the saddle pal of the "Back in the Saddle" singing cowboy champion Gene Autry.

Autry used many horses as Champion over the twenty-plus years that he made films and TV shows, but there were three official Champions (their real names were Baldy, Wags, and Champ). The original Champion (Baldy) had three white stockings (the right front leg did not have a stocking) and a blaze face. The second Champion, Champion Jr. (Wags), had four white stockings and a narrow white blaze on his face, while the third Champion (Champ), who worked on *The Gene Autry Show* and *The Adventures of Champion*, had four white stockings and a wide white blaze on his face.

To further complicate matters, Autry also had a second horse named Champion Jr. that worked personal appearances with the cowboy star. And there was a pony named Little Champ, who was used in several films and during public appearance tours.

As for the horses' main film and TV credits, before World War II Autry used the original Champion in his films. This horse died in 1947 of a heart attack at the Melody Ranch while Autry was out of the country. Champion Jr. was used in Autry's movies after the war, while Champ was used in Autry's feature films of the 1950s and the two TV series.

Marilyn Eldrenkamp, a horse enthusiast,

Singing cowboy giant Gene Autry shares a private moment with his original screen Champion (Baldy). Check out the ornamental pistol at the bottom of the bridle.
Courtesy of Marilyn Eldrenkamp.

as well as a Gene Autry fan for many years, has always kept a keen eye on the horse on screen. "The first Champion used in Gene Autry movies originally appeared in the serial *Phantom Empire* in 1935, and his last movie appearance was in Gene's last film before the war, *Bells of Capistrano* [1942]," says Eldrenkamp. "He was a Tennessee Walker and was bay in color with three white socks. [Bay color is brown with black "points." His mane and tail were black, and the lower part of his legs above any socks was also black.] He had a T-shaped blaze and moved with the typical Tennessee Walker gait.

"The second Champion was known as Champion Jr. He appeared first in *Sioux City Sue* [1946], and, I believe, his last film was *Cowtown* in 1950. He appeared to be at least part Arabian, and I think he was called Boots. He had four high white socks, and a narrow blaze which ended in a diamond shape on his nose. I believe he was considered to be the best and most dainty when it came to the tricks and was the only one used to jump on top of a specially built piano. He will be best remembered for his role in *The Strawberry Roan.*" (He was not a roan, by the way. A roan has gray hairs sprinkled through

Gene Autry is ready to be back in the saddle again on his second Champion, Champion Jr. (Wags), who took over the role after the first Champion died in 1947.
Courtesy of Marilyn Eldrenkamp.

The star of Gene Autry's television series was Champion Number 3, named Champ but affectionately called Po by the folks of the Melody Ranch. Champ lived to be about forty years old. He died on May 9, 1990, and was buried on Autry's ranch beside all seven other horses that served Autry well. That's Little Champ at right.
Courtesy of Marilyn Eldrenkamp.

the coat. He was reddish brown and would have been called a chestnut or sorrel.)

"The third Champion was used in the rest of the Columbia films, from 1950 through 1953's *Last of the Pony Riders*, and in all of the TV shows," Eldrenkamp says. "He was also a chestnut or sorrel in color and was, I believe, also part Arabian. His mane and tail were of a lighter color. He also appeared in *The Adventures of Champion* and was on the cover in the later Gene Autry and Champion comic books. The first issue cover was a photograph, and later ones were artwork, usually by well-known cowboy artist Sam Savitt."

The late Johnny Agee, who worked Tom Mix's horse, was the trainer of Champion, coming to work for Autry in 1936 or 1937. Said Agee of his charge to a writer in the 1952 *Who's Who in Western Stars*, "He dances to any rhythm, kneels, marches, bows, unties knots with his teeth, laughs, kisses, and signs his name—all on cue. Champ is smart, but it's his confidence in Gene that counts. Even a horse knows he can trust a man who names him beneficiary of a $25,000 life insurance policy."

Champion was very popular in his heyday and received as many as a thousand pieces of fan mail a month. And in 1940 he was reportedly the first horse to fly across the United States, traveling in a TWA DC-3 airplane that had a private stall positioned in the rear of the plane—all according to Autry's instructions.

Autry told writer David Regan in 1957 about Champion: "He wasn't the first horse I owned and rode in pictures. The original horse was named Lindy, and he was foaled on the day that Lindbergh flew the Atlantic. Tom Mix had ridden him in pictures and called him Tony Jr. I bought him from the owner, a man named Johnny Agee. He was old even when I bought him. I was in Nashville working. A fellow with the group had been scouting horses for me. He came and told me this fellow named Granger Williams had this colt, just a year old, that was exactly like Lindy, painted the same and everything. You couldn't tell them apart. I bought him for one thousand dollars, a lot of money in those days."

Some years later, in his autobiography,

Back in the Saddle Again, Autry wrote: "*The Strawberry Roan* . . . marked the debut of Little Champ, the son of the second screen Champion. I used three different Champions in my movies (although they all had their own understudies). Little Champ's sire had been a Tennessee Walking Horse, a dark chestnut with a flaxen tail and mane, the beautiful face and four white socks to the knees. He was marked exactly like the first Champion, and I paid fifteen hundred dollars, the most I spent for a horse."

Bill Catchings, who became Roy Rogers's stunt double in the 1950s, worked for a time with Champion trainer Agee. Catchings recalls, "Johnny Agee trained Tom Mix's horses, and Autry bought the horse when Mix died. Agee trained the new Champion, and I worked with him in 1947 and 1948. I was the legs for Agee, who was then eighty-eight. He had the brains and the voice."

One gentleman who knew almost all of Gene Autry's Champions on a personal level was Henry Crowell. Crowell began working for Autry in 1949 as an opening act during Autry's personal appearances. In 1962 Autry persuaded Crowell to become the foreman of his Melody Ranch in Newhall, California.

"Gene had eight different horses that appeared as Champion over the years in films, TV, and personal appearances," Crowell says. "The last [and third] Champion died on May 9, 1990. I put him to sleep."

Crowell can tick off the names of all eight steeds that one time or another portrayed the part of Champion:

1. Baldy (Champion Number 1, who died in 1947)
2. Wags (Champion Jr. and Champion Number 2)
3. Champ (Champion Number 3, aka Po)
4. Boots
5. Willie
6. Melody
7. Little Red
8. Red Cloud

Crowell says the horse originally named Lindy had its name changed to Melody in honor of the Melody Ranch.

"The new [third] Champion, called Champ, was a Morgan and quarter horse," Crowell says, "and he did all the personal appearances. He and Willie did all the close-up work in the two TV series, and Willie was the Champion in *The Adventures of Champion.*

"Willie was a nice-built horse. Gene really liked Champ and Willie. Those were the two he would bring out if somebody came out for an interview. Champ [Champion Number 3] was the best at tricks. He marked, he crossed his legs, he would smile, he would charge. All of the horses were really docile horses. Little kids could handle them. My daughter—she handled Champ."

The man behind the last years of the Melody Ranch wound up there because of his prowess on the trampoline. That was the act he was performing at a fair in Keokuk, Iowa, when he was discovered by Autry, who truly loved a good trampoline act. After Crowell helped repair a truck that transported

A couple of young cowgirls sit astride Champ for a picture-perfect postcard shot of Gene Autry, Gail Davis (the star of *Annie Oakley*) and Champion.

Courtesy of Marilyn Eldrenkamp.

Champion and Little Champ, Autry hired the gymnast as his opening act, a gig that lasted for about ten years.

Crowell says that all of the later Champion horses lived into their forties, and all are buried on the Melody Ranch.

Autry aficionado Marilyn Eldrenkamp shares a bit more information on her silver-screen memories of Champion and of her own trip to Melody Ranch in the late 1980s. "Other Champions include Lindy, which was originally owned by Tom Mix, and was one of his Tonys. He seemed to be used mainly as a stand-in horse, but had a good scene in *Yodelin' Kid from Pine Ridge* in a trick sequence. He probably was also used in personal appearances.

"The horse I know as the later 'tour' Champ also filled in many movie scenes and may be remembered in *Gaucho Serenade* in the picnic scene along the river where Gene sang 'A Song at Sunset.' I saw him often in the 1950s on tour with Gene and Little Champ. He was very versatile and seemed to have a great unflappable disposition.

"Little Champ, which was a very pretty small horse or pony, was a great crowd pleaser. He did tricks on tour—the most memorable was walking the plank. He also would jump through hoops and would run underneath the tour Champ while the latter stood on wooden boxes.

"The last Champ was a horse whose nick-name was Po, and who was used by Gene in his very last tours and to pose with Gene in later years whenever the occasion demanded. He lived to a very advanced age and was allowed to live at the Melody Ranch until his death. Gene refused to sell the final portion of the ranch until the horse's death. In his final years, he was no longer the chestnut/sorrel color but was gray all over."

Animal trainer Bob Blair says that *The Adventures of Champion* was the first TV show he worked on as he helped with Rebel, the German shepherd. "Rebel was played by J. R. and was owned by Frank Barnes. He was the best-trained dog in the business," says Blair of the animal that also appeared in *The Adventures of Rin Tin Tin.*

Frank Inn says that he borrowed the dog from Barnes, and his partner Neil Gazeley and Blair worked it. "Before Barnes died, he gave me the dogs to keep over here, so I had two sons of Rin Tin Tin here and had them until they died of old age."

Blair also recollects that Ace Hudkins

trained the horses Champ and Willie on the series. "I remember old Willie, the horse used for running loose. Willie would charge anybody."

No matter which Champion appears on screen, it's certain that he's a winner as well as a wonder.

General Hospital

ABC, 1963–present (still in production)

*Starring **Friday** as **Friday**, a **bunch of ducks** as **Sigmund**, and dozens of human actors.*

With about twenty-five years behind him in the acting-animal business, Rob Bloch counts his dog Friday as the most incredible of all the creatures he has owned.

The wheaten terrier mix played Robert Scorpio's dog on *General Hospital* for about three years, and, says Bloch, "He was the dog that built my company with one paw tied behind his back. He was so good, he was scary. When he looked at me, there was a magic between him and me. The relationship I had with the dog was unbelievable. If I have two more like him in my career, I'll be a happy camper. There was something special about that animal, just remarkable."

Bloch discovered the canine in an animal shelter in Carson, California, in October 1982, when the dog was about one year old. "I got him on a Friday. That's how he got his name. That evening they were going to put him to sleep. When I saw him lying in the run [at the pound], he would hear something, walk over, and look around very calmly. He would see what there was to see, and lie back down. I thought there was a mind at work there—not just a dog but a thinking being. He's not nervous, not neurotic, but just taking a look at who's coming. It was no big deal but the thought pattern in him . . . he was just a wonderful, wonderful animal."

Bloch began working Friday on the typical movie-type behaviors, and after two or three years of working on various projects, the dog caught on (in a way no other dog seemed to). "It was like all of a sudden something inside clicked as if to say, 'Oh, *this* is what we're doing.' From then on he was unbelievable.

"When he first began on *General Hospital*, he was used a lot. Then he slowly fell into being one of the characters and wasn't on a lot. Friday developed a friendship with Kimberly McCullough, who played Robin on the show. He never really locked with the Scorpio actor, but in the last show for actors Tristan Rogers and Finola Hughes, who were leaving the series, they had a car wreck and both of their characters were killed. These were Robin's parents, so now they had her living with her aunt, played by Emma Samms as Holly.

"There were no bodies, but they had the funeral, and Robin was in denial that her parents were dead. So they had a scene with Friday in the girl's bedroom. She's doing her homework, and the dog steals her pen, and now she realizes her parents are dead.

"The director talks to Kim because this is a heavy scene, and they kept the dog there, so I backed away, and the little girl stares at the camera and starts shaking and crying. Friday gets up, and he looks over at the girl and starts licking her tears. It was unbelievable. We couldn't breathe. The director said, 'Stop the tape, cut!' Everybody stood there and nobody could move."

Bloch relates one more tale about his wunderdog: "We did a commercial job with BellSouth—probably the most difficult animal work I've ever done. This has Friday working all day in pouring-down rain. The dog and myself and another trainer and a humane officer are out in the rain all day.

Rob Bloch's dog Friday, one of the canine world's greatest gifts to the soap opera genre, showed his natural thespian skills on ABC's *General Hospital*.
Courtesy of Rob Bloch / Critters of the Cinema.

"The dog has to work to the camera and stand with his nose pressed against the window while it's raining, and a girl is talking on the phone inside the house. Friday gets on his hind legs and dances around in circles to get her attention that he wants in. Then he's walking on his hind legs carrying an open umbrella in his mouth. Next he's wearing yellow slickers, and finally, at the end, all you see is rain pouring down, and he's holding a snorkel in his mouth and wearing a mask.

"The dog just shined, and the commercial won a Clio Award," says Bloch. Friday also worked in the movie *Tomboy* and was on *Perfect Strangers, Cagney and Lacey*, and *Star Trek: The Next Generation.*

"He was just a magnificent animal," Bloch says. "He lived in the house, while most of my dogs and cats live in the kennel. He wanted to be with people. That was his thing—sleeping in my bed and being with me. He was definitely a people person."

Bloch said Friday passed away in the mid-1990s. "Most of my animals (just like Friday) are buried out behind the house in a cemetery. I go right beside him when I die," says the dog lover.

Bloch also supplied other creatures for *General Hospital*, mainly the quacking kind. "They wanted a Peking duck. His name was Sigmund the duck," Bloch says. "The story line had everybody having turkey for Thanksgiving, so Lucy [actress Lynn Herring] wants duck for Thanksgiving. She orders range-fed duck from Long Island. The duck comes live, unknown to her, so now she is going around trying to find someone to dispatch the duck for duck dinner. She walks all over town with the duck in a birdcage. I thought the duck was a one-shot deal, but we got called back for the Valentine's Day show. Her boyfriend got Sigmund and brought him back. He gives her a locket and a box, and Sigmund is in the box.

"So the duck came back and became a semi-regular. When they spun off to *Port Charles,* it became a semi-regular there. We originally used three ducks to play the one, but I had given those ducks away, and so I got some more ducks.

"We used two different groups. The first ones were named Sigmund, Freud, and Blackie. There were four ducks in the second batch: Rock, Rhythm, Blues, and Cowboy. Rhythm did most of the work."

Bloch says he worked the ducks with a food reward system. He gave them duck food, mainly a mash from the feed store, and a little bread or lettuce.

Bloch, a Brooklyn native who dreamed of sportscasting Dodger baseball games as a youth, came to the Sunshine State and made friends with a woman who had a Doberman with a problem. He used logic to solve the dilemma. He realized he was good with animals and then attended Moorpark College. During a visit to Hubert Wells's animal ranch, he encountered a tiger close up. It was love at first sight.

Over a period of several years, he worked with some of the best in animal show business: Steve Martin, the Blair Bunch, Karl Lewis Miller, Moe Di Sesso, and Frank Inn Animals. For the past twenty-one years, Bloch has owned and operated Critters of the Cinema, which furnishes mostly dogs and cats for commercials and television.

Gentle Ben

CBS, 1967–1969, 56 episodes

Starring ***Bruno as Ben,*** *Clint Howard as Mark Wedloe, Dennis Weaver as Tom Wedloe, Beth Brickell as Ellen Wedloe, and Rance Howard (real-life father of Clint) as Henry Boomhauer.*

This series features the pursuits of a food-loving bear and his youthful master, the son of a game warden in the Florida Everglades.

Gentle Ben star Bruno and a brother were orphaned in Wisconsin as cubs and were acquired from a private party a few years later by Ralph Helfer for his Africa USA animal ranch, which was originally located in Soledad Canyon near Los Angeles and specialized in "affection training" for animals. (Bruno was lucky to be away from the ranch during a wildfire one year and also bearly survived a flood there during another year before being permanently moved to Florida.)

As Bruno became full grown, he appeared in movies and TV series for famed producer Ivan Tors, but got his big break as the title character in the film *Gentle Giant* in 1967, which led to the series *Gentle Ben.*

Clint Howard goes in for a little R and R with Ben the bear of *Gentle Ben* fame.

Helfer talks about Bruno and the other bears used on *Gentle Ben*: "The Canadian black bear can weigh six hundred pounds or more and has a much better pelt [than American black bears]. We had four Canadian blacks for *Gentle Ben*. Bruno was the lead for *Gentle Ben*. Bruno was everybody's favorite, and he could do many things. He not only had the facial look, the gentle look, but he was great with the boy.

"Bruno did most of his own work. He would ride those big boats with the fans in the back, and he would do his own attacks. He was always grabbing the bad guy. We had a game we played during lunch. We would run around him in a circle, and he would catch us in his arms, and we would wrestle, which was fun. When he got tired, he would sit on you.

"The bears were great. We had a run-through bear. He had two cages. He was not good with people, but we would open the cage at one end, and all he knew was to run, and he would run to the other cage where there was food. We'd put the heavies (bad guys) midway between the two cages, so it looked like he was running after them. Once he reached his cage, the heavies would bail out of the way."

Actor Clint Howard recalls, "It was fun having all the animals around and the adventure of being down in Florida with my dad working on a show. Bruno was the main bear, and then Buck was a little smaller, a little younger and thus more agile. So between Buck and Bruno, they did probably seventy-five percent of the work. There was another bear called Drum who liked to work in the water. The other bears, even though bears go in the water, didn't seem to enjoy going in the water as much as Drum. But once a bear gets in the water, you can't really tell what kind of bear it is, which was good because Drum didn't look very much like Bruno or Buck.

"But Buck was a really good double for Bruno. Buck was a little smaller but facially looked a lot like Bruno and it was hard to tell the two of them apart. We could tell them apart, but nobody else could. Drum actually was brown; they had to keep spray painting Drum. They were physically kind of slow, and we were always waiting for them to hit their marks or waiting for them to do what they were supposed to do."

When asked whether food was a good motivator for the bears, Howard is quick and definite in his reply. "Totally. They didn't really care about anybody. They just were going from point A to point B because there was food. The trainers did tricks like putting cookies in my pocket or smearing honey on my hand. Or they'd use Lifesavers or anything sweet. Bears have a real sweet tooth. And I didn't have any real problems with the bear.

"One time the bear sat on me, which was pretty uncomfortable. It was hot down in Florida, and Canadian black bears are just not used to that heat and humidity, and in the grind of trying to get a day's work done, we were shooting fast. We would do an episode of *Gentle Ben* in three days. We were flying. But there was one instance I remember—I was pulling on his chain trying to get Bruno to move, and he got tired of that and kind of somehow worked his way around and sat on me, as if to say that he wasn't going to have this little kid pull him around. And, of course, the animal trainers were right there. Vern DeBor and Monty Cox got him off.

"Ralph Helfer owned the bears, but head trainer Monty Cox and Vern Debor were the two day-in and day-out animal trainers. They would handle all the animals. Besides the bears, we had raccoons and all sorts of things.

"The only time I really ever got hurt was one of the very first days I worked with one of the raccoons. The raccoon didn't have teeth, but he had his claws. They had to leave the claws in the raccoon because they ate with their hands. For the scene, I remember I was supposed to pick Charlie [the raccoon] up. Charlie was supposed to come to me, and I was going to pick him up, and it was a pretty normal routine. It was a normal trick for the raccoon to do, and we did the scene several times. Finally, the raccoon realized where he was supposed to go, and instead of allowing me to pick him up, he climbed me, and I had scratch marks up and down my chest that were bleeding, and it hurt and scared me and made me mad—especially the fact that by the next day, they had invented this leather vest that I would wear under my costume. I was thinking, 'How come you guys didn't think of this before?' You know, the bear never came close to hurting me like the raccoon did."

And so it is that the ursine star of the series was in the end the one who truly lived up to the description "gentle."

The Ghost and Mrs. Muir

NBC and ABC, 1968–1970,
50 episodes

*Starring **Scruffy as Scruffy**, Hope Lange as Carolyn Muir, Edward Mulhare as Capt. Daniel Gregg, Reta Shaw as Martha Grant, Kellie Flanagan as Candy Muir, Harlen Carraher as Jonathan Muir, Charles Nelson Reilly as Claymore Gregg, Guy Raymond as Peevy, and Dabbs Greer as Noorie Coolidge.*

Based on the 1947 movie, *The Ghost and Mrs. Muir* is set on the New England Coast at Gull Cottage overlooking Schooner Bay. A widow, her two children, and housekeeper settle in, only to find that the ghost of a nineteenth-century sea captain haunts the house.

The heart-warming Cinderella story behind Scruffy's rise to TV stardom began in an animal shelter in Sherman Way, California.

Hollywood animal trainer Karl Lewis Miller, whose career covers many great creatures from cinema and TV, was the one who discovered Scruffy and nurtured him to fame. He recalls, "I just wandered through the dog shelter at Sherman Way [in the Los Angeles area] one day, seeing what was there. I passed the kennel, and he was the coward, this one little dog sitting way back in the corner. I started shooing the other dogs out of the way and I made some little noises, pretending I was going to feed him. His little tail started wagging, because someone gave him some attention.

"I checked the papers on him and in another two days he would have been put to sleep. I went back, and it was his last day there. I took him, only because he was on my mind. So I brought him home, this happy but snotty little mutt. He was playful when he wanted to be, but if you tried to do something with him, he'd hide under the bed or coffee table. He didn't want to be handled.

"I had him for a couple of weeks, and at about the same time, director Gene Reynolds was putting together *The Ghost and Mrs. Muir* and he was casting for the dog Rusty. In the movie he was a cairn terrier, I think. Reynolds had called every competitor to show dogs to play the part, and my partner, Lou Schumacher, showed him many dogs, but Gene said no to all of them.

"That day I happened to carry the little mutt from the pound along for the ride. Schumacher said to Reynolds, 'You've seen everyone else's dog. We've got one more dog in the car—it won't hurt to take a look.' Reynolds said, 'OK, go out and get the little dog.'

"I brought in the dog, who doesn't have a name at the time. I had been calling him pup or dog. I bring him in, and he's struggling, really straining the leash, barking and scrambling. Reynolds said, 'Turn him loose and see what he does.' I explained how this is a pet dog, not a Hollywood-trained performance dog. So the dog goes over and sniffs, knocks over a trash can, jumps on the couch, and Gene said, 'That's him, that's Rusty, that's what I want, a natural-looking dog.'

"I said, 'You got to be kidding.' 'He's untrained,' Lou told Reynolds. But this dog acting natural was exactly what he wanted. So we walk out the door and we've got four weeks to train this dog. I get the pilot script and it gives a description: cute and ratty-looking scruffy dog, so out of that description, I named him Scruffy.

"We had this challenge of training this dog in less than four weeks' time, and in the pilot he had a lot of stuff to do. I take him home and start training him. It was real hard getting the basic obedience, plus the movie tricks: bark on cue, back up, crawl, etc. I'm training him, but you can tell I'm having to do a rush course. He doesn't want to do the tricks, but his attitude is, 'OK, if I've got to go to school, I'll go to school.' And all the time I'm trying to perk him up. He'd play ball with me and eat chicken and hot dog morsels, but he wouldn't do it with a happy attitude. He'd love for me to pat him, but he wouldn't give me a tail wag. Four weeks of this, and I got him to lie down, crawl, come back, and speak, but every time his ears are laid back and his tail's back behind his legs. He looked so grouchy—his response to being put into a military academy.

"So the first day's call comes, and I'm sweating it. I go to present the dog, to meet the crew and cast, and he's going to work against his wishes. Bring in Rusty, they tell me, so I go out, get the dog, and I'm trying everything to perk him up.

"He lagged behind me walking to the stage. This dog just looks so browbeaten. I open up the door, and he lunges forward on the leash, and there are the two kids. They see the dog and they go 'Rusty! There's Rusty,' and they start running over to him. He sees the kids and goes bananas. He started wagging his tail, and so I figured out that wherever he lived before, he must have had kids. He loved them, and from that day on his tail was always wagging. It was a very scary situation for me to go to work that day, but when those kids saw that dog . . ."

Kellie Flanagan and her canine costar Scruffy indulge in a spirited checker game between filming scenes for *The Ghost and Mrs. Muir.*

That problem was solved, but Miller recalls that another funny thing happened on the first day of shooting. "When they asked me, 'What's his real name?' I said Scruffy. The kids play with the dog a little bit, and I'm saying 'Scruffy, sit,' and 'Come, go to them, good Scruffy.'

"We go to do the scene, and the little boy had to use the dog's name, Rusty, in the dialogue, but he couldn't remember the Rusty name. He kept calling the dog Scruffy. Gene Reynolds would say 'Cut! Do it again. The dog's real name is Rusty. Come in and say 'Hello, Rusty,' and the boy would come in and say, 'Hello, Scruffy.' Finally Gene gave up and said, 'I tell you what. We're gonna change the dog's name to Scruffy.'"

Miller says that the twenty-three-pound Scruffy was a wire-haired fox terrier with questionable ancestry. When *The Ghost and Mrs. Muir* went off after two seasons, Scruffy found he had been typecast and he couldn't get a job. "He was literally out of work for a couple of years because everyone in Hollywood knew his personality. He was out of work until an episode of *Barnaby Jones* where they had to have one heck of a trained dog to do every trick in the book. We purposely left him ungroomed, sprayed him down with women's hair spray color, and then he got the part. I didn't tell them he was Scruffy. That broke the ice from then on. I left him ungroomed, and he did *Kung Fu.* He worked continuously after that. He even did the TV pilot for *The Thin Man* as Asta, but that pilot didn't sell."

Among the talented pooch's other TV credits were *Happy Days, The Rockford Files, Mannix, The Streets of San Francisco, CHiPs,* and a most memorable Chuck Wagon Dog Food commercial—where the chuck wagon races through the kitchen and startles the family dog.

Scruffy passed on in 1981 at age fourteen, one of the luckier dogs of Hollywood fame and fortune.

Trainer Karl Lewis Miller's story is also a good one. A native of New York State, in the late 1950s he was sent at age seventeen by the military to California to guard Atlas missile sites. When troops were asked to volunteer for a sentry dog program, he held up his hand.

Working in the vicinity of Santa Barbara and Hollywood, Miller met Jack Weatherwax, the brother of Rudd Weatherwax of *Lassie* fame, who told him to come to Hollywood and see what he could do. So in 1964 Miller tried to get a job as dog trainer in the movie industry, but "nobody needed a young whippersnapper." Just at that time the TV show *Hogan's Heroes* was developed, and Frank Inn remembered Miller and his military experience.

"That's what got my foot in the door. During that time Frank Inn was in his heyday with shows like *The Beverly Hillbillies, Petticoat Junction,* and *Green Acres.* I worked for him for about four years on an apprenticeship level."

Here Miller observed one of the best trainers in the business, Genny Kerns, who was working for Inn with the dog Higgins on *Petticoat Junction.* Miller says, "I used to watch Genny, and I got so involved in watching her work and her mannerisms. When she left the show *Petticoat Junction,* I took over and worked the last season.

"When I left Frank, I went to work for Lou Schumacher, another animal supplier. He supplied 20th Century Fox with most of their animals, so I ended up at Fox for several years. Then I did shows like *Land of the Giants, The Brady Bunch, Longstreet, Punky Brewster,* the bionic dog on *The Bionic Woman, Run Joe Run,* and others. I was so busy that I was sometimes doing four shows a day. After working for all the suppliers at the time, I eventually formed my own business, Animal Action, in 1978."

His first job on his own was furnishing Harry, the black dog in *The Amityville Horror*, who with Scruffy became a member of the Animal Actors Hall of Fame. Miller has since gone on to work some of the most famous canine roles in the movies, from *Cujo* and *K-9* to *Beethoven* and many others.

The Greatest Show on Earth

ABC, 1963–1964, 30 episodes

Starring Jack Palance as Johnny Slate and Stu Erwin as Otto King.

The Greatest Show on Earth is the under-the-tent story of the Ringling Brothers and Barnum & Bailey Circus and of how Ringling ringleader Johnny Slate handles the problems of the troupe that makes up the circus.

The exotic cast of creatures used in *The Greatest Show on Earth* was furnished by Ralph Helfer. He remembers, "We had hundreds of animals and all of that circus paraphernalia—cages and tents with camels and llamas and zebras and elephants.

"Jack Palance was great to work with. Whatever he was asked to do with an animal, he did it right away. In a way, he was a lot like Clint Eastwood. He had a good attitude."

Among so many animals, Helfer recalls that his elephants Debbie and Modoc were used a lot on *The Greatest Show on Earth.*

Jack Palance embraces a little big cat in a publicity pose for *The Greatest Show on Earth.*

Green Acres

CBS, 1965–1971, 170 episodes, 1 TV movie

*Starring **Arnold as Arnold Ziffel, Eleanor the cow,** Eddie Albert as Oliver Wendell Douglas, Eva Gabor as Lisa Douglas, Pat Buttram as Mr. Haney, Tom Lester as Eb Dawson, Alvy Moore as Hank Kimball, Hank Patterson as Fred Ziffel, Barbara Pepper and Fran Ryan as Doris Ziffel, Frank Cady as Sam Drucker, Kay E. Kuter as Newt Kiley, Sid Melton as Alf Monroe, and Mary Grace Canfield as Ralph Monroe.*

Green Acres is a comedy about the unreal adventures of a city couple, a lawyer and his socialite wife, who move to a run-down farm and try to adjust to life in the country. They never do.

Arnold the pig proved to be one of the most popular animal stars of the 1960s. He had to have been in hog heaven with four PATSY Awards for his acting talent.

The porcine performer played the beloved pet of farmers Fred and Doris Ziffel, who loved him like a son. Among his tricks for the show were opening doors, turning on the TV set, carrying roller skates in his mouth, pulling a wagon, and holding newspapers in his mouth. He could also grunt on cue. In addition, the fertile minds of the writers of *Green Acres* had the animal imitating the bark of Lassie, delivering newspapers, and speaking three languages. And Arnold was a couch potato pig. In the Ziffel home, he was partial to John Wayne westerns and broadcasts by CBS newscaster Walter Cronkite.

More than a dozen pigs filled the bill as the Ziffel pet. Frank Inn remembers the first Arnold, which he got from a farmer in his hometown of Mooresville, Indiana. "I got a call from *Green Acres* for a pig, and it didn't have to do anything. It was just going to be in a baby buggy, so I got a pig and tied its feet and laid it on its back and nursed it on a bottle. I fed it so that it didn't squeal, and we did a gag at the railroad station and used it in a couple of more gags, and it grew up.

"It got big, and I had a man butcher the pig, and the day after, it was ready for us to eat. We were sitting down to have a nice meal from it and the phone rang, and the producer was asking for the pig to be back on the job by Monday. I had to go out and buy another pig and try to get by. When the show went on hiatus, I went back to Indiana and bought two baby pigs. They were about two or three weeks old. I fed them on a bottle, and they followed me everywhere I went. They started using the pigs on *Green Acres* and the pig became a star."

Inn says he never did eat a bite of the first *Green Acres* pig after that telephone call. As for the Arnolds that followed, he allowed them to retire on a farm, and some of them lived to be over ten years old.

"I had one [Arnold] pig that got to be six hundred pounds," says Inn, who added that he fed dog biscuits to the pigs as treats for a job well done.

Arnold Ziffel gives Porky Pig and Miss Piggy a run for their bacon as the most popular pig on television. He starred with Eddie Albert and Eva Gabor on *Green Acres.*

While the majority of pigs playing Arnold were Yorkshire pigs, the original Arnold was a Chester white male with a pedigree.

For the first two seasons or so of *Green Acres*, Arnold didn't perform any tricks per se. But once the writers started coming up with stunts, a trainer had to get busy. Glen Garner did more work with the Arnolds than any other. He recalls the assignment. "I was not the original trainer, but I did the bulk of it. At first they had animal handlers who used wrangler methods and herded the pigs around and tempted them to cross from one point to another to get to food.

"You can train a dog and it can work for ten years, but a pig is a hog in ten months. They can hit three hundred pounds before they're a year old. The writers wanted a cute little pig about a foot tall and weighing thirty to forty pounds, but after about six to seven months, about the time you got the pig trained, it gets to be big."

Because of the growing pains, Garner says he trained two pigs a year. They were the same age, and whichever one seemed to be learning best became Arnold, and the other became Arnold's backup. Garner says most of the Arnolds were purchased from a large hog breeding farm near Acton, California. "They were usually pure white, so they were enough alike so we did not have to worry about doubling. The animals did not respond to their names, so my number one pig I called Arnold. The other, usually a female, I would call Sugar, or if number two was a male, I'd come up with anything. Arnold was usually a male, but there's a disadvantage because males grow faster and the plumbing starts to show after six months."

Garner says the first trainer on the show got things going in the right direction with conditioned-response training. "We were coming up with really good stuff. We began to teach them to earn the reward, but that it did not come immediately. I used a little clicker, and when the clicker sounded, it told the animal 'You've done right. You're gonna get a reward.' That let the pig know instantly, and it speeded up the process and allowed us to work at a greater distance [away from the animal]."

Sunglasses and director's chair? Yep, Arnold got star treatment. After all, he did bring home four PATSY awards.

Garner says the pigs ate commercial pig chow when they were fed at the kennel, but when he worked them on the set he used a kind of dog food that came in little chunks. "When the pig was just starting to work, I could cut it into eight pieces and give them one-eighth as a reward, and as the pig grew I increased it to one-fourth and then one-half and by the end of the year, the whole chunk. I had a leather pouch attached to the belt on my waist. The food was moist, and the pig could take it in its mouth, take two chomps and swallow and was ready to go again.

"Pigs are extremely smart. I was tickled to death because previously I never knew they had that kind of intelligence," says Garner. "It was fun. I had a ball. They would give me a script on Monday and want to shoot on Wednesday. Some of that stuff was no more than two days' training."

Garner trained the Arnolds well, but there were other chores. "Every morning before I took them down there, I gave the pigs a bath. I used human hair shampoo. What's good for humans is good for the pigs. In the morning, they would smell real sweet but usually by noon they smelled like pigs again."

Garner, who worked with the Arnolds for three full seasons, says the pigs were transported to and from General Services Studio, where *Green Acres* was filmed, in aluminum dog crates. He recalls that the pigs were clumsy, and the Ziffel home had linoleum on the floors. Because the pigs would slide around on the floors, they had to tack carpet over the linoleum.

What happened to the year-old Arnolds?

"By the end of the year," says Garner, "the pig was really well trained but too big. There was a man who had property behind Frank Inn, Lionel Comport, and he supplied animals for barnyard scenes, like a pigpen or a hen house. When Arnold got too big for *Green Acres,* Frank Inn gave him to Comport Animal Rental. He was thrilled to be getting a trained pig."

During the last few seasons of *Green Acres,* Arnold was trained by Moe Di Sesso, who says he had to change the pig every six months because they grew so fast. "I always had another one coming along," says Di Sesso, who called his pigs Arnold if they were male and Annie if they were female. "I'd rather train a pig any day than a dog. I can train a pig to do anything. Pigs are food-oriented. The last pig on the show once had to open a mailbox, go back to the wagon, take a newspaper out, put the newspaper in the mailbox, close the mailbox, and pick up the wagon and go on to the next house."

While on hiatus, some of the Arnolds saw the world. For publicity purposes, Arnold toured 4-H Clubs and schools around the country, and he occasionally went on TV shows like *What's My Line?* and *The Tonight Show*. The pig's popularity spawned Arnold fan clubs, and he received bags of fan mail.

"We went everywhere," Inn says of trips with the pig, "and that was what caused the fan mail to start. I'd go to these 4-H Club meetings, and all these clubs from each state started sending fan mail."

Inn adds, "Eva Gabor got fan mail, and one day Arnold got a letter, and she said, 'Oh, isn't that cute. Arnold got fan mail.' Then one day Arnold got four letters and she thought that was cute. Then one day a man came in with two big mail sacks and dumped them on the floor in the studio, and Eva said, 'I never got so much fan mail,' and the man said, 'These are for Arnold,' and she said, 'Oh, that dreadful pig.'"

"I used to answer a lot of his fan mail," says Tom Lester, who played Eb. "He'd get a slew of it from young girls. I'd sign pictures with my left hand, sort of like a kid. I'd write, 'Love, Arnold Ziffel. P.S. Please don't eat bacon.'"

Sampling a bit of the light classics before a nightcap, Arnold of Hooterville was a cultured pig.

Gabor had other troubles with Arnold. Inn says that she came on *The Tonight Show* once with the pig on a leash. "All at once she said, 'What are you doing?' And he had peed on her dress. It got so they called her for talk shows, but they wanted her to bring Arnold. One night Johnny Carson was doing his opening monologue, and she came out and interrupted him, saying, 'Would you babysit my pet?' and she ran back offstage and came back in leading Eleanor the cow."

Eleanor, who also appeared on *Green Acres*, racked up considerable credits of her own. She appeared in a number of *Lassie* episodes and later appeared on *The Waltons*. Never a temperamental cow, she was not bothered by the attention slathered on her stable mate.

And that's life down on the farm.

Hart to Hart

ABC, 1979–1984, 111 episodes, 10 TV movies

*Starring **Charlie Gray as Freeway,** Robert Wagner as Jonathan Hart, Stefanie Powers as Jennifer Hart, and Lionel Stander as Max.*

Hart to Hart is about a millionaire industrialist and his journalist wife who live the good life as jet-setters out of Beverly Hills. They are quite in love as they solve crimes wherever they roam.

The little terrier mix belonging to the detective duo of Hart and Hart was owned by Bob Blair of the Blair Bunch. Trainer Henry Shannon first spotted the dog at an animal shelter, and comrade Rob Bloch was there the day Shannon brought the dog back from the kennel. Bloch recalls, "He was a mess. His name was Charlie, Charlie Gray. He was a little one. Henry brought him back and put him up on a table and said, 'Sit.' The dog sat. He said, 'Lie down.' The dog lay down. He said, 'Charlie, on your feet.' The dog stands on all fours. This dog is doing all this stuff. He even had him speak. This was a very well-trained dog.

Lionel Stander, Stefanie Powers, and Robert Wagner, right, are all smiles as they pose with their pooch, Freeway, played by Charlie Gray, on *Hart to Hart.*

"So I gave him a little hand signal to sneeze, and he sneezed. Henry had trained a sneeze on him. Charlie was wonderful and very energetic with a very good feeling of self." Bloch went on to work the dog in a Lipton's iced tea commercial with Don Meredith.

Shannon says that Charlie was "an even-tempered dog, and he learned easy."

When asked why he chose Charlie, Shannon responds, "His happy-go-lucky look. I got him out, and he wasn't afraid. He had his tail up, and he walked with a bounce. You need a dog with an outgoing personality, like a salesman, always on."

Shannon adds, "Charlie loved the stars, Stefanie and R .J. [Wagner], and they loved him. It was like love at first sight."

Director Earl Bellamy recalls the canine as a cute dog, who worked very well. "Whenever Stefanie and R .J. would get into an argument, you would see the dog run and jump on the bed or sofa, and it would go beneath the pillow and stick its head out. Then it was like a tennis match, the eyes would go from side to side. We had a lot of things in the script for him to do. He would always follow the butler around. The butler would talk to him, and the dog would do a cute thing and then Lionel Stander would give him something to eat."

But no tea.

Shannon recalls that the dog with plenty of pluck died of natural causes at about sixteen years of age.

The Hathaways

ABC, 1961–1962, 26 episodes

Starring the ***Marquis Chimps (Enoch, Charlie, and Candy)****, Peggy Cass as Elinore Hathaway, Jack Weston as Walter Hathaway, Harvey Lembeck as Jerry Roper, Barbara Perry as Thelma Brockwood, and Mary Grace Canfield as Amanda Allison.*

The Hathaways is about a perfectly normal family of five but for one exception—the three kids are chimpanzees. The father sells real estate, while the mother is the booking agent for her three "kids" who are show-biz performers.

The trio of simian stars in *The Hathaways* did it all in the 1950s and '60s: the chimps entertained in vaudeville, circuses, and television. They were frequent guests on *The Ed Sullivan Show*, where they performed numerous tricks, including riding bicycles and making all sorts of amusing faces, and they were guests several times on Lucille Ball's *Here's Lucy* TV series.

The Chimps were owned and trained by Englishman Sammy Woods, who billed himself and the monkeys as Gene Detroy's Marquis Chimps. Woods, later Detroy, began his career as a low-wire act in British vaudeville. He started training the chimpanzees in the late 1940s.

Detroy's nephew, Dan Westfall, who inherited the last members of the amazing animal act, relates what happened next. "Danny Kaye saw them playing in the London Palladium and invited my uncle over to the States in the early 1950s. They made nearly thirty appearances on *The Ed*

Ed Sullivan greets two of the Marquis Chimps on his show in 1959.

Sullivan Show, and from there, they did some circuses, but they were mainly a night-club-theater act. They worked Vegas for years at various hotels. Their last engagement was a five-year run at the Tropicana in the late 1970s.

"He got Charlie when he was about four in the late 1950s. The people that had him couldn't handle him, so they called my uncle. He says Charlie was timid and scared, so he had to take him home in a crate and he was screaming away. He turned out to become one of the best."

Westfall says that Detroy trained about twenty different chimpanzees over the course of the thirty-year career of the Marquis Chimps. Their name came about because in the early stages of the act Detroy had a chimp named Marquis. Someone in American show business, perhaps Kaye or Sullivan, suggested that Detroy call the act the Marquis Chimps. He liked it, so the name stuck.

Enoch sits on the knee of the assistant trainer of the Marquis Chimps.
Courtesy of Mary Grace Canfield.

More than three different simians played the threesome on *The Hathaways*, Westfall says. One very special chimpanzee named Susie, who lived to be more than forty and died in the late 1990s, appeared on *The Hathaways*.

Westfall says his uncle told him that Susie once gave Peggy Cass quite a scare. "Peggy Cass was holding her hand, and Susie grabbed Peggy's hand and stuck it in her mouth and clamped down on it. She didn't bite down hard, but it scared Peggy, and she took off running to her dressing room. Peggy didn't like the chimps that much, but they really were well behaved."

Westfall also says that Lucille Ball used to call his uncle and ask if the chimps could come over to her house so that she could play with them.

The great character actor Mary Grace Canfield, who costarred on *Green Acres* as Ralph Monroe, played the housekeeper, Mrs. Allison, on *The Hathaways*. She remembers the Marquis Chimps with fondness. She also reveals a closely guarded show-biz secret: Charlie was a girl! (Psst, Susie was a boy.)

"Charlie was quite a spiffy dresser—sports jacket, long trousers, etc.," says Canfield. "On sound stages, there is a portable coffee table with all kinds of goodies—doughnuts, Danish treats. Sometimes they're free, sometimes you drop a few coins in a box. The trainer used to give Charlie some quarters and send him over to buy coffee and a doughnut, and I think he was also given a cigar. These Charlie would take back to his dressing room, sit back, and enjoy.

"One time Charlie and I had a scene in which I had to carry a bucket of water with him—each holding on to the handle. Charlie decided to bite me between my thumb and forefinger. His trainer was, of course, terribly upset and rushed me to the emergency room of the nearest hospital for a tetanus shot."

Enoch mugs for the camera.
Courtesy of Mary Grace Canfield.

Canfield adds, "The pressure to perform was extremely stressful on these chimps, and often they simply did not want to work. They let go with terrible screams when they're angry or frustrated, and the sound can break your heart. The trainers, however, were very loving with the animals; nevertheless, they had to deliver—time was money—and this sometimes involved some disciplining. The trainers always had a handful of jelly beans, which they dispensed as rewards or bribes.

"Enoch was my favorite. When I came onto the set in the morning, he would spot me, get my attention with hooting calls, come over to me, take my hand, and twirl me around in a kind of joyful dance step. I had to roller-skate once with Enoch, and he had better balance than I did.

"We became so accustomed to interacting with these likable animals. This episode with Candy, the baby (she was usually dressed in ruffled petticoats and crinoline dresses), will demonstrate. I once mistook my dressing room for Candy's. When I opened the door to what I thought was my dressing room, I came upon Candy, petticoat up to her waist, sitting on a potty. I gasped with embarrassment, apologized profusely for invading her privacy, and left in a hurry. The reality didn't hit me till later.

"These chimps did not always sit on pots—they wore diapers and did they smell? Sometimes! The trainers couldn't always keep up with it, though they tried.

"I once worked with another chimp on the series *My Sister Eileen.* That chimp refused to work and climbed up into the rafters, refusing to come down, screaming his head off. As I recall, there were guns fired off to scare him down—hardly a well-thought-out strategy."

Hathaways actress Barbara Perry recollects that the chimps "were not that adorable.

Enoch and Charlie take it easy in lawn chairs.
Courtesy of Mary Grace Canfield

Jack Weston gives Candy a feeding on *The Hathaways.*

They were not studio pets. They would snap at you."

But it was another member of the crew who left the most memorable impression on her mind. "The monkeys had a dwarf as their stand-in, a Mexican," says Perry. "We were upset that a human would be a stand-in for a monkey. Someone mentioned it to him, and he said, 'But I'm feeding a whole family of people on my salary.'"

After one season, ABC canned *The Hathaways,* stand-in and all. The Marquis Chimps returned to the road, but they were pioneers for other simian-starring series, most notably the Saturday morning series *Lancelot Link, Secret Chimp,* and NBC's prime-time 1980s show *Mr. Smith,* starring C. J. the orangutan.

Westfall had another uncle, Tony Gentry, a cousin of Detroy, who also worked with movie monkeys. Gentry trained Jiggs, the chimp who played Cheetah opposite Johnny Weissmuller in some of the MGM *Tarzan* films. There were actually four chimps that Gentry had named Jiggs (Jiggs I, II, III, and IV), and Jiggs IV at the age of sixty-eight was still thriving as of early 2001.

Hee Haw

CBS and syndicated, 1969–1993, 585 episodes

Starring ***Kingfish, Beauregard, Beauregard Jr., Buford,*** *and country music's greatest performers.*

The *Hee Haw* hounds fit in nicely with the barnyard full of singers, pickers, comedians, and entertainers that kept the show on the tube through parts of four decades.

Hosted by Roy Clark and Buck Owens and featuring mood-setting bloodhounds Kingfish, Beauregard, Beauregard Jr., and Buford, the show starred a cast of dozens, plus big-name guest stars numbering in the hundreds. This country music variety series featured ultra-corny jokes and well-distilled country music.

Right square in the middle of the whole *Hee Haw* gang of Cornfield County is Buford, the fourth and final hound dog of the long-running variety show.
Courtesy of Gaylord Program Services, Inc.

Before going too far into the *Hee Haw* hounds, know this: six dogs worked on the show, but there were only four official hound dogs:

1. Kingfish the Wonder Dog, 1969–1970
2. Beauregard, 1970–1975
3. Beauregard Jr. (real name "Beauford"), 1976–1979
4. Buford, 1980–1989 (approximately)

The other two dogs were Buddy "the Wonder Dog," a trained golden retriever from Carson City, Nevada, who performed in skits for several seasons in the mid-1970s, and Melvin, a bloodhound, who worked the second half of the 1975 season (after the death of the original Beauregard) as Beauregard Jr.

Now, back to the beginning: The original *Hee Haw* hound was owned and raised by Nashvillian Bobby Gropp. Kingfish "the Wonder Dog" was born in Gropp's house in Brentwood, Tennessee. "I just named him Kingfish because he was the biggest male puppy of my first litter of bloodhounds," says Gropp, who got his first bloodhound out of Horn Lake, Mississippi. Gropp's dog got his break one day when his phone rang and somebody asked him if he had any bloodhounds.

The original *Hee Haw* hound, Kingfish "the Wonder Dog," checks out a contract with his friend Tandy Rice.

"Yeah," he answered, "I got about thirty-five of 'em."

Gropp responded to the invitation and brought Kingfish to downtown Nashville for an audition, and the dog was hired. Gropp recalls, "He was on a couple of years. Then they asked me to sign the name Kingfish over to the production company for nothing. I said, 'Naw, I'm not going to give you the name of the dog.' It was a lot of trouble to bathe the dog and stay all day at the studio. We finally parted ways."

Kingfish began his acting career at the age of two. "He used to get fan mail. It was amazing," says Gropp, who also had one of his bloodhounds appear in the Burt Reynolds film *W. W. and the Dixie Dance Kings* (1975).

Contrary to rumors, Kingfish was never used by lawmen as a tracking hound for escaped convicts, but Gropp did have several trained bloodhounds that he ran with the Tennessee State Prison's hounds on practice runs.

Gropp says of Kingfish, "He didn't get no special treatment. Kingfish stayed in the pen with the rest of the dogs. But when he went to work [on *Hee Haw*], that air-conditioned studio made him real lazy. He'd just fall out on the floor where you put him because that cold concrete felt good."

Kingfish died of old age at ten, and Gropp buried him in his backyard in Brentwood.

The next star hound of *Hee Haw* was Beauregard the first. He was registered with the American Kennel Club as Earthman's Beauregard P. and was raised by Douglas Earthman in the Green Hills area of Nashville.

Beauregard came to the attention of the show via Gene Evans, who worked at the Tennessee State Prison. Evans found Earthman through a veterinarian in Nashville, and the two worked as partners. Evans acted as Beauregard's manager and took him to the *Hee Haw* tapings, while Earthman cared for the dog year-round as a pet.

Earthman says, "We auditioned and had exactly what they were looking for as far as color and type of dog. After the interview, they wanted to name him Wheeler the Wonder Dog, but I protested that the name was not as good as his own name. The writers talked about it and agreed."

Beauregard was about three when he went on the show, and he had some basic obedience training. He was a somewhat active dog although he played a lazy old hound dog. "He was alert, very personable, and friendly. He had a lot of spark to him and seemed to

Beauregard plays his role out perfectly as the moonshiners (from left, Grandpa Jones, Archie Campbell, Gordie Tapp, and George Lindsey) perform "Gloom, Despair, and Agony on Me."

Courtesy of Gaylord Program Services, Inc.

always know where the camera was," says Earthman.

Beauregard was in the scenes with four men performing the "Gloom, Despair, and Agony on Me" song skit, and he was in the "Moonshine Shack" scenes where two characters would lie on burlap bags (the dog lying between them) telling a joke. He was also in the "Pickin' and Grinnin'" scenes with Buck Owens and Roy Clark and all the cast.

"Cathy Baker was the one most involved with the dog. She spent a lot of time holding his leash on the set," says Earthman.

The flop-eared, sad-eyed Beauregard died June 30, 1975, of kidney infection at the Hillsboro Animal Hospital. He had just completed taping the final episode for the fall-winter season. He was eight-and-a-half years old. His death was reported in the *Nashville Banner* by entertainment writer Red O'Donnell, who also covered the funeral.

"He was popular with viewers of all ages—and received fan mail comparable to that of some of our human stars," said *Hee Haw* producer Sam Lovullo at the time. "Additionally, during his entire time with us, he never once demonstrated temperament or viciousness. Beau was a very kind dog. A real pet. A real star. He definitely will be missed."

The bloodhound was buried at a ranch near Fairview, Tennessee, in a special wooden casket. Beauregard's son Melvin stepped into the role next, but only temporarily.

"Melvin did the second half of the season that Beauregard began. He had an accident, and his eyes got infected and because of physical injuries, he couldn't work anymore. Melvin was friendly enough but didn't have that star quality. He became just a backyard pet," says Earthman.

So at the beginning of the 1976 season, Earthman introduced Beauregard's grandson

Beauregard Jr. slums with Roy Clark, left, and Jimmy Dean in front of the Moonshine Shack on *Hee Haw*.

Courtesy of Gaylord Program Services, Inc.

Buddy was a golden retriever from Nevada who performed in skits for three seasons on *Hee Haw.*

Courtesy of Gaylord Program Services, Inc.

(son of Samson) who was born in December 1975 and named Beauford, but was called Beauregard Jr. He filmed the next four years of *Hee Haw.*

Earthman says that Beauford was a little taller, lankier, and darker red than his grandfather, but both Beau and Beau Jr. had the characteristics of purebred bloodhounds. Beauford left the show around 1979 and died in 1985 of an internal illness.

The fourth official *Hee Haw* hound dog was really named Buford. He was owned by Joe and Anita Hostettler (the technical director and a makeup artist, respectively, for *Hee Haw*).

"We had the fourth hound dog. He belonged to our children," says Joe Hostettler. "Buford was about three when we found him in Spring Hill, Tennessee. Sam Lovullo told me he needed a bloodhound and that if I would get one, it would help send the kids to college, so I put some feelers out and found a fellow in Spring Hill who had coon dogs. Buford was the lone bloodhound."

The Hostettlers got trainer Rick Baccari to put some basic obediences on him, such as sit, down, and stay, so that they knew he would stay pretty calm on the set. Hostettler says of the hound who worked on *Hee Haw* from about 1980 to 1989: "He was just an old farm dog, but he minded and was a fairly smart dog. Buford had a great personality and was just a real good dog. He was named an honorary member of the House of the Tennessee legislature, and he appeared in photos for Smokey Bear campaigns. We had a paw print made up for autographed pictures. He was pretty much a celebrity." Buford died in 1989 from an intestinal illness and was buried in a dog cemetery in southwest Nashville.

Both Hostettler and Earthman recalled the only non-bloodhound who worked on *Hee Haw.* "Buddy was a real smart golden Labrador from Nevada. He could do about anything," says Hostettler. "They had him driving a car. He was on for three seasons and was a specialty dog used to do tricks and such. They used Buddy for some running skits where Goober goes to town or where George Lindsey and Gailard Sartain would do crazy things."

Buddy was owned and trained by Bill Williamson, and, indeed, the dog could sit in the driver's seat of a car with his paws on the wheel and his eyes fixed straight ahead. Buddy died in November 1983 at age fifteen and turned the wheel over to his son Beaver.

It was not all laughs with the dogs on *Hee Haw*, however. When asked to describe the dogs, series regular George Lindsey does so in one word: "Flatulence. Those dogs ate a lot of beans."

Hostettler is in complete agreement: "Buford would expel gas every once in a while and that would clear the set."

And *Hee Haw* executive producer Sam Lovullo remembers this quality about the dogs as well. "I think the dog always created a lot of odor. He would fart sometimes, and we'd have to wait till he was through. We would recognize that it was time to stop production and get him outside. But the dogs were well mannered. The person who really took an interest and a liking to the dogs and who helped us tremendously in the studio was Cathy Baker, who loves animals. I think she was really our lifesaver. She knew when to step in and keep things moving. But there were times the dog would just get up out of place and go to the moonshine shack and start invading the Hee Haw Honeys."

Lovullo adds, "The one thing that I believe is important, and I was very adamant about, is that the dogs would not be tranquilized. We never, never tranquilized the dog. I have a great compassion for animals. As a youngster, I had a number of animals at home, not a bloodhound, but I treated them just like human beings. There were times while doing the show that maybe perhaps the dog wasn't feeling well and the behavior pattern wasn't the best, and I was forever pushed to put in a 'calmer,' so to speak—to tranquilize him—because we were slowing up production, and I would say no. I would rather cancel the spot than do that. So what you saw was real."

Cathy Baker, who always ended the show with a friendly "That's all!" can't remember exactly why she became the keeper of the dog on the end of the leash when the cameras were rolling, but she says, "I loved dogs. I always had to have on overalls, so I guess it was sort of, 'You're here. You keep the dog.' I was probably playing with them."

Baker distinctly remembers how Beauregard's handler, Gene Evans, was always squirting cologne on the hound. "You can't cover up the smell," she says. "Beauregard was such a dear dog. He was ideally situated at the moonshiners' porch between those two men. There was not a mean bone in his body. All of them were so sweet."

And being the one holding the leash, she also remembers that the hounds were doggone strong. "If they decided to go someplace, they'd take off, and off I'd go, sliding off the stage," says Baker. "If they decided to leave, you left."

That's all!

Here's Boomer

NBC, 1980–1982

*Starring **Boomer (aka Johnny)** as **Boomer.***

Here's Boomer is about a little shaggy dog who wanders in and out of people's lives spreading a little sunshine. Some critics referred to the series as "TV's answer to *Benji.*"

The star of *Boomer* was a Burbank dog-pound dog rescued by trainer Ray Berwick. Probably born in the spring of 1976, the floppy-eared Boomer was eighteen inches high, weighed forty-five pounds, and had brown eyes and a brown-and-cream coat.

Johnny the dog visits Johnny *The Tonight Show* host as the canine star of *Here's Boomer* hears the greeting "Here's Johnny!"

Before his work on *Here's Boomer,* he starred in *The Red Hand Gang,* an NBC Saturday morning series during the 1977–1978 season.

Berwick said in a 1980 NBC publicity release when the show began, "We want people who see Boomer to go out and save a dog from the pound . . . to say to themselves, I'd love to have a dog like that."

He remembered the day he found Boomer. "I was looking through a group of cages and there he was. At first he was suspicious of me. But, eventually, he came up to say hello. Never once did he beg me to save him even though he probably knew what his next stop was. He had lots of dignity and class."

When the animal trainer brought him home, his wife wanted him to get rid of the poor dog after the pooch got into a tussle with her favorite poodle. "I told my wife he's just like a kid. Not long after that, she got to like him and he stayed with us. Boomer and the poodle became great pals."

According to Berwick, Boomer was fairly independent of other animals, especially dogs. He said in the press release, "He prefers the company and friendship of people. He's a real people dog. Many trainers will tell people not to touch the animal, but not me. Some trainers fear too many people will divert the animal, and they will lose control. I don't do that.

"Boomer was extremely bright and quick to grasp a command or suggestion. He never quits on me. Some dogs give up when the going gets rough in a training session. Boomer easily took to my hand signals and word repetitions . . . the two key elements in training an animal."

After a few years of intense training, Boomer could talk, lie down, roll over, climb a ladder, go right and left, act sick, put his feet up, put his eyes down, and lower his head. "He can scratch a flea on cue or sneeze with his head up or even fake a limp," said Berwick in the 1980 press release. The dog's skills landed him guest roles on *Baretta* and *Starsky & Hutch*.

"Boomer was Ray's dog, and he was named Boomer, although he was originally named Johnny," says Karl Mitchell, who served a five-year apprenticeship under Berwick from 1975 to 1981. In fact, the working title of the series was "Here's Johnny."

Mitchell continues, "He was just a mutt dog. He was four years old when the *Boomer* series came along. Ray had adopted him and trained him, and he was the back-up dog for Jeff, who became the *Little House* dog. Jeff was the big star of the Universal Studios Tour show, which played before ten thousand people each day. After Jeff got on *Little House*, it was time for the number two dog to come up and that was Johnny, because he had been trained to do the show.

"Then Ray got this idea to do *Boomer*. Ronald Reagan was president at the time, and he wanted the networks to have more family-oriented shows. So NBC went with Ray's story. Johnny, all of sudden, could not do tour shows because he was Boomer.

"He was a little shaggy mutt who was always out and doing stuff. Boomer was good at being goofy. He was so exuberant with his behavior, smiling all the time and wanting to play—just a lovable dog."

While Berwick owned Boomer, his nephew Bryan Renfro trained the dog. Working with animals was and still is in Renfro's blood because his father was Rennie Renfro, the man who trained many a star dog in the heyday of 1930s and 1940s Hollywood features. Rennie's apt pupils included the dog Spook and its pups in the series of *Blondie* films.

Bryan Renfro first went to work for his uncle in 1970 after serving in the Army. "Ray Berwick told me, 'I can give you a job at Universal cleaning cages.' I went up there and knew nothing about animal training. I just started watching and listening and learning. The first thing I ever trained was a macaw parrot named Tuffy. I taught this bird to do everything. Then I realized here was something that I could do.

"The unique thing about working at Universal Studios is that you were working with a variety of animals: dog, cats, birds, rats, you name it," says Renfro.

Bryan Renfro reminisces a bit about Boomer. "He was the first dog I had trained. He was a bit of a scrapper, a tough little dog. He was a sweetheart. He wasn't the smartest dog, but he had a lot of heart. Our training philosophy was use everything positive under the sun—food or a rag or a ball, whatever they liked. We used different rewards for Boomer, and as for food, we used chicken and beef.

"I remember one difficult thing where he

had to go into the bathroom and turn on the bathtub tap. He had to fill the bathtub up so it would overflow.

"He had to learn a lot of picking up and pulling things and untying himself and taking off his collar. For one episode I had to teach him to put his feet up and push a revolving door all the way around but not go outside," says Renfro, who also worked on the TV series *Baretta*, *Little House on the Prairie*, and *Rin Tin Tin K-9 Cop*, and the Hallmark Hall of Fame TV movie *The Snow Goose*.

Honey West

ABC, 1965–1966, 30 episodes

Starring ***Bruce the ocelot****, Anne Francis as Honey West, John Ericson as Sam Bolt, and Irene Hervey as Meg West.*

Honey West is about a Los Angeles detective who solves crime with brains, wit, science, and technology.

Honey West was one of television's first female detectives, and she was a cool customer. How cool? Well, her personal pet was an ocelot, and you can't get much cooler than that.

Several cats were used to portray Honey's pet named Bruce, provided courtesy of Ralph Helfer and his company.

"We used a number of ocelots," says Helfer. "They are not the easiest cats to work with. They're feisty and more like a domestic house cat: they refuse to take instructions. Bruce was played by two or three of our best ocelots. They're gentle animals, just sweet, but that's all they were. The ocelot is one of the most difficult, the same as training a bobcat. Smaller cats are not as trainable. The bigger they get, the more trainable. The same is true of bears, cougars, and tigers. Small species are generally more difficult to work with than larger."

Helfer says star Anne Francis got along fine with her pets. "She was a sweetheart, one of the few that didn't mind if the ocelot scratched her a little bit when it jumped out of her lap. She was a real animal lover.

Anne Francis starred as Honey West, the only detective to keep an ocelot (Bruce) as a pet.

"We did the show, and everybody was happy with it. We ended up calling the key ocelot Bruce since everybody called it that. So we eventually adopted that name."

Helfer says that all of the cats came from South America and that their life expectancy is usually fifteen years. The ocelots are referred to as "miniature leopards."

And Helfer shared a secret that ocelots weren't the only exotic cats used as Honey West's pets. "Occasionally, we would use a margay, a smaller version of the ocelot. The margay is a subspecies of the ocelot." (The word 'margay' is an Indian term for 'little ocelot.')

Helfer adds, "Our cats were good as long as you didn't push them. They were a lot like a cheetah, absolute dolls to be around, sweet and lovable, but if they don't want to do anything, they won't do it."

Not even if Honey sweet talked 'em.

Hooperman

ABC, 1987–1989, 42 episodes

Starring ***Little Britches as Bijou,*** *John Ritter as Detective Harry Hooperman, Debrah Farentino as Susan Smith, Barbara Bosson as Capt. Celeste Stern, Clarence Felder as Officer Boris Pritzger, Sydney Walsh as Officer Maureen DeMott, Joseph Gian as Officer Rick Silardi, Felton Perry as Inspector Clarence McNeil, and Alix Elias as Betty Bushkin.*

Hooperman is a comedy drama about a peaceable cop who works with a tough superior on the San Francisco police force. After his landlady is murdered, he inherits her crummy apartment building and has to deal with complaining tenants, the handywoman he has fallen in love with, and a yappy terrier that intensely dislikes him.

John Ritter's canine costar in *Hooperman* was a fierce little female Jack Russell terrier named Little Britches. The dog was owned and trained by Hollywood's pioneer female animal trainer, Cindy James, the first woman trainer to gain membership in the Los Angeles Teamsters Union in 1954.

James, who was the stepdaughter of the late Edgar Rice Burroughs, the author who created *Tarzan of the Apes*, got Little Britches from a woman detective when the dog was four months old. James called Britches "the dog from hell." She recalls, "The original owner couldn't handle her. She just didn't have the time, and I wanted to try a Jack Russell. I had heard they were tough as a Doberman, and I had had good success with Dobermans."

When the TV series began, Little Britches' character, Bijou, belonged to Hooperman's landlady, and the mutt hated the cop. But after the landlady died, Hooperman took the dog in as his own, and they gradually became friends of sorts.

"Britches got along with everyone on the set. She liked everybody. She was very energetic, very outgoing," says James. "She would only do the attack work off cue, but in the beginning she did a lot of pants-leg attacks on John.

"There was one time in a scene where an actor was sitting on the couch with John Ritter, and Britches sat between them. The actor was supposed to lean in and say something to John but was too afraid. 'She's ferocious,' the actor said to the cast. But she didn't bite anybody."

James says that star Ritter kept a basketball goal on the set where he practiced shooting hoops, so she brought in a little goal for Britches and taught her to slam dunk a Nerf ball.

Little Britches' favorite food was Rollover, a Canadian product similar to a big bologna roll. As for vices, she would drop everything to catch mice. "Oh, she liked mice," says James. "If there was a mouse in a wall in the production office, she would go right to it. Just forget getting any work out of her."

James's Jack Russell worked in various films, TV shows, and commercials for thirteen years. Among her credits were the feature film *Harry and the Hendersons*, a commercial for Kibbles and Bits where Little Britches jumps over the back of a bulldog, an MCI commercial where she snarls in the face of Jim Carrey, and commercials for Church's Chicken.

James kept Little Britches in her house, and the dog slept in her bedroom. The feisty little star died in 1999 at age fourteen.

Animal trainer Cindy James paved a path for all of the women trainers that followed. She persevered in a position that had been predominantly male since the early days of moviemaking in Hollywood.

Born in Los Angeles, James spent much of her childhood in Hawaii with her mother and her stepfather, Burroughs, who gave her her first dog, Mothball. She returned to Los Angeles to complete junior high and high school and always liked animals, especially horses.

By the time she graduated, she was working for trainer Earl Johnson, performing tasks in the kennel, and doing obedience training with dogs. That job led to a meeting with veteran movie animal trainer Henry East, who gave James her first feature film job, training the dogs in the Walter Brennan/Brandon DeWilde classic *Goodbye, My Lady*, a 1956 release about a boy and his dog in the Southern swampland.

Throughout the 1950s, James worked with dogs on live television shows and on the programs of stars such as Bob Hope, Jack Benny, George Burns, and Red Skelton.

John Ritter and the feisty Little Britches made uneasy partners as Harry Hooperman and Bijou on *Hooperman*.

In the meantime, she showed dogs in American Kennel Club shows and had some top dogs of her own, including a trained toy poodle, Frosty, who was all of ten inches tall. Frosty's fame got James and her dog into several Bob Hope feature films and helped open some doors.

By the late 1950s and into the early 1960s, James was training animals for the famous duo of Hal Driscoll and Bill Koehler, the team responsible for the animal actors of many great Disney films. She worked with many of the creatures on the movies *Swiss Family Robinson, Big Red, The Shaggy Dog, Toby Tyler, The Incredible Journey, Savage Sam, Bristle Face*, and *The Ugly Dachshund.*

During that time, her own dog, Hobo, starred with Doris Day and David Niven in the feature film *Please Don't Eat the Daisies.* And James trained the hound dog that appeared to have rabies and was shot by Gregory Peck's Atticus Finch in *To Kill a Mockingbird.* She later worked with Peck again as her dog, Son, finished off Peck's evil Nazi character in *The Boys From Brazil.*

During the 1960s, James freelanced for both Koehler and Frank Inn, but for the most part worked with a slew of famous TV pets in shows where Inn's company furnished the animals. Those credits include a variety of critters on *The Beverly Hillbillies,* Arnold the pig on *Green Acres,* Tramp on *My Three Sons,* Higgins on *Petticoat Junction,* and Waldo the dog on *Nanny and the Professor.* James also worked with many of the dogs that starred in the series of *Doberman Gang* movies.

In the 1970s, Cindy James, Glen Garner, Carl Spitz Jr., and Fred Dean began to run Frank Inn Animals, as Inn gradually retired from training. James moved the company from Los Angeles to Sedona, Arizona, and operated the firm until her death in 2001.

The company's motto was "Trained dogs, working cats, clever critters. Renting insects to elephants for over fifty years."

Hopalong Cassidy

Syndicated, 1948–1951,
52 sixty-minute episodes
NBC, 1952–54, 52 half-hour episodes

*Starring **Topper as Topper,** William Boyd as Hopalong Cassidy, and Edgar Buchanan as Red Connors (in the NBC TV series). Among his saddle pals in the hour-long shows were Jimmy Ellison as Johnny Nelson, George "Gabby" Hayes as Windy Halliday, Russell Hayden as Lucky Jenkins, Andy Clyde as California Carlson, and Rand Brooks as Lucky Jenkins.*

Fifty-two of actor William Boyd's sixty-six *Hopalong Cassidy* feature films of the 1930s and 1940s were edited and packaged into sixty-minute episodes for television in 1948. He edited twelve more of the features into a dozen thirty-minute shows and packaged them along with a new series of forty thirty-minute episodes for NBC from 1952 to 1954.

Set at the Bar 20 Ranch in Crescent City of the Old West, *Hopalong Cassidy* features the exploits of a good guy who always wears black as he defends justice on the range. In more than sixty feature films and forty television episodes, Topper was Hopalong Cassidy's number-one horse, after making his debut in 1939's *Renegade Trail*. (The actor rode a white steed named King Nappy in about a dozen of his earlier films.)

Star William Boyd, who was revered by children everywhere as their beloved "Hoppy," purchased the horse, a pure white Arabian stallion, soon after he married his wife Grace Bradley Boyd, and it was Grace who gave the horse his name, after a novel by Thorne Smith that she was reading at the time. (That book, *Topper*, eventually became a Cary Grant movie.)

Grace says, "He found Topper and me the same year. He had a horse, but it was not what he wanted, so we went to this ranch to look at a horse we had heard about, and we both fell in love with him. He would go anywhere if Bill was on him. When the kids were pulling hairs out of his tail [at public appearances], he would never move."

Topper was cared for and trained by Mike Nimeth. Nimeth also was responsible for transporting the horse to personal appearances for Boyd. The duo did a lot of work for Cole Brothers Circus. And the white horse traveled in style in a custom-made black-and-white trailer (to smartly match Hoppy's outfits). The trailer also had portholes that allowed Topper to take a look outside.

The horse had a remarkable memory, according to Grace Bradley Boyd, and he loved attention. "He was such a ham. One morning we were up in the mountains on the set, and Topper was all gorgeous and preening himself. He knew he looked beautiful. He would step out and stretch out his whole body. This morning he stretched a little too far, and he lost his balance and he fell over, and you could see that horse blush. He kind of gradually got himself up, and he kind of looked around to see if anybody noticed. It was a riot."

She recalls other funny moments with the white stallion. "There was one scene where they rode off, and Topper hit a bucket on the side of the road, and it made a big noise. They had to do the scene over, but everyone had laughed about it because it was very funny. So they set it up again, and they had moved the bucket off to the side. They started off nice and fresh, and what did Topper do but go off the path and stick his foot in the bucket for another laugh.

"He remembered the first time he ran in front of the camera, the chase was on, and they would come in barreling full speed and go past the camera and then everybody stopped. They did the scene again and came tearing through, and Bill nearly went over the horse's head, because he just jammed down his feet and stopped. You had to watch him every minute because he was so smart. Bill wouldn't let him do any tricks. He said this movie takes place in 1890, and this isn't any singing cowboy, and this isn't a trick horse. He wouldn't let Topper do any tricks."

Grace says that Topper had pink skin and blue eyes, and that Nimeth kept the horse's teeth filed so folks couldn't guess its age. And one more Topper beauty secret: Nimeth put cold cream on Topper's nose as a sunscreen, while Grace used her own special brand. "The horse used to sunburn. He had that pink nose. I would come out with Elizabeth Arden's eight-hour cream and put that on his nose to help him," she said. "He was manicured. Mike would have him shod, get his hooves all beautiful, and put clear nail polish on him. He was well taken care of."

For many years in the 1950s, William Boyd adorned himself in his Hoppy costume and rode Topper in the Rose Bowl Parade. They made their annual Pasadena appearance in 1961, and several days afterward Topper passed away at twenty-six years of age.

"Topper went out to his trailer and just never woke up. Three weeks later, Mike died of a heart attack," said Grace. "Once Topper went, there would be no more parades, and he wouldn't ride another horse." The two deaths were taken as a sign by Boyd to hang up his Hoppy spurs, so he retired the character.

Horse trainer Kenny Lee was good friends with Nimeth and also did some work with Topper. "I worked with the horse on *Hopalong Cassidy.* That is the only horse he ever rode [in the TV series]," Lee says. "He was an old give-out horse by the time that *Hopalong Cassidy* got to TV. When they finished that series, he was too old to be making pictures. Boyd, he didn't want to ride anything else.

William Boyd was the good cowboy who wore black and rode a white horse, Topper, whom he purchased in 1937, the same year he married Grace Bradley.

"Mike Nimeth wrangled and took care of that horse from the time the company bought that horse for Boyd until he died. Topper had black ears. He wasn't a true white horse, but he sure looked it on the screen. Topper was the only name they ever called him. He was just a good old gentle saddle horse."

When William Boyd and Topper made a July 4, 1951, appearance in Omaha, Nebraska, the *Omaha Morning World-Herald* newspaper interviewed Topper with questions interpreted by his friend and trainer Mike Nimeth:

Between chews on a ration of oats at the Hillside Stables, Topper was at first a bit testy but mellowed when he heard the Omaha kids wanted to know about him.

"It is about time someone gets to hear what I have to say. This guy Cassidy has been getting all the plums. I'm the only horse he has ever owned in the movies—been with him fourteen years, in fifty-four pictures. He got me when I was a kid three years old, and I've been lugging him ever since. Then when we cash in, they put out Hopalong Cassidy guns, hats, and Hopalong this and Hopalong that."

Snorting his disgust, Topper asked, "Why don't they put out Topper bridles, Topper saddles and blankets? I've been in the big time as long as he has. I've traveled twenty-five thousand miles in the past fifteen months with him. Five days ago . . . in Hollywood, now look at me—1,800 miles away from home and carrying Cassidy . . . on my back again.

"All I've heard since I got to Omaha is about those horses out at Ak-Sar-Ben. They run six furlongs with a 110-pound jockey and think they have it tough. They ought to take a gallop over some rough country with Cassidy blasting those pistols past their ears."

He glanced complacently at his luxurious specially-built trailer with his name on the side.

"That cost Cassidy a pretty penny. Bet none of those fancy swishing nags over at the track has got one like it. If I had to do it over, I would play it again with Cassidy."

Blinking a sleepy eye, Topper excused himself, "I'm due at the American Legion fireworks display at 8:30 P.M.—got to get some shut-eye."

Like an old trouper with an eye on attendance, he added, "Tell the kids there are thousands of tickets left—box office opens at 5 P.M."

Rand Brooks, who starred on TV's *Rin Tin Tin*, made about thirteen feature films with Hopalong Cassidy and his horse. "Topper was a wonderful horse, solid as a rock. He lived a good long life," says Brooks.

The only horse Hoppy ever loved is buried at Calabassas Pet Cemetery, north of Los Angeles.

I Love Lucy / Dennis the Menace

I Love Lucy: CBS, 1951–1956, 179 episodes

*Starring **Danny as Fred,** Lucille Ball as Lucy Ricardo, Desi Arnaz as Ricky Ricardo, Vivian Vance as Ethel Mertz, William Frawley as Fred Mertz, and Keith Thibodeaux (Richard Keith) as Little Ricky.*

One of the most popular sitcoms of all time, *I Love Lucy* is about a wacky redhead whose harebrained schemes always backfire and make her husband mad at her. But he still loves Lucy.

Dennis the Menace: CBS, 1959–1963, 146 episodes

Starring ***Danny as Fremont,*** *Jay North as Dennis Mitchell, Herbert Anderson as Henry Mitchell, Gloria Henry as Alice Mitchell, Joseph Kearns as George Wilson, Sylvia Field as Martha Wilson, Billy Booth as Tommy Anderson, Jeannie Russell as Margaret Wade, Gale Gordon as John Wilson, and Sara Seeger as Eloise Wilson.*

Dennis the Menace is based on the Hank Ketcham comic strip about a mischievous little boy who, while trying to help others, generally makes matters a mess.

The little dog featured on both *I Love Lucy* and *Dennis the Menace* was a wheaton cairn terrier that Frank Inn retrieved from an animal shelter.

"I was doing the animals on Lucy's show, and they called me and wanted this puppy to be Little Ricky's dog. I got this puppy and put Bob Blair to working with it," says Inn. "He trained that puppy, and it worked the *I Love Lucy* show several times."

"Danny was his real name," says Blair of the pup that played Little Ricky's pet Fred. "He was sort of shy." Blair says he was mostly used for atmosphere on *Lucy*, but sometimes he had to run in and jump up on the couch and hide his head under the pillow.

Keith Thibodeaux, who played Little Ricky on *Lucy*, remembers Fred and how life imitated art. "I liked dogs, and I really liked that little dog. I liked him so much that I wanted to take him home with me, but I couldn't, of course, because he was an actor. But it was a good little dog, and I wanted one like it. As a result of that, Lucy told my Dad, 'Thibby, you need to get Keith a dog.' And so I believe we did get a dog because of that."

Danny scored a major coup in 1959. He became one of the stars of *Anatomy of a Murder* and worked on the big screen with

Little Danny boy starred as Little Ricky's pet on *I Love Lucy* and as Mr. Wilson's pooch Fremont on *Dennis the Menace.* But in between the two TV roles, he found time to star with Lee Remick in the feature film *Anatomy of a Murder.*

Jimmy Stewart, Lee Remick, and George C. Scott. It took a little tomfoolery by Blair and Inn to get that part, but it paid off.

"We showed several dogs to director Otto Preminger, and he said no to all of them," says Blair. "Finally, I pulled out Danny, because he was so shy. Otto says, 'No, I need a ladies' dog.' So I went back, and Frank and I talked it over. I said, 'I bet if it was a blonde, he would like it.' So we bleached him a blonde and took him in again and showed him to Otto, and he said, 'That's the dog.'"

Danny had a major part in *Anatomy of a Murder* as he played Lee Remick's pet, the little dog who carried the flashlight for her in his mouth. "There was a big courtroom scene that the dog had to go through, and Otto wanted it all in one piece. We had to do it in pieces, so I got with Jimmy Stewart every chance I got," says Blair. "Danny had to come out of his crate and go jump in Jimmy's lap. Well, Danny was a little dog, and Jimmy was a tall fellow. I had to show him how to do it, so it would work. I had cues on Danny so that when he would see that little flashlight, he would go over and turn it on. In the courtroom he runs over and jumps in George C. Scott's lap."

Danny performed admirably, and the movie wrapped. "Then at the cast party, Otto said he wanted Danny to be there too," Blair says. "So I brought Danny and put his crate in the hat-check room, and Preminger's wife came over and says, 'Bring Danny over to Otto's table.' By then we had dyed him back for other shows, so he was dark now. I walked over to the table with the dog, and Otto says, 'Who's that?' I told him, 'That's Danny,' and I told him the whole story. He laughed about it."

After *Lucy* and *Anatomy of a Murder*, Danny moved on to *Dennis the Menace*, where he played Fremont. "He was a really nice dog," says Blair. "Jay [North] used to like to take the dog for a walk. I kept Danny at my house when I was working with him. We had to keep him happy. If something happened that he wasn't familiar with, he would go into his shell. He couldn't stand loud noises."

Jay North, who starred as *Dennis the Menace*, barely remembers the dog that belonged to his neighbor, good ole Mr. Wilson. "That was a sweet animal that I used to play with. I don't have any memories, but I used to pet it. I didn't know the dog other than as Fremont.

"I do remember there was a chimp one time in an episode. It bit me on the hand. The chimp was very temperamental. When I grabbed his hand to hold him, he bit me on the hand. The doctor had to look at it, but it was not very deep a wound.

"There was another dog, a stray, that I was playing and roughhousing with over in the park at the Columbia Ranch, and they called me over to location for the scene. I went running, and the dog saw me running with the slingshot in my back pocket, and he took off after me and missed the slingshot and bit me on the behind. I had to have stitches and a shot."

Henry Shannon, who worked for Frank Inn as a trainer, did some of his first TV work on *Dennis the Menace* with Danny. The thing that stands out in his mind is that they had the pooch in the dirt a lot. "Danny was a good little dog, who spent a lot of time digging up holes in Mr. Wilson's back yard," Shannon says.

Frank Inn's Danny had a stable mate named Snuffy (owned by Inn's partner, Neil Gazeley) who was very similar in looks. Snuffy had a nice role in the 1957 Frank Sinatra film *Pal Joey*. Snuffy was part cairn terrier and won his role at an audition at a fancy restaurant on Sunset Boulevard.

The producers of the film held a publicity stunt where they had all the dogs apply for the job on *Pal Joey* by asking the trainers to have their dogs eat a bagel off a plate. "Some of those dogs ate the plate and everything," says Inn. "We taught this dog so that it would pick up a bagel and dip it in a bowl of soup and lay it down on the plate and eat the soft part." So it was that *Pal Joey*'s pal became Snuffy.

In the Heat of the Night

NBC and CBS, 1988–1994, 150 episodes

*Starring **Hunter as Beauregard,** Carroll O'Connor as Chief Bill Gillespie, Howard Rollins as Chief of Detectives Virgil Tibbs, Anne-Marie Johnson as Althea Tibbs, Alan Autry as Sgt. Bubba Skinner, David Hart as Dep. Parker Williams, Hugh O'Connor as Dep. Lonnie Jamison, Geoffrey Thorne as Dep. Willson Sweet, Crystal Fox as Sgt. LuAnn Corbin, Denise Nicholas as Harriet DeLong, Dan Biggers as Dr. Robb, Carl Weathers as Chief Hampton Forbes, and Randall Franks as Officer Randy Goode.*

Based on the novel and 1967 Oscar-winning film of the same title, *In the Heat of the Night* is about a police chief and his force in Sparta, Mississippi, adjusting to the addition of a black chief of detectives.

Beauregard, Chief Gillespie's pet dog, was played by a black Labrador retriever with a bit of rottweiler by the name of Hunter. He was owned and trained by Bryan Hudson.

Handler Laura Levy took Beau to work on the show during its last three seasons, and says, "He was a great dog. He knew about a hundred tricks. Bryan had trained him well, but he didn't have a lot of distinct roles. Basically it was bark or sit up and go. He was kind of there as just the family pet, so they didn't make him do a lot of tricks.

"He was just sweet and loving. He had a certain spark in his eye. He liked to work; he loved it. He had a lot of energy, a lot of spunk, and a lot of drive."

But one thing Hunter didn't have was a tail. "He did not have a tail. He had his tail docked when he was young, but nobody ever saw that he didn't have a tail," Levy says.

The biggest problem the dog had on the set was the dilemma facing the cameraman

Carroll O'Connor and Hunter take a break for a snapshot while on location in Georgia for *In the Heat of the Night.* *Courtesy of Laura Levy.*

of getting the lights right on a black dog. "It was the funniest thing," Levy says. "He practically had to have his own lighting crew because he was black. It's hard to get a black dog to show up, especially in Carroll O'Connor's office on the show because he had a black couch. They had a difficult time getting him to show up."

Levy says that star O'Connor loved dogs and even brought his own pet boxer to the set. "Carroll O'Connor was a huge dog lover. Hunter was like a mascot on the set. Everybody knew him. The whole set was a family, and when he wasn't working, he would run around and get petted by everybody."

As for motivation, Levy says Hunter liked playing with tennis balls.

Jungle Jim / Bomba the Jungle Boy

Syndicated, 1955, 26 episodes

*Starring **Tamba the chimp,** Johnny Weissmuller as Jungle Jim, Martin Huston as Skipper, and Norman Fredric as Kaseem.*

Created by Alex Raymond, *Jungle Jim* is a series about a guide who performs heroic deeds in the jungles of Africa, mainly in Kenya. Assisting him are his son and servant.

After the glory years of swinging as Tarzan and Boy on the silver screen, actors Johnny Weissmuller and Johnny Sheffield, respectively, went down separate jungle paths in a series of low-budget films: Weissmuller as *Jungle Jim* and Sheffield as *Bomba the Jungle Boy.*

Both had chimp sidekicks, and one chimp in particular, named Peggy, worked with each of them.

Weissmuller made sixteen *Jungle Jim* flicks between 1948 and 1955, and then the character jumped to television. Jim's main animal pal in both the films and TV shows was named Tamba, and the chimp was played, for the most part, by Peggy.

Animal importer-exporter Trader Horne brought Peggy out of Africa in the late 1940s. He took her to the World Jungle Compound, which Horne co-owned at the time, and had her trained by "Chief" Henry Tyndall.

Weissmuller's son, Johnny Weissmuller Jr., recalled that his father worked with many, many chimpanzees while making the *Tarzan* and *Jungle Jim* movies. He says that often the producers used multiple chimps on one shoot to play Cheetah or Tamba.

"They preferred to work with females because the males were more aggressive. They would use the males for the aerial work and the females for close-ups," says Weissmuller. "The males had a glary, feral look which the directors liked, but they didn't like to work with them."

The son of Tarzan/Jungle Jim recalls that they often brought some of the chimps home with them because his father had to spend time with the animals to work better with them before the camera.

Peggy was first seen in the 1950 Jungle Jim flick *Mark of the Gorilla* and became an official sidekick in *Captive Girl* that same year. In this film for the first time she was given the name Tamba (she was billed on posters as Tamba "the Talented Chimp").

But jungle hijinks weren't the only tricks in Peggy's bag. Peggy costarred in *Bonzo Goes to College* in 1952, for which she copped a second-place PATSY Award, and by this time she was generating her owners twenty-five grand a year. She reportedly began biting folks about this time, and when she became pregnant in 1954, she lost her *Jungle Jim* gig to another chimp, billed as Kimba.

When *Jungle Jim* went from films to a TV series in 1955, Jim's chimp sidekick retained the name of Tamba, but it is highly unlikely that it was Peggy in the role.

Veteran director Earl Bellamy helmed the first four episodes of the *Jungle Jim* TV show, and he recalls that the chimpanzee was very fond of Weissmuller. "The chimp would do anything for him at all. Johnny would pick him up and hug him. It was just like he belonged with Johnny," says Bellamy.

"I had a funny experience," Bellamy adds. "There was to be a scene of the chimp shooting a rifle. We gave it to the trainer a week before we had to do the scene. He rehearsed, and it went just great. So when it came time to shoot, the chimp was there, and we said, 'He's ready.' So we started the scene and all was going fine. Then it come time for the chimp to load the rifle and shoot, and he

Peggy smirks as Kimbbo the chimp alongside Johnny Sheffield in *Bomba and the Jungle Girl* in 1952.

Courtesy of Fred Goodwin.

Peggy plays Tamba ("the talented chimp") to Johnny Weissmuller's Jungle Jim in *Voodoo Tiger* in 1952. The actress in the flower-printed sarong is Diane Garrett.
Courtesy of Geoff St. Andrews.

quit and ran to the highest part of the stage. We coaxed and got him down."

The director says the trainer's name was Jimmy. "He sure worked with that chimp a lot and knew what it was doing." And Bellamy is sure that it was not Peggy or Jiggs, another famous chimp of the day.

In the earlier film series, Jungle Jim also had a dog named Skipper and a crow named Caw-Caw. The crow was probably the famous black bird of Hollywood, Jimmy (trained by Curly Twiford), or his protégé Jimmy Junior (trained by Moe Di Sesso). When *Jim* went to a TV series format, Jim had a son named Skipper, who had a dog named Trader (in one episode only).

As for Sheffield, he made a dozen *Bomba the Jungle Boy* films (based on Roy Rockwood's series of books for boys) between 1949 and 1955. Peggy was his chimp co-star. Her character was named Kimbbo.

During the 1960s, both film series, *Jungle Jim* and *Bomba the Jungle Boy*, got lots of airplay on television stations as syndicated Saturday morning shows. They were billed in some markets under the banner of "Jungle Theater."

Lancelot Link, Secret Chimp

ABC, 1970–1972, 26 episodes

Starring ***Tonga as Lancelot Link, Debbie as Mata Hairi, Henry as Commander Darwin, Tammy, Corky, Charlie, and many other simian stars,*** *plus the voices of Dayton Allen, Joan Gerber, Steven Hoffman, Bernie Kopell, and Malachi Throne.*

Lancelot Link was an unusual addition to the Saturday morning lineup in that the cast was entirely made up of apes, all chimps except for one orangutan, Henry. A spy spoof, the show starred good guy Lancelot Link who partnered with Mata Hairi as APE (Agency to Prevent Evil) battled CHUMP (Criminal Headquarters for Underworld Master Plan). The villains included Baron von Butcher, Creto, Duchess, Dr. Strangemind, Wang Fu, and Ali AssaSeen. Musical interludes were supplied by a chimpanzee rock band, the Evolution Revolution.

Frank Inn was the mastermind behind the cavorting chimps in *Lancelot Link.* His TV and movie menagerie included about twenty chimps, which furnished the players for the series. "I started out with a chimp on *The Beverly Hillbillies,* Debbie, who played Cousin Bess [Debbie also played Jenny, the Space Bloop, on *Lost in Space*]," says Inn. "I would buy two chimps every year and train both of them. When I did *Lancelot Link,* I had several chimps, and then I went out and bought some more older chimps that were retired but were controllable.

"Tonga was the big chimp who starred as Lance. He was a huge chimp, but he was as nice a doggone chimp as you could ever have."

The sole orangutan on *Lancelot Link* was named Henry, and he belonged to trainer Darrell Keener, whose other credits included handling the chimpanzees on *The Beverly Hillbillies.*

Among other stunts the chimps performed was riding anything that would move, including miniature horses, little automobiles, boats, and motorcycles. "We started them out riding a motorcycle with training wheels. It was just like riding a tricycle, and it wouldn't fall down," Inn says. "Then, eventually, they could hold their balance and ride around in a circle. To get them to stop, we set the carburetor so it could go only so fast. Then we had them wave their hands, and they would come off the throttle and the motorcycle would stop.

"One day we had a chimp sitting still on a motorcycle, but he had tinkered with it, and the throttle was not under control. The gate was open, and he hit the gas and went right through the gate and down the street. We went running down the street trying to catch him, and one of my trainers disappeared around the corner chasing him. The next thing I know, I look behind me and here they come down the street. I got out in the street in front of the chimp and signaled for him to wave, and the motorcycle stopped. The cops were there and didn't know who to give the ticket to, me or the chimp."

Trainer Hubert Wells, who worked such series as *Born Free, Bring 'Em Back Alive,* and *Lucan,* was one of the main chimp men on *Lancelot Link.* He remembers what a big job the show was. "Every day was interesting. These chimps had to do everything like the spies in the *James Bond* movies. We had as many as fifteen chimps a day, but they were not all working at the same time, and we had five trainers on the set. We took every precaution and nobody got bit," says

Lancelot Link, played by Tonga, seems deep in thought. No doubt another hilarious mission is about to ensue. *Courtesy of Photo History.*

Wells. "Tonga played Lancelot. He was a huge animal, very keen, about fourteen years old and very good-looking.

"One day we were filming in the Santa Monica mountains, and one of the chimps, Corky, got lost. He was dressed like an Indian brave with feathers and war paint on his face and moccasins on his feet. We looked and looked for him and couldn't find him. Later that day he was returned by a hippie that looked pretty much just like him, except the hippie was not wearing war paint."

Another experienced chimp trainer on the show was Wally Ross, who started in animal show business in the late 1950s. Ross recalls, "Darrell Keener was the head trainer, the top honcho. I was a principal trainer, and there was a bunch of chimps. We put makeup on 'em, and we had them looking like Japanese chimps, and there were German chimps wearing monocles.

"Each principal trainer handled about three chimps. The main chimp I worked was Corky. He was a very good-looking chimp and easy to put makeup on. He did a lot of the girl parts. I also worked with the chimp that was the drummer in the chimpanzee band."

Ross worked on the films *Project X* and *Dr. Doolittle*, among others, but his career took him down an interesting side road. "I worked with sea lions in circuses, so the government hired me when it began the Man in the Sea project using sea lions, porpoises, and whales to be assistants to man in the sea," Ross says.

After *Lancelot Link* completed its two-year run, Inn sent his chimps on a performance tour around the world. Stops included Japan, Hawaii, and South America. He eventually sold most of them, including Tonga and Debbie, the stars of *Lancelot Link*, to the trainer in charge of the touring show. The others he donated to an organization that raised and cared for chimps. He heard later that the *Link* chimps were resold to a trainer in Florida.

"One day I went to watch them working on the set of the movie *Project X* [about 1986—fourteen years after *Lancelot Link*]," says Inn, "and the biggest chimp I have ever seen came running after me, and he jumped on me, and I'm down on the ground afraid. This was a chimp I had raised from a baby, Moe, and he had me down, not trying to hurt me, but he recognized my walk, and he was loving me."

As for the ape appetites of the *Lancelot Link* spies, Inn fed them bananas, apples, all kinds of fruit, and oatmeal. Nobody likes spying on an empty stomach.

Voice actor and comedian Dayton Allen, who did the talking for Lancelot and other characters on the show, gives another per-

spective. He says it was hard work, long hours, but great fun. Allen says, "I was doing the voices, and they had these chimps come in and do the live action, and immediately we'd play it back and see the mouthing, and then we would lip-sync it.

"They gave the chimps bubble gum. They loved to chew it. That way we could match the voices to the mouth. They were trained well enough to chew gum in different rhythms. I did a lot of ad-libbing as we followed the mouthing. They were great comic copycats, but we had timing problems because you never knew what they would do. So we said whatever came to our mind and it was funny.

"I loved them. I thought they were fantastic. They were very friendly, but sometimes the chimps were not in the mood or they would be preoccupied, and we had to wait for them to think it over."

Allen says the chimps looked forward to getting into costumes and makeup, such as moustaches, beards, and wigs. "The chimps loved it. They thought they were stars. They were real hams."

Allen also remembers there were two seven-foot-long couches in the studio, and in between breaks, everybody would make a rush to get on the couches and stretch out—even the chimpanzees. "Everybody doing the voices couldn't wait until after their bit was done to go and lie down, because it was tiring," says Allen. "The couches were the only places to lie down, and the chimps would come over and lie down with you. I went over to lie down once, and I put my hands in back of my head, and I looked over and the chimp playing Lance did the same thing. They were very intelligent."

Land of the Giants

ABC, 1968–1970, 51 episodes

*Starring **Chipper as Chipper,** Gary Conway as Steve Burton, Stefan Arngrim as Barry Lockridge, Don Marshall as Dan Erickson, Heather Young as Betty Hamilton, Deanna Lund as Valerie Scott, Kurt Kasznar as Alexander Fitzhugh, Don Matheson as Mark Wilson, and Kevin Hagen as S.I.B. Inspector Kobick.*

Set in 1983, *Land of the Giants* follows a band of earthlings whose suborbital flight passes through a "space warp" and lands in a world filled with human giants. There these "little people" are menaced by giant adults, children, insects, and animals while they try to repair their plane for escape.

A trio of canines handled the dog chores on the Irwin Allen sci-fi fantasy series. The primary dog was Chipper, "an all-American dog, a cross between Hollywood and Vine, possibly a cocker spaniel and poodle mixture" according to owner Karl Lewis Miller, who recollects finding the dog at either the Burbank or Sherman Way animal shelter.

"Chipper did not have any big major

Stefan Arngrim holds the only Earth creature smaller than he was during their journey to *Land of the Giants*.

physical feats to do on the show, but the dog always had to be around. He had to bark and alarm the little people when something was astray or when someone was coming," Miller says. "He usually gave notice to the little people that giants or giant animals were coming by growling or running away from being stepped on."

The cast member who really knew Chipper was Stefan Arngrim, who was just a youngster when the show was produced. "There were three dogs: Chipper, Chip, and Little Chip. The camera-friendly close-up dog was Chipper, and then Chip was the stunt dog who did all the climbing and jumping and stuff, and Little Chip was the stand-in. Little Chip used to stand around with the second team while they were lighting the set," Arngrim says.

"The dogs tended to work the same schedule as I did," Arngrim remembers. If you were under eighteen, you were only allowed to work eight hours a day and that includes one hour of lunch.

Arngrim says, "Chipper, who was a little bigger than the other two, was female. She was a sweetheart, and we got along very well. She was not really a trick dog, but she had a very sweet temperament, and put up with the rigors of having to work with humans. She looked great on camera and was wonderful at stealing scenes. She was good at doing things incredibly cute.

"Just before we started, Betty Burke, the trainer on the set, recommended that Chipper come and spend the weekend at my house and that we kind of hang out together, so when we started the pilot, Chipper came home with me for a weekend, and we became friends. All the dogs were so well trained and so well cared for and looked after by Betty.

"Kurt Kasznar and Chipper had a very interesting relationship. Kurt sort of liked to play the curmudgeon-cantankerous personality off screen, but he really was a sweetheart. He played the W. C. Fields sort who acts like he hates kids and dogs. He and Chipper used to have these one-way conversations quite frequently where Kurt would tell

Chipper, 'I know what you're up to. You want a spin-off. I know with your little brown eyes, you're trying to steal the scene.' Chipper would sit there and listen innocently.

"Chip, the little stunt dog, was a male and very enthusiastic. He was quite extraordinary, and he did all kinds of things. He could make his way up a rope as long as it was slanted."

While Arngrim and the dogs got along like gangbusters, there was one day when a bear decided it was way past his snack time. Arngrim recalls, "We had an episode that involved a giant circus and they had a full-grown bear, a black bear, I think. The bear apparently had a real fondness for Coca-Cola and Hostess Twinkies. This was his preferred treat, so the trainer kept a case of Cokes and a bunch of Twinkies to one side of the set.

"We worked pretty long hours, and Harry Harris was directing and having difficulty with the shot with the bear. This bear had on a collar with a chain, mostly for effect, but her chain was bolted into the soundstage floor. The floor was nothing more than a couple of layers of plywood, so it was not going to hold a full-grown black bear if it wanted to leave.

"The trainer came to Harry and said, 'The bear needs to take his break now. He would like his Twinkies and his Coke. Could we give him a break?' Harry was running behind, and said, 'OK, just give me one more minute,' like all directors do.

"Harry pushed the time maybe a little too far, and the bear finally decided he was done and didn't want any more rehearsals or shots and he stood up and rather calmly pulled the chain out of the ground. He made his way across the set as a sea of people parted. The bear kind of growled and made very fierce noises as he made his way to the table and had his Twinkies and Coke. There was a good twenty seconds where we didn't know what was going on as five of our biggest grips grabbed a hold of that chain and were dragged fifteen feet across the floor."

The actors never had such "hunger pang" problems with the canines. The star Chipper of *Land of the Giants* died peacefully of old age at owner Miller's home.

Lassie

There have been (so far) seven formats for Lassie television shows:

1. Jeff's Collie (syndicated title): CBS, 1954–1957, 103 episodes

*Starring **Lassie,** Tommy Rettig as Jeff Miller, Jan Clayton as Ellen Miller, George Cleveland as George "Gramps" Miller, Donald Keeler as Sylvester "Porky" Brockway, and **Porky's dog Pokey.***

The series is about a boy and his faithful collie dog, who live with the boy's widowed mother and grandfather.

2. Timmy and Lassie (syndicated title): CBS, 1957–1964, 247 episodes

*Starring **Lassie,** Jon Provost as Timmy Martin, Cloris Leachman and June Lockhart as Ruth Martin, Jon Shepodd and Hugh Riley as Paul Martin, George Chandler as Petrie Martin, Andy Clyde as Cully, Todd Ferrell as Boomer Bates, and Boomer's dog Mike.*

This series is about an orphan discovered by Lassie and adopted by the Martins. He and Lassie find great adventures in the countryside around the farm.

3. Lassie and the Forest Rangers: CBS, 1964–1970, 143 episodes

*Starring **Lassie,** Robert Bray as Ranger Corey Stuart, Jed Allan as Ranger Scott Turner, and Jack DeMave as Ranger Bob Erickson.*

Lassie finds a new master, a forest ranger, as the dog helps protect the forests and endangered humans and animals.

4. Lassie the Wanderer: CBS, 1970–1971, 22 episodes

*Starring **Lassie.***

Lassie roams the countryside helping people and animals in need.

5. Lassie on the Ranch: Syndicated, 1972–1973, 44 episodes

*Starring **Lassie,** Larry Pennell as Keith Holden, Larry Wilcox as Dale Mitchell, Skip Burton as Ron Holden, Pamelyn Ferdin as Lucy Baker, Joshua Albee as Mike Holden, and Sherry Boucher as Sue Lambert.*

Lassie finds a temporary home in the country with a kind rancher and his family.

6. The New Lassie: Syndicated, 1989–1991, 46 episodes

*Starring **Lassie,** Will Nipper as Will McCullough, Christopher Stone as Chris McCullough, Dee Wallace Stone as Dee McCullough, Wendy Cox as Megan McCullough, and Jon Provost as Steve McCullough.*

The collie finds a home with a middle-class family in a California suburb.

7. *Lassie: Animal Planet, 1997–1998, 52 episodes*

*Starring **Lassie and two non-Weatherwax dogs (one named Buster),** Susan Almgren as Dr. Karen Cabot, Corey Sevier as Timmy Cabot, Walter Massey as Dr. Donald Stewart, Tim Post as Ethan Bennett, Tod Fennell as Jeff Mackenzie, and Natalie Vansier as Natalie.*

The final *Lassie* series of the twentieth century is set in a small town in Vermont, where a widow returns to raise her son and work as a veterinarian. The boy finds a collie to share his life.

Television's greatest animal star of all time? It's gotta be Lassie, paws down.

How do you argue with a television series that ran in its various forms for nineteen straight years and more than 650 episodes (not counting animated episodes), spanning almost half a century? You don't. Lassie, as *TV Guide* announced in 1993, is "America's favorite pet."

The credit must go to a beautiful series of Lassies and one man, the late Rudd Weatherwax, who trained the collies to be the dog that practically every man, woman, and child at one time or another wished for as their own best friend.

The origin of one of television's greatest characters goes back to a 1938 issue of the *Saturday Evening Post.* Between the covers was a short story, "Lassie Come Home," by Eric Knight. The heroic dog, Lassie, was modeled after the writer's own dog, Toots. The tale proved so popular that it was quickly turned

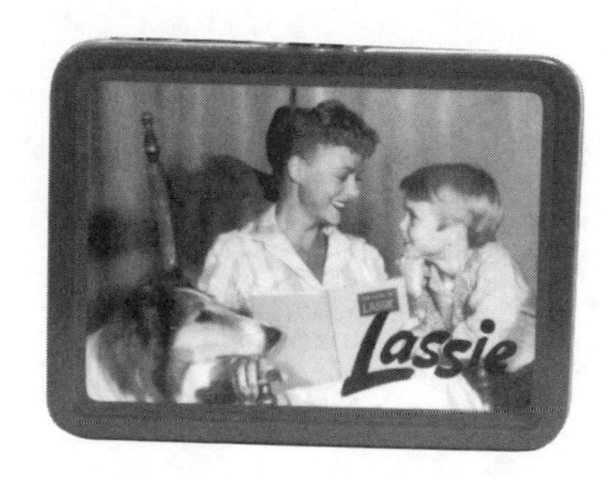

into a novella, and in 1939 the book sold a million copies.

Writer and patriot Knight, who was killed in World War II, never saw the first *Lassie* feature film. But MGM's 1943 *Lassie Come Home* was a bona fide smash, and Lassie became a star.

Robert Weatherwax, son of the late Rudd Weatherwax, explained how his father brought Lassie into the limelight. "My father got that dog [the original movie Lassie, whose real name was Pal] from a guy who

Lassie's first favorite boy was Jeff Miller, played by Tommy Rettig. Rettig and Lassie were together for more than one hundred episodes, which were syndicated under the title of *Jeff's Collie.*

Timmy (Jon Provost), Jeff Miller (Tommy Rettig), and Porky (Donald Keeler), left to right, spend time in the woods.

couldn't train him. He was chasing motorcycles. My father tried but couldn't break him, and the guy just didn't want the dog, so he gave it to my father, who didn't really want him. He farmed him out.

"Then the movie came along, *Lassie Come Home*. They had their star dog, and they asked my father if he would get a collie as a stand-in. So Father got his collie back, never expecting the movie to be big. The original dog failed on a river-crossing shot. It wouldn't go into the water. So Father brought Pal. He choreographed the scene. He didn't want the dog to just come out of the river. He had him come out and collapse."

Director Fred Wilcox said at the time, "That dog that jumped into the river may have been Pal, but it was Lassie who crawled out. Your dog is my star, I don't care what anyone says!"

So Knight created the story, and Weatherwax created the real-life dog. And Pal the stunt dog became Lassie the superstar.

Today the Weatherwax name is one that is rich in the annals of Hollywood's top dogs. The family's story began on a ranch in New Mexico, where Rudd and brothers Frank, Jack, and Mac were raised. Their father used collies to guard their sheep and goats. As a youngster, Rudd taught a pet lamb to open and close a latched gate, and he trained a white rat to chase mice out of the house.

The family moved to Los Angeles in 1917 while Rudd was still a teenager. He had a dog named Wriggles that he taught to fetch and carry. Always interested in movies and an especially keen fan of Rin Tin Tin, Rudd was working as an extra in a film one day and was called upon to play a Western Union boy. Instead of delivering the message himself, he had Wriggles carry the telegram in his teeth.

Rudd's son Robert relates what happened next. "Well, he was a kid with a fantasy. He wanted to work dogs in movies. That was always what he wanted to be. So after they moved to Hollywood, he got the job as a stand-in and had Wriggles carry the paper to the house. Dog trainer Henry East saw my father [do that] and asked, 'Would you like a job?'"

Rudd jumped at the opportunity, and eventually worked two of the most famous dogs in the movies, Asta of *Thin Man* fame, and Daisy, owned by Rennie Renfro, of the *Blondie* film series.

Later, Rudd realized there was no reason he couldn't work for himself, so in 1940 he launched his own business, while brothers Jack and Frank Weatherwax also became animal trainers. The Weatherwax siblings trained hundreds of dogs over the years for film and television, including Toto, John Wayne's dog in *Hondo* (a brother to Lassie), and Spike, the dog star of Disney's *Old Yeller*.

But it was via Lassie that Rudd blessed America and the world. He reflected on his first meeting with Lassie in a long-ago CBS press release: "This collie chased cars, and this man brought her in to have her cured of it. The man didn't care much for the dog. He didn't even come back, just phoned and said to keep the dog for the bill" (a seventy-dollar training fee).

What a gift.

After that first hugely popular *Lassie* feature film, released on October 7, 1943, others followed. An MGM press release of the 1940s read: "Lassie knows more than 100 different commands, but he is simply too nice and too polite to snarl. Lassie can swim rivers, climb mountains, lead children home from the woods, and carry a baby chick in his mouth, but if a scene requires him to snarl, the director must bring on a stunt dog."

The *Lassie* films ran their course through the 1940s. A *Lassie* radio show debuted on the ABC Radio Network in 1947, and Pal furnished the actual on-air barking (but no snarling). By the early 1950s, MGM saw no future in more *Lassie* movies. The studio owed Weatherwax and his Pal $40,000, so they came to an agreement.

"We don't need to deal," Rudd told the giant studio. "Just give me all rights to *Lassie* and you keep the money owed." MGM agreed.

"It looked like a pretty stupid deal at the time," Weatherwax later admitted, "and for a while it seemed to prove to be that way. But I always loved Lassie."

Weatherwax need not have worried, as Lassie's fortunes were only beginning, thanks to the young medium of television. In 1954, the collie became the star of his own show, and America watched.

During the first years of *Lassie*, thirty-three million viewers tuned in every week to watch a dog and his boy, and Lassie received two thousand pieces of fan mail a week. During its first two seasons, *Lassie* won the Emmy Award for best children's program.

At the beginning of Lassie's fifth season in 1958, his family featured June Lockhart as Ruth Martin, Hugh Reilly as Paul Martin, and Jon Provost as Timmy.

In 1948 Lassie enjoys a treat at the table of his best friend Rudd Weatherwax.

Lassie was a handsome star. The sable-and-white male collie boasted a full white collar, a narrow white blaze down the nose, and four white feet. Although the TV character of Lassie was female, only male dogs played the role, mainly because male collies don't fully lose their coats (they gradually shed throughout the year) and because they are bigger than female collies.

Lassie lived on the Weatherwax Ranch in California and enjoyed a double bed, his own hi-fi, and a large toy chest. While the TV series was sponsored for many years by Campbell Soup Company, Lassie dined on homemade steak stew, veggies, and garlic, with a side order of cottage cheese. On the road, the dog star of dog stars ate Dinty Moore beef stew and lapped bottled water.

Lassie's first favorite boy, Tommy Rettig, told in many interviews how Lassie hand-picked him for the role of Jeff. "The decision as to who got the part was essentially left to Lassie," Rettig said. "I spent a week with Rudd and Lassie out in North Hollywood at the Weatherwaxes' home. The other finalists did too. The fact was that Lassie liked me better than he did the other two kids."

The same thing happened to Jon Provost, who portrayed Timmy, boy number two in Lassie's TV life. Provost recalled, "I watched the show when Tommy [Rettig] was on it. I was in Japan making a movie. I was six. They were looking for a new boy to replace Tommy.

"I got back from Japan and met with the producers and directors, and they said, 'Yes, you are the one we want, but we have to see how you get along with Lassie and how Lassie gets along with you.'

"I had grown up around animals, and I knew there had to be that bond, because you couldn't fake it. They had me go and live with Lassie for a week at Rudd Weatherwax's ranch in the San Fernando Valley. That one week of living with Lassie and doing normal things proved the point that we got along great. It was a kid's dream to go to that ranch and play a week with Lassie."

During that week Provost also met Pal, the original Lassie, who by this time was deaf and blind. The Weatherwaxes referred to him as "the Old Man," a term of respect. Pal had the run of the house and, even though he couldn't see, never bumped into anything.

The first Lassie Provost teamed with was Lassie II, who was also aging. "He was old," says Provost, "probably twelve when I met him, and he was great, very calm and relaxed. But we didn't have any strong feelings between us. He was Tommy's dog."

Provost worked with Lassie II for about two seasons, until illness brought Spook, Lassie II's brother, aboard to fill in while Lassie III was being broken in. Spook was appropriately named, as Provost explains. "There was an incident on the set with me, June Lockhart, and Lassie [Spook]. The camera was coming in toward us, and the dolly grip tripped and let go of the dolly. The whole thing was rolling down the ramp with nobody to stop it. The dolly came off the track and knocked over the lights, which spooked the dog. That caused him to get nervous and not want to work, so they replaced him with Baby [Lassie III].

"Baby was my favorite. I loved that dog. We worked together for a good four years, and we were really allowed to bond. When Rudd would find a replacement dog that was going to take over, he would take that puppy and raise it on the set, so it could become familiar with the workings of the studio. That was what he did with Baby, and I think it is why we bonded. I kind of grew up with him before we started working together.

"He was definitely the best-looking dog and the smartest that I worked with. He was not only smart but really intelligent and able to really understand things that were going on. A lot of times over the years I would leave Los Angeles and go with Rudd and Lassie to his ranch and spend the weekend there.

"One time when we were out at Rudd's ranch, where there was a small pond, I was fishing and Rudd was reading the newspaper. He ran out of cigarettes, and the pond was a quarter of a mile from the house. He said, 'Lassie, go up to the house and get me a pack of cigarettes.' Baby went up to the house and about five minutes later here came Baby with a pack of cigarettes."

Provost not only worked and played with Lassie, but he also toured the United States with America's favorite dog. "We worked nine months out of the year and for three months we were off on hiatus. During that time, we usually took a month and toured the U.S., usually just me and Lassie," says Provost. "We would mainly go to the big cities and the big theaters. Rudd would go through a few tricks, and Lassie and I would give autographs, but one thing that we did in every town we went to was to visit the children's hospital. We would go to the different wards, and the looks on those kids' faces: 'Hey, Timmy and Lassie!'"

Incidentally, Provost's "Timmy" costume now resides in the Smithsonian Institution.

The *Lassie* series rolled on for nineteen years and reoccurred in the 1980s and 1990s. Along the way, Lassie has picked up such nicknames as "The Bark," "Greer Garson in Fur," "America's Favorite Pet," and "The Environmental Dog."

Lassie has captured PATSY Awards and Emmy Awards, has appeared on nine *TV Guide* covers, has a star in the Hollywood Walk of Fame, and was the first animal inducted into the PATSY Hall of Fame. There was also an animated version of *Lassie* when CBS aired *Lassie's Rescue Rangers* on Saturday mornings from 1973 to 1975.

Robert Bray starred as Ranger Corey Stuart on *Lassie* in the mid-1960s.

Here's a rundown on all the classy Lassies. There have been nine, the latest a collie originally called Laddie, who took over the role in early 2001.

"All the dogs were named Lassie. The names that Ace Collins listed in his definitive book [*Lassie: A Dog's Life*] were all names of the pups before they took over from their father," says Joan Neidhardt, the one behind the "rebarkable" Web site, www.lassie.net. "Think of it sort of like a breeder that gives pups a temporary name, until they go to a new home or new owner. When a dog is chosen to become the next Lassie, the name is changed permanently to Lassie. If you call Lassie by any other name, he won't respond."

Pal, the first Lassie, was the dog who performed in all of the MGM movies and starred in the CBS-TV pilot at age fourteen. Lassie I died in 1958 at the ripe old age of eighteen and was buried on the Weatherwax ranch.

Lassie Jr. became Lassie II. He was the only Lassie whose name really was Lassie. The son of Pal, he was the first TV dog Lassie and he played three years with Jeff (Tommy Rettig) and two years with Timmy (Jon Provost). A cancerous tumor forced Lassie II off the show in 1959.

An unofficial Lassie took his turn briefly before the cameras next. Spook, brother of Lassie Jr., filled in during the spring of 1960 and the fall of 1960. Seen walking with Timmy in the opening credits of the "Lassie and Timmy" era (the syndicated version), Spook was easily frightened by all the action on the set and was happy to retire quickly and quietly.

Baby, named after Jean Harlow, became Lassie III in 1960. He worked alongside Timmy and continued for two seasons of the "Ranger" era. Starring as Lassie for six years, Lassie III died of cancer in 1966 at age eight, and was the only Lassie who did not live a long life.

Mire was Lassie IV. He filled the role for five years of the "Ranger" era, while his brother Muck earned his pay as his stand-in. Lassie IV lived to be nineteen.

Lassie V was Hey Hey, the last of the TV Lassies until the late 1980s. He was Lassie in the syndicated version of the show. His TV

Among Lassie's forest ranger pals were Jed Allan as Scott Turner, left, and Jack DeMave as Bob Ericson.

career ended in 1974, but he starred in live shows across the country for many years and died at eighteen.

Boy, son of Hey Hey, was Lassie VI. He starred opposite James Stewart in the 1979 feature film *Magic of Lassie* and danced on the stage of Radio City Music Hall with the Rockettes among other feats. Hey Hey died in 1989.

The Old Man was Lassie VII. He was the last Lassie trained by Rudd Weatherwax, while his training was completed under the hand of Rudd's son Robert. This collie starred in *The New Lassie*, the syndicated series that ran from 1989 to 1991.

Howard is Lassie VIII. He made his Lassie debut in 1993 at the Tournament of Roses Parade, has made numerous public appearances, and is the great-great-great-great-great-grandson of Pal. Howard starred in Animal Planet's *Lassie* series of the late 1990s.

And now there is Lassie IX, the dog artist formerly referred to as Laddie.

"Lassie's been everywhere," says Robert Weatherwax, who brought Lassie VIII and Laddie, his successor, to the Louise Mandrell Theater in Pigeon Forge, Tennessee, in the fall of 2000. It was the first time anywhere in the world that two Lassies performed publicly together. "My Lassie VIII is eleven, and I am retiring her at the end of the year and bringing on the new Lassie, IX," the trainer announced at the time.

Indeed, in October 2000 Lassie VIII retired, and Laddie walked onto the stage in East Tennessee as Lassie IX.

Lassie is buddies with Pamelyn Ferdin as Lucy Baker and Larry Pennell as Keith Holden during the 1972–1973 TV season.

"Lassie is an actor, not a trick dog," Robert insists. Among the things he has Lassie do on stage is a re-enactment of the first stunt when Pal swam the river and crawled up on the riverbank.

By the way, at most Lassie public appearances, fans can get Lassie's autograph. The photograph is stamped with a copy of the paw print of the original Lassie, Pal.

Robert Weatherwax says it takes several thousand hours to train a collie before it can begin to play Lassie. He gets Lassie to react by using his voice. "If I was using hand signals, I could not always place myself in the proper position. When I am dealing with a dog that does one hundred tricks, I could never separate all the hand signals. In the last Lassie movie, when the truck driver gets killed, I controlled how Lassie looked through my voice. I talked to him with a certain tone of voice and his head dropped. The most important lesson I learned from my father was to interpret the dog's role and direct him in such a way that the dog's acting is believable."

The late Robert Bray, who played Ranger Corey Stuart in the third *Lassie* TV format, expressed amazement, during an interview in 1966, at Lassie's intelligence, and at how the trainer handled him. He commented, "The other day we had a scene in which Lassie had to walk into a room, stop, look offstage, and then bark. The trainer gave Lassie a hand cue

Actor Jon Provost has had a lasting relationship with Lassie for more than thirty years. At left, he visits with Lassie VII, the star of *The New Lassie* in 1989, while at right he bonds with Lassie as a boy.

for the offstage look in the rehearsals. But when the camera started, the trainer's hand cue was not necessary. Lassie played the scene like a human. In fact, we have more trouble with humans missing cues and their stage marks on this show than we do with Lassie."

What is the magic of Lassie?

"Mother, apple pie, John Wayne, and Lassie. An institution—that's what my father called Lassie," says Robert Weatherwax. "My father was a genius. Lassie has a great image. He is honest, he's forthright, he stands for things people like to have. The collie dog has great beauty and that heritage.

"Older men and women walk up to me to shake my hand, and they say, 'We want to thank you and your father for giving us this wholesome, clean image throughout our childhood and throughout our children's childhood.' They appreciate Lassie being there all those years and being handled by one family. It's very heartwarming to hear people say thank you."

Robert has his own special memories of Lassie. Pal was his own personal pet. "The dog was born in 1940; I was born in 1942. I've been with Lassie forever. I thought everybody's dog was like this. He was the family dog; he lived in the house. I was the boy who worked with Lassie during my father's training sessions. I was the one he taught Lassie to give the kiss, nudge his arm, and things like that."

As a boy, he also became close friends with the late Tommy Rettig, Lassie's costar on *Jeff's Collie*. "I spent a lot of time with Tommy. He came out [to the ranch] to play with Lassie. My father liked to have the children come over and stay with the dog a while. We were good friends."

Ace Collins, the official Lassie historian and author of *Lassie: A Dog's Life*, says there are several reasons Lassie has remained a hero forever. "One is the simple fact that Lassie never did anything in a movie or a television show that a real dog couldn't do. We believe everything he did and that our dog could do it. And two, Lassie always represented what each of us should be. Lassie was more than a dog. Lassie represented the best that each human could be. So you had a dog that was believable and that in a very real way was a role model for everyone who watched the dog perform.

"Beyond that, it was the magic of Rudd Weatherwax. Lassie acted. There was something about the Weatherwaxes and the dogs they worked with. They were incredible."

Collins, a friend of Robert Weatherwax and Lassie, is one lucky dog himself. He has a sister to Lassie IX as the family pet.

In the meantime, Robert Weatherwax upholds the family tradition. He says, "I'm the last one that does this. I learned under my father. He passed the torch. We'll do it until I retire. You can't have a great dog and keep him in kennels and get him to act like he does. He must be in tune with my moods. You can only reach a dog like that by having him near you all the time."

Weatherwax shares one last tale. "I remember one time, someone came into the house and Lassie was lying on the couch, and the man said, 'You let that dog lie on the couch?'

"My father said, 'My dog bought that couch. He allows me to lie on the couch.'"

Life Goes On

ABC, 1989–1993, 83 episodes

Starring ***Bullet as Arnold ("the semi-wonder dog"),*** *Bill Smitrovich as Drew Thatcher, Patti LuPone as Libby Thatcher, Christopher Burke as Charles "Corky" Thatcher, Kellie Martin as Rebecca Thatcher, and Monique Lanier and Tracey Needham as Paige Thatcher.*

Life Goes On was one of TV's first dramas about a family with a mentally challenged child, in this case son Corky, an intelligent boy with Down syndrome who, though a few years behind the usual schedule, takes high school classes with his younger sister. The series looks at family life and dilemmas confronting young Rebecca, who wants to be accepted by her peers but at the same time is protective of her brother.

Arnold, "the semi-wonder dog," played by Bullet, sits for a family portrait with *Life Goes On* siblings Monique Lanier (left), Kellie Martin, and Christopher Burke.
Courtesy of Joann Curtis.

Bullet, the dog star of *Life Goes On,* was a mix of pit bull and Lab. He came into the hands of owner/trainer Richard Calkins at three months of age. "A friend brought him to me when he was a puppy. The dog jumped all over me and that was it. I loved him," says Calkins. "I taught Bullet things to help him act, to fit in whatever situation the director wants and to look natural. He got along great with the cast, and they all loved him, especially the boy. Chris Burke and the dog were real close. On the set they had time to spend together, so Chris would come around and play with Bullet. He liked to have him do a couple of little things, and the dog was crazy about him."

"Chris loved that dog. He loved Bullet," agrees Joann Curtis, who worked Bullet on the series and later adopted the dog as her own. "Chris would put his arms around him and kiss that dog. Sometimes he got a little too squeezy.

"He was not a mean dog. He was very loving, very affectionate, but very difficult. He would ride in the car with me and sit in the front seat. When I went to get gasoline, I would look over at him, and he would have his teeth back at everything. He was very particular about people [gas station attendants] coming near the car and watched every move they made. He had a protection thing over the car. And nobody could step in my driveway. I always knew who was coming. With Bullet, you didn't need a security system.

"He was a fantastic dog, marvelous. I had him in my home for fifteen years. He was my family, just like having a kid. I got so attached to the dog that I bought him off of Richard, and I retired him.

"He lived a very wonderful life. He had his own bedroom, his own TV, and his own VCR. I would play cartoons. He loved them—he loved Tweety Bird. I treated him like Lassie." Curtis, by the way, is the daughter of the late, great Lassie trainer, Rudd Weatherwax.

Bullet died in 1999 of kidney failure. "I cried when he died," says Curtis, who also owned the basset hound Pokey, who starred on *Our House.*

Original owner Calkins concurs that Bullet was one heck of an acting dog. "The thing he did the best was look natural. There was one episode of *Life Goes On* that they built around him," Calkins says. "There was a real cute gag in it where the lady of the house, Patti LuPone, walks into a casting office where they have thirty or forty dogs in a room. He walks in the door and sees a really cute white dog wearing a bow, and he falls in love. You get a look out of Bullet, and they go to a dream sequence where there's a huge field, and the boy and girl dogs start from different ends and jump over hedgerows and run and meet and cuddle in the middle."

Calkins said that Bullet, whose only other major credit was in a commercial for the Arizona state lottery, loved to eat everything, but one taste treat especially tempted him. "His favorite thing in the whole world was pizza crust from Palermo's in Hollywood on Vermont. This dog could single that pizza crust out from anything you could imagine."

And, well, that's *amore!*

The Life and Times of Grizzly Adams

NBC, 1977–1978, 37 episodes, 1 TV movie

Starring ***Bozo as Ben,*** *Number 7 as Mad Jack's burro, Dan Haggerty as James "Grizzly" Adams, Denver Pyle as Mad Jack, Dan Shanks as Nakuma, and Robbie Cartman as John Bishop.*

Set in the American wilderness of the 1850s, *The Life and Times of Grizzly Adams* is about a man accused of a crime he did not commit. He takes refuge in the countryside where he turns mountain man and happily coexists with the animals of the forest, especially a grizzly bear that he rescues as a cub from a mountain ledge.

The TV series was loosely based on the

true story of a bankrupt man who left Massachusetts and went into the wilderness where he killed and captured wild animals for profit, including a grizzly named Ben that wound up in a zoo in San Francisco.

The ursine star of the Grizzly Adams series was an almost-human bear by the name of Bozo. Owned and trained by Lloyd Beebe of the Olympic Game Farm in Sequim, Washington, the bear came into Beebe's possession in the early 1960s.

"People called her Bozo when she was little. We called her Boz," says Lloyd Beebe, a trainer of animals for Disney nature films and movies for twenty-eight years. Beebe's creatures have been featured in *Night of the Grizzly; Where the Red Fern Grows; The Legend of Lobo; The Living Desert; Vanishing Prairie; Those Calloways; Charlie the Lonesome Cougar; Nikki, Wild Dog of the North;* and *Never Cry Wolf,* among others.

Dan Haggerty starred as Grizzly Adams and Bozo was his bear Ben in *The Life and Times of Grizzly Adams.*

"Bozo was the best bear I've ever been around in all my life," swears Ken Beebe, Lloyd's son and the man who trained her for the majority of episodes of *Grizzly Adams.* "She was the best bear in the world, without a doubt. We got her at Deer Forest Park near Chicago. She was a sweetheart even then [at about age three].

"I think the guy that had her used to train bears for circuses. He must have been really rough on them. He had the two of them, and the other one wasn't any good, but Bozo kind of took it to heart—we taught her by being good to her. Everything she did, we gave her something or spent a lot of time with her. We loved her, and she loved us. I think she was glad we got to own her because we treated her like one of the family.

"She was very good; she could get upset a little bit once in a while. She was just as perfect as you could get. She was a lot better than most of the people who worked on the show. She was the kind of a bear you would just forget she was a bear. We treated her more like a big dog. She didn't like to be startled or surprised. Occasionally she would react like a bear, but when she was working, she was great."

"She was in every show," Lloyd says of

Bozo, "but we always had other bears. We might have used three or four, but she did it all. Once in a while we'd get stuck. Maybe one of them would start shedding, so we'd try not to use that one, but we had to use Boz."

At four hundred pounds, plus some, and standing somewhere between six and seven feet tall, "Boz was the first-unit bear," Ken says. "Rosie was the second unit [the bear that reacted with other animals and was used for long background shots], and Hoko was the third-unit bear. They were all good bears, but Bozo was the number one bear."

The Life and Times of Grizzly Adams was shot mostly in the mountains of Utah near the Wasatch National Park and Park City. Lloyd Beebe bought thirty acres of land with shade trees for the animals. In reality he practically built a new game farm in Woodland, Utah.

As the winter weather closed in on Utah, the crew moved south to places like Payson, Arizona, and Ruidoso, New Mexico.

"Dan Haggerty got along fine with Bozo. He was good with animals," says Lloyd. "He had been sort of an animal handler, and he was good with bears."

Actor Haggerty had been a professional animal trainer several years before he accepted the role of *Grizzly Adams.* He worked for nearly a year in Brazil on a *Tarzan* feature film and worked his own wolves and a pair of Siberian tigers in *When the North Wind Blows.*

He attributed his show-biz success to his love of animals. Haggerty told an NBC publicist in the mid-1970s, "I love 'em all. I've trained more than thirty African lions. At one time, we had five lion cubs in the house."

Haggerty also trained wolverines, eagles, elephants, chimpanzees, hawks, and wild boars. So when it came time to do a slow dance with a grizzly bear for a couple of seasons, he was the man for the job, and Bozo was the right bear.

TV Guide's Bill Davidson once wrote: "Who can forget the memorable scene in which Bozo awakened Haggerty by pulling the blanket from his bed, then chased him coquettishly through a meadow, then allowed Haggerty to chase her—equally coquettishly—and finally rolled over on her back in the grass to allow Haggerty to scratch her belly."

Of course, Bozo didn't work for peanuts. Lloyd says, "When Bozo was working, she got $3,500 a week. That bear, she'd do anything we wanted her to do. She rode up on a ski lift with us for that opening scene on a snowy mountain.

"She would follow along with Grizzly Adams. She had to do different things for different scripts. For one show she had to cook something on a fire, turn a stick while

it's cooking. Anything we could dream up. We had her rescuing little baby rabbits and carrying them around without hurting them. One time there were these little geese that got lost, and she let them follow her and she takes them back to the nest. She'd learn all those things.

"We'd never know what the next script was until like the Thursday night the week before. So we had to figure out the animals that would be needed. The different animals had to be ready to do things. For the bear, it would only take five minutes to teach her. She knew when people were getting ready to take pictures. She was always waiting for it. We gave her good bites of something we knew she liked. Once in a while we'd give her an ice cream cone, but she loved wieners."

She also had a sweet tooth. "She liked all sweets, hot dogs, peaches, fruit, marshmallows," says Ken Beebe. "We went through a lot of marshmallows. People in the store looked at me kind of strange when I bought several cases every week."

But Bozo wasn't above calling it a day before the director had finished. "They'd shoot so much that they would run out of film, and she might say, 'Hey, it's quitting time,'" Lloyd Beebe recalls.

The Beebes had one bear that had taught itself to throw rocks, so when Grizzly Adams was building a fireplace or piling up wood, the bear would toss him rocks or wood. That bear they renamed Rock Thrower.

And the Beebes furnished plenty of other woodland creatures for the TV series. Those included raccoons, coyotes, foxes, and Mad Jack's burro, Number 7. "We had about three of those burros," says Ken. "One we just used for braying. There were a couple that were really good."

They still have one of the burros used on the show (it may be Number 8) at their game farm eighteen miles south of Victoria, Canada, on the Olympic Peninsula of Washington state.

Grizzly Adams wasn't ole Boz's only acting credit. She was the mother of the grizzly in the 1970 film *King of the Grizzlies*, while she made her feature film debut in 1966's *Night of the Grizzly*.

"She was a very good bear, but she was a pet," says Lloyd Beebe, who has trained more than thirty bears over the years.

"Bozo died in 1999 at thirty-nine years of age," Lloyd says sadly of the bear that was like a member of his family. She is buried near a grove of old-growth fir trees on a hill at the game farm along with many other special animals the Beebes have known and loved. And Boz leaves a legacy.

"We got her daughter, who looks just like her," says Lloyd with a smile.

Little House on the Prairie

NBC, 1973–1983, 206 episodes

*Starring **Barney as Jack, Jeff as Bandit,** Michael Landon as Charles Ingalls, Karen Grassle as Caroline Ingalls, Melissa Gilbert as Laura Ingalls Wilder, Melissa Sue Anderson as Mary Ingalls Kendall, Lindsay and Sidney Greenbush as Carrie Ingalls, Karl Swenson as Lars Hanson, Richard Bull as Nels Oleson, Katherine MacGregor as Harriet Oleson, Alison Arngrim as Nellie Oleson Dalton, Jonathan Gilbert as Willie Oleson, Dabbs Greer as Rev. Robert Alden, Victor French as Mr. Isaiah Edwards, Merlin Olson as Jonathan Garvey, Patrick Laborteaux as Andy Garvey, Matthew Laborteaux as Albert Ingalls, Linwood Boomer as Adam Kendall, and Dean Butler as Almanzo Wilder.*

Based on the books by Laura Ingalls Wilder, *Little House on the Prairie*, set primarily in Walnut Grove, near Plum Creek, Minnesota, is the story of a homesteader and his family trying to survive, along with their neighbors and friends, during the late 1870s and 1880s.

"The dog on *Little House on the Prairie* was really named Barney," says trainer Genny Kerns, who worked with Barney in the *Little House* pilot episode and for the show's first season. "Barney mostly had to stay with the girls. He was a little shaggy mixed dog, bigger than Higgins (who starred as Benji). Just a real cute mutt with a happy personality. Melissa Gilbert is an animal nut, and she loved that dog, adored that dog."

Barney can be seen in the opening credits of the first season as Gilbert and the family dog run down a grassy hillside. That scene, by the way, was shot in Sonora, California.

Kerns recalls, "Barney was a very fine dog. When we did the interview with Michael Landon, they had looked at a lot of dogs. They had asked for a large, short-haired dog. I begged Hal Driscoll [the dog's owner] to let me show them Barney. 'Let me put him in,' I asked. So I took him along, and as soon as Michael saw him he says, 'Make him follow me.' I said, 'Go with,' and he did, and Michael said, 'That's the one I want.'

"He was a good picture dog, not brilliant like Higgins, but a good basic dog. He always barked on cue and hit his marks. I think he came from the Van Nuys pound. He was a good, basic, happy little working dog. His double's name was Jack.

"They changed dogs after I left and went with trainer Ray Berwick and a border collie after that."

Thus, the Ingalls family found themselves with a Scottish border collie named Bandit as the second season of *Little House* opened

Clockwise from left, posing with Barney, who played Jack on *Little House on the Prairie*, are Lindsay Greenbush, Karen Grassle, Michael Landon, Melissa Sue Anderson, and Melissa Gilbert.

with the episode "A Day at the Fair." This dog was named Jeff, and he had been the star dog at the Universal Studios Tour show, where Berwick and his assistants supplied and trained all the animals.

"Jeff was almost all white except for a little bit on the tail and the mask on the face," says Bryan Renfro, Berwick's nephew and the principal trainer on *Little House* once the second season began. "That's why Michael Landon called him Bandit [on the show], because of the mask on the face. It looked like the Lone Ranger mask with the black over the eyes.

"Ray had trained Jeff years earlier for the show at Universal. Ray and I both took him down to the studio, and Michael liked him right away. Michael Landon was great to work for because he knew exactly what he wanted.

"Jeff was a big border collie from Scotland. There were three from the litter: Jake, Jeffrey, and Joey. Jeffrey had to learn to do film work because he had been performing in a live show. He was middle-aged by this time, but he was a good dog."

Renfro recalls one difficult scene. "There was an episode with Ray Bolger playing a man who had come into town and fallen in love with the widow. So the kids, Melissa and Matthew Laborteaux, were trying to eavesdrop on the house and they had brought Bandit. They looked up in the window and the dog put its feet up and looked into the window, and they see a black cat on the table and the dog jumps in through the window up on the table going after the cat, and the dog and cat go all through the house and you hear the crashing and banging.

"Jeff was highly intelligent. He was very animated and wanted to go all the time. He learned things quickly. We had a double, who wasn't as animated. We sometimes used him for just lying around, and his name was Bandit."

Jeff, the border collie, worked at least three seasons on *Little House*. After retiring, he became one of Ray Berwick's pets and lived in Berwick's backyard where he passed away in peace.

The Little Rascals (Our Gang films)

The series of 221 Our Gang *films was produced between 1922 and the mid-1940s. It was syndicated in earnest as* The Little Rascals *for generations of television viewers beginning in 1955.*

*Starring **Pete (aka Petie) the Pup** and a cast of dozens of wonderful kids, pesky adults, and assorted pets and animals.*

Tracking the history of the *Our Gang/Little Rascals* films is one of the most difficult tasks in all of entertainment. Others have followed and will follow that trail. We'll keep our focus as much as possible at the canine level, which unleashes enough difficulties of its own.

Virtually all of the *Our Gang* films that are considered the true "canon" of the series were created before the invention of television. However, Pete the Pup qualifies as a TV pet because the re-release, beginning in the 1950s, of many of the *Our Gang* films into television syndication as *The Little Rascals* has had a bigger impact on many TV viewers of all ages than much of the made-for-TV programming in the last fifty years.

Many dogs played Pete the Pup. All of the Petes were American pit bulls, but they were trained to be naturally friendly and gentle rather than vicious and aggressive, as many modern pit bulls are trained to be.

There were also Pete-like pups who preceded (and succeeded) Pete—for example, Pal, the first *Our Gang* dog to appear fairly often. It was Pal's son who became the first real Pete and also the first *Our Gang* dog with the trademark ring around his eye. (It was a man-added ring from the dog's previous film work.) And by the last core *Our Gang* film, *Tale of a Dog* in 1944, it was a non-bulldog named Spotty that played a dog called Smallpox in the pivotal role. (Oh, for Pete's sake!)

The fact of the matter is that numerous dogs played Pete the Pup over the years. As with other celebrity animals, stand-ins and doubles would often make appearances on behalf of the "star" actor animal. While actor Pete was busy working on films, any number of Petes hit the publicity circuit doing personal appearances as Pete the Pup. And of course in the films themselves, there were some stunt Petes and doubles, but probably not all that often.

"The several Petes were very smart dogs,"

Pete the Pup, this time with the ring around his right eye, warbles into the microphone in an episode of *The Little Rascals.*

wrote *Our Gang* member Tommy "Butch" Bond in his 1994 book, *Darn Right, It's Butch: Memoirs of Our Gang.* "Harry Lucenay had worked with the original Pete, but the later Petes learned from Tony Campanero. . . . He handled those dogs by his dominating personality. I remember him looking at Pete and sternly commanding, 'Sit !' or 'Go!' And Pete would do as he was told. Was it fear, love, or just plain obedience? I don't know."

Pete the Pup (that is, the role as played by whichever of owner Harry Lucenay's string of Petes was best able to perform a particular behavior on film at the time) was central enough to the *Our Gang* franchise that he was, like some of the human actors he worked with, under a lengthy (especially in dog years) contract with Hal Roach Studios.

When Lucenay and Roach parted ways around 1932 (by then Lucenay was using the second dog to play the main Pete), Tony Campanero began training dogs to play Pete the Pup. It is his first Pete (the third true Pete) that was considered by many *Our Gang* members to be the definitive Pete the Pup—and is still considered so by many *Our Gang* fans to this day.

There's no doubt that the third Pete was a good dog, but it may also be that his popularity is attributable to his being lucky enough to be in some of the best *Our Gang* films and to have his era coincide with the emergence of George "Spanky" McFarland as perhaps the quintessential Rascal. (It also could be that subsequent Petes acted progressively more anemic.)

Whichever Pete the Pup is your favorite (and for some fans it's a favorite pastime just to spot how the ring around Pete's eye changes shape and moves from eye to eye—even within the same film), one thing is certain: With a span of popularity of nearly fourscore years, Pete the Pup is the most enduring dog star in the history of film.

Tommy Bond may have summed up Pete's role in *Our Gang* as well as anyone when he wrote in his 1994 memoirs, "The Gang wasn't complete without Pete. We were a family."

The Littlest Hobo

Syndicated, 1963–1965, 65 episodes
Canadian TV and syndicated, 1979–1985, 114 episodes

Starring ***London, Toro, Hobo ("Bo"), Thorn, Lance, Litlon, Venus, and Raura as London.***

The Littlest Hobo is about a vagabond German shepherd that wanders from place to place, through cities and the countryside, helping people and animals in a variety of ways. After performing good deeds of derring-do, he always continues on his way, preferring life on the open road.

The Littlest Hobo television series is a Canadian icon. It would not be fair to compare the German shepherds that portrayed London, the main character, to Lassie,

From left, Lance, Hobo, London, and Thorn shared the fun as Canada's top dog, London, the canine character on *The Littlest Hobo.*
Courtesy of Charles P. Eisenmann.

because of their unique qualities and talents, but in many ways, *The Littlest Hobo* of the 1960s and 1980s was to Canada what the *Lassie* series of the 1950s and 1960s was to the States.

The TV show has its roots in a 1958 feature film, also titled *The Littlest Hobo,* that opens up with a German shepherd riding into a California town on a freight-train boxcar.

But the real story behind *Hobo* goes back twelve years earlier to when professional baseball pitcher Charles P. Eisenmann bought a dog in 1946. A native of Wisconsin, the athlete served in the U.S. Signal Corps during WWII. After the war he traveled to California and opened a Los Angeles nightclub.

"I bought the dog in Los Angeles and called him London because I was stationed in London during the war. I left the dog at the nightclub with a friend while I played baseball," says Eisenmann, who played in the Pacific Coast League and the International League while under contract to the Brooklyn Dodgers and Chicago White Sox.

"I started teaching the dog, not training, using a common-sense attitude like you would teach a child. I didn't use words like 'come' or 'heel.' It contradicted everything I had read about dogs in training books, but the dog began responding intellectually.

"London was a great dog, but at that time I was still involved in baseball. Later the dog traveled with me to baseball games. After I quit the San Francisco ball club, I became sports editor in Carney, Nebraska [where he wrote a sports column titled *Doggone Truth*], and I became manager of the local ball club. London would take the jacket out to first base if the pitcher got a hit, and one night the other team's manager wanted to kick the dog off the field. I motioned to the dog to come up, and he pushed the manager out of the ballpark."

The night these antics occurred, *Life* magazine happened to be there with a photographer. The magazine did a three-page feature called "The Dog That Made the Team."

Eisenmann recalls, "We did the first film with only the one dog, London, shooting in Los Angeles. It took almost a year because we could only shoot when I was back in town from playing baseball. In that original *Littlest Hobo*, you see the dog doing practically everything after he comes into town on a freight train. He was just a dog and never belonged to anybody."

The success of the feature film eventually led to the 1963–1965 TV series, which was shot around Vancouver, British Columbia, except for three episodes that were filmed in Toronto. Among the guest stars in the original 1960s series were Edgar Bergen, Noah Beery Jr., Jim Davis, Pat Harrington Jr., Henry Gibson, and Keenan Wynn.

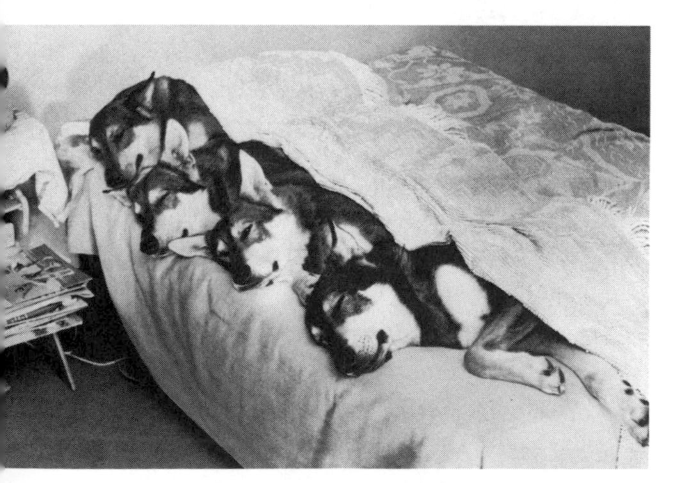

Four little Hobos take a dog nap.
Courtesy of Charles P. Eisenmann.

"I did the first series with London—the second in a series of three dogs by that name. Basically, the one dog would do about ninety percent of the show, and the only time we used the other dogs was just to run or jump. In my lifetime," says Eisenmann, "I have had three Londons, as well as dogs named Toro (one of my great dogs), Litlon, Lance, and Hobo; and two females, Venus and Raura. They were all registered German shepherds.

"All the dogs were educated with a vocabulary range of about 1,500 words, but my top dog had a 5,000-word vocabulary. You spend fifty-two years with dogs, twenty-four hours a day, and you learn what a dog is."

Not only did Eisenmann teach his dogs well, but he also taught them to be trilingual: "We are talking about dogs knowledgeable in three languages—English, French, and German.

"I toured eight months out of the year doing personal appearances in about every city in Canada and the United States from 1965 to 1979. Nobody ever had dogs this great in filming. Most dogs were conditioned to sounds, whereas I would teach a dog that a word had a meaning, not just the sound of it."

Using as many dogs as he did, Eisenmann had to be careful to select dogs that looked alike. He describes London as looking "almost like a timber wolf, a very light face, light eyebrows, white around a kind of brown neck, almost like it was drawn, and a flash of light color back of the front leg and a light chest with two brown markings.

"I had to work on that color, because it was very difficult to get it so that one could pass for the other. I would breed two females that I kept in Ontario. They would mate and I would keep the top dog out of the litter."

Before he wound down his career in 1992, Eisenmann figures he and his dogs performed three shows daily for eight months out of eighteen years. And he says that meant living in a hotel with five dogs, usually all males, but he never saw them get in a fight. Along the way, the troupe appeared on such TV programs as *The Today Show, The Mike Douglas Show, The Tonight Show,* and *Betty White's Pet Set.*

The Littlest Hobo series was reborn in color in 1979 and besides being a Canadian hit (it was filmed in and around Toronto, Ontario), it aired in sixty foreign countries and nearly forty American cities.

Actors who worked opposite London in the second series included Anne Francis, DeForest Kelly, Sheldon Leonard, Patrick Macnee, Barry Morse, Vic Morrow, Leslie Nielsen, Abe Vigoda, and Ray Walston.

And there was a twelve-year-old youngster named Megan Follows, who costarred with her entire family in a three-part episode titled "The Spirit of Thunder Rock." Follows went on in the mid-1980s to star in the title role of *Anne of Green Gables,* the highest-rated miniseries in the history of Canadian television.

The actress recalls that her mother and father portrayed her parents in the three-parter, and her brother and two sisters played her siblings. "My father played a geologist, and we were visiting him while he was doing his work. Then there was an earthquake. The villain was a poacher, and I was kidnapped and hidden in a cave or something like that. The dog has to save me or lead my parents to where I was.

"I remember that there were about seven dogs, and each dog had its own specialized area, like barking or running. I do remember if you were doing a scene with a dog, Mr. Eisenmann would be shouting commands at the dog, and it was hard for me to concentrate on my lines. You were essentially acting with a dog, and the trainer was near, and you'd have to block out the sounds of the trainer.

"I think he definitely loved his dogs. I remember the one called Bo a lot. The dogs had their own trailer, but they did not socialize."

For the second version of *The Littlest Hobo,* Eisenmann used a variety of dogs with different talents. "Toro was star of the first season, then Hobo [Bo] took over the last five years [also worked in those years were London Number 3, Lance, and Thorn]. Toro was the biggest dog among them, about 125 pounds, and did most of the work. Almost all of them lived to be thirteen to fifteen. Toro lived to be fifteen," says Eisenmann.

"I learned a great deal from each dog. The dog has the capacity to be hurt by words thrown at him. You have to be real careful with mind-over-matter language. My dogs became very alert in watching what I did, and I would say words to equal a given end. They were all educated, so it made it quite easy to switch them.

"The only time I used a dog other than the star would be to use a faster dog or a lighter dog, but not because the other star dog didn't know what to do. I always gave safety the first call.

"The dogs all had a capacity for shooting a film. Each dog would know automatically what I wanted just like an actor or an actress. These dogs had the capacity to do just about anything."

The only calamity of all of his years of television production was when his dog Thorn made a jump across a river and his hips came out of joint. The dog had to be put down.

Eisenmann and his dogs left the road and public appearances behind in 1992. Today he keeps just one German shepherd, Raura. His legacy remains with several feature films, 179 TV episodes of *The Littlest Hobo*, and three books: *Stop, Sit, and Think*; *The Better Dog, The Educated Dog*; and *A Dog's Day in Court*.

The Lone Ranger

ABC, 1949–1957, 221 episodes

*Starring **White Cloud and Tarzens White Banner as Silver;** Pet as Scout; Victor as Victor; Clayton Moore and John Hart as John Reid, the Lone Ranger; Jay Silverheels as Tonto; and Chuck Courtney as Dan Reid (the Ranger's nephew).*

Six Texas Rangers were trailing outlaw Butch Cavendish and his Hole in the Wall gang when they were ambushed and left for dead. An Indian passing through the valley discovers the sole survivor and nurses him back to health. Together, Tonto and the Lone Ranger form a duo that upholds law and order across seven states of the Old West. The Ranger wears a black mask as a disguise and uses silver bullets as a reminder of how precious human life is.

With its origins in the 1933 radio show, the video version of *The Lone Ranger* began every episode with the words: "A fiery horse with the speed of light, a cloud of dust, and a hearty hi-yo Silver! The Lone Ranger! With his faithful Indian companion, Tonto, the daring and resourceful masked rider of the plains led the fight for law and order in the early West. Return with us now to those thrilling days of yesteryear. The Lone Ranger rides again!"

We return now to the early days of the TV show that starred a horse named Silver. But who was that white horse? Uncovering his identities proves more difficult than removing the Lone Ranger's mask. Parts of the horse's history remain clouded, but many facts about the two main star Silvers have been revealed.

The first Silver on the TV series probably

worked only the pilot, which was actually a three-part series explaining the origin of the Lone Ranger.

"The horse was owned by Fat Jones of Fat Jones Stables," says horse trainer Kenny Lee, who grew up on Fat Jones's ranch. "Bud Pope was the wrangler and ramrod on that show, and when the pilot sold, the horse went to the Hooker family and trainer Bud Pope."

Horseman Ken Taylor, a good friend of the late Clayton Moore, also believes the first white horse was used only in that three-part pilot before the show was sold to a network.

Now enters the first star Silver of the show. "He was just a great, great horse. Silver was dog gentle, and Clayton loved him," says Bill Ward, the horseman who owned the original Silver and who also worked the series as a stunt double for star Clayton Moore.

"Silver's real name was White Cloud, and he had a brother, a younger horse, not quite as full-bodied but more athletic, who was named Blanco. Silver was about twelve years old when *The Lone Ranger* began filming in July 1949," Ward says. "Silver, Blanco, and Traveler [a third white horse] all had pink skin and black eyes. All three had Tennessee Walking Horse in their breeding.

"All of the horses that did the first bunch of *Lone Ranger* episodes were owned by the Hookers [a father and his three sons, Bud, Joe, and Hugh]," says Ward, who was familiar with the family because he worked at their stables in exchange for horseback riding favors when he was a teen.

"When they made *The Lone Ranger*, they needed white horses. The producers came to

Clayton Moore's Lone Ranger and Silver chase after bad guys in another adventure of *The Lone Ranger*.
Courtesy of Dick Warlock.

the Hooker farm and looked at their horses and rented them from us. Scout [Tonto's mount] was originally named Pet, and he was another of the Hooker horses."

The Hookers brought the horse that became Silver from Texas by way of Vallejo, California, Ward recollects. Hugh Hooker and Ward later became partners in supplying horses for TV and film. In about 1949, Ward bought all the horses from the Hookers, building up a nice herd for his Studio Stables, which, Ward says, furnished riding stock to many of the independent production companies of the 1950s. That included the horses for such such TV fare as *Sky King*, *The Adventures of Annie Oakley*, *The Adventures of Champion*, *Buffalo Bill Jr.*, and *Range Rider*, plus the Gary Cooper western film classic *High Noon*.

But back to the fiery white horse with the speed of light.

"Silver did most everything. Either I was

riding him or Clayton did it. Clayton could ride pretty good. He could do the stirrup mount and ride off on Silver," Ward says.

Moore, who died in December 1999, recollected in his 1996 autobiography, *I Was That Masked Man*, that the original Silver was out of the Hooker stables, just as Ward states. Moore wrote in his book, "First I had to attend to the horse—after all, where would the Lone Ranger be without Silver? I went to a well-known horseman, Hugh Hooker. He and his family raised and trained horses out in the San Fernando Valley and often provided mounts for the movies.

"Hugh had two white horses for me to consider, but we never used the second one; he was not as handy or as good-looking. The first horse was the stallion that I used. He was a gentle and good-looking stud. . . . Although his name was Silver on the screen, on the set we nicknamed him Liver Lip. You can see in some of the publicity pictures he had a big bottom lip. We made fun of him because the bit he used had a copper roller and he would tongue that copper roller so his lip would hang down."

Silver's owner, Ward, tells more about his fine horse. "I broke Silver and had him where he would stand for anyone and anything. He was a gentle horse, and you could do anything in the world with him if you rode him properly. I remember one scene in the feature film when we were at Kenab, Utah, and I was up on top of a mountain, a couple of hundred yards up, and they were shooting from the ground. They wanted to see the Lone Ranger on the horse from the ground, so I had to be so close to the edge of a straight-down drop that I couldn't see the ground on the right of me, and Silver just went on right around.

"The horse would get barley for breakfast and alfalfa hay for the evening. He didn't do any tricks, but he reared good. He was about seventeen hands tall and full flesh all the time. I washed him off every morning with cold water.

"When I quit doubling the Lone Ranger, I turned the job over to Allen Pinson. The last time I rode Silver was in the first *Lone Ranger* feature film" (*The Lone Ranger*, released in 1956).

Stuntman Pinson recalls that there were possibly three horses that served as Silver when he worked the series between 1955 and 1957: one white horse for the rear, one for close-ups, and one for running scenes. Pinson also remembers that "Clayton did all the rears. He got extra pay for that," a fact that Moore verifies in his book.

"Silver Number 1 was brought back for one scene in *The Lone Ranger* movie," Moore wrote. "Remember the opening scene in front of Lone Ranger Rock, where Silver rears up? That's me. I did all the rearing of the horse. . . . Because every time they used that shot to advertise the show, I got fifty dollars."

By the early mid-1950s, the first Silver had pretty much finished his work with the masked rider, other than some guest appearances in the 1956 *Lone Ranger* film. He had also worked in the 1950 feature film *Baron of Arizona*, and by the time a second *Lone*

The Lone Ranger and Tonto, Clayton Moore and Jay Silverheels, are poised for action as their steeds Silver and Scout relax beneath the western sky.
Courtesy of Louise Thomas.

Ranger feature film, *The Lone Ranger and the Lost City of Gold*, was released in 1958, Ward's Silver was getting some age on him but was still in pretty good shape. "I ended up selling him to Ace Hudkins when I went out of the business in the late 1950s," Ward says.

Veteran stuntman Bobby Herron recollects the white horse coming to his stepfather Ace Hudkins's stables. "We had the horse. He loved to get you against the wall and lean on you—not hurt you, but lean on you so you couldn't get out. The horse had a sense of humor. Silver was by then an older horse and only used for close-ups. He didn't have much schooling, but he was good to do the big rear."

Now we move on to a new Lone Ranger and a new Silver.

Actor John Hart played the Lone Ranger from 1952 to 1954, and he rode a different white horse. "We became good friends over the fifty-two episodes that I did. He was half Arabian and half saddle bred," Hart says of his Silver. "He was a beautiful white horse. He was a stallion and high-strung, and everybody had trouble riding him. He threw most people off.

"When I got the job, I took him out and rode him for weeks before we started shooting. We got to be friendly and went out on some of the trails in Griffith Park. He behaved beautifully for me. He had a beautiful high-running gait.

"You couldn't miss this guy. He was such a beautiful horse, no pink on him, black nostrils, just pure white, a gorgeous horse. I really cared for that horse."

Earl Bellamy, the director of many episodes

The second man to play the Lone Ranger on television was actor John Hart. He rode a different Silver than Clayton Moore used in the earlier episodes.
Courtesy of John Hart.

of *The Lone Ranger*, remembers the second Silver. "It was a beauty and pretty well trained. He had a great head," he says.

Clayton Moore clearly knew the difference between the two main mounts, as he explained in his book: "The first one was the horse we called Liver Lip because of his protruding lower lip. He had a dark spot on his hindquarters that had to be dyed white before filming. The second one came along while John Hart was starring as the Lone Ranger. Though it was rarely visible on the show itself, the horse 2 had a black spot in his left ear—the only black spot he had on his body. That's how I can tell the Number 1 horse from the Number 2 horse in photographs. Otherwise they were nearly identical."

Moore continued, "I never took the Number 1 horse on tour. Both were specially trained for motion pictures, but Silver Number 2 was very camera-wise. Sometimes we used a motor to start the camera, and his ear would twitch when he heard it; he knew when the camera was on.

"I worked out Silver Number 1 very often. The second horse, bought for John Hart, stayed with Glenn Randall."

Where did Silver Number 2 come from? He was foaled on a farm near Danville, Iowa, on September 2, 1945. Since his daddy's name was Tarzen, and he was born on Victory in Japan Day, the horse was christened Tarzens White Banner.

The original owner and trainer was Virginia Lee Perry. She sold the horse at age four to Charles Van Dyke of Peoria. Van Dyke sold the animal to *Lone Ranger* producer George Trendle in 1949. The savvy Trendle gave the stallion a new name, Hi Yo Silver, which he had registered. The second star Silver, who was 15.2 hands tall and weighed 1,150 pounds, was ridden by Hart and later Moore and, after the series and movies were done, was used in special appearances.

In the spring of 1954, the ownership of the *Lone Ranger* changed hands, and Jack Wrather came into possession of the TV show and all the character names connected to it, including Silver and Scout.

Louise Thomas knew Wrather's horses as well as anyone, as she cared for Silver Number 2 and his partner, Scout. Thomas says, "The last Silver was born in 1945. He was owned by Jack Wrather. Clay [Clayton Moore] and my ex-husband Wayne Burson [the stuntman for Tonto, Jay Silverheels] and I worked for the Wrather Corporation. Wrather took the show on the road in 1957 to 1958 [on tour to fairs, rodeos, Madison Square Garden]. We had Silver and Scout. We kept them at our ranch in Shadow Hills near Sunland, California.

"We had Silver when he died. He was a standard bred. Silver was one of the few horses with pink skin. After Wrather made the tour of all the fairs (a losing affair financially), Clay and Wayne and I formed a company. We rented the horses and names from Wrather and went on tour ourselves."

The company of Moore & Burson created a ninety-minute show, and in the course of two summers (1959–1960) covered much of the U.S. and Canada with the masked man, Silver, and Scout. Thomas recalls, "Silver was wonderful, but he didn't really do a lot of tricks. He would lay down, and Clay would spread a blanket over both of them. Then Silver would reach over and pull the blanket away. He would count. Clay would do his gun twirling. We had a skit where we took Chuck Courtney along, the actor who played his nephew, Dan Reid. Courtney rode a horse we called 'Son of Silver.' Its real name was Bishop, and he looked just like Silver." (In the TV series Reid rode a horse named Victor.)

"Clay always would hug Silver at the end of a night," Thomas says. "He really truly loved the horse. There was something between the two of them."

Louise's four children were the lucky ones, as they kept Silver and Scout practically as backyard pets. She says her children exercised the two horses daily. Silver, who weighed about 1,200 pounds, liked children. "He was a horse you could trust," she remembers.

Of Scout, Tonto's mount, she recalled that he, too, was a great horse. "He was a spotted pinto with beautiful markings. He was a little feistier than Silver."

Wrather eventually sold Scout to a movie studio after the series wound down. Thomas and her family began boarding Silver and Scout in 1956. Silver Number 2 was retired in 1962 and died January 1, 1974, at twenty-nine years old on the Burson ranch in Shadow Hills, California, of old age.

"He was such a sweetheart," Thomas says of the famous white horse of Hi-Yo! fame.

Besides Silver Number 1, stuntman/horseman Bill Ward had another white horse that became famous. Named Traveler, because Ward admired General Robert E. Lee, who had a white horse named Traveler during the Civil War, this horse had been raised by Ward since he was a yearling.

"I always was looking for a white horse. Someone told me about a horse in Burbank. I went to look at him and he had not been broke nor ridden. I think I paid four hundred dollars for him," says Ward.

Traveler was a stunt double for Silver on *The Lone Ranger*. Ward said in one interview:

"Traveler did all the stunt work for the first two years, but Clayton never rode him ever. There was another white horse that we used for insert scenes, and we used a white horse named Ratchethead on the features."

Ward later said that Traveler in fact did not work the western series. He did recall that cast horses, such as Silver and Scout, earned twenty-five dollars a day, while the other horses got five dollars.

"I did a picture with Traveler called *The Merry Widow* [released in 1952] and also *Snowfire. The Ballad of a Gunfighter* was the last picture he made," Ward says of Traveler. "He was a hard horse to break."

Stuntman Whitey Hughes, who worked on *The Lone Ranger*, exercised Traveler many times in the early 1950s, and he shares some golden memories. "That horse was a very difficult horse for some men to be around. Ward kept the horse in stables near the Griffith Park area [of Los Angeles]. He'd ask me to exercise Traveler. I'd put the bridle on him and ride him all around Griffith Park Trail.

"He was a beautiful animal. Bill [Ward] had a fellow that put that rear on him. He was a high-school horse, one that had been trained. He did a lot of little tricks like counting and lying down, but he was not really a highly trained trick horse. Traveler had dark eyes, the eyes that they liked, and he was very nice and gentle except with certain people. If he didn't like a person, he'd take after them."

"Traveler was a nice horse, a good-looking horse—snow white," another top-notch trainer, Kenny Lee, says. Years later, the horseman worked his own hand on five different Silvers that were used in the 1981 feature film *The Legend of the Lone Ranger*, one of which really had the name Silver.

Stuntman Jerry Vance, a close friend of Bill Ward, remembers Traveler well. "I met Bill Ward at Studio Stables in Burbank in about 1952. He had Traveler then, and the horse was just phenomenal. He followed Bill around like a puppy.

"Bill would jump from a tree or a roof onto Traveler, and he could always trust him to stand. Bill could stand as far away as you could stand and still see him, and move his hand and make Traveler rear up. That horse was so handy. Bill was standing in a riverbed one time, a good five foot up to the bank, and he was being chased, and Bill just turned around and kicked Traveler, and he jumped right up on the ledge and took off. Nine times out of ten when you saw Traveler, it was Bill Ward in Clayton's costume. Bill trained him with hand signals, and he would use body language to talk to Traveler.

"He loved carrots, of course. He weighed about 1,100 pounds and stood 16 hands tall. He had a very thin neck, more like an American saddle bred. When he moved, he held his head up high. Traveler was a thin horse, not heavyset. He never put much weight on, and he had black eyes that were kind of pretty. Bill took real good care of him. Nobody could clean his stall except Bill Ward. Oh, he could be stubborn.

"He was a very popular horse in town, especially in the 1950s. He was in a lot of romantic and swashbuckling movies. Maureen O'Hara rode him. Barbara Stanwyck rode him. He liked ladies. He just didn't like guys cleaning his stall. Traveler didn't like to be heavy handed."

"Traveler was difficult with some people. I got along with him pretty good," says stuntman Dick Warlock. "I remember one time he bit Bill Ward and picked him up by his shoulder and actually threw him in the air. But he was good with me and high spirited. I rode Traveler when I doubled Marty Robbins in *Ballad of a Gunfighter* [1960]."

"Traveler did a lot of heavy stuff in that film," Vance recalled. "He hid behind rocks, and Bill Ward jumped off a stagecoach onto him."

Eventually Traveler came into the hands of Richard Saukko, recalls Warlock. "Saukko would dress up as Tommy Trojan, and he rode the horse at USC [University of Southern California] football games."

Saukko passed away in 1992, but his widow, Pat Saukko, continues the tale of how one of the Lone Ranger's horses became a mascot for the USC Trojan football team.

In 1959, Saukko started riding Traveler in the Rose Parade, his widow says. Then in 1960, Bill Ward was getting into horse racing and wanted to retire his horse. Saukko offered a home for Traveler, and Ward was satisfied the horse would be well treated. Because of Saukko's appearances in the Tournament of Roses Parade, horse and rider began making other appearances.

In 1961, the Tournament of Roses referred Saukko and his horse, Traveler, to USC officials as a possible riding team for USC football games at the Los Angeles Memorial Coliseum. Thus Saukko and Traveler began their role as Tommy Trojan and a university mascot.

"Traveler was born a Tennessee Walking Horse with some Arabian blood in 1948. Ward gelded him two weeks before Saukko got him in 1960, and Richard rode the original Traveler at USC football games 1961 through 1967," Pat Saukko says.

When the original Traveler became lame, Saukko got a second white horse named Little Society, a purebred Tennessee Walker, whom Saukko rode from 1968 to 1978. A third Traveler, a purebred Arabian stallion named Ibn Bent Sulejman, then appeared from 1979 through 1988. In 1988, the stallion's son took over the Traveler duties as mascot. Saukko rode officially at the USC football games until 1988, when Saukko's health started to fail. Saukko and Traveler made their final appearance as a team in December 1991. After Saukko passed away in March 1992, his widow continued parading and bringing Traveler to the football games as the beloved mascot. In 1996 an Andalusian gelding started appearing as

Traveler. There have been four riders since Richard Saukko, but the Saukko family has remained the proud owner of Traveler.

Pat Saukko recalls that her late husband once told her that Fernando Lamas rode Traveler in the 1952 film *The Merry Widow* and that Leo Carrillo, Pancho of TV's *The Cisco Kid*, rode Traveler in many Rose Parades. The original Traveler died in October 1975 of old age and was buried on a ranch in Chino, California.

And like the Lone Ranger had Tonto, Traveler had his own saddle pal, a strawberry roan named Red, which also belonged to Bill Ward. "Red was Traveler's buddy. Red quieted Traveler down, and when Red was with him, Traveler behaved," says Vance. "Every time you saw an extra riding a sorrel horse with a blaze face in *The Lone Ranger*, that was Red, and Red was also in *Ballad of a Gunfighter*."

So, who was that white horse? Hi-Yo, Silver! of course.

Longstreet

ABC, 1971–1972, 24 episodes

Starring ***Blanco, Snow, and Blizzard as Pax;*** *James Franciscus as Mike Longstreet; Marilyn Mason as Nikki Bell; Peter Mark Richman as Duke Paige; Ann Doran as Mrs. Kingston; and Bruce Lee as Li Tsung.*

Set in New Orleans, *Longstreet* is about an insurance investigator who has lost his wife and his sight in an explosion after some enemies tried to keep him off their case. With the aid of an electronic cane and a seeing-eye dog, he continues to solve cases for the Great Pacific Casualty Company.

Pax, the white German shepherd who aids James Franciscus in *Longstreet*, was played most of the time by Blanco, who was trained by Karl Lewis Miller.

In the early 1970s, the white German shepherd was not a popular breed, but the oddity of the type got Blanco the job.

"We had a hard time casting dogs," says master trainer Miller. "Producers and directors always want to be the deciding factor, so we go through with dozens of animals. They looked at numerous German shepherds, but couldn't find what they wanted.

"Lou Schumacher and I explained that we couldn't get a real seeing-eye dog in the movies because of legalities, and because the stop-and-go-pace would detrain a seeing-eye dog, and because movie commands would detrain a seeing-eye dog."

The pair made their point, so here came the regular German shepherds. "They're looking at every combination of German shepherd you can see: black shepherds, brown shepherds; and they kept saying, 'We need something different.'

"Schumacher said, 'I have a friend that has a white shepherd. Do you want to look at a white shepherd?' We took the white shepherd in, and they said, 'Hey, now that's different.'

"We emphasized the point that they were not so popular, but they were unusual. And white stands for peace, and Pax means peace, and since we would be shooting lots of night shots, the white dog would show up great."

The white was right. So Miller and Schumacher got to work. "We had to get on the phone looking for more white shepherds as backups. I ended up acquiring four white shepherds and enough preparation time to figure out which one is the best lead dog."

Miller recalled that two of the white shepherds were acquired from private parties, one came from an animal shelter, and the fourth from a breeder. "So the four dogs went into training for the same purpose. They were all great dogs personally, but one was very explosive in his actions, not aggressive, but he would go nuts and at other times he would be calm.

"With another one, because of the skin pigmentation, we actually had to color his nose black to make it look like the other ones."

Miller dropped one of the four, but *Longstreet* proved to be the only show where all three dogs could literally have played the part of Pax, and few folks would have noticed the difference. "Blanco was the character dog, the expressive dog," says Miller, "but he wasn't physically fit to do the jumps and the action. He was good by the fire and would stay calm, and he was good for snarls. Another dog was good for running and jumping and attacking, and the other dog we saved for lining up the lights in rehearsal.

James Franciscus was a blind criminal insurance investigator who used an electronic cane and had a white German shepherd as a pet and partner. The dog was portrayed by three shepherds: Blanco, Snow, and Blizzard.

"It was the one show where I could interchange any one for any particular scene, and I did it a lot with Blanco, Snow, and Blizzard. And that is Blanco you see in all the photographs."

Mad About You

NBC, 1992–1999, 164 episodes

*Starring **Maui as Murray,** Paul Reiser as Paul Buchman, Helen Hunt as Jamie Buchman, John Pankow as Ira Buchman, and Hank Azaria as dog-sitter Nat.*

Set in New York City, this show follows the newly- and then not-so-newlywed adventures of filmmaker Paul and wife Jamie Buchman, a sometime public relations executive, and their high-strung group of friends and family.

Maui is a border collie mix who was born around 1986. Trainer Betty Linn talks about how Maui got into show business: "My boss, Boone Narr, owner of Boone's Animals for Hollywood, found Maui and his mother, Bingo, at the animal shelter. Bingo did the movie *Bingo,* and Maui was her double in that movie. Then he did a few commercials and this and that and then he landed the role of Murray on *Mad About You.*"

But Maui wasn't the original choice for the role. Linn says, "They chose a dog named Smiley, a boxer mix, who was a very, very good dog, but he wound up not being cut out for that particular four-camera show. Smiley was more of a movie dog as opposed to a sitcom dog, I think. A great, wonderful dog, but just maybe not quite cut out for that particular show."

Maybe it was his work ethic that gave Maui an edge for a show like *Mad About You.* Linn says, "His motivation was mostly because he wanted to work. He is not a chow hound, so he really doesn't care about treats. He likes to play with balls and toys but, again, not as a real motivation like a lot of dogs. He really did it because he liked it and he wanted to please you, and so if I walked up and gave him a pat and told him 'good dog,' that was the best thing you could do for him.

"Once he got used to audiences and the clapping and whatnot, I would take him up into the audience after he was finished with his hardest scenes, and then I would let him just cruise around the audience. He loved it, I mean he just loved the attention of people petting on him and everything. He almost loved it too much.

"Maui just sort of loved all people. The one thing about him is he wasn't really an in-your-face sort of dog. He didn't love to lick people or he didn't want you to be right in his face or he didn't want you to pull him toward you and that kind of thing. He loved to be petted, but he wasn't one to come and jump on you and lick you in the face."

Still, he enjoyed the perks of his profession and station. "He had his own dressing room on *Mad About You,* and whenever we would travel, he'd get a first-class seat next to me and then usually get picked up in a car, either a town car or limousine. He's had so many limo rides. I always laugh because I say that I just sort of rode around on his coattails and got treated very well because of him. And the hotels were always very happy to see him. I would always leave his photograph with his paw prints and that kind of made everybody happy. Some of the best hotels would bring him a certain doggie platter. One place brought this big red doggie sleeping bag for him to sleep on and a crystal water bowl and stuff like that."

If Maui was treated like a king, it's not surprising, because he was top dog on one of TV's top shows of the 1990s. Betty Linn says, "I think what made him the best for that show is that he knows a lot of behaviors, good ones, but he can also take direction very, very well and hit a 'mark' that isn't there. For a four-camera show, that's so important because you can't talk. It's all with hand signals, and you're behind four cameras that are moving very quickly. So he would learn. I could put a piece of tape on the floor and show him the tape and send him to it once or twice and then pull the tape up, but he knew that mark. You didn't have to go touch his foot on the mark—he just knew, so once the tape was pulled up, he knew that.

Maui ties one on as Murray on *Mad About You.*

"Sometimes on four-camera shows, animals can get confused because they are entering or exiting the same direction in several scenes on the same night. So you just put your tape mark down if he's got to enter the same way. I'm back at the camera doing a point that means go to your spot or your mark or go to the person or go get up on the couch or go put your feet up somewhere. And so I could just remind him once before we're shooting and he was great. He just would pattern very, very well."

Most of all, Linn says, Maui knew how to be natural. "There's a fine line between having animals really, really, really into you and working very snappy and doing their tricks, or being a little more relaxed, which is where I sort of kept Maui, where he didn't have to stare at me all the time. He could look around the room, he could feel comfortable to turn and watch the actors as they would come and go, but still be able to take a cue from me. Getting an animal to be loose is very difficult because you always want your animal just right there and to take the cues just really quick and really sharp, but often when you have that you don't have an animal that looks very natural. They're always staring at the trainer or the trick comes really snappy. So I let Maui relax to the point where he could be natural. He came across just like he was the Buchmans' dog. He was just there."

Linn remembers one time when Maui was especially convincing in naturalness. "There was a show where they wanted him to lick himself and the dialogue was something to the effect of, 'Yeah, I wish I could lay around and lick myself all day' or something like that. The production people came to me and said, 'Do you think you could do this?' and I said, 'Yeah.' So I trained it. It was a behavior, and I could hold him so that he had his head down and then I point, because I can't talk. I point and that cue in that particular scene meant for him to start licking himself between his legs. Well, the audience and everybody thought it was real—that he was doing it and we didn't want him to. They roared! If the audience doesn't think it's trained, I guess you're doing your job pretty well."

Linn has several favorite *Mad About You* episodes that featured Maui. "I would say obviously the most famous episode featuring him was 'Go Get the Mouse,' where Murray is chasing an invisible mouse. He would run into walls and whatnot. It was very, very fun to shoot.

"Another memorable episode was 'The Last Scampi,' in which Maui's real mother, Bingo, plays Murray's mother, Mona. We did a whole scene in the park with her." Another episode that stands out is "Just My Dog," where the Buchmans decide Murray should audition to do a TV commercial. "That was very difficult," says Linn, "because there was a scene in that where Maui had to do a 'work away.' Doing a work away and doing tricks on a four-camera show is incredibly difficult, but between the director and me and the actors, there would be a little space in between the lines of dialogue where I would say sit or lie down or roll over, so that he could hear my voice and do the behavior while he was facing away from me. It turned out excellent, and I was very happy with him."

To keep Maui fresh, Linn usually did a lot of scoping out of his scenes with the rest of the cast and crew before beginning work with Maui for the scenes. "They would tell me what they would want, and I would say OK, and then I would train the behavior with Maui on my own while everybody else wasn't there. I wouldn't want to burn him out on a lot of the things I was training him on. I would usually come out for the first run-through and then prepare to work with him.

"There was a show called 'Home' where Murray got the next door neighbor's dog pregnant, and she was in the room having puppies. The director wanted to know if Maui could pace, and I said, 'Sure,' and found out which way and this and that. I trained it—again it was just two taped marks, and I just pointed one way and then the other, one way and then the other. And nobody had seen this yet and so for the run-through, they wound up laughing so hard they couldn't even go on with the scene. This happened three times or so. The director finally just had to say, 'OK, OK, just stop Maui. We've got to go on with this scene.' Things like that happened a lot because Maui was really a character and did some really funny things."

After *Mad About You*, Maui did a few movies, including *Airhead*, and commercials for Pizza Hut and others. He also was the first celebrity dog to use Program dog food. But he is now enjoying a well-deserved retirement and living the good life by the pool in Boone Narr's backyard with mother Bingo. His friend Betty Linn drops by occasionally to visit.

Magnum, P.I.

CBS, 1980–1988, 162 episodes

Starring ***Whiskey, Brutus, and Dominique as Zeus and Apollo;*** *Tom Selleck as Thomas Magnum; John Hillerman as Jonathan Higgins; Roger E. Mosley as T. C.; and Larry Manetti as Rick.*

This hour-long drama follows the laid-back investigations and hunches of private detective Thomas Magnum as he operates from the mansion (managed by Higgins and his Dobermans) in Hawaii, which he is allowed to use in exchange for his expertise at security.

Though they lived in a tropical paradise on *Magnum, P.I.*, the Dobermans owned in the series by Higgins didn't always live the good life. According to trainer Scott Hart, "One came from like a junkyard-type area. That was Whiskey. And Brutus I bought just by looking at a photo. He was out of Oklahoma, I believe. And then the third main dog that we used was Dominique. Then we had assorted other back-up dogs that would last for a year or two, but wouldn't be happy or whatever."

As far as which dog played Zeus and which played Apollo, Hart confesses, "Well, you know, they were interchangeable, but Whiskey, Brutus, and Dominique were the three main ones, and all three were there pretty much through the whole series. Actually, the very first year they used local dogs and brought me over to train them. But after that, they asked me to get all of my own dogs.

"We used Dominique, since she was the female, to do a lot of the leaping. But they all liked leaping on a back or doing the take-downs or things like that. We always used her because she was the little one, and it gets kind of tiring after five or ten takes of having a one-hundred-pound dog jump on you. She did great at that. She was our little speed demon.

"It took Whiskey about a year or a year-and-a-half before he'd trust people. But we'd always take the dogs to the little parties that they'd have pretty much after each day. Whiskey would go in, and people would toss him sushi or things like that, and then he started realizing that not everybody was trying to set him up to hurt him, and he started having a lot of fun after that.

"Brutus was cowed by Whiskey because Whiskey was the old junkyard dog that wasn't going to put up with the young stud, so we had to really watch the two. They always worked together, but Whiskey was always the more aggressive, and we had to make sure nothing happened. Brutus always kind of watched Whiskey as much as he watched me, but they both did very good hits or studio attacks, which are a lot different than what a normal attack would be."

Brutus may have been the meekest of the dogs on land, but in the water, he was pure Neptune. "Brutus was a real retriever in the ocean," says Hart. "But Whiskey didn't like the ocean. He'd go in and do stuff, but Brutus would dive down and retrieve stuff off the bottom of the pond where we were working, and he was the best one working in the water."

So what was it that motivated the killer instinct in the *Magnum* Dobermans? "We actually got written up once. It was in the *National Enquirer* that the killer Doberman on *Magnum P.I.* was actually working for chocolate doughnuts. Whiskey, who was the problem child at that point, did love chocolate doughnuts. He'd eat a chocolate doughnut before he'd eat meat, but we couldn't give it to him because it wasn't all that good for him. He could have some but not a lot. There was one scene when the dogs had to keep watching John Hillerman, who played Higgins on the show. What we did was give John this Texas doughnut. It was this huge, huge chocolate doughnut, and he held it over his head as he paced back and forth in front of them as he was talking, and the dogs' eyes never, never left him."

Hart adds, "Brutus and Whiskey were two pretty amazing dogs. It was very interesting working Whiskey and getting him to trust everybody. He wanted to play, but he just didn't know quite how when I got him, so when he would play with the ball, he would always end up popping it. Or if he grabbed you by the hand when you were playing with him, he'd break skin. He just didn't understand. He was playing and having a good time, but he didn't understand how strong he was, which scares the heck out of a lot of people, to see all of a sudden they're bleeding, while I'm trying to tell them, 'Oh no, he's just playing.'

"By the third season, you could just put the dogs next to John Hillerman and go grab a cup of coffee. They knew never to leave his side. Wherever John was, they knew they were supposed to be there, too.

"We had one funny gag with them where they were supposed to have gotten into Robin Masters's wine cellar. Just as a gag—I didn't tell the director—I taught the dogs to hold a wine bottle in their mouths, and I had them laying with their feet up in the air with this wine bottle. That was a pretty funny gag, but they figured that drunken dogs wouldn't get past the censors."

Another moment that involved gagging was invisible to the censors. "There was a time where John Hillerman had to walk down the staircase," recalls Hart, "and it was the day after we had to feed each of the dogs probably four or five pounds of raw prime rib. So that next day they had to walk down the staircase with John and stop three-quarters of the way down where John and Tom had to carry on this conversation. What was happening was the dogs were letting off gas something fierce. Nobody knew it till they said cut, and both John and Tom about fell over because it was so bad."

Hart continues, "The dogs did quite a few things when they finished *Magnum*, but we did about an eight-year run. So they were almost semi-retired when we finished. The movie *Armed and Dangerous* is the main one after *Magnum* that comes to mind. But we did a number of things. They passed away quite a while back. The oldest one lasted a little over fourteen years, just about fifteen, and the last one to pass away was about twelve-and-a-half or so. For Dobermans they lasted quite a while. Whiskey was the oldest, Dominique was the youngest, and Brutus was the middle boy."

In an animal-training career that spans more than three decades, Hart has worked the gamut of animals. "Actually, lately a lot of my work has been with house cats. I started with elephants and big cats and chimps. Just lately for some reason, the last maybe six or seven years, it's been a lot of house cats" (including a Persian in some of the widely aired Fancy Feast ads).

But there will always be a soft place in this Hart for a threesome of doughnut-loving Dobermans. "They were all pretty great dogs," he says with affection.

Married . . . With Children

Fox, 1987–1997, 262 episodes

*Starring **Buck as Buck, Lucky as Lucky,** Ed O'Neill as Al Bundy, Katey Sagal as Peggy Bundy, Christina Applegate as Kelly Bundy, David Faustino as Bud Bundy, David Garrison as Steve Rhoades, Amanda Bearse as Marcy Rhoades (D'Arcy), Tim McGinley as Jefferson D'Arcy, and Kevin Curran as the voices of Buck and Lucky.*

The Bundys are one of Chicagoland's most unforgettable and also famously undistinguished families. Al's work as an uninspired shoe salesman makes him the kingly provider of the Bundy household, where wife Peggy does as little work as possible and where kids Kelly and Bud excel at immodest, but mostly harmless, no-goodness. Leave it to family dog Buck to observe all and occasionally share his musings with the audience.

Trainer Steven Ritt of Acting Dogs talks about the dog who landed the role of the likable canine in a TV family that did everything in its power to be irresistibly unlikable. "Well, actually, I answered an ad in the *Los Angeles Times.* Buck came from a home in Bel-Air. He was approximately two years old. That was in '85 or '86. They had him for sale because he is a purebred briard. The gentleman actually ended up giving me the dog. He thought I would be a good home.

He was a wealthy man and didn't feel right about actually taking money for the dog. They had to get rid of him because they raised two litter-mate males together, and they were fighting a lot."

Ritt sensed early on that the dog (then called Mike, but soon to be officially renamed Buck) would have a flair for motion picture and television work. "He was unique in the sense that briards are usually all black or all blonde, and he's what they define as an overlay. He had the tan face and legs and the grays and silvers and blacks in his body, and his ears were left natural, uncut and not cropped like they normally do with a briard."

Married . . . With Children was almost but not quite Buck's first acting work. "He did a Janet Jackson music video, 'When I Think of You,' as his first thing," says Ritt. "He's in the opening of the video. Then, during the second season of *Married*, he did the movie *Scrooged* with Bill Murray, and he had a scene with Bill in there."

But Buck's big break came with *Married . . . With Children.* Ritt recalls, "When we went and 'showed,' they were actually looking for an older, lumbering, lazy, large type of short-haired dog. At that time, Buck was young and full of energy. Briards, the males, are generally high energy with a lot of drive.

"I tried to convince them that they didn't want to start with an old lazy dog because then, if the show became successful, the dog wouldn't last. Plus, if there were actually any kind of tricks or actions, you just really don't want to start with an old dog. So I showed them things like walking easy, which is easy on your side, head down, on your back, and things that made him look like he could be older. Well, before I had gotten home after the showing, they had called and said they wanted him.

"Buck was always capable of a lot. He had a lot of tricks on him. After they saw he was easy to work with, they started writing him in more episodes. He did three or four a year that were centered around him where he'd be the 'A' story line. It just progressively got to where they used him more and more."

Ritt says that Buck's fellow actors got along swell with their canine pal. "They all really loved him, especially Ed O'Neill. He probably liked the dog more than he liked me," Ritt says with a laugh. "They were good buddies, and Ed was always willing to work with him and do whatever he had to do to get whatever shot or scene. There was actually quite a bond there between the two. He always took time out in between shots. Whenever he had extra minutes, he'd go sit and hang out with Buck and pet him."

But when the cameras were rolling, it was all work. Says Ritt, "Four-camera live is generally harder than film, where you can cut and get isolated shots. It's all hand signals, and we'd have scenes that would be twelve and fourteen minutes long sometimes. You've got to build up your dog's lapse of memory time because there would be pages before he'd have to enter and then hit marks or do tricks at the marks. And then of course you know it's all to one beat with a large show. If he's one second too soon or too late with something, the joke doesn't work. It's a little more involved than for a film dog because of getting them used to staying and waiting and not jumping a cue and building up their memory."

So how did Ritt keep Buck motivated? "Depending on what he had to do, I would change treats and I'm not really one to withhold food to get a lot of food motivation because then you get a dog that looks like he's anticipating and looking at the trainer too much."

Ritt studied dog psychology, pet behavior and obedience, and protection training, and apprenticed for several years under respected trainer Bob Weatherwax. He recalls, "I think one of the nice comments I get from people is how natural Buck looked and how he fit in with the Bundys, and it wasn't like panting anxiously looking at a trainer. With a live show, because a dog has got to see hand signals, it's a fine line. You do want them to stare at you when you need the look to see the hand signal, but the rest of the time I would actually let people pet him and so you then get a lot of different looks over at the people and reaction to them.

"The main thing is you don't want to stop a scene. So you do want to make sure your dog is doing the action properly, and then once he is getting action properly, I start to focus on where the look is and getting natural—once he knows the action well.

"Then that final day of the live show or the day before, I'll start worrying about getting looks—again, once he's got the action down—and have the cast feed him or come pat him. Or I'll turn my back and that's a sign to kind of drift around with your head and do what you want. So he kind of knew my body language, besides the hand signals, like the different poses of my body, whether it be relaxed or whether my energy gets up and I'm staring at him, or whether it's almost time to be ready to watch a hand signal and do a trick or now it's OK to just kind of be a dog."

Ritt adds, "We always did two live shows a night. So you could either do great the first show and then have to keep it up for the second, or you had a chance to redeem yourself if things didn't go good at the first show."

And Ritt proved right on the mark in his early counsel to use a young dog in case the

Buck takes his place at the foot of his *Married . . . With Children* TV family, clockwise from top left, David Faustino, Christina Applegate, Ed O'Neill, Katey Sagal, and Amanda Bearse.

show became a hit. Buck worked long into the run of *Married . . . With Children*, but then Ritt decided to retire him. "He worked up until he was like twelve-and-a-half, and he was still able to work, but it was getting hard for him to distinguish hand signals at a distance. Rather than replace him with another briard, which I actually had in the wings, the producers felt there would ever be only one Buck, and they didn't want to try to fool the audience. So they went completely with a different direction, and I actually have a dog still now that did the last two seasons or so—Lucky, the cocker."

Ritt explains further: "They wanted to go in a different direction, so during one hiatus I had a dog they were going to use [to replace actor Buck in the role of the Bundy Buck], and then about two months before we were going back, they decided they wanted to start with a puppy. They had written a story that involved a puppy, and Buck getting reincarnated as a puppy. So I went out taking pictures of a lot of different dogs and brought them to the producers. They actually picked one dog I had taken a picture of at the Lancaster Animal Shelter. They said they liked that look and wanted him. It was a cocker, but by the time I went back the next day to get him out of the shelter, they had euthanized him.

"But they liked that look, so I tried real hard and went to different breeders and rescues to find that look. I eventually did and acquired Lucky at about ten weeks old. I had two months to get him ready, so he was actually doing a live camera show at almost five months old. For the opening titles, where he picks the dollar after all the Bundys get money, he was five months old. He was so short and couldn't reach, so we had to put a little thing behind there, a little padding for him to step up on and jump behind the couch."

As for Buck, Ritt says, "Buck actually lived another year after that. He passed away at thirteen-and-a-half in '96."

But luckily the engaging performances that Buck and Ritt created together live on in popular *Married . . . With Children* reruns. And his Bundy replacement, Lucky, continues to see regular work in a variety of film and TV shows.

Maya

NBC, 1967–1968, 18 episodes

*Starring **Paro as Maya,** Jay North as Terry Bowen, and Sajid Khan as Raji. Narrated by Marvin Miller.*

Maya, set in India, is about an American boy searching for his father, a white hunter who is believed to have been killed by a man-eating tiger. He joins forces with an orphaned Indian boy and his pet elephant, who are fugitives. On the back of Maya, the boys ramble the Indian countryside.

The TV series *Maya* was spun off of the

1966 feature film by the same name, which starred Clint Walker, Jay North, and Sajid Khan. The majority of the feature film and practically all of the TV series was shot on location in India.

"All the animals were from an Indian circus, the Gemini Circus, which was a big circus that traveled through India similar to Ringling Brothers and Barnum & Bailey in the States," says Jay North. "All the animals we used came from that particular circus. The elephant Paro was a very sweet elephant. I had to be trained to grab the elephant's ears and walk up the trunk, or she would put her leg up and you'd have to climb up that way.

"I remember that she liked peanut butter sandwiches because my mom and I made them and fed her. We became very, very close although there were times when she would rear up like a horse and buck us off. They did have another elephant, Gunga, that they used at times as a substitute. It took a while to get acclimated to working with these animals."

North recalls working with tigers from the circus, including one named Gemini, a beautiful five-hundred-pound Bengal tiger. "We shot a scene one day in a special compound made out of bamboo poles. It was like a big stockade, but it was camouflaged with green trees and bushes. I was in there with the cat on my own shooting a lot of footage. We shot a lot of different shows with the tigers and elephants and snakes, and it was a very interesting experience.

"The elephant could rear up and walk on her two back legs. She could roll down and

Shot on location in India, *Maya* starred Sajid Khan and Jay North as two boys who crossed the country on the back of an elephant named Maya.

fall on the ground and pretend she was sick. We always had this kind of candy that we fed her when she was good in a scene. We would tap her forehead with the candy, and she would reach down with her trunk and put it in her mouth. We kept her well fed."

Before North starred in *Maya*, he made another feature film with wild animals, 1965's *Zebra in the Kitchen*, costarring Martin Milner, Andy Devine, and Jim Davis. "I worked with a mountain lion whose name was Sierra as my pet. The boy I play sneaks into the city where he lets all the animals out of the zoo. I remember that trainer Ralph Helfer wanted me to spend at least four weeks with the big cat, who was very playful. Once he got rambunctious and tackled me, but he was more like a kitten, and he liked to be scratched and petted. And he liked whipped cream. I would squirt whipped cream on his face and he would lick it.

"We used another mountain lion, Sheba, who was the mother of the male. She occasionally doubled for her son in the film. I didn't have much physical contact with the other animals, just the two mountain lions."

While young North was in India making *Maya*, animal trainer-owner Helfer recalls that the most difficult part of shooting the movie was a scene where tigers attack an elephant and its young offspring. This was all done at Africa USA with no actors other than the animal ones.

"We filmed that scene at our ranch, and it took months and months of work to get an elephant and a tiger to be responsive, to be friends if you will. That shot is what sold the series because it was so difficult," Helfer recalled.

"Debbie was the star elephant, although we used other elephants. That was Debbie used in the fight scene, and the two tigers were Sultan and Patrina.

"Jay North used to come out to the ranch and get used to the elephant. He would jump up on the elephant and do what he had to do. Children are a lot easier to work with animals than are adults, because they trust you, and they love animals. We didn't have a problem convincing a child whether an animal was good or bad."

Helfer explains that they used at least three different elephants to play Maya in the big action sequence for the feature film, but the most important thing was to have an elephant "that has a great look." He says, "Debbie was a very handsome elephant and good on camera. There were other elephants that did certain performances, but Debbie was a 'moush,' a sweetheart. She was like Modoc [Helfer's great movie star elephant]. She was one of our favorites. She was very big, about four or five tons, and had a good heart. Never in her entire career did she do anything negative.

"We trained her to do so many behaviors that she didn't forget, whether squashing a watermelon or playing baseball with you. We'd put a dime lying flat on a piece of glass, and she would pick it up with her trunk.

"She would always get her feelings hurt if a trainer got onto her for not getting it right the first time. She would do a belly rumble, almost like crying, and put her head down close to yours."

As for unusual hobbies, Debbie was a pachyderm painter. "We had her doing elephant art, where we would give her a board and paints and a brush, and she, at her own discretion, would choose colors and paint unusual paintings," Helfer says. The trainer says that he believed Debbie, an Indian elephant, had come into the States via Florida. "She was not zoo-born," he says. "She was a good elephant."

Helfer explained that elephants in the wild do not have as long a life expectancy as those in captivity because injuries can kill them and, when they lose their teeth, eating becomes a big problem. "In the wild, they do good to live to fifty-five years, but you can add another ten years in captivity because of veterinary care and more personal attention. In captivity when all the teeth are gone, we put them on molasses and grain and barley, and they can eat that and that keeps them alive."

As for what happened to one of his biggest stars, Helfer says, "Debbie went to a good friend with some other animals. She could well still be alive."

Me and the Chimp

CBS, 1972, 13 episodes

Starring ***Jackie as Buttons,*** *Ted Bessell as Mike Reynolds, Anita Gillette as Liz Reynolds, Scott Kolden as Scott Reynolds, and Kami Cotler as Kitty Reynolds.*

Me and the Chimp is about your everyday ordinary Southern California suburban family, except for one thing: they have a chimp as a pet. Named Buttons, because he loves to push buttons, the family chimp's curiosity creates interesting problems for his favorite humans, especially the father who thinks the chimp doesn't like him.

Simian star Jackie was owned by Lou Schumacher and trained for *Me and the Chimp* under Bob Riedell.

"She was about three or four when the show began. She was a good, smart chimp," says Riedell. "Chimps are like people. Some are smart. Some are mediocre and can't even learn their name. Their intelligence varies. But Jackie was a smart one and had a great personality, and I never worked her under stress.

"On *Me and the Chimp,* I sort of trained as we went. We did one show a week, Monday through Friday. Saturdays and Sundays I went into the studio with the script and trained her to do what she had to do in two days.

"She was partially trained when we started the series and knew the basic commands. You just had to show her a couple of times, and she picked it up. The best trait a chimp can have is to get along with people.

Ted Bessell starred as a young father whose family gains the addition of a chimp named Buttons, played by Jackie the chimp, in the sitcom *Me and the Chimp.*

Jackie had that. She liked me and she liked animals. She had a good temperament.

"She was just great with Ted Bessell and Anita Gillette, but I had to watch her around the kids because kids are quick. For a dream sequence set in the West, Jackie did a gunfight with Ted in the middle of the street. I taught her to do a quick draw with bananas as pistols."

Riedell not only worked with the chimp star, but he and his family also lived with the chimp for fourteen weeks, when he brought her to his house. "She wrestled with the kids under my supervision. They played hide and seek; they played tag and threw the ball around."

And Jackie picked up a few behaviors from the Riedell dinner table. The trainer says, "By having her down to dinner with my wife and two kids, by watching them eat and drink is how she learned to pick up a glass and use a fork.

"At night going home, I would put her in a grocery basket, and the people at the store got to know her. We'd go down the produce aisle, and she would take out whatever she wanted, put it in the basket, then take it out, and put it on the counter. So she'd pick out her own dinner every night.

"If we came within a half-mile of any McDonald's, she would go bonkers. She loved the cheeseburgers and milk shakes. She knew where every McDonald's was. And she loved Wrigley's chewing gum."

Before turning to a sitcom, Jackie made her mark in a Disney feature film. "She had done all the close-ups and carrying-in stuff in *The Barefoot Executive.* I remember taking her to lunch in the commissary, and there would be me and Jackie and Kurt Russell on one side of the table. Wally Cox, Tim Conway, Harry Morgan, and John Ritter were on the other side of the table cracking jokes so much that Kurt and I were laughing so hard we couldn't eat. The chimp couldn't care less."

Another celebrity star pal of Jackie was Lucille Ball. Jackie guested on *The Lucy Show* over the course of several years and accompanied Lucy to meet Johnny Carson on *The Tonight Show* at least three times. "We did one scene with Lucy down on her knees talking to Jackie, and Gale Gordon comes out in an ape suit," Riedell says about a scene from *The Lucy Show.* "Well, the chimp took a double take, screamed and went flying up into his arms like it had found heaven. Then when we did it with the tape rolling, Jackie knew Gale was in there, and he would run up and jump on him but there was no screaming and no arms outstretched like 'this is my mother who has been missing for thirty years.'"

Lucy liked to play with Jackie off the set, and Riedell relates the story that one day Lucy called and asked them to go with her to daughter Lucie Arnaz's new apartment. "We rode with Lucy in her limo, but first we went over to Jimmy Stewart's house, and Jimmy got down on the floor and played with Jackie. Lucy took us to John Barrymore's house to show him the chimp and then to Milton Berle's (but he wasn't home) and then to Ross Martin's [*Wild Wild West* costar], and then on to Lucie's for the party."

"Jackie was just a good animal and good with people. After working with her for about five years, Lou Schumacher gave the chimp to another trainer," says Riedell, who began training animals in 1956. He first worked with Ralph Helfer on weekends and then got into it full-time, working on TV shows such as *Daktari* (with Zamba the lion and Judy the chimp) and *Lancelot Link* and in movies such as *Toby Tyler* and *Zebra in the Kitchen.* Riedell also worked for six years at UCLA in their space biology laboratory, where he trained ten chimpanzees to be potential astronauts.

Perhaps the greatest perk Jackie and Riedell received during their star run was the use of a free vehicle. "We had the official chimp van," Riedell recalls. "The owner of Galpin Ford in Los Angeles, Bert Beochmann, was a friend of mine. He was always into marketing and creative ideas. He asked me to come down there and he would supply me with the van. It was customized, all carpeted and painted outside with a big banana on it. It said 'official chimp van' on the front, and had 'Buttons, star of *Me and the Chimp*' written on the side with the CBS logo."

Riedell and Jackie may have been living the life of *Me and the Chimp,* but they were certainly no chumps.

Meego

CBS, 1997, 13 episodes (only six aired)

Starring ***Barkley as Barkley,*** *Bronson Pinchot as Meego, Ed Begley Jr. as Dr. Edward Parker, Michelle Trachtenberg as Maggie Parker, Will Estes as Trip Parker, and Jonathan Lipnicki as Alex Parker.*

Meego was a short-lived comedy series about an alien who crash-lands on planet Earth. Three youngsters find the interplanetary traveler and convince their single-parent dad to keep him on as a nanny while he tries to repair his spaceship.

All dogs go to panting, but not all dogs go to pant-leg attacks. Meet Barkley, a smooth-coat, short-legged Jack Russell terrier who is the undisputed canine champion of pant-leg attacks of TV and film. The canine fireball weighs all of seventeen pounds.

"He's probably worked more than any other dog in Hollywood but never had a big hit," says Barkley's trainer, Doree Sitterly Bayliss, who has worked with Animal Actors of Hollywood since 1982. "Because he's not on *Frasier* or *Wishbone,* nobody knows who he is. But he is famous for his pant-leg attacks. My dream is, if we ever get a biography, to have a whole tape loop of every pant-leg attack he has ever done. Ninety percent of his work, he's grabbed somebody's pant leg. He's very safe about it. He's never bitten anyone. When I tell him 'out,' he let's it go and that's it."

A short list of Barkley's victims includes

Barkley bares his fangs.
Courtesy of Doree Sitterly Bayliss.

Demi Moore, Drew Carey, Dana Carvey, Ray Walston, Paul Rodriguez, and Lisa Kudrow. He's performed his signature move on such TV shows as *The Pretender*, *Malcolm in the Middle*, *Love Boat: The Next Wave*, *Caroline in the City*, *The Drew Carey Show*, *Friends*, *Tales From the Crypt*, *L.A. Law*, and *Full House*.

He's acted in gobs of commercials for clients such as Purina, Dentyne, Cheer, Nike, Kellogg's Frosted Flakes, Nintendo, McDonald's, Tyson Chicken, Levis, Radio Shack, and the U.S. Postal Service.

Up to now, Barkley's only starring TV role is as Barkley on *Meego*, where he communicated with the alien portrayed by Bronson Pinchot. "Barkley communicated by making dog sounds, and Bronson could understand him," says Bayliss. "He's always been a very verbal dog. He makes a lot of funny, different sounds. He'll mimic me, and he loves to sing along with people. He knows a growl and a bark on cue. He also knows a few other sounds, and if I get him going, he'll make really silly sounds. Bronson could take off on whatever sound came out."

Bayliss considered *Meego* a plum role for Barkley, especially considering that the producers allowed her to give input to the scripts, a luxury producers rarely allow a trainer. And Barkley also had his own dressing room and a very special kid. Bayliss says, "Jonathan [Lipnicki] had to work a lot with Barkley. He ended up being wonderful with Barkley. He's a very funny little kid. Once Jonathan was a guest on *The Rosie O'Donnell Show*, and she asked him about Barkley, and he said, 'I'm the human treat machine.' Jonathan told her that Barkley gets lots of dog money.

"When we reward a dog, we pay him, so on the set whenever Jonathan was just standing around, I'd give him a treat and say, 'Here, pay him,' and he would treat Barkley."

Bayliss acquired Barkley after she lost her first Jack Russell, Petey, to a rattlesnake bite. A dog breeder was hoping to breed one of her dogs with Petey since Petey came from Africa. When the breeder discovered that Petey had died, he invited Bayliss to come take a look at her pups. "Barkley sort of stood out from the rest," says Bayliss. "He was so cute. We tested his personality, and my friend [and fellow trainer] Cristie Miele said, 'He's the one.'"

Almost immediately after he left his birthplace, Cedar Hollow Ranch in Williams, Oregon, Barkley made his movie debut. At the ripe old age of six months, he popped up in the film *Don't Tell Her It's Me.* "He didn't know much, but he had the looks and the personality, and we trained as we went along," says Bayliss.

Next came the Jim Varney comedy vehicle *Ernest Goes to Jail.* Bayliss relates how Barkley got the assignment. "The dog character, Rimshot, was described in the script as a mop. They were thinking shaggy, weird-looking little dog, and we showed several dogs, and then Barkley walked in, and the director said, 'That's it. That's the dog.'

"He really had a character, and he had to learn how to behave on the set, so we had to do some serious training. After that, it seemed like he went from one job to the next. We taught him more tricks and gave him more training as each one came along."

Bayliss considers Barkley the character dog of Hollywood. "Barkley is one of those dogs that just loves work. He loves being on the set, and he loves sitcoms with a live audience. You can train him for a week, and you wonder if he's gonna get it, and then on set he does it. Other trainers tell me when the cameras start to roll, don't worry, he'll do it. Barkley knows when the camera are rolling."

Bayliss says one of Barkley's greatest challenges was the film *Clean Slate,* where he had to wear a patch over one eye. The patch caused a depth perception problem. He saw everything two feet to the left.

"We had to come up with all kinds of things, like trying to get him to eat food that wasn't there or bite someone's hand that wasn't there. All the stunts in the movie were very obscure, even just getting him to wear the eye patch. Only four days before shooting did he finally accept the eye patch. We went down to the wire."

For the *Ernest Scared Stupid* flick, Barkley had to be trained to drive a truck. "He had to learn to work different kinds of mechanisms in the garbage truck—how to honk the horn, shift gears, and work the steering wheel.

"There were a lot of trolls in the film, and he learned to really dislike the trolls. One of the actors who played a troll said, 'Barkley hates me.' I told him, 'No, Barkley hates you when you're the troll.'"

A plum TV role for Barkley came up in an episode of *Family Law* where he proved that

Barkley poses with his favorite Earth boy Alex Parker, played by Jonathan Lipnicki, in the 1997 CBS series *Meego*.

Courtesy of Doree Sitterly Bayliss.

every dog must indeed have his day in court. "He played an aging dog commercial star who was getting taken out of his contract because of age discrimination and being replaced by a younger dog. So he had to be in court and show he could perform as well as the other dog."

And exactly how old is Hollywood's foremost character dog? "Like most actors, he lies about his age," says Bayliss. "He's still working."

Another top TV credit was an episode of *Friends*. "In that episode, Phoebe went to look for her father. She went to his house in a cab and knocked on the door, and Barkley came around the side of the house and made a pant-leg attack on her. He held her and the rest of the cast hostage in the cab. He jumped up on the window and was snarling at them. It was very funny," says Bayliss.

Barkley, who well may be the busiest Hollywood hound of the 1990s, had a recurring role as the neighbor dog on *Full House*, opposite his pal Comet. Among his many feature film credits are *American Beauty*, *Volcano*, *This Boy's Life*, and *Problem Child 2*.

But all work and no play is not the story of Barkley's life. Bayliss treats him to fine, home-cooked meals. "He will eat just about anything, but I cook beef and liver and chicken for him. I freeze that and cut it into smaller pieces. He also eats chicken dogs from the health food store."

As for leisure time, Barkley has a basket full of twenty-five toys, which he loves. He's especially fond of soft, stuffed toys with squeakers, and he likes rubber fish toys.

Bayliss rarely leaves Barkley out of family plans. "He pretty much goes most everywhere with us. He rides in the basket of my bicycle with me. He loves going for walks, out on the boat, sailing, and jet skiing. We even take him on vacations."

Barkley is definitely a character and one very lucky dog.

Mister Ed

Syndicated, 1961; CBS, 1961–1965, 143 episodes

*Starring **Mister Ed (formerly Bamboo Harvester) as himself**, Alan Young as Wilbur Post, Connie Hines as Carol Post, Larry Keating as Roger Addison, Edna Skinner as Kay Addison, Leon Ames as Gordon Kirkwood, Florence MacMichael as Winnie Kirkwood, and Allan "Rocky" Lane as the voice of Mister Ed.*

Mister Ed is the story of a horse and his man. Oh, the horse can talk, too, of course, of course. But Ed will talk only to his owner, architect Wilbur Post (he's the first person that Ed has found who's worth talking to), which leads to all kinds of humorous adventures.

The idea of a *Mister Ed* TV series began with some short stories about a talking horse named Mister Ed that began running in *Liberty* magazine and the *Saturday Evening Post* in the late 1930s. Soon afterward, the

Francis the Talking Mule movies (based on the novel *Francis*, but likely influenced somewhat by the Mister Ed tales as well) became a big hit in theaters. *Francis* director Arthur Lubin became aware of the *Mister Ed* stories himself in 1957 and subsequently purchased the rights to the *Mister Ed* character and stories from the estate of writer Walter Brooks.

In association with George Burns, Lubin developed a pilot for a *Mister Ed* TV series in 1958. The flawed production (which did not include the eventual famous *Mister Ed* horse or the eventual human stars) did not sell. Two years later, Lubin and Burns resuscitated the talking horse idea with the help of Al Simon and Filmways Television. They formed the Mister Ed Company and sold the series into syndication with a pilot that used a second horse, who was still different from the Mister Ed that the world would soon come to know and love.

Mister Ed, Alan Young, and Connie Hines certainly "walked the walk" of Hollywood stardom, but more important, all three could "talk the talk."

Trainer Les Hilton, who learned his trade under Will Rogers and Jack Lindell and had been trainer for the *Francis* films, scoured the Amcrican West for just the right horse for the role. He eventually found his famous Mister Ed at the home of Carl Ward, a few miles from his North Hollywood home.

The horse's name was Bamboo Harvester. Foaled near El Monte, California, in 1949, the golden palomino was sired by Chief Tonganoxie and his dam was Zetna. Both had strong Arabian bloodlines (she was sired by Antez, an Arabian imported from Poland). Like his grandsire (The Harvester) before him, Bamboo Harvester was a champion show horse and a frequent participant in parades, including the Rose Parade.

Loretta Kemsley, daughter of trainer John Kemsley (as well as a trainer herself) and an across-the-road neighbor of Les Hilton during the *Mister Ed* years, recalls, "A saddlebred-Morgan cross, Ed was a grandson of The Harvester, a founding sire of the Palomino Association, whose distinctive silvery tone shimmered through his golden coat and was passed down, including to Ed."

Struck by Bamboo Harvester's engaging eyes and sensitive demeanor, Hilton declared that in the 1,100-pound horse, he had found his Mister Ed. Filmways paid the asking price of $1,500, and Bamboo Harvester was gelded and officially renamed Mister Ed.

Now came the crunch. Hilton had just a few weeks to get Mister Ed trained to begin production for the series, which would spend its first season in syndication before moving to CBS for four seasons.

Alan Young talks about renowned trainer Les Hilton. "Les was the show. I mean, he and the horse. Without Lester, everybody agrees it couldn't have been done. He picked out the horse. He was commissioned by the Mister Ed Company to pick out the finest horse he could get. Ed was never a trained horse; he wasn't a trick horse. He was a parade horse at best, but he was very docile, and as Lester told me, you've got to pick out a horse that's docile and inquisitive and then you can get them to do anything you want. That was Ed."

Says Loretta Kemsley, "Born in 1949 and registered as Bamboo Harvester, Ed had traveled throughout the United States, winning championships in prestigious arenas like Madison Square Garden. I first met Ed at the Los Angeles County Fair in Pomona, still considered the largest fair in the world. Each year, the Palomino Association sponsored an exhibition barn and Bamboo Harvester was one of their prime attractions. People would wander through the barn, admiring each palomino in turn, but would gather in front of Bamboo Harvester's stall, which was lined with trophies and ribbons. At that time, the future Mister Ed was owned by the president of the California Palomino Association [Carl Ward]. Needless to say, the horse barns, especially the palomino barn, were a favorite haunt of mine.

"Les looked at a lot of horses before he picked him, and one of the things that made him outstanding for the choice was that he liked learning and he liked playing games with people. He wanted to be in the middle of what people were doing and to have the attention. And of course the more tricks he did, the more attention he got. No doubt what made him a good show horse was having the presence of mind to know that 'I'm here to do something and I must do it right.' Of course, later on when he became Mister Ed and had all the props around at home, he would naturally show off for people."

Kemsley adds, "Mister Ed resided in the last stall on the left of this long, white shed row barn at Les's place. At various times, several of the best-known equine stars lived there. Black Diamond and Francis the talking mule were two that preceded Ed. While Ed lived there, the stall immediately to his right was the home of Pumpkin [also called Punkin], his stunt double. Both of these charismatic palominos became my good friends.

"Pumpkin's gold was slightly darker, the color of a newly minted gold coin. However, the most notable difference between Ed and Pumpkin, a registered American quarter horse, was the golden moon in the center of Pumpkin's blaze. When he was standing in for Ed, this moon was covered with white makeup. Years later, Pumpkin starred in the Snak-Pak commercials as a talking horse—a direct result of his training by Les Hilton. In the Snak-Pak commercials, his golden moon was fully visible.

"Ed dominated the barn even though [at fifteen hands high] he was two inches smaller than Pumpkin. The sheer force of Ed's personality dictated the daily routine. People weren't allowed to say hello to Pumpkin first or Ed would sulk, grabbing the short rope affixed to the top half of his Dutch stall door and slamming it shut. It didn't do any good to apologize. Ed would be out of his stall and into his corral by then, hiding behind the barn and refusing to return. Ed demanded to be first in all things: the meals of alfalfa hay at sunrise and sunset, cleaning his stall, the mid-morning grooming, the noon ration of oats and barley, and even the afternoon training sessions. If Les brought new toys, Ed insisted on playing with them first."

Kemsley recalls, "The one problem with Ed that Les did have, which was fairly easily solved but it took a while to get the right combination, is that Ed figured out how to unlock his stall door and Les had to experiment with different types of snaps because Ed was quite good with his lips.

"They had a two-horse trailer that they kept in Les's yard. It was white with green lettering that said, 'I'm Mister Ed.' And of course they made parade appearances. After Pumpkin was seasoned enough, they used Pumpkin more for the parade appearances than Ed because Ed was just too valuable to take a chance on getting hurt.

"When fans visited, which was often since his trailer sat out front, Les greeted them cordially but was careful to steer them toward Ed and discreetly shoo Pumpkin away. No amount of coaxing would induce Ed to perform for fans if they stopped to admire Pumpkin. Having completed a career as a show and parade horse before becoming a movie star, Ed was used to basking in the spotlight. People would drop by to visit. It wasn't a secret that he was there, and Les was always very accommodating and he would take them out back. As soon as Ed saw that he had visitors coming, he would start in with his routine with the phone and with the pencil to dial the phone and so on."

Kemsley continues, "Pumpkin, younger by several years, was content to play second fiddle. As a three-year-old, his babyish interests were different than the well-seasoned Ed. Pumpkin lacked the worldly demeanor Ed found so natural. He preferred to romp free in the arena behind the barn. During the training sessions, Pumpkin was as likely to play as he was to work. Not yet understanding the importance of exact timing, Pumpkin tried to shorten the training sessions by anticipating Les's next commands. This was fortunate for me. Les asked me to be Pumpkin's assistant trainer. By working for two people, it would make it harder for him to anticipate the routines. A young teen, I was thrilled to be handed this honor by a trainer of Les's caliber. To say I was diligent would be an understatement. I was as overzealous as Pumpkin—wanting to please Les in any way possible. Our combined enthusiasm must have been a source of amusement to Les.

"For many years, I'd watched, shy and silent, from Les's fence, intent on capturing every detail of his training methods and their results. Once I was sure I understood, I'd practice on Dad's ponies until I could duplicate the tricks and performances. Les, also a person of few words, didn't seem to mind his quiet disciple. He never asked me to leave and sometimes appeared to exaggerate his cues so I'd be sure to learn them."

Alan Young adds his praise for Hilton. "Les was not only a great trainer—he was a fine man. You didn't get to know him very quickly. In fact, I was sitting there one day after about five or six shows and I said, 'I really don't ride well, Les.' And he said, 'Yep, I know.' That's all. I said, 'Could you get me some training?' 'Yep.' So I went out to his little spread, and he got me on Ed and started me in riding lessons, and then he got me a regular trainer so I could take lessons. Lester was recognized as one of the finest large animal trainers, if not *the* finest, in Hollywood. He worked with elephants, you name it. He was so nice. He shared everything he knew if he liked you. I got to know him quite well. We became very friendly, but he was quite a taciturn individual."

Loretta Kemsley adds this observation: "Les was an extraordinary trainer and was really more into the horses than he was into the people but he would tolerate the people for his horses, and I'm sure that's the kind of relationship that he had with teaching Alan to ride because it wouldn't have been his favorite chore but he would have done it to help out Ed."

Kemsley elaborates further on the training techniques for Mister Ed: "Cueing movie horses is an art in itself. The cues must be subtle and yet visible from a distance so the trainer and his shadow remain out of camera range. Movie horses are always focused on the trainer. If the trainer is in the wrong place behind the camera, the horse appears to be looking in the wrong direction on screen. To keep the apparent focus right, Les had to be able to work from every angle and from behind huge lights and other bulky equipment. Most cues also must be silent, contained in hand and body gestures rather than words. Stars like Ed must be able to work at liberty—that is, with no restraints from bridles, halters, and ropes.

"Les was a gentle, methodical trainer. He communicated well with horses and understood what inspired them to excel. He started his horses with word commands and body movements designed to excite the horse into doing the desired action. As soon as they responded even slightly, he'd stop and praise them, sometimes using carrots as a reward. This encouraged them to try again, becoming bolder in their response each time they were rewarded.

"Once they knew the trick thoroughly, Les began replacing the word commands with physical cues. Les used whips as cues but never whipped his horses. The whips were an extension of his arm, indicating which way to look or move. They were also used to tap the horse in the beginning stages of a trick. This led the horse to understand that a whip pointing at his leg would mean to move the leg. Specific movements meant specific things. A whip suddenly raised high meant to rear. A whip held to the left, with the tassel shaking, meant to look to the left. Without the tassel shaking, it meant to move to the left.

"Ed followed Les's commands exactly—looking always to the whip to learn what Les wanted next. One day, I was riding my horse, Diamond, and stopped by to see Les. My friend Maggie was riding with me. Les asked us to stand in two spots in the arena. In a third spot, he put a barrel. As we stood there, he had Ed canter around us in a cloverleaf pattern, using only hand and whip cues. Ed never faltered or changed speed. He always watched Les. The viewer, if they were alert, could watch Ed's eyes and ears and tell where Les was hiding behind the camera because Ed never stopped watching him."

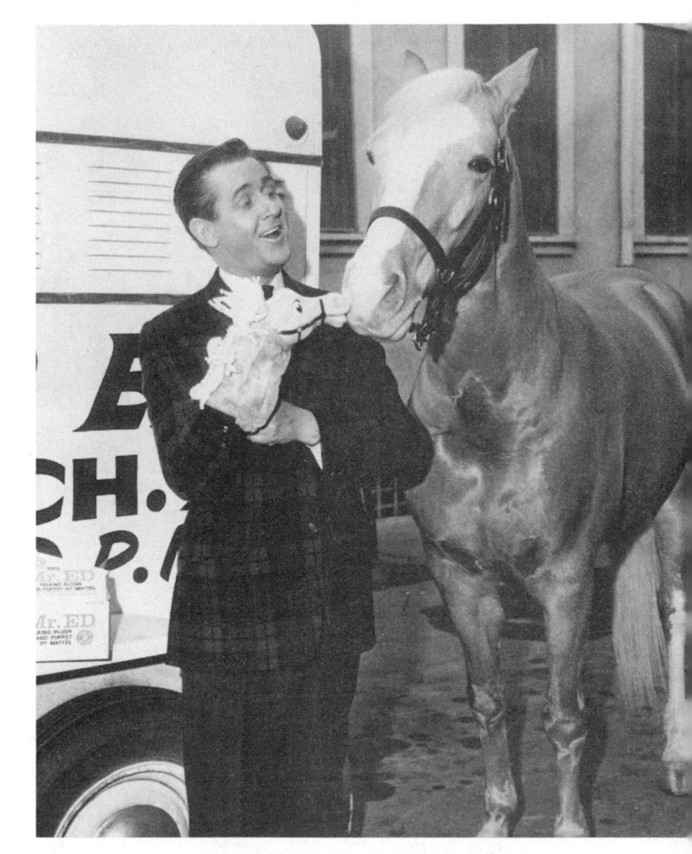

Alan Young shows Mister Ed one of the toys spawned by *Mister Ed* the series, a hand-puppet of Ed that talks after you pull its string. Ed didn't seem to "carrot" all.

Alan Young recalls that Hilton would use both spoken commands and visual cues. "Les would say, 'Pick it up, pick it up, Ed. Pick it up and then pull it. Pull it with the drawer.' But when it was just the two of us—Ed and me—Lester told me little places to touch Ed that would make his head turn and things like that, but most of it was spoken."

Young adds, "Les told me that it wasn't so much teaching Ed what to do as it was unteaching him after he did so that he wouldn't do it every time he came on the set. Les had great techniques in that way. He was very gentle with the horse. He would spank him now and again, but it was just his little crop over the hoofs, which of course didn't hurt Ed a bit. But the noise just made him feel so embarrassed, you could just see Ed almost blushing when he got spanked. He would try to look at Lester like 'what did I do wrong?' and Lester would have to pull him back into line again but he did. He was so smart."

In those situations, Young says, Ed often would seek comfort from Young. "Lester was the father, and I was the mother. Ed would come to me for consolation," Young remembers fondly.

He adds, "Ed would do three or four things in a row in one take and get applause after it. One take. For example, one time he came in, pulled open a drawer, took out a bunch of carrots, closed the drawer with his nose, dropped the carrots on my desk, walked into his stall, and pulled the door shut—all in one take. It was just incredible, but Lester of course was lying on the floor telling him what to do because they wouldn't be printing that sound. He would be telling him what to do, but of course Ed remembered it anyway because Lester would run him through it a few times. It didn't take long. Oh, he was wonderful.

Alan Young and Connie Hines were Wilbur and Carol Post, the masters of Mister Ed on *Mister Ed*. Or was it the other way around?

"Ed was the most thoughtful animal," continues Young. "He used to roll his eyes. That meant he had to go to the bathroom, and I don't know whether Les taught him that or not but Les was quite amazed at it and very tickled of course because then we had a very lovely stage."

While it is indeed nice that the star steed helped keep a tidy set, let's get down to that question that everybody wants to know: Just how did Ed talk?

"Well, I started one rumor," says Young, "and it was that he put peanut butter under his lip. I started that one, but we didn't want to tell people what he did. The kids just thought he talked because the credits said 'Mister Ed played by himself' and we felt he talked. I mean, I felt he talked because he was so intelligent that when I was acting with him I felt I was acting with another actor. You get carried away, you know."

But Young goes on to explain his actual observations about Ed's talking. "It was a soft nylon that Les slipped under his lip. The thing is, of course, that Ed tried to get rid of it. He would do it on cue. That's where the cleverness came in. Les had something that he pulled. It was soft, it didn't hurt Ed at all, but then he would lay the crop across Ed's forelegs to make him stop and then he would take it off and give a little tug and Ed would begin again. After the second year, it was hard to shut him up because as soon as he heard my voice cease he'd start moving his lips or he heard Rocky Lane's voice." (That's Allan "Rocky" Lane, the B-Western movie star from decades earlier who was the uncredited, barely hoarse baritone voice of Mister Ed.)

Young continues, "In the beginning, he had to have a little nylon attached to it so that would cue him—the tingling, I guess, got him. In fact, I think we had the ASPCA on the set the first day of shooting, but they never had to come again because Lester was most protective of Ed—just like a mother."

Loretta Kemsley also has distinct memories and observations about how Mister Ed talked. "That was a closely guarded secret so as not to disillusion the public. I know Les would share the secret if he was still alive. Even though it's been more than forty years, I still feel uneasy breaking the pledge I made to Les. However, it is time for others to know how this gentle man worked this magic. It wasn't with peanut butter, as is often imagined. Peanut butter would make a horse use his tongue excessively, but would not affect his lips, much like a person trying to get peanut butter off the roof of his mouth.

"Les first trained Ed to move his lips on cue. This took a lot of patience and rewards. Ed liked the attention so much he wouldn't stop 'talking' on cue. He'd keep going until Les walked away. To overcome this, Les had to devise another method. Fans have noted that Ed always appeared wearing a halter. Some fans even spotted a slender line running from the halter to a place off camera. They interpreted that line as a cue to move his head. The line had another purpose. It ran from one halter ring, under Ed's upper lip, and back to the other halter ring, then off camera to Les's hand. Les would wiggle the line to tickle Ed's lip, cueing him to talk or stop talking. The line was a common, clear fishing line found in any hardware store. Because it was clear, it was hard to spot on camera, although not impossible as those alert fans proved."

So there you have it—not quite from the horse's mouth but about as close as we're ever going to get. The fishing line was used only to let Mister Ed know when to start and stop talking, but not actually to manipulate his lips. That was all Mister Ed himself.

But talking wasn't Ed's only talent. Loretta Kemsley describes some of his other star qualities. "Ed was virtually unflappable by noise and commotion. This was important on the movie set where crews would be dragging equipment and cables virtually under his feet. One of Ed's best qualities was his ability to concentrate despite the confusion and noise on the set. Before the camera rolled, Les would practice the scene with Ed. Once the cameras were rolling, Ed would perform as directed, usually only needing one take.

"Although Ed was beautiful to look at, by

far the most appealing trait he brought to the show was his personality. He loved attention and would perform for long hours as long as he was the star of the show. This vanity was evident in his scenes. Off camera, he was the same as the horse everyone grew to love on camera."

Kemsley adds, "In front of Ed's stall were all the familiar props from the movie set: the table with the telephone, the pencil for dialing, the sunglasses, and whatever would appear in upcoming stories. This gave Ed a chance to work with new props and become familiar with the required tricks before doing them on the set."

Kemsley recalls some of Ed's famous tricks: "The only trick Ed disliked was hitting a baseball with a bat. This was for a show with Leo Durocher and the Los Angeles Dodgers ["Leo Durocher Meets Mister Ed"]. Ed had to hold the bat in his teeth. He didn't like the way it felt when the ball hit the bat. Les asked me to help him with this trick because it took two people: one to stand beside Ed and encourage him to hold the bat, the other to pitch the ball. Ed finally gave in and hit the ball on cue, mostly because he was bored. He knew we'd quit once he did the trick we wanted.

"Another trick that amazed fans was Ed riding a surfboard. This was relatively easy to train. Ed was used to riding in horse trailers, which don't have the best shock absorbers and sometimes have none at all. Ed was accustomed to having a floor moving and bouncing under his hoofs. The hard part fell to the prop men who had to create a realistic 'surfboard' that was strong enough to hold his weight, which was over a thousand pounds. Ed trusted Les, and Les trusted the skill of the prop men. Even so, he worried that the 'surfboard' might not be strong enough when Ed stood on it. Fortunately, the trick went off without a hitch."

One other big mystery that is still a source of much confusion surrounding Mister Ed concerns his demise. Once again, Alan Young and Loretta Kemsley help set the record straight.

First Alan Young: "I think it [Ed's death] was 1973 or '74—no later than that. (There was another rumor that went around that a different horse was Mister Ed, but it wasn't true.) I'd talked to Les on the phone and he told me about Ed's death, so I rushed right up there. Of course, Lester was retired by then. He retired with Ed, and he was just heartbroken. The reruns were on the air then every day and he said, 'Al, I just can't watch it anymore.' He almost had a tear in his eye. He didn't last long himself after that.

"It was in the papers here. In fact, there was a picture of me in the paper with the horse, and it said Mister Ed is dead, and I got flowers sent to my house. They thought it was me. I think it was carried on the air, but maybe not on the networks. It happened very quietly because the show was off the air and nobody was wanting to see anything about it because it was a bit of an accident that it happened."

In his 1994 memoir, *Mister Ed and Me*, Young elaborated further, describing how Les Hilton had been out of town and a caretaker was looking after Ed. "No one is quite sure what happened exactly," Young wrote, "but it would appear that Ed decided to lie down or perhaps take a roll in the grass, which was not his usual routine. He was a heavy-bodied horse with long slender legs, not always strong enough to get himself back on all fours without a lot of flailing and struggling.

"The poor 'sitter' came out to see Ed on the grass puffing and heaving and thought the horse was having a seizure. He held Ed's head down to stop him from struggling. Ed was used to this from his training and lay quietly. The man then shoved a tranquilizer pill of some sort in his mouth."

He concluded, "It might have been the fact that Ed was not used to the medicine or some other reason Lester couldn't figure out, but, within hours, Ed was gone. He was cremated in Los Angeles, and where his ashes were scattered, only Lester knows."

Loretta Kemsley last saw Les and Ed in the late 1960s. Here is what she recalls about Ed's death. "I read in the paper a few years later that Ed had been put to sleep due to arthritis. It was a sad day. Arthritis is not only painful for horses but a severe problem. Their legs are vulnerable at all times because they are so small compared to the weight they carry. When arthritis strikes, it can cripple them completely. They become afraid to lie down, lest they can't get up again. Horses that can't get up will die a slow death and can injure themselves while thrashing around trying to rise. I didn't question the need for this humane act but couldn't help crying for my old friend. I miss him still and treasure the memories that Les, Ed, and Pumpkin left behind." (Les Hilton himself passed away on February 27, 1976.)

Other credible accounts place Ed's death as happening in 1968 and attribute his death to having to be put down because of either a broken leg or severe arthritis complications similar to those described above.

The common thread of the these various histories is that Ed died between 1968 and 1974 (our wager is on Alan Young's estimate) and that his death was associated with some sort of arthritic difficulty with his legs.

One thing for sure is that the Mister Ed formerly known as Bamboo Harvester is not the same horse, also purported to be Mister Ed, that died in Oklahoma on February 28, 1979. At best, that horse was perhaps a horse used in one of the *Mister Ed* pilots or maybe in a one-time publicity photo for the *Mister Ed* series. That horse is buried in Oklahoma with a fund-raised monument. But he is not the famous Mister Ed.

As for the real Mister Ed, everyone who knew him has only praise for him and his show. Says Alan Young, "I have great gratitude for the show because it was a wonderful thing for me. It was not as exciting as some of the things I did, but in another way it was more exciting than anything because to watch this horse . . . I could talk about him all day long.

"Every animal that came on the set he would get along with—even the zebras (and of course horses don't much care for them) and elephants (which horses also don't care for). He trusted Lester—that's the whole thing. I mean, Ed had birds all over him on one show and he went right along with that.

It was just fine with him. Maybe he didn't like it, but he never showed it.

"He trusted Lester and Lester loved him. And of course the wranglers that worked on the show were very kind also. They were very protective of Ed. He was . . . I'll use the word 'spoiled,' but he never took advantage of it. Some people say that horses are the dumbest animals in the world because they have to be led out of a burning building, but I don't think that's true. I think they're very smart. They're a bit like cats in that they mind their own business to a great extent so people think they're dumb, but he's an example of a smart horse."

That is Mister Ed.

Morris the Cat

His real name was Lucky and was he ever. He became Morris, the star of Nine Lives cat food commercials.

Trainer Robert Martwick describes how his career with famed finicky-eater Morris evolved. "I had a boarding, training, and grooming kennel and supplied most of the commercial animals in the Middle West for about fifteen years. There was no other supplier here. I worked basically with dogs, and then when cat food started to come to the fore, I worked more with cats. In one job, I needed an orange cat for atmosphere.

"I had a friend, Sylvester Carter, over at the Hinsdale Humane Society [in the Chicago area], and I called him and asked him if he had any orange cats, and he said, 'Yeah, actually I've got about four of them, but you know what day it is.' By that, he meant that the anticruelty folks came out in Chicago and did the job of putting them to sleep.

"So I went over there and I looked at all of them. One was hiding in the corner and another wasn't eating. Then I walked up to this one kennel, and this cat seemed very bold, very outgoing. His food dish was empty, and I turned him out because I had permission, and I put him on the floor, and he didn't run or look or hide. He turned and rubbed up against me a little bit. I dropped his metal food pan, and he looked around at me as if to say, 'What the hell are you doing?' But I did that because I knew he was going to be under strobe lights in the studio and with lots of noise.

"Anyway, I took him and he did a little job. We probably spent five minutes to get the shot, and so I went back and I told Sylvester that I'd like to keep him. Sylvester said, 'Well, you'd better keep him or he's going to be gone.' So I kept him, and as the years went on and I got more into the cats, I got quite a bit of work. And at that time I called him Lucky—lucky for him and lucky for me. He did a couple of very good commercials and quite a number of still shots.

"He was loose in our office at the kennel all the time. Customers would come in, and he would sit on the desk and look at their big dogs like, 'What the hell are they doing here?'

He quickly adapted. Then I got a call to have some cats audition for the Nine Lives commercial. They wanted six or seven cats. Because the guy that was the director was already a friend of mine, I said, 'I've got the cat. You don't need any others.' He said, 'Well, our ad agency wants to look at cats,' and I couldn't blame them.

"So I took down six or seven cats, including a couple of very pretty cats and all workable. But I saved Lucky till the last. The ad people were sitting in this conference room. Instead of going in with Lucky, I opened the door and shoved him in. He went over and did what he always does. He jumped up on the table, and by chance, walked over and bumped into the guy who was the art director. And that guy said, 'This looks like the Clark Gable of cats.' That's an understatement." Lucky had become Morris.

Lucky is all smiles with his trainer, Robert Martwick.
Courtesy of Robert Martwick.

"We went to make the commercials," Martwick recalls, "and they were planning a long shooting session. We shot the commercials in about half the time they expected, and I don't remember how many it was in that first segment. They always tried to do two to four at a time once they set the studio, in order to save the money. Morris was very good about being able to sit still. That was his nature basically. Also, he kind of liked people, and he didn't mind being handled. He would get tired of it after a point. There were a few times I just had to tell people, 'No, we're not working. We're done.' But Nine Lives allowed me to make that call. They gave me a lot of respect.

"Anyway, after about a year, Morris's commercials were so popular that we got a call from a writer for the *Cleveland Plain Dealer* who asked if she could have him at a pet show down there, a charity thing, and then a brand new shopping center. The ad agency didn't particularly like it, but the guy that was the salesman for Nine Lives in that area talked them into agreeing because it would be good for him.

"So I went down there, and in four hours we went through about two thousand pictures. It was unbelievable. People drove all the way from Columbus, Ohio, from Ft. Wayne, Indiana, and everywhere to see him. And that was the kickoff of him going on PR work. After that, they finally decided we should do a tour where he did the Northeast because that was where Nine Lives was much more prominent at that time. We did about forty cities or something like that. And on that tour, we'd fly into a major city, and then, of course, that included smaller cities around there, which I would be doing in a rental car, and Morris loved it.

"Now this was the first Morris. And he made something like fifty-five commercials [Lucky also starred opposite Burt Reynolds in the 1973 film *Shamus*] and then when he died in 1978, the estimated guess of his age was nineteen and that was very close. It was news in all the magazines and newspapers. So then I found this other cat, Morris II, who was not the same temperament. He was more of a cat. (The first Morris was more like a dog.) He was a very good cat, but he was not quite as outgoing as the first one. But he still stood up to a lot of punishment—a lot of traveling and sitting in a chair for half an hour. I never allowed him to do any more. And he died in 1997.

"We traveled about a couple of million miles. It wears you out. But they did treat me well. They put me in first class, and Morris always traveled onboard with me, and for a while, the airlines would say, 'Bob Martwick traveling with Morris the Cat.' Well, that became a very dissatisfying thing because I couldn't relax. The people would be all over us. So we just stopped that and I just carried a cat on. If people would ask if there was somebody unusual or interesting, I'd tell them who it was, but not very often. I did see the United States—every major city except two, out of fifty, plus over one hundred more. And I did like to travel, so that wasn't too bad."

There has been a Morris III and now there's a Morris IV, but Martwick is not their trainer. "I was kind of happy to get out of it as it changed from Nine Lives to a bigger corporation. The whole thing changed, and they weren't making any more commercials and that was kind of the fun part. So it was kind of time for me to get out."

With that, we'll do the same.

Mr. Smith

NBC, 1983, 13 episodes

Starring C. J. as Cha Cha/Mr. Smith, Leonard Frey as Raymond Holyoke, Tim Dunigan as Tommy Atwood, Laura Jacoby as Ellie Atwood, Terri Garber as Dr. Judy Tyson, Stuart Margolin as Dr. Klein, and Ed Weinberger as the voice of Mr. Smith.

Mr. Smith was a comedy about a circus orangutan named Cha Cha who drinks a bottle of experimental enzyme that turns him into a talking primate with an IQ of 256. The government renames him Mr. Smith and makes him a special consultant because of his brilliance. Meanwhile he lives with a regular family in the suburbs of Washington, D.C.

The star of *Mr. Smith* was one great orangutan named C. J. Owned by Ralph Helfer, the man behind Clarence the cross-eyed lion, Judy the chimp, Modoc the elephant, and Zamba the lion, C. J. had thick reddish gold fur, beady eyes, and the strength of four men. In his prime, he weighed 275 pounds, most of it seemingly in his belly.

"C. J.'s outstanding talent and personality made him famous throughout the industry. Always in demand, he did a number of movies, television shows, cameo spots in TV series, and magic shows. C. J. was a star. He was to the animal world what Laurence Olivier was to the human," Helfer wrote in his 1990 book *The Beauty of the Beasts.*

"He was a gentle animal, a lover of people, animals, and life in general. He rode horses, traveled in cars, and kissed the people he liked," Helfer wrote. "However, if someone had ticked him off for some reason, he would ignore the person by turning his back."

Helfer talked more about his beloved orangutan in an interview in the fall of 2000. "C. J. was fabulous. Paramount came to us because he was such a winner, and he was getting quite popular. We considered him a member of the family. He would watch television at night. He loved westerns and eating popcorn."

Helfer says the simian would snack at his house on Cokes, cheese, fruit, candy, and popcorn, and he loved the westerns because of the horses. His favorite show was *Gunsmoke.*

Mr. Smith was about an orangutan who has an accident and develops an incredibly high IQ as well as the ability to talk. "We had to use a mechanical orangutan to match him hair by hair, so that we could do that in-sync dialogue," Helfer recalls.

Thus, a special-effects team built a computer model of C. J. that could move its eyes, lips, arms, and body and that could talk. The funny thing, Helfer says, is that after time, some people began to believe C. J. really could talk.

"C. J. had his own trailer on the lot just like a movie star," Helfer says. "He had his own director's chair, the star chair. When he went on the set, he would go to his chair and lounge. He had his own wardrobe that was very expensive. He had turtleneck sweaters. He'd put on his glasses. He'd dress himself and undress himself. He was incredible." The wardrobe featured everything from tuxedos and hats to shoes, coats, pants, and suits—all custom made.

That's not all. Like many stars of TV series, C. J. even sat in on all

C. J. took control as a brilliant Washington, D.C., consultant in *Mr. Smith.*

C. J. the orangutan became a movie star as Clint Eastwood's buddy Clyde in *Any Which Way You Can* in 1980. A few years later, he starred in his own TV series, *Mr. Smith*. His real-life best pal was Ralph Helfer.

Courtesy of Ralph Helfer.

the script conferences. He knew verbal commands like stop, stay, sit down, stand up, and wave, and he did his own stunts. The orangutan even had a pet white toy poodle, named Cheetah.

C. J. was probably best known for his movie-starring roles opposite Clint Eastwood and Bo Derek. Helfer says that C. J. fell in love with Bo Derek at first sight as they made *Tarzan* in Sri Lanka.

And he got along great with Clint Eastwood in *Any Which Way You Can.* "Clint was great. I told him he should have been an animal trainer. He was so good with the animal—that casual appearance he has on the screen is really him; therefore, he worked really well with animals," says Helfer. "He was never a man to use force in any way, verbally or physically. C. J. took to him right away. Many times trainers were not needed. Clint would bring him over, and he knew what he had to do. They would go to lunch together."

From an early age, C. J. played with tigers, lions, and bears. A duckling lived with him in his cage back on the ranch. He could use a flush toilet just like a human, and he liked to ride in a truck with his arm hanging out the side. When folks recognized him and would yell 'Clyde,' he'd give his famous right-turn hand signal.

Helfer tells the story about how he and C. J. once went into a 7-Eleven store and C. J. picked up bubble gum, candy bars, peanuts, and Cokes. He waited in line behind Helfer. When his turn came, he gave the cashier a twenty, took his change and bag of goodies, and walked out just like a regular joe.

"He was hysterical. He was as human as an animal can get," says Helfer. "He would listen. He would mimic. He had a certain wardrobe that he liked and others that he didn't. He liked certain colors."

While Helfer was away in Brazil making a movie, C. J. died of a heart attack. The trainer paid tribute to one of his all-time favorite creatures in his book with these words: "C. J. was a teacher, a loyal friend, and a pal. My relationship with him—like the one I had with Zamba, my lion—epitomized that special something that happens to people who really allow animals into their hearts. What you were before it only enhances by having the animal enter your world, and vice versa."

Helfer, who was born in Chicago and came to California as a boy, began working in the business as a teenaged stuntman. After performing stunts with wild animals, he became a trainer and since the late 1950s has supplied animal performers for more than five thousand feature films, TV shows, and commercials. His animals have won twenty-two PATSY Awards. Today he is a safari guide and a writer.

My Friend Flicka

CBS, 1956, 39 episodes (filmed in color but originally aired in black and white)

*Starring **Wahama and Goldie as Flicka,** Gene Evans as Rob McLaughlin, Anita Louise as Nell McLaughlin, Johnny Washbrook as Ken McLaughlin, Frank Ferguson as Gus Broeberg, and Pamela Beaird as Hildy Broeberg.*

Set at the Goose Bar Ranch in Coulee Springs, Wyoming, in the early 1900s, this series features the tales of a boy and his horse. Flicka is Swedish for "Little Girl." The TV series was inspired by the 1943 movie *My Friend Flicka,* which was based on the stories by Mary O'Hara. There were two other film sequels, *Thunderhead, Son of Flicka* in 1945 and *Green Grass of Wyoming* in 1948.

When ten-year-old Canadian lad Johnny Washbrook signed on to star in the TV series *My Friend Flicka,* he proved a quick study in the saddle. He had to be. He had never ridden before.

The young boy and the nine-hundred-pound chestnut horse became a perfect fit. "Flicka was absolutely beautiful. I was totally in love with her," says former child actor Johnny Washbrook. "Because of that show, I grew to love horses. I was a real city slicker, born in Toronto. I did not know how to ride until I got the series.

"When they bought her, her real name was Wahama, but they changed it to Flicka. An Arabian mare, she was four years old when we began shooting the series. It was a very exciting time of my life. I can recount it with vivid detail. After they screen-tested me, they took me out to meet Flicka the next day. I had reddish auburn hair, the same as the coat of Flicka. We got along great. They started me on riding lessons with just me, Flicka, and the trainer.

"I rode every day for an hour for several weeks before shooting began. I soon became spoiled. Flicka was so well trained. I felt at times that I only had to think what I wanted to do, and she would sense it and she was so receptive to any commands. Later, when other friends asked me to go horseback riding, I went a few times, but I found that horses at public stables were not so well trained as Flicka and I didn't enjoy going."

My Friend Flicka was filmed at the 20th

Century Fox Studio and at their lot in Malibu Canyon, known as the Fox Ranch. Flicka (Wahama) and Goldie, Flicka's double, were trained by Les Hilton.

"Les Hilton was a very likable, soft-spoken man. He was well-known for training horses in movies," recalls Washbrook. "Les was gentle but firm. He was the kind of person that people respected and he was well liked. It was no wonder he got along well with animals. He certainly had a way with horses."

Because the TV series required scenes with animals, it necessitated a lot of retakes. That meant rising costs.

"*My Friend Flicka* was the first venture into television for 20th Century Fox, and they had enjoyed a reputation as being the producer of first-class motion pictures," says Washbrook. "When they took on the *Flicka* series [they had done the original film when Roddy McDowall played the boy], they treated it like one of their motion pictures. They were striving for the same level of perfection as they did with their movies, and they did so many retakes that the shooting schedule exceeded the budget. That created a lot of problems. We did thirty-nine episodes the first year. The second year they continued to keep me under contract, and I saw more scripts being written but there were delays."

For reasons still unknown to Washbrook, there never was a second season of *My Friend Flicka*. But he packed a saddlebag full of memories of the horse into those thirty-nine episodes: "I did love her and loved to ride her when we were filming the series out in Malibu Canyon. I often attempted to ride Flicka between scenes or at lunchtime. The movie studio was also filming a war movie out on their property, a war movie starring Robert Wagner. He was fifteen years older than me, so he was probably twenty-five, and we became friends.

"One day he decided he was going to teach me to drive an army Jeep. I rode Flicka bareback over to the location, and after visiting, I got on Flicka to ride back. Now Flicka had a tendency to be very high-strung, and I often had to keep a tight rein, and just at that moment when I was losing control, she started to take off. The next thing I knew I was doing a somersault over her head. She had a quirk where she would put her head down to the ground and give a quick little buck. She got away from me and ran straight back to where the other horses were." Washbrook was left behind with more than just a wounded pride.

"This was so typical of so many of the *Flicka* episodes where my character Ken would get into trouble and Flicka would come back to the ranch and there would be no Ken with her," Washbrook recalls. "But this time it happened for real, and you can imagine the shock of the company—here comes Flicka and no me on her. It didn't take long for them to find me. My wrist had a minor break.

"Sometimes it was rather comical to see the degree to which the writers of the episodes expected Flicka to perform. It is one thing to have a well-trained horse, but to read in the footnotes where they would suggest that I would have some dialogue, and Flicka was scripted to then look at me quizzically or with some emotional, underlying feeling . . ." Washbrook laughs at the notion.

"There was one scene I recall and for some reason Flicka reared up on her hind legs, which was quite a jolt and shock for me, but at the same time it was quite a thrill as a ten-year-old.

"Flicka was well trained, naturally being able to shake her head yes or no on cue. Les would be off camera signaling her. I felt totally relaxed around her and never felt afraid or nervous about her hurting me or stepping on me, just total confidence and trust."

While Flicka and Washbrook got along fine, the first stand-in was another story. "It was different riding Goldie. Generally speaking, I didn't ride her," recalls Washbrook. "She was used for the dangerous stunts and fast chases because Flicka was naturally high-strung and they had to keep her more under control and could not have her be involved in anything that would be dangerous.

"I rode Goldie a little, but I did have a double, a girl [probably Steffi Epper]. The reason was because in those days there weren't too many kids who could ride that well at ten years. She came from a large family of stunt riders. Her father was Gary Cooper's stuntman, and her brothers and sisters all worked in the movies. So they cut her hair and dyed it red to match mine.

"There was one horse I remember that they used for bucking when bad guys would steal Flicka and get on her. That horse wasn't used very often. But Goldie was on the payroll all the time and was used frequently."

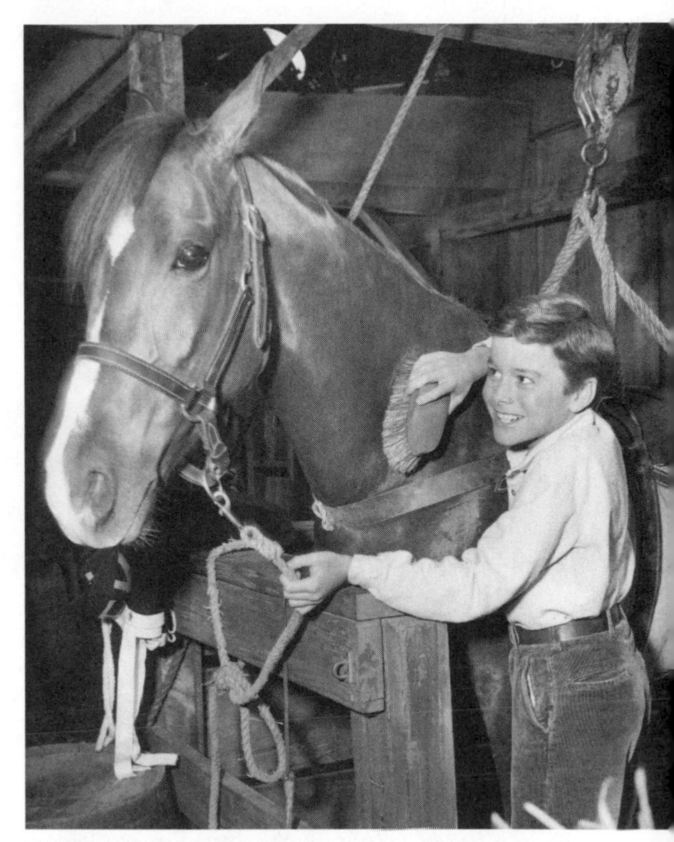

Johnny Washbrook works Wahama over with a currycomb on *My Friend Flicka.*

Washbrook tried to keep up with the whereabouts of Flicka after the series shut down. "Eventually 20th Century sold Flicka to a man who owned a ranch in New Mexico. He bought her for his daughter. Many years later, when I had moved to New York City to do more theater work, I ran into somebody who told me they had been working on a movie on this man's ranch in New Mexico, and Flicka was still there. So I phoned the man and talked with him about how Flicka was doing.

"Then some years after that I learned

through secondhand information the rest of the story. It turned out that the man subsequently sold Flicka to somebody else. Because of a medical condition, Flicka should not have been bred, but she was, and she died from complications during pregnancy."

The overall job still left young Washbrook with positive feelings. "I remember one episode where there was the risk of Flicka going blind. It was titled 'Blind Faith,' and like so many of those episodes, it had a good moral. I remember the message my mother was trying to get through to me was to have faith the size of a mustard seed in hope that Flicka would be all right. I used to get quite involved emotionally with the stories and Flicka, and I really threw myself into it. To this day I am a great horse lover because of that experience."

Les Hilton not only trained the horses for TV's *My Friend Flicka*, but also worked in the classic 1943 feature film of the same title. One of Hollywood's top horse trainers, Hilton worked with many great animal stars.

One was Misty, an almost-black thoroughbred stallion owned by Fat Jones. Hilton worked Misty (Mist-A-Shot), renowned as a great fighting stallion, in the movie *Flicka*, along with his mentor Jack Lindell, who trained the two lead horses, Flicka and Thunderhead.

Hilton had one of the longest careers of any horse trainer in Tinseltown. Besides TV's Flicka and Mister Ed, he worked a passel of great movie horses. Another was Black Diamond, whom he considered the most versatile of all the horses he ever trained.

Hilton was just a young cowboy when he came to Hollywood, and he was fortunate to learn under Jack Lindell, who was considered by many experts the greatest horse trainer in the business. Lindell worked out of Fat Jones Stables and trained Rex, "King of the Wild Horses," a particularly wild horse who was the most famous of them all in the 1920s and 1930s and was the first horse to star in his own series of films.

Fat Jones for many, many years had the largest stable of movie horses. He once said, "I look at a thousand horses to buy maybe ten, and only four or five of them make it in pictures."

His most beloved horse was Misty, known as "the John Barrymore of movie horses," who played in about seventy films. When Misty had to be put to sleep, Jones locked himself in his office all day.

In the late 1960s, Fat Jones Stable in North Hollywood had barns, saddle sheds, a blacksmith shop, and corrals settled on eleven acres. The beasts included horses, mules, oxen, and burros, and there were all types of wagons, stages, buckboards, and the like.

Fat Jones began renting his first horse when Hollywood was young, around 1912. When *Cimarron* was made in 1929, he was hired to gather in 1,100 horses and 400 wagons from all across the Southwest.

Not only were the Jones stables the home of the four-footed stars, but such cowboy actors as John Wayne, Randolph Scott, Gary Cooper, Joel McCrea, Ken Maynard, William S. Hart, and Tom Mix also bought horses from him. His most lucrative horse was name Steel, who was ridden in the movies by Clark Gable, Robert Mitchum, Joel McCrea, John Wayne, Randolph Scott, Ben Johnson, and Robert Taylor, among others.

During the 1940s, Fat Jones Stable was a comfortable place to hang out for cowboys who drifted in from the ranches of America. Some stayed around long enough to become stuntmen.

Jones died in 1963.

The second most famous place to find good horseflesh was the Hudkins Brothers' Stable, run by Clyde, Ace, and Ode Hudkins. They were as famous for stunt horses as Jones was for star horses. And this is where Roy Rogers found his Trigger.

And so it was that for the first fifty years of American motion pictures and into the first two decades of television, Fat Jones, the Hudkins brothers, Glenn Randall, Jack Lindell, Les Hilton, and Ralph McCutcheon were the men who made many a horse as famous as the two-legged stars who rode them.

My Three Sons

ABC, CBS, 1960–1972, 369 episodes

*Starring **Spud, Speed, and Hobo as Tramp;** Fred MacMurray as Steve Douglas; William Frawley as Bub O'Casey; William Demarest as Uncle Charlie; Tim Considine as Mike Douglas; Don Grady as Robbie Douglas; Stanley Livingston as Chip Douglas; Barry Livingston as Ernie Douglas; Meredith MacRae as Sally Ann Douglas; Beverly Garland as Beverly Douglas; and Tina Cole as Katie Douglas.*

My Three Sons is the story of a widower, who is an aeronautical engineer and does his best at raising three (well, actually, four) sons with assistance from the boys' uncles.

The main two dogs that played Tramp Douglas were named Speed and Spud. The latter dog Frank Inn retrieved from one of his favorite haunts, the Burbank animal shelter.

The dogs who played Tramp were mixed briards, and they were especially nice dogs, according to Inn. He says, "Fred MacMurray thought Tramp was great. Sometimes he would send me off with Tramp to where his wife, June Haver, was helping at a children's hospital.

"Tramp won three first-place PATSY awards over the thirteen-year run of the series. He didn't do nothing fancy. He was just a dog in *My Three Sons*, but he was good."

Tramp weighed about sixty-five or seventy pounds and was served homemade dog food. The chef was Inn. "I fed 'em all the same," says Inn. "We made our own dog food. We'd go down and get chickens from the butcher, and we'd get rabbit, and cook the meat up, take all bones out, and mix it with oatmeal. That was our dog food."

Stanley Livingston, who played Chip on *My Three Sons*, knew Tramp as well as anyone

The third Tramp on *My Three Sons* was played by Hobo, a grandson of Spud. He stands still for a Douglas family portrait in 1971.

Courtesy of Stan Livingston.

who worked on the show. After all, he was a boy and Tramp was a dog.

He remembers working with both Spud and Speed. He thinks the two shared most of the workload the first few seasons, but after that Spud was his TV pet. "Spud did the bulk of the work. He was the friendlier of the two dogs," says Livingston.

"Basically the dog just walked through scenes," he adds. According to Livingston, "Spud was better animated and a better-looking dog, but he wasn't as controlled as Speed. Occasionally, in the middle of a scene, Spud would just bolt or run in circles. Speed may have been a little bit better trained.

"Spud seemed to have his own mind-set, but he had a lot of show-dog kind of training and was very friendly. I remember wrestling with him. He was like Pluto, big and slopping all over, almost like too big for his brain. He would come running around corners and his feet would go out from under him. He was just the most affectionate dog. You could call him over and he would jump up, put his paws on your shoulder, and slurp your face."

John Stephens, production manager on *My Three Sons*, says of the dogs that played Tramp, "We used Spud mostly. He went for almost the length of the series. He did all of the close-ups and the tricks. We used Speed in the long shots. He was the more athletic of the two.

"Tramp was a real, real sweet dog, a great dog, never missed a cue. He was just always there. . . . If the tricks were difficult, we

Fred MacMurray was the father of three sons and a dog in *My Three Sons*. The dog is Tramp, and the three sons are (clockwise from the dog) Stanley Livingston, Don Grady, and Tim Considine.

Fred MacMurray, who played the father on *My Three Sons,* holds Speed, who played Tramp, in 1960.
Courtesy of Stan Livingston.

Chip Douglas (Stanley Livingston) shows up with a boy's best friend, his dog, in this case, Tramp, on *My Three Sons.*

would isolate the shot with just the dog and call it a 'Tramp shot.'"

Genny Kerns, who worked on the show for the first three seasons, says the directors "were all just crazy about the dog. Spud was just a real happy-go-lucky, friendly, sweet, and actually, a well-trained dog, but he didn't do anything sensational because nobody required it of him."

Livingston says there was an obvious physical difference between the two Tramps. "Spud had a longer nose. Speed's is shorter and darker." He also remembers that in the later seasons, they started using a grandson of Spud, a dog named Hobo (no relation to an earlier movie star sheepdog of the same name), and they colored him to match the markings.

Before *My Three Sons,* Livingston worked in the feature film version of *Please Don't Eat the Daisies,* where he made the acquaintance of Hobo, Cindy James's sheepdog that saw plenty of action. Livingston recalls, "All I did was play with Hobo. After the film was over, Cindy James gave me a shaggy dog, Patches, the brother of Hobo. We lived in a pretty small apartment in Hollywood, so after two years, my parents called Cindy and traded Hobo in for a poodle. But my brother Barry and I would take the dog up to Hollywood Boulevard, and we would roller skate with the sheepdog. We would put two leashes on the dog, and he would pull us."

Livingston also paid visits to TV pets at other studios during the 1950s and 1960s. He used to feed and play with Cleo of *The People's Choice*, and he met the famous Mister Ed.

"I discovered next door was Mister Ed. I brought carrots from home and sugar lumps. I would go over and feed him and pet him, but he never said anything, and I would think, 'How come this horse doesn't talk?' I was pretty young," says the third son and the friend of three Tramps.

Nanny and the Professor

ABC, 1970–1971, 65 episodes

*Starring **Bozo and Waldo as Waldo,** Juliet Mills as Phoebe Figalilly (Nanny), Richard Long as Professor Harold Everett, David Doremus as Hal Everett, Trent Lehman as Butch Everett, Kim Richards as Prudence Everett, Eileen Baral as Francine Fowler, Patsy Garrett as Florence Fowler, and Elsa Lanchester as Aunt Henrietta.*

Nanny and the Professor follows the lives of a widowed college math instructor, his three children, and their mysterious housekeeper, Nanny, who, with a touch of psychic powers, spreads happiness.

There were two dogs who filled the bill of dog star for *Nanny and the Professor*, and they were as different as day and night. Both were owned by Frank Inn. The first Waldo was not an Old English sheepdog but missed being one by only a tail. According to Inn, he looked exactly like one, except that he had a tail.

Henry Shannon handled most of the training of the two Waldos and knew their characters pretty well. "The first dog was eight or nine and had belonged to another trainer," says Shannon. "Frank finally bought him and then we found out he didn't know many tricks. His name was Bozo, and he did the first two years of the show. He was kind of a quiet dog, sort of laid-back. You couldn't use him for high-speed scenes or vim-and-vigor things. He kept to himself, but when you said, 'Action!' he was ready to go. He liked to eat, and we had to watch his weight."

The sixty-pound canine knew some basics such as sit, lie down, and speak, Shannon says, but "we had to teach him to walk with people. He was with the kids most of the time. He liked them, and the kids seemed to like him."

One of Shannon's favorite episodes centered on Waldo digging up dinosaur bones. "A truck goes by and a bunch of dinosaur bones fall out. Waldo takes them and buries

Where's Waldo? David Doremus knows that he's on the set of *Nanny and the Professor* in 1970.

them in the backyard, and then Jim Backus, playing a paleontologist, keeps digging the bones up and the dog keeps burying them."

By the second season, a Waldo-in-waiting was brought aboard. Since he was going to take over the role of Waldo, they named him Waldo.

"We brought Waldo along to get him set experience. You can train all you want in the backyard or park, but under different circumstances, it's a whole new ball game," Shannon says of young Waldo, who was a purebred Old English sheepdog.

"Waldo was very active. Frank bought him from a breeder at about six or eight weeks old. He was really happy-go-lucky. Everything was whoopee with him. He was bouncy, very active, kind of a hyper type. You had to watch him closely. He was so full of energy. It was hard for him to stay still sometimes. When the kids laughed, he thought it was time for him to go. He was almost like an untrained colt, like a kid himself."

Waldo was particularly adept at little head cocks and little woofs for close-ups. And Shannon recollects that after his *Nanny and the Professor* days, the sheepdog did a lot of group work.

Patsy Garrett, who played neighbor Florence on the series, had her own dog on the show, Fifi, a little poodle. But she, too, remembers Waldo: "He was great big and fluffy. Nanny didn't pull a lot of magic tricks on him. Waldo was just their big old household dog, and whatever she said never seemed to surprise this dog. She would fly in the air, and he would just look at her.

"He didn't do any tricks, and usually went with the children. The first dog, the old one, would go off and sleep somewhere, and we couldn't get him to react to much. But he was a very loving dog, very nice and easy to be around."

Garrett went on to work in Purina cat food commercials for ten years, including the famous one where she dances with a cat in the kitchen. And she acted in the original *Benji* film as Mary the housekeeper and returned for roles in *For the Love of Benji* and the TV special *Benji Christmas.*

The cast of *Nanny and the Professor* worked with other critters during the course of the series, including guinea pigs Mertyl and Mike, rooster Sebastian, and baby goats Jerome and Geraldene, who were kids, of course, to Nanny.

National Velvet

NBC, 1960–1962, 58 episodes

*Starring **Blaze King as King,** Lori Martin as Velvet Brown, Ann Doran as Martha Brown, James McCallion as Mi Taylor, Arthur Space as Herbert Brown, Carole Welles as Edwina Brown, Joey Scott as Donald Brown, Carl Crow as Teddy, and Rickey Kelman as John Hadley.*

The TV version of *National Velvet* was loosely based on the 1944 film starring Elizabeth Taylor. Unlike the film, the TV series was set in the American Midwest, where a twelve-year-old girl chases her dream of entering her horse King in the Grand National Steeplechase. While her parents operate a dairy farm, Velvet and her friend Mi, a handyman and ex-jockey, train the horse to race.

Horse trainer Kenny Lee had a problem: how to train a stallion to work with a twelve-year-old girl with little riding experience for a new TV series. The dilemma began when the producer of *National Velvet* picked the star horse without checking into its background.

"The producer saw the horse in a show ring one day in Palo Verde, California. It was a three-year-old stallion, and he bought him without checking with any trainer or horseman," says Lee. "He wasn't even broke to ride when I got him, but he got him because he had the bald face and stocking legs and looked a little like the original horse in the feature film. He decided 'that was the horse for me.'

"Now a stallion is not a plaything for a twelve-year-old girl. Lori Martin didn't know anything about a horse, and I figured it was just too dangerous when they hired me. So I had him altered. He settled right down and was a perfect gentleman for the rest of his life. When he was a stallion, he would bite you and he wasn't the best mannered. As luck would have it, once he was altered, he turned out to be a fine gentleman."

Lee says the horse who starred as King was fine with Lori from the get-go. "Before we started shooting, they gave me six weeks with Lori to try to teach her to ride and get along with the horse. She was as good a student as the horse. She learned how to ride well. She did most of the riding in the show, but for some of the big jumps, like water jumps and things, they used a double. She liked the horse, and the horse liked her."

National Velvet was filmed on a sound stage at the MGM Studios. For outside shots, like chases across the meadows, scenes were filmed at the Jans Ranch in Thousand Oaks, California.

"He just had a great personality," Lee says of the horse. "I'll never forget one show where he was supposed to be sick, and I had him lying down in a stall. Lori comes over and sits down next to him. We put his head in her lap, while she was sitting there. That scene had to last a good ten minutes. They did the master shot with two cameras and then had to cut in to close-ups, and that horse lay there like he knew they were making a picture and that was what he was supposed to do."

The series ended after two seasons, but the production company kept King because they thought they might do a spin-off with Velvet's little brother Donald and his Shetland pony in the spotlight. A pilot was shot, but it didn't sell.

In the spring of 1962, King and his equine costars were shipped out of the Sunshine State. Lee recalls, "I sold the horse for the company after the show was over, and he went to Bob Frisch, whose family owned the Big Boy restaurants [a hamburger chain in Ohio in the early 1960s]. I sent him and his double back there. The double was named Chief, and you could hardly tell them apart."

Lee took both horses and the Shetland pony to a children's home outside of Cincinnati. There he put the animals through their paces as he showed the new owners all their different tricks. "They had several horses there," Lee says. "Basically, all they did with them was just turned 'em loose in a big indoor arena and let the kids sit in the bleachers and watch 'em."

Lori Martin starred as Velvet Brown in 1960, when the classic *National Velvet* tale became a TV series. The horse, named King, was trained by Kenny Lee.

So King found a nice retirement home, and while he probably didn't go for burgers, Lee says, the horse loved a sweet concoction that combined sweetened grain, raisins, barley, rolled oats, and molasses. M'm, m'm, horse granola.

The Norm Show

ABC, 1999–present,
54 episodes

*Starring **Tony** as **Wiener Dog**, Norm Macdonald as Norm Henderson, Laurie Metcalf as Laurie Freeman, Ian Gomez as Danny Sanchez, Amy Wilson as Molly Carver, Bruce Jarchow as Mr. Curtis, Max Wright as Max Denby, and Artie Lange as Artie Henderson.*

The Norm Show is about a pro hockey player who is kicked out of the league for cheating on his taxes. He is sentenced to five years of performing community service, so he becomes a New York social worker.

Tony the dachshund is none other than Norm Henderson's Wiener Dog on *The Norm Show.*

Courtesy of Animal Actors of Hollywood.

One of TV's hot dogs of the new millennium is Wiener Dog as played by Tony, a miniature smooth-coated dachshund.

Trained by Janine Aines of Animal Actors, Tony was selected by Aines after she looked at more than a hundred different dachshunds for the role. The producers and writers of *The Drew Carey Show* also created *The Norm Show*, and they gave Aines three weeks to get a dog before the cameras.

"That was such a small amount of time, but I didn't really have the dog that I thought was needed. Dachshunds are tough. They're hounds, and they're probably the hardest to train because they're bred for using their noses," the trainer says.

Then she went to check out some dogs with a breeder in San Diego, and that's where she spied Tony. "I saw him, and there was just something in his eyes. I can't tell you what it was," says Aines. "But his owner said, 'He's not available. He's my stud.'

"I told her, 'I like your dogs, but I want this dog,' and she says, 'You can pick any dog but not him.'

"When I was leaving, she says, 'All right, I'll sell him to you' because she could tell I would take really good care of him."

From the get-go, Tony was a challenge. "When we got him, he really knew nothing. He couldn't even walk on a leash well, but he didn't know any bad training habits. He was totally green, so we started working. About a week before the show, I was really sweating it out. I took him everywhere with me.

"Finally we did the pilot, and he was very good, and he has been excellent ever since. On the pilot, we had gotten another dachshund from another animal company for safety as a backup. The pilot was very hard, even for a well-trained dog. The older, seasoned dog had a bit of a problem, so I told Tony, 'Come on, kiddo.' I was like, 'If you do this for me, you can stay at my house forever.' I think the little guy knew what I was saying."

Now six years old, Tony is staying at Aines's house.

He does have a helpmate on the set, Lexus, and also Andy, who is basically Wiener-Dog-in-waiting. "We have two doubles," says Aines. "One is female and completely different. Tony is mellow, easy-going, kind of takes everything and doesn't care about noise. Lexus, the female, is kind of kamikaze, crazy. Nothing upsets her, but Tony is real slow, deliberate, and detailed.

"Everything on *Norm* is very detailed work. With Lexus, if we need crazy runs or barking or being silly in someone's arms, she would be the one to do that.

"The second double is a puppy, Andy, who is about four months old. He goes to the show and is sort of growing up on the set, kind of like going to kindergarten class. He's kind of comic relief for the actors.

"Tony is really special. He likes actors, and he likes Norm a lot. If he is sitting on Norm's lap, he is always trying to sneak him a little kiss. He runs to the door when I bring him to the set. He's really a lot of fun to work because he's so sweet. They have been writing some clever little things for him to do. Because of his legs, he is limited physically. He can't jump on the couch.

"But Tony can type on a computer keyboard, and he can play dead and retrieve, and change channels on the remote TV. He brings things to Norm, but the thing he does best is just staying there. Things are never quiet and calm on the show. It's pretty chaotic and loud. People are always running around.

"One of the hardest things for him is to go to an actor and be picked up. Little dogs don't like to be picked up that much, and you have to pick them up properly."

Of course, there are fringe benefits of being friends with human television stars. "One of the actresses, Faith Ford, has given him a 'pooch pouch,' a cute little bed, for Christmas. He loves to cuddle up there and burrow. It was made specially for dachshunds."

As for diet, Tony gets chicken as a reward and generally feasts on Iams dog food. Lexus, says Aines, is Tony's best friend, and the couple shares a big dog run whenever they're not in the house. "Tony hangs out in the kennel with Lexie and is very good with the puppy," she says.

And Tony is one affectionate hound. "He's a cuddler. If you're watching TV, he wants to be on your lap and stay there all night long."

Among Tony's other credits are the feature *15 Minutes* and commercials for Kraft Macaroni & Cheese and Harry's Bread (in France).

Northern Exposure

CBS, 1990–1995, 110 episodes

*Starring **Morty as himself**, Rob Morrow as Dr. Joel Fleischman, Janine Turner as Maggie O'Connell, Barry Corbin as Maurice Minnifield, John Corbett as Chris Stevens, Darren E. Burrows as Ed Chigliak, John Cullum as Holling Vancoeur, Cynthia Geary as Shelly Tambo, Elaine Miles as Marilyn Whirlwind, and Peg Phillips as Ruth-Anne Miller.*

To pay off his medical school tuition loan, Dr. Joel Fleischman ends up with a four-year hitch in the tiny town of Cicely, Alaska, where a friendly moose wanders the streets, a retired astronaut is the big businessman, and there's a one-woman air shuttle service. And that's just the tip of the iceberg of interesting characters and story lines.

When the *Northern Exposure* production crew made its casting call of the wild for a moose, they found just what the doctor ordered in Morty, one of many moose under the care of Charlie Robbins, a biology researcher at Washington State University. *Northern Exposure* was filmed in Roslyn, Washington, and as it turned out, Robbins was studying the behavior and habits of moose not too far away at the Washington State George Hudson Biological Reserve.

While moose are not known for being the most cooperative and trainable of animals, Morty did respond fairly well to one motivation in particular: bananas. Armed with bunches of tasty bananas, the production crew barricaded sections of downtown Roslyn and then, with cameras rolling, let Morty wander around under the watchful eye of Robbins and other handlers.

Morty, who stood six feet tall and weighed about eight hundred pounds, was just a couple of years old when he started the series. As he aged, he became even less trainable than he already was, so the *Northern Exposure* crew resorted to using earlier moose-reel footage of Morty when they needed shots of him in later episodes.

One extra benefit of Morty's celebrity from being on *Northern Exposure* was that it drew

Dr. Joel Fleischman (Rob Morrow) meets one of the fine citizens of Cicely, Alaska, Morty the Moose, on *Northern Exposure.*

added attention to the important research being done by Charlie Robbins at Washington State. Among the things Robbins and his team have studied is why it is that the life spans of moose in captivity are less than half the usual life spans of moose in the wild.

Though they made the discovery too late to help Morty, who died of inflammatory bowel disease at age six, Robbins and his team found that a diet deficient in cobalt and copper seems to be a major factor linked to the early deaths of captive moose.

It's the kind of healthful finding that would have made Cicely's Dr. Fleischman proud. And no doubt Morty would have been pleased to know that he was part of a research effort that will help his fellow moose.

100 Deeds for Eddie McDowd

Nickelodeon, 1999–2001,
31 episodes

Starring ***Rowdy as Eddie McDowd, Mushu as his pug friend,*** *Seth Green (first season) and Jason Hervey (second season) as Eddie's voice, Brandon Gilberstadt as Justin Taylor, Morgan Kibby as Gwen Taylor, Danny Tamberelli as Spike Cipriano, William Francis McGuire as Doug Taylor, Catherine MacNeal as Lisa Taylor, Diane Delano as Brenda May, Richard Moll as the Drifter, Josh Hammond as Flaco, David L. Lander as Caesar (a dog), Joe Piscopo as Salli, and Brenda Song as Serifa.*

100 Deeds for Eddie McDowd is about a school bully who has been transformed into a skateboard-riding dog that must do one hundred good deeds to turn back into a kid. He is befriended and adopted at the pound by the last boy he tormented.

It takes a special dog to play a boy who has been turned into a dog, and Rowdy, a five-year-old Australian shepherd mix, is it. Discovered at the animal shelter in Castaic, California, Rowdy was plucked from obscurity by his owner and trainer Cristie Miele because of his looks and his attitude. "He's a very striking dog, and he's very friendly and outgoing," says Miele, who gave him his name because "he just seemed Rowdy."

Miele continues, "He does almost everything a movie dog can be trained to do. He'll cover his eyes, he'll crawl on the ground, but mostly his strong point is his ability to do successive behaviors in a row. He can come into a room, look to his left, go over and put his feet up, then bark and lower his head like he's sad, and he's good at interacting with different people at the same time.

"He is very into working. He likes to perform. That is first and foremost on his mind: 'Please, let's go to work. Let's get in the van.' He's pretty happy-go-lucky but very serious about doing his job. He seems to like everybody. Every week we seem to have a different guest dog, and he gets along well with the other dogs."

Rowdy plays Eddie McDowd, a dog who once was human, and Brandon Gilberstadt is his human master in *100 Deeds for Eddie McDowd.*
Courtesy of Nickelodeon.

Eddie McDowd was Rowdy's big break. Previously he had done a few commercials and an episode of *ER.* Under the auspices of Worldwide Movie Animals, Rowdy auditioned with many other dogs for the title role.

When the producers noticed his unusually good looks and how well he worked, plus saw that he had a double (it is often hard to have a double for a mixed breed), Rowdy won the role in a cinch. By the way, his double is Newman (named after another actor, Paul Newman).

"The dog lives with a family in *Eddie McDowd* and can talk to the boy Justin, with whom he gets along very well. Otherwise, he talks to the other dogs," Miele says. "It's a dog show and a children's show. The story line is always cute, and there is often a moral. Eddie still thinks like a bully but in the end does what is right."

She adds, "He has a sidekick in the pug, Mushu, who was the dog in the film *Men in Black.* He likes to play with other dogs." Miele should know. She has ten different dogs in her house, including Comet of *Full House* fame. A New Jersey native, Miele studied at Moorpark College and became a volunteer at Animal Actors of Hollywood, where she was eventually asked to help build up the dog department. She has been a professional trainer for fifteen years.

Rowdy's favorite feat for *100 Deeds for Eddie McDowd* is riding a skateboard. "He thinks that it is the greatest thing on earth," Miele says. "His attitude seems to be, 'This is so easy. You say, "Jump on this," and they roll me to you.' We literally could not keep him off of it."

And when the camera is turned off at the end of the day, Rowdy enjoys a good rip and tear. "We call it agitating," Miele says. "He'll play tug-of-war. He can go all day and still be happy and energetic by the end of the day. As for food, he loves everything. He's a bottomless pit. That helps give him the drive to work. He eats a lot of cooked chicken for treats."

The PATSY Awards

The PATSY Awards (Picture Animals Top Star of the Year) were given out by the American Humane Association Society between 1951 and 1986 for noteworthy performances by humanely trained animals in movies and television. These awards recognized the animals, as well as their trainers and handlers.

Animals were eligible for a PATSY Award when they appeared in a feature film meeting American Humane Association standards. Television animals qualified for nomination by performing in American Humane Association–accepted network programs or first-run syndicated shows of at least thirty minutes in length.

Each year the American Humane Association polled hundreds of entertainment editors, writers, and critics to determine the winners of the first-place PATSY trophy and the second- and third-place awards, which were plaques.

The Award of Excellence was given when the vote determined a deserving performance.

The Craven Award was named to honor the late Richard C. Craven, who became the first director of the American Humane Association of Hollywood office in 1940. The award was given to animals that ordinarily have no opportunity for a starring role, but excel in training, rearing, jumping, and "fighting."

The original PATSY ceremonies were held at Hollywood's Carthay Circle Theater in 1951, where Ronald Reagan presided as master of ceremonies. The event drew thousands, including movie fans and actors, who watched Jimmy Stewart give Francis the Talking Mule the very first PATSY award.

The winners over the years follow (please note that the names of the winners are most often the animals' screen character names and not their real-life names).

1951

1st: Francis (a mule) in *Francis the Talking Mule*
2nd: California (a horse) in *The Palomino*
3rd: Pierre (a chimp) in *My Friend Irma Goes West*
Craven Award: Jerry Brown (a falling horse), owned and trained by Ace Hudkins
Awards of Excellence:
Flame (a dog) in *My Pal*
Lassie (a dog) in *Challenge to Lassie*
Black Diamond (a horse) in *Black Midnight*
Jackie (a lion) in *Samson and Delilah*

1952

1st: Rhubarb (a cat) in *Rhubarb*
2nd: Francis (a mule) in *Francis Goes to the Races*
Craven Award: Smoky (a fighting horse), owned and trained by Fat Jones
Awards of Excellence:
Chinook (a dog) in *Yukon Manhunt*
Diamond (a horse) in *Flame of Araby*
Corky (a dog) in *Behave Yourself*

1953

1st: Jackie (a lion) in *Fearless Fagan*
2nd: Bonzo (a chimp) in *Bonzo Goes to College*
3rd: Trigger (a horse) in *Son of Paleface*
Craven Award: Bracket (a jumping horse), owned by Hudkins Stables
Awards of Excellence:
Francis (a mule) in *Francis Goes to West Point*
Tramp Jr. (a dog) in *Room for One More*
Cheetah (a chimp) in *Tarzan's Savage Fury*
Chinook (a dog) in *Yukon Gold*

1954

1st: Sam (a dog) in *Hondo*
2nd: Francis (a mule) in *Francis Covers the Big Town*
3rd: Jackie (a lion) in *Androcles and the Lion*
Craven Award: Cocaine (a falling horse), owned and trained by Chuck Roberson
Awards of Excellence:
Baron (a dog) in *Back to God's Country*
Peggy (a chimp) in *Valley of the Headhunters*
Jackie (a lion) in *White Witch Doctor*

1955

1st: Gypsy (Beauty, a horse) in *Gypsy Colt*
2nd: Francis (a mule) in *Francis Joins the WACS*
3rd: Esmerelda (a seal) in *20,000 Leagues Under the Sea*
Craven Award: Flash (a falling and lying down horse), owned and trained by Henry Willis
Awards of Excellence:
Shep (a dog) in *A Bullet Is Waiting*
Satin (a tiger) in *Demetrius and the Gladiators*
Beauty (a horse) in *Outlaw Stallion*

1956

1st: Wildfire (a dog) in *It's a Dog's Life*
2nd: Francis (a mule) in *Francis Joins the Navy*
3rd: Faro (a dog) in *The Kentuckian*
Craven Award: Flame (a dog), owned and trained by Frank Barnes

1957

1st: Samantha (a goose) in *Friendly Persuasion*
2nd: War Winds (Beauty, a horse) in *Giant*
3rd: Francis (a mule) in *Francis in the Haunted House*
Craven Award: King Cotton (a horse), owned and trained by Ralph McCutcheon
Awards of Excellence:
Silver (a horse) in *The Lone Ranger*
Lady (a dog) in *Goodbye, My Lady*
Bascom (a dog) in *Hollywood or Bust*
Note: Beginning in 1958, separate PATSY Awards were given for performances in film and for television (Performing Animal Television Star of the Year).

1958

Motion Pictures

1st: Spike (a dog) in *Old Yeller*

2nd: Beauty (a horse) in *Wild Is the Wind*

3rd: Kelly (a dog) in *Kelly and Me*

Awards of Excellence: Toby (a horse) in *Hoofs and Goofs*

Television

1st: Lassie (a dog) in *Lassie*

2nd: Cleo (a dog) in *The People's Choice*

3rd: Rin Tin Tin (a dog) in *The Adventures of Rin Tin Tin*

Craven Award: Trigger (a horse), owned by Roy Rogers, trained by Glenn Randall

Awards of Excellence: Flicka (a horse) in *My Friend Flicka*

1959

Motion Pictures

1st: Pyewacket (a cat) in *Bell, Book, and Candle*

2nd: Tonka (a horse) in *Tonka*

3rd: Henry (a rabbit) in *The Geisha Boy*

Awards of Excellence: King (a dog) in *The Proud Rebel*

Television

1st: Lassie (a dog) in *Lassie*

2nd: Asta (a dog) in *The Thin Man*

3rd: Rin Tin Tin (a dog) in *The Adventures of Rin Tin Tin*

Craven Award: Baldy (a rearing horse), owned by Fat Jones Stables, trained by William "Buster" Trow

Awards of Excellence: Jasper (a dog) in *Bachelor Father*

1960

Motion Pictures

1st: Shaggy (a dog) in *The Shaggy Dog*

2nd: Herman (a pigeon) in *The Gazebo*

3rd: North Wind (a horse) in *The Sad Horse*

Television

1st: Asta (a dog) in *The Thin Man*

2nd: Lassie (a dog) in *Lassie*

3rd: Fury (a horse) in *Fury*

1961

Motion Pictures

1st: King Cotton (a horse) in *Pepe*

2nd: Spike (a dog) in *Dog of Flanders*

3rd: Mr. Stubbs (a chimp) in *Toby Tyler*
Skip (a dog) in *Visit to a Small Planet*

Television

1st: Tramp (a dog) in *My Three Sons*

2nd: Lassie (a dog) in *Lassie*

3rd: Fury (a horse) in *Fury*

1962

Motion Pictures

1st: Cat (a cat) in *Breakfast at Tiffany's*

2nd: Pete (a dog) in *The Silent Call*

3rd: Flame (a horse) in *The Clown and the Kid*

Television

1st: Mister Ed (a horse) in *Mister Ed*

2nd: Lassie (a dog) in *Lassie*

3rd: Tramp (a dog) in *My Three Sons*

1963

Motion Pictures
1st: Big Red (a dog) in *Big Red*
2nd: Sydney (an elephant) in *Jumbo*
3rd: Zamba (a lion) in *The Lion*
Television
1st: Mister Ed (a horse) in *Mister Ed*
2nd: Lassie (a dog) in *Lassie*
3rd: Tramp (a dog) in *My Three Sons*
Craven Award: Mickey O'Boyle (a fighting horse), owned by the Hudkins Brothers and trained by Glenn Randall

1964

Motion Pictures
1st: Tom Dooley (a dog) in *Savage Sam*
2nd: Pluto (a dog) in *My Six Loves*
3rd: Raunchy (a jaguar) in *Rampage*
Television
1st: Lassie (a dog) in *Lassie*
2nd: Mister Ed (a horse) in *Mister Ed*
3rd: Tramp (a dog) in *My Three Sons*

1965

Motion Pictures
1st: Patrina (a tiger) in *A Tiger Walks*
2nd: Storm (a dog) in *Goodbye Charlie*
3rd: Junior (a dog) in *Island of the Blue Dolphin*
Television
1st: Flipper (a dolphin) in *Flipper*
2nd: Lassie (a dog) in *Lassie*
3rd: Mister Ed (a horse) in *Mister Ed*
Craven Award: Little Buck (a trained falling horse), owned by Gary Combs and trained by Les Hilton

1966

Motion Pictures
1st: Syn (a cat) in *That Darn Cat*
2nd: Clarence (a lion) in *Clarence the Cross-Eyed Lion*
3rd: Judy (a chimp) in *Merlin Jones*
Television
1st: Flipper (a dolphin) in *Flipper*
2nd: Lord Nelson (a dog) in *Please Don't Eat the Daisies*
3rd: Higgins (a dog) in *Petticoat Junction*
Craven Award: Smokey (a trick horse in *Cat Ballou*), trained by Al Yank

1967

Motion Pictures
1st: Elsa (a lion) in *Born Free*
2nd: Duke (a dog) in *The Ugly Dachshund*
3rd: Vindicator (a bull) in *The Rare Breed*
Television
1st: Judy (a chimp) in *Daktari*
2nd: Flipper (a dolphin) in *Flipper*
3rd: Arnold (a pig) in *Green Acres*
Craven Award: Smokey (a trick horse)

1968

Motion Pictures
1st: Ben (a bear) in *Gentle Giant*
2nd: Sir Tom (a cougar) in *The Cat*
3rd: Sophia (a sea lion) in *Doctor Doolittle*

<u>Television</u>

1st: Arnold (a pig) in *Green Acres*

2nd: Clarence (a lion) in *Daktari*

3rd: Ben (a bear) in *Gentle Ben*

TV Commercial: Zamba (a lion) for Dreyfus Fund

1969

<u>Motion Pictures</u>

1st: Albarado (a horse) in *The Man in the Gray Flannel Suit*

<u>Television</u>

1st: Arnold (a pig) in *Green Acres*

2nd: Timmy (a chimp) in *The Beverly Hillbillies*

TV Commercial: Chauncey (a cougar) for Ford Motor Company

1970

<u>Motion Pictures</u>

1st: Rascal (a raccoon) in *Rascal*

<u>Television</u>

Series: Scruffy (a dog) in *The Ghost and Mrs. Muir*

Non-series: Algae (a seal) in *The Ghost and Mrs. Muir* (single performance)

Craven Award: Kilroy (a falling horse), owned by Henry Wells

1971

<u>Motion Pictures</u>

1st: Sancho (a wolf) in *The Wild Country*

Tramp, who performed the role of Tramp on *My Three Sons*, receives a PATSY Award in 1963 with a little help from his friends, owner Frank Inn and best boy Stanley Livingston.

Courtesy of Stan Livingston.

<u>Television</u>

Series: Arnold (a pig) in *Green Acres*

Non-series: Margie (an elephant) in *The Boy Who Stole an Elephant* and Lassie puppies (dogs) in *Lassie*

1972

<u>Motion Pictures</u>

1st: Ben (a rat) in *Willard*

Television
Series: Pax (a dog) in *Longstreet*
Non-series: Ott (a horse) in *Lassie*
Craven Award: Cocaine (a horse) for outstanding stunt work

1973

Motion Pictures
1st: Ben (a rat) in *Ben*
Television
Series: Farouk (a dog) in *Ironsides*
Non-series: Ott (a horse) in *Bonanza* (single performance)
Commercial: Morris (a cat) for Nine Lives cat food
Animal Actors Hall of Fame: Lassie

1974

Motion Pictures
1st: Alpha (a dolphin) in *Day of the Dolphin*
Television
Series: Midnight (a cat) in *Mannix*
Non-series: Caesar (a dog) in *Trapped*
Commercial: Scruffy (a dog) for Chuck Wagon dog food

1975

Motion Pictures
1st: Tonto (a cat) in *Harry and Tonto*
Television
Series: Elsa (a lion) in *Born Free*
Non-series: Ginger and puppies (a coyote family) in *The Indestructible Outcasts*
Commercial: Lawrence (a red deer) for the Hartford Insurance
Animal Actors Hall of Fame: Benji
Note: The format of the awards was changed again in 1976 with the categories becoming Wild Animal, Canine, Equine, and Special. The Grand PATSY Award was initiated with one Grand PATSY a year, including all categories.

1976

Grand PATSY Award: Fred (a cockatoo) in *Baretta*
Wild Animal: Billie (a chimp) in *Swiss Family Robinson*
Canine: Tiger (a dog) in *A Boy and His Dog*
Equine: Ott (a horse) in *Run, Joe, Run*
Special: Fred (a cockatoo) in *Baretta*

1977

Grand PATSY Award: Fred (a cockatoo) in *Baretta*
Wild Animals:
Neal (a lion) in *The Bionic Woman*
Heller (a cougar) in *Shazam*
Lawrence (a red deer) in Hartford Insurance ad
Snoopy (a raccoon) in *Guardian of the Wilderness*
Bruno (a bear) in *Wilderness Family*
Valentine (a camel) in *Hawmps*
Canine:
Gus (a German shepherd) in *Won Ton Ton, The Dog Who Saved Hollywood*
Five Dobermans in *The Amazing Dobermans*

Bourbon in *Call of the Wild*
Kodiak and sled team in *Call of the Wild*
Equine:
Shoshone in *Mustang Country*
Yoyo in *Banjo Hackett*
Yoyo in *The Shaggy D.A.*
Gus (a mule) in *Gus*
Unnamed horse in Top Choice dog food commercial
Special:
Seventeen (a cat) in *Dr. Shrinker*
Jojo (a raven) in *Duffy Moon*
Fred (a cockatoo) in *Baretta*
Animal Actors Hall of Fame: Scruffy

1978

Wild Animals: Farcas (a wolf) in *Lucan*
Canine: Sam (a yellow Labrador retriever) in *Sam*
Equine: Domengo in *Peter Lundy and the Medicine Hat Stallion*
Special: Amber (a cat) in *The Cat From Outer Space*
Craven Award: Sandy (a dog) in the Broadway production of *Annie*
Note: No awards were presented from 1979 to 1982 due to a lack of funding.

1983

Wild Animals: C. J. (an orangutan) in *The Fall Guy*
Canine: Boomer in *Here's Boomer*
Equine: Kit Kat in *The Fall Guy*
Special: Jeckel (a bull) in *Knight Rider*
Human/Animal Bond Award: O. J. (a dog) in *Skeezer*, owned and trained by Robert Weatherwax

1984

Wild Animals: the panthers in *Manimal*
Canine: Tundra in *The Love Boat*
Special: Merlin (a hawk) in *Manimal*
Animal Actors Hall of Fame:
Neal (a lion) owned and trained by Ron Oxley
Harry (a black Labrador/Great Dane mix) owned and trained by Karl Lewis Miller
Human/Animal Bond Award: Am (a seal) in *The Gold Seal*

Genny Kerns and Barney, who played Jack during the first season of *Little House on the Prairie*, make a grand appearance at the PATSY Awards show in 1974.

Courtesy of Genny Kerns.

1985

Wild Animals: J. R. (an orangutan) in *Goin' Bananas*
Canine: Folsom in *Body Double*
Equine: Silver in *The Yellow Rose*
Human/Animal Bond Award: Sneakers (a puppy) in *Highway to Heaven*

1986

Wild Animals: Dee (a chimp) in *Simon and Simon*
Canine: Samson, Magnum, and Lucan (Dobermans) in *Reno Williams: The Adventure Begins*
Equine: 'Tis No Trouble in *Sylvester*
Special: The cats in *Alfred Hitchcock Presents*
Note: After 1986, the PATSY Awards were discontinued because of a lack of funding.

The People's Choice

CBS, 1955–1958, 104 episodes

Starring ***Bernadette as Cleo,*** *Jackie Cooper as Sock Miller, Patricia Breslin as Mandy Peoples Miller, Paul Maxey as Mayor John Peoples, Margaret Irving as Gus Miller, Dick Wesson as Hex Hexley, Elvia Allman as Miss Larson, and Mary Jane Croft as the voice of Cleo.*

The People's Choice is about an ornithologist studying to be a lawyer who falls in love with the mayor's daughter and winds up a councilman and head of a housing development. His dog, Cleo, observes the action and through overdubbing makes sarcastic comments to the viewers.

Frank Inn, the man behind Cleo, the famous basset hound of *The People's Choice,* worked for some of the top dog men in Hollywood, guys like Henry East, Rennie Renfro, and Rudd Weatherwax.

He had just begun working independently when he got a phone call to come down to General Services Studios where they

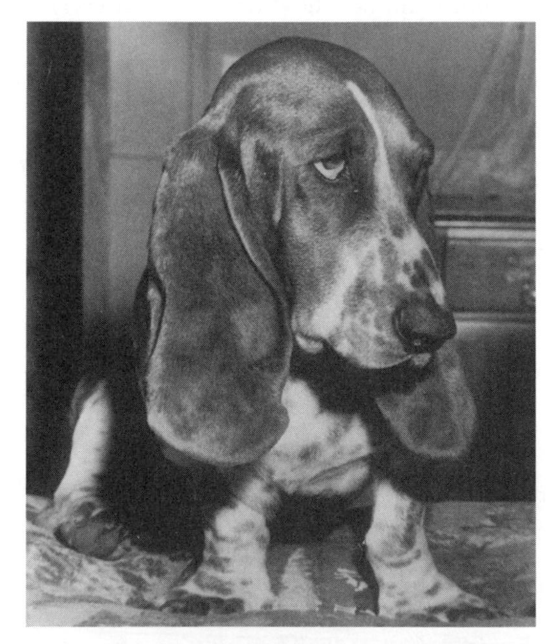

The basset hound star named Cleo on *The People's Choice* was trainer Frank Inn's beloved Bernadette.

Jackie Cooper and Patricia Breslin starred with Bernadette, as Cleo, in *The People's Choice*. The audience heard Cleo's thoughts, but her masters, the Millers, didn't have a clue.
Courtesy of Kevin Marhanka.

were looking for a dog for a Jackie Cooper TV pilot. When Inn got to the studio, he was a bit intimidated by what he found. Inn recalls, "When I went down, I walked in and there sat Rudd Weatherwax with a dog named Pokey, a basset hound I had trained; Henry East was in there with a bloodhound I had trained for him, and Rennie Renfro was there with a dog I had trained for him.

"I didn't even have a dog, no basset hound or bloodhound. The producers took me right past the others. They hadn't even looked at the other dogs. They told me that they were looking for a sad-eyed dog, probably a bloodhound or basset hound, and I said, 'The best trained basset hound is the one Rudd Weatherwax has out there.' They said, 'We know about it. We want a guy that trained Lassie.' I told them, 'That's the guy.' They said, 'We know about it.'

"They said they wanted a sad-eyed dog, and they looked at these other dogs but didn't give them an answer. They told me to see what I could find and show them in two weeks. So we looked at basset hounds. We found one we could rent from a lady, and she told me where some puppies were that were related, about ten or eleven months old. So I go and found this one that they had sold twice and given away once, but the people couldn't housebreak it.

"Boy, you talk about a sad-looking dog. This one was. My partner took the dog and put it in the car. We pooled our money. The dog cost eighty-four dollars, and when we got back to the car, the dog had taken the car keys and chewed the leather strap off of the key chain and chewed a couple of holes in the seat. Anyway, I went to work on the dog, and two weeks later, we made the pilot."

In the meantime, Inn was hired to work some dogs in the film *Giant* in Texas, where he also assisted Ralph McCutcheon with his great horse, Beauty, on the movie. "I was in Texas for several weeks when I get a call. They want me to come home because they wanted to start the series," says Inn. "When I got home, I found the dog was just a little on the thin side, so I told my wife to take good care of this dog. She did—she fed it too well and it got overly fat. I had two weeks to get it in shape and train it to do the stuff, but we did it.

"The dog didn't have a lot to do, but Mary Jane Croft did the voice, and we got a PATSY with Cleo. She was on there for three years.

"She was rather a timid dog, but she did everything I taught her. She would pose like a seal, and you could put a balloon on her nose. She would drag her hind legs like a seal. She'd play dead. Later, we made personal appearances everywhere with Jackie Cooper for the March of Dimes."

Inn recalls that Jackie Cooper liked to say, "My boy tells me 'Everybody at school knows who you are. You're the man that works for that dog.'"

Cleo's real name was Bernadette. She died of a heart attack at age twelve or thirteen, and her remains are in a bronze urn that will be buried with Inn. She was obviously one of his choice creatures.

Petticoat Junction

CBS, 1963–1970, 148 episodes

*Starring **Higgins (who later became Benji) as the unnamed family dog (occasionally referred to as "Boy")**; Bea Benaderet as Kate Bradley; Edgar Buchanan as Joe Carson; Jeannine Riley, Gunilla Hutton, and Meredith MacRae as Billie Joe Bradley; Pat Woodell and Lori Saunders as Bobbie Joe Bradley; Linda Kaye Henning as Betty Joe Bradley; Smiley Burnette as Charley Pratt; Rufe Davis as Floyd Smoot; Frank Cady as Sam Drucker; Charles Lane as Homer Bedlow; Mike Minor as Steve Elliott; Hank Patterson as Fred Ziffel; June Lockhart as Dr. Janet Craig; and Elvia Allman as Selma Plout.*

Petticoat Junction is about a widow, her three beautiful daughters (lots of curves—you bet), and their Uncle Joe, who operate the Shady Rest Hotel near Hooterville along the CF & W Railroad line.

The first scene Higgins ever did for television was the one that was used for the closing credits of *Petticoat Junction.* The Hooterville Cannonball is rolling down the tracks. The little dog is seen trailing after it. Little did his owner, Frank Inn, know that little Higgins was on the track to stardom.

Inn found the dog, which was a mixture of schnauzer, poodle, and cocker spaniel, as he did many of his finest animal actors, at the Burbank animal shelter. Inn recalls, "I got a call from the man who worked at the shelter, and he said, 'I got a cute puppy that you ought to have.' 'That's fine. I'll come down and look at it,' I told the man.

"I went down there, and he had this one puppy there, about six months old. He had gotten two or three new litters in. This was kind of a feisty pup, and the man didn't want to put it up with the other pups because it would fight them, and he didn't want to put him to sleep. So I brought him home. The man didn't even charge me."

At the time, Inn was spending much of

his time directing the numerous animals that worked on *The Beverly Hillbillies*. There was one episode where Elly May goes to an animal shelter and brings about forty dogs back to the Clampett mansion.

In one scene, Granny comes to the front door, hits a big pot with a spoon, and says, "Soup's on!" and all forty dogs charge the door, run over Granny, and leave footprints on her back. *Hillbillies* creator and producer Paul Henning thought it was the funniest scene he had ever seen. It left such an impression on him that he told Inn he thought a cute little dog would help his new TV series, *Petticoat Junction*.

Henning looked over about a half a dozen dogs that Inn brought with him, and Henning selected the dog that Inn had taken from the animal shelter. "That one there looks like a good one. Do you think it can follow a train?" Henning asked Inn.

"I took the dog, and we did a scene with it chasing a train along the railroad track, which they used for the credits. When we were shooting that scene, I stood on the back of the train and called the dog. That was the day President Kennedy was shot," says Inn, remembering that the shocking news stopped work for the day.

The dog that would later become Benji was on his way. The funny thing is that on *Petticoat Junction* he was the star without a name—a character name, anyway.

Inn explains how he came to call the real dog Higgins. "After we started on *Petticoat Junction* and had the stuff with the train, I was gonna call him Casey Jones. But then

There's a little hotel called the Shady Rest at the junction. Come and be the guest of Kate Bradley (Bea Benaderet) and her family, from left, Betty Joe (Linda Kaye Henning), Uncle Joe (Edgar Buchanan), Billie Joe (Jeannine Riley), Bobbie Joe (Pat Woodell), and their dog (Higgins) on *Petticoat Junction*.

they decided they were gonna have a contest and name the dog. They started the contest, but it was never completed. So all through *Petticoat Junction* he was just known as 'dog.' They never called him Higgins, but we called him Higgins at the kennel because of another TV series, *Hazel*, with the maid. They were planning another TV series about a butler, similar to Hazel, and that's what made me think of the name Higgins."

Inn says that Higgins was a very outgoing, aggressive dog, yet very much under control. He gives much of the credit for its training to Gerry Warshauer (who today goes by the name of Genny Kerns).

"She was one of the best trainers that ever was. I taught her step by step, but she didn't have to learn from me," says Inn.

Frank Inn holds his famous dog Higgins, who came out of retirement to become one of the most famous movie star dogs of them all, Benji.

"Genny had a good knowledge of what to do. Then, when I suggested something out of the ordinary—things I thought she could never get the dog to do—then she would do it. Higgins was one of the smartest animals I've ever seen. He probably did more things than any of the other animals I had."

Genny Kerns, the trainer Inn credits for much of Higgins's success, began working for Inn at age seventeen. She started on *The Beverly Hillbillies* and continues even today to work on some of the best TV shows and feature films using animal actors. She remembers one of her favorites. "He was such a great dog. Higgins was his name, but he didn't have a name on *Petticoat Junction.* Paul Henning was going to have a contest to name the dog, but he never got around to it," says Kerns, echoing Inn.

"Higgins was a once-in-a-lifetime dog. He was a dog that had a sense of humor. He wanted to do nothing but find out what you wanted him to do, and he did it with enthusiasm every time. That dog would know when there was a 'Cut!' and a mess up, and he would go back to his 'number one spot,' and if it was a good take, he would go back to his corner to rest.

"He'd yawn on cue or sneeze on cue. One of the gags, in one episode where the girls weren't dusting the hotel enough, had the camera on the dog, and he would sneeze. In one scene, he did a combination of behaviors as Uncle Joe describes a scene in a play, telling the dog what to do. He has to cross the room, take a piece of paper out of a safe, take the phone off the hook, pull a cord from a lamp, and get in a kid's car, all in one take. He was just an unbelievable dog.

"Everybody adored that dog. His favorite person on the set was the camera operator, who had a habit of eating tuna fish sandwiches in the afternoon. I have the sneaking suspicion that he gave a few bites to Higgins. Higgins liked hot dogs, hands down. He would always go for a bit of a doughnut or Kentucky Fried Chicken."

Kerns once took Higgins on a ten-day national publicity tour. "He was so wonderful and captivating. We went to the St. Regis Hotel in New York. They served the dog breakfast in bed there. We went to the White House, just on the outside. We were on *To Tell the Truth* and did numerous interview shows."

Kerns shared the fun of working with the talented dog with Karl Lewis Miller, another renowned trainer, who also worked several years for Frank Inn. "That dog was fantastic. I didn't have to train him, just show him what to do," says Miller, who worked with Higgins during the final season of *Petticoat Junction*, when he replaced Kerns, who had left to raise her children.

Miller recalls, "With this dog, they could throw me the most complicated actions, and I never had to train him. I would just show him what to do and he could do it.

"At the end of a cut, if he heard 'Cut, print it!' he ran off the stage to his crate to lie down and relax. They had customized his crate into a lavish, Southern colonial house. This was an aluminum crate that had pillars in front. He had his own little dressing room there. We called them dressing rooms because they're not cages to the dogs—more like a man's den or a woman's sewing room. It was a place to get away from the pressure of film-making. So when he heard 'Cut, print it!' he would run around the corner and lie down.

"His door was always open. He just lay there and watched the activities. When they're ready to shoot, they move on to the next setup, get the lights all set, and the crew is ready for the actors to come in. They honked a horn that was mounted on the side of the camera. That was the signal for 'everyone back on set.' When he heard that horn, he'd jump out of the crate and into my lap, and I'd take him onto the set for the next scene."

According to Miller, he was a special dog, but he was also typecast—Higgins couldn't get work after the series ended. After seven seasons of *Petticoat Junction*, Inn decided to retire the TV star. But then a man with a script titled *Benji* came calling.

Joe Camp, the writer and producer of *Benji*, looked at practically all of Inn's dogs but didn't see what he was looking for. Miller says, "Joe was walking out Frank's driveway, and he sees in Frank's front yard this little brown mutt lying in the shade.

"'What about that dog?' he asks. Frank says, 'No, that dog's too old. He's done his job.'

Frank Inn enjoys the company of his third Benji, who carried on in the role that Higgins made internationally famous.

Lotsa curves? You bet. The Petticoat Junction lassies, from left, Jeannine Riley, Linda Kaye Henning, and Pat Woodell, didn't always go swimming in that water tank shown in the opening credits. Their favorite dog was named Higgins, but was only referred to as "Boy" during the course of the TV series. Later Higgins became a movie superstar as Benji.

'Wait,' said Camp. 'I see one dog I'm interested in. Give me a minute?' So Frank says, 'OK.'

"Camp says, 'Let me have a moment with him,' and he goes into the yard and calls the dog, and the dog comes up and wags his tail. Joe is just walking around Frank's yard, and he tells the dog to sit and lie down and bark, and Frank keeps telling him, 'He's retired.'

"Joe Camp says, 'Frank, take him out of retirement. This dog is Benji.'"

Frank Inn adds more details to the Benji story: "When Joe Camp came out looking for his Benji, I was ready to retire. He was on his way out before we talked money. I told him I wanted $50,000 and ten percent of the profits, and he said 'I can't do that. I don't have that kind of money.'

"I finally made a deal because this was the last picture that I was gonna do. I made a deal for $9,500 for seven weeks. Joe had looked at about three hundred dogs by this time, and then he saw this old dog I had retired, lying in the yard.

"'That looks like the dog I wrote about,' Joe said to me. 'What can he do?' I said, 'He can do just about anything.'

"'Can he come to the window and yawn?' I said, 'I don't know why not.' I picked the dog up and threw him up on the roof of the house, about a two-foot throw. I had the dog go up behind the chimney and walk down to the edge of the roof and yawn.

"Then Joe asked me to have him do something else. About two hours later, he said, 'I'd like to see that dog in the picture.' I told him the dog was old, but we made a deal. I started riding a motorcycle and having the dog run along beside me for exercise. I taught him to dive into the water and all the other stuff in the script. We started shooting and after the end of seven weeks (the agreed-upon time), he paid me in full."

The only problem was that filming was not complete, so Inn and Camp worked out another deal. Inn and Higgins would complete the movie, not for cash, but for a part of the profits.

The dog spent about seven more weeks in front of the camera, and then, when the movie was released, Camp asked Inn and Higgins to go on a ten-week personal appearance tour. Inn agreed, but even after all the publicity, the film was still not clicking at the box office.

Inn says that Camp pulled the film from theaters and waited for school to be out so that more youngsters would have time to get into the theaters. "This time the picture just boomed and went off like a bang. My first percentage check was for $30,000. I signed a contract with Camp, and we went on from there," says Inn, who realized several million dollars from the *Benji* deal.

Now Inn faced a new problem: he had an old dog and movie fans wanted more Benji. "The public wanted more Benji and so did Joe Camp," Inn says, "so I trained his daughter, and she worked for fifteen years. She died at sixteen years, and I have one now who is thirteen that has carried Benji on."

Inn bred Higgins, the original Benji, many times. "He was still breeding when he was fifteen or sixteen, and he bore a litter of pups almost every year. I never sold a one. I gave most of them to friends who wanted them, to a lot of handicapped people, and many were used for hearing dogs."

The second movie-star Benji was Benji's daughter Benjean. The third in the line of stars was also called Benji and lived with Inn until he died at age fourteen in the fall of 2001. But there were more Benji offspring than Inn could shake a stick at.

"When we made *Benji the Hunted*, we used Benjean, three of her brothers, and two of Benji's grandsons. I had eight dogs on *Benji the Hunted* that looked like Benji," he said.

Inn did all of the training on Benjean, whom he described as "a very timid dog who developed into a very aggressive one because of the training."

For the thousands of miles that Inn, Benji, and Benjean traveled over the years, they used the "Benjimobile." Inn still has the last one, a thirty-three-foot-long motor home of 1979 vintage.

"Benji and I were responsible for more than a million dog adoptions around the United States," says Inn. "We got fifty to sixty thousand pieces of fan mail a year for Benji. When people asked, 'Where can I get a dog like Benji?' I told them to go to their local animal shelter."

And where are the remains of the first Benji? "Higgins died at eighteen," says Inn, but in answering the question he must go back to the early 1960s. "When Cleo [Inn's famous basset hound on *The People's Choice*] died, she was twelve or thirteen, and I was working at the studio when my wife called and told me she had taken Cleo to the vet. Cleo had collapsed in the backyard, and the veterinarian told her to go home and get a crate for an oxygen tent. The vet just wanted her out of there because he knew the dog was gone and didn't want her there crying.

"Cleo passed on, and we left the dog there to do whatever they do with dogs. A couple of weeks later, the veterinarian took us out to dinner. He gave me a bronze urn with Cleo's ashes in it. He had had her cremated. From that time on, I had all my motion picture animals cremated. When I die, they are going to line my casket with all these urns of my cremated animals. The only bronze urns are of Cleo, Higgins, and

Benjean. All the rest are in these little casket cans."

Frank Inn, says Karl Lewis Miller, "was the first versatile animal trainer for the movie industry. Frank Inn trained anything and everything. In my lifetime, Frank Inn is the granddaddy of them all. When I came in, he was the busiest man in Hollywood."

The grand total of Inn's animals (more than a thousand) and their TV and movie works may never be equaled, but he insists on giving the credit for his success to God. "God has given me this chance to have a beautiful life. My wife, Juanita, and I had fifty years together. You know the word 'dog' is 'God' spelled backward," says Inn. "I think that is more than a coincidence."

Please Don't Eat the Daisies / The Doris Day Show

Please Don't Eat the Daisies: NBC, 1965–1967, 58 episodes

Starring ***Lord Nelson as Ladadog,*** *Patricia Crowley as Joan Nash, Mark Miller as James Nash, Kim Tyler as Kyle Nash, Brian Nash as Joel Nash, Joe Fithian as Tracey Nash, Jeff Fithian as Trever Nash, Shirley Mitchell as Marge Thornton, Dub Taylor as Ed Hewley, and Ellen Corby as Martha O'Reilly.*

Based on the Doris Day film of the same title, which was based on the book by Jean Kerr, *Please Don't Eat the Daisies* is about a very untypical suburban family consisting of a mom who hates housework and works as a newspaper columnist, her husband who is an English professor, and their four young sons.

The Doris Day Show: CBS, 1968–1973, 128 episodes

Starring ***Lord Nelson as Nelson,*** *Doris Day as Doris Martin, Denver Pyle as Buck Webb, Fran Ryan as Aggie Thompson, James Hampton as Leroy B. Simpson, Philip Brown as Billy Martin, and Todd Starke as Toby Martin.*

The Doris Day Show is about a widow and her two sons who live on a ranch with her father and staff while she commutes to San Francisco as a secretary for a magazine. There were several format changes over the course of the series.

Television's most famous sheepdog was renowned Tinseltown trainer Hal Driscoll's Lord Nelson. Lord Nelson starred in two 1960s TV series, *Please Don't Eat the Daisies* and *The Doris Day Show,* and also popped up in the short-lived Mickey Rooney series, *Mickey.* He had been in more than twenty television shows, including *Dr. Kildare* and *The Man From U.N.C.L.E.*, and had worked with Lucille Ball and Jack Benny before he got the *Daisies* job.

Born in the spring of 1961 in San Fernando, California, the purebred Old English sheepdog's mother was Bridewell's Beauty, and his father was a chap named Cheyenne Sam.

"We always called him Nelson, but his full name was Bridewell's Lord Nelson," says longtime Hollywood dog trainer Genny Kerns. "Hal Driscoll owned him. He bought him from a big breeder who had come to California from England. Hal Driscoll and William [Bill] Koehler were partners in a company named Allied Movie Dogs. Hal Driscoll was a horse trainer by trade, and he hooked up with Bill Koehler, whom they called 'Mr. Obedience' because of his dog training work."

Koehler was chief animal trainer for Walt Disney Studios for twenty-three years. He created the "Koehler Method of Dog Training" and wrote six books about dog obedience during his fifty-year career.

Together Koehler and Driscoll did a lot of movies for Disney: *Big Red*, the original *Incredible Journey*, *That Darn Cat*, *The Ugly Dachshund*, and *Please Don't Eat the Daisies* (a non-Disney feature).

The team trained the star of Disney's *The Shaggy Dog*, named Lillybrad's Sammy's Shadow (called Sam for short), who looked remarkably like Lord Nelson. In fact, several of Lord Nelson's network biographies credit him as the star of *The Shaggy Dog*. The only problem is that he wasn't yet born when the 1959 film was made.

Nelson's first regular TV series was *Please Don't Eat the Daisies*. For the role, he was named after the favorite collie of children's author Albert Payson Terhune, who penned *Lad, a Dog*. The book became so popular that two subsequent adventures about Lad the collie were published. (The original Lad lived from 1902 to 1918.)

Mark Miller and Patricia Crowley are the parents of four red-haired boys and share an Old English sheepdog named Ladadog. The dog behind the mop of hair, Lord Nelson, won a PATSY Award for his talent.

Joe Fithian, along with his identical twin brother, Jeff, played Tracey and Trevor Nash, the youngest freckle-faced kids on the sitcom. Joe Fithian fondly recalls Lord Nelson, the only dog used in the series: "He was the friendliest, most gentle dog you'd ever know.

Mark Miller and Patricia Crowley go through a pile of *Please Don't Eat the Daisies* fan mail with Lord Nelson.

And he smelled gorgeous because he was groomed like a queen. The dog was always powdered and groomed beautifully. He was not only beautiful, but smart and wouldn't hurt a flea. On the show, of course, the dog used to answer the phone, run through the house, and do anything."

Many scenes in the show revolved around Ladadog's wild abandon as he ran at full clip through the house. "I remember one scene where my brother and I were supposed to run up the stairs and pretend like the dog knocked one of us down and then deliver a line," says Fithian. "The dog went by so quickly he actually knocked one of us down, but he knocked the one of us down who didn't have the line. The director said, 'Cut! What happened?' and I remember one of us said, 'I'm not the one he's supposed to knock down!'

"Lord Nelson had a zillion tricks," Fithian continues, "and you could get face to face with him, with all that hair over his eyes, and he'd lick you."

Veteran Kerns worked for Driscoll for several years and was on the set of *The Doris Day Show* when she got to know Lord Nelson. She recalls, "I worked the chickens (the show was set on a ranch) and helped Hal with the dog, who was probably four or five then. He was a gorgeous Old English sheepdog, one of the first dogs here that started to influence the popularity of the breed.

"Nelson was one of the smartest Old English sheepdogs I have ever seen, then or since, and he was a beautiful dog. He was big and fluffy and very smart. He probably weighed ninety pounds because what you see is mostly hair." (His NBC publicity biography states he weighed 104 pounds when *Daisies* debuted.)

"Nelson was Hal's house dog. Hal loved that dog, and he got special treatment," says Kerns. "He was great with kids, just a wonderful all-round dog. As for tricks, he just did the standard picture dog stuff: speak, go with someone, go put your feet up, get on your side, get on your feet, go pick it up. He ate anything and everything, and I know he got table scraps a lot."

According to his official press biography, Nelson ate one meal a day, but what a meal: three pounds of food consisting of one pound of raw meat and two pounds of Kibble and extra vitamins and sea kelp.

The canine thespian arrived at work daily in a station wagon. On the set of *Please Don't Eat the Daisies*, he had his own canvas-back chair with his name emblazoned in red and gold on the back.

"He's a regular ham," said Patricia Crowley at the time. "Just let a member of the press walk on the set and Lord Nelson takes over. It is almost as though he can scent printer's ink."

And the dog did get lots of ink. By the start of the second season, he got his own mailbox in the NBC mail room and received over seventy thousand pieces of mail before the second season premiere episode.

Lord Nelson began his schooling at the age of four months and was a quick study. "He's what we call a natural," Hal Driscoll told publicists in the mid-1960s. "From the time he was a pup, he was alert and fast to learn. This is a bit unusual in a thoroughbred. If you notice, most of the trained motion picture dogs are of mixed breeds. He's a dog with a drive to work that would match any devoted performer's. He'll take a routine, embellish it, adding his own flashy tricks and personal touches to the set pattern."

Among his other tricks of the trade: he could bark on command, jump through a window, climb a ladder, put his feet on a table, sit in a chair, drink coffee with the crew, and look alert—tail thumping and ears bristling—when the phone rang.

Kerns recalled that Doris Day truly adored Nelson and she once said that he was "a dog among dogs. . . . I loved him very much."

"She was really good with the dog," says Kerns. "They didn't demand a whole lot of the dog because he was part of the family. We mostly put the dog in the scene and let him run around with the kids."

Owner/trainer Hal Driscoll pampers the lumbering sheepdog known as Lord Nelson with *Please Don't Eat the Daisies* star Patricia Crowley.

The top dog practiced a bit of nepotism on *Please Don't Eat the Daisies.* He hired his own brother Lord Beaverbrook as his stand-in. And Nelson had a reputation as a big spender who cared about his appearance. Every time he went to the beauty salon for a bath and comb, the tab was $27.50, and it took an hour a day to comb his coat thoroughly.

The PATSY Award winner from TV's *Please Don't Eat the Daisies* died of old age in about 1971 or 1972, according to Kerns.

Punky Brewster

NBC, 1984–1986, 88 episodes

*Starring **Sandy as Brandon the "wonder dog,"** Soleil Moon Frye as Penelope "Punky" Brewster, George Gaynes as Henry Warnimont, Eddie Deezen as Eddie Malvin, Cherie Johnson as Cherie Johnson, Susie Garrett as Mrs. Betty Johnson, Ami Foster as Margaux Kramer, Casey Ellison as Allen Anderson, and T. K. Carter as Mike Fulton.*

Punky Brewster is the story of an abandoned seven-year-old Chicago girl who is "adopted" by an old bachelor who manages an apartment building. This sweet little tomboy slowly brings happiness into the old man's world.

Former child actor Soleil Moon Frye has very warm and very real feelings about the dog she had as a pet in her TV role as Punky Brewster. "Brandon was like a human being," she says. "I really think he was the smartest dog in the entire universe. He skateboarded and could go up to a water fountain and get a drink of water. He was such a human being.

"I think animals are so human. We forget that they do have feelings and they are sensitive. I loved Brandon. He was like my pet. They promised me they would give him to me when he turned twenty-one (in dog years), but they didn't.

"He'd push me on the skateboard, and we'd go skateboarding together. He'd come in every morning and chomp on me. He was so much fun."

Karl Lewis Miller, the man behind many television animal actors, was the guy responsible for Brandon, along with his trainer Glen Garner. "The golden retriever who played Brandon on *Punky Brewster* was actually named Sandy," Miller says. "He started as a puppy on the show, so he got trained while they were doing the show.

"We got Brandon from a reputable retriever breeder. Using him at a young age was unusual for me because typically I dislike raising puppies. I don't have the time for all the special care of puppyhood. I like to get young dogs nine months of age and train them.

"The show was about this Little Orphan Annie–like girl, and her companion was a puppy, a golden retriever. So from the pilot episode, we had to supply the puppy, and the puppy grew up on the show.

"Glen Garner was my right-hand man for fifteen years, and I had him assigned to that project. Any dog, such as Eddie on *Frasier*, for example, you could have the right dog to go to work but the wrong trainer or you could have the right trainer but the wrong dog. To have the right dog with the right trainer is where you get good work. And Glen was right for Brandon.

"We did conditioned behaviors. We don't want to break the spirits of animals too young, so Glen would condition this puppy to do behaviors. So when we came back for the second season, he was a young dog. By this time, the dog had some discipline and obedience training put into it, and now the writers could write more different gags for the dog to do."

Veteran trainer Glen Garner loved working with Sandy. "There's never been a sweeter dog," Garner says. "He was very, very devoted, very willing. He had average intelligence for a golden retriever. We started out with two brothers, Sandy and Brandy, and used them interchangeably as puppies, but Brandy got darker and larger and had a different shape to his head. It got to where they could tell the dogs apart in screenings, and so they said, 'Choose one and make it Brandon.' It was a tough decision—I liked both very much. Brandy was physically more capable, but Sandy has that instinct, the desire to please. I'll never ask for better than him. I cried when he died."

"Sandy later did the original *Watchers* feature film with Corey Haim as well as many bit parts on other shows," says Miller of Punky Brewster's favorite pet.

As for a bit of great TV trivia, Sandy was called Brandon in the series after NBC president Brandon Tartikoff, who created the show and suggested the title *Punky Brewster* after a childhood friend by that name. The real-life Punky Brewster actually guest-starred in one episode of the series.

Trainer Glen Garner was a native Californian who served in the military at Fort Carson, Colorado, training sentry dogs to go to Korea in the mid-1950s. After service, he went to work for Carl Spitz Sr. at his dog training school in 1957. In the mid-1960s, Garner hooked up with Frank Inn and made his TV debut in 1965 as a Marine dog trainer in an episode of *Gomer Pyle, U.S.M.C.* ("Gomer Un-Trains a Dog"). He later worked for Miller before going in with partners to purchase Frank Inn's company.

Sandy played Brandon, Punky Brewster's pet dog. Soleil Moon Frye (right) played Punky, and George Gaynes was her guardian.

Garner mainly trained domestic animals, but he did a few stints with a pelican on *The Flying Nun.* "Sally Field was scared to death of the pelican, but she worked with it. Pelicans are not overly intelligent," he says.

Garner, who believes there are three things that make a dog trainable (intelligence, instincts, and the physical ability to do things), also shared his talents on the sets of the feature films *Cujo, The White Dog, Beethoven, Beethoven II,* and a couple of *The Doberman Gang* movies.

Rin Tin Tin K-9 Cop

The Family Channel, 1988–1993, 106 episodes

Starring ***Rocky and Ike as Rin Tin Tin,*** *Jesse Collins as Officer Hank Katts, Andrew Bednarski as Stevie Katts, Denis Akiyama as Officer Ron Nakamura, Brian Kaulback as Officer Dennis Brian, and Denise Virieux as Officer Renee Daumier.*

Rin Tin Tin K-9 Cop picks up about one hundred years after Rinty, the main character's forefather, patrolled the old West. However, this time the German shepherd is a police dog battling urban crime. This Rin Tin Tin is cared for by a policeman and his teenage nephew.

Filmed for the most part in and around Toronto, *Rin Tin Tin K-9 Cop* featured German shepherds from owner Gary Gero of Birds & Animals Unlimited that were worked by head trainer Roger Schumacher and his partner Bryan Renfro, who doubled as a stuntman on the series.

For Renfro it was a chance to experience another side of the business. "Roger Schumacher and I came up to Toronto to do that show. Gary Gero had wanted me to do a movie, *Steel Magnolias,* or go with Roger and help on *Rin Tin Tin.* I wanted to get out of animal work and do more stunt work," Renfro says. "It was a great show to work on. Besides dog attacks, we had dogs running and jumping in and out of cars, and all kinds of stunts.

"That first season, Rocky was the main character dog we used. Roger had twelve weeks to get him trained. I was helping him—doing the dog attacks.

"A dog named Luke did all the running and jumping, and there was a dog named X that did all the attack work. We had another dog, a younger dog named Ike, that we also used for running stuff. After the first season, Ike became the lead dog, and he did the next four seasons."

Schumacher adds, "We found Rocky in Vancouver. He was a good dog. We crammed a lot of stuff into him in twelve weeks. During the first season we brought more dogs over from Germany. One of those was Ike, who I raised on the show. We planned on using him the next season, and he turned out to be the cream of the crop.

"Rocky'd come in and do anything you wanted him to do, but he was not as smooth as you'd like. He'd act like he was getting bored, but Ike loved it. Ike was special.

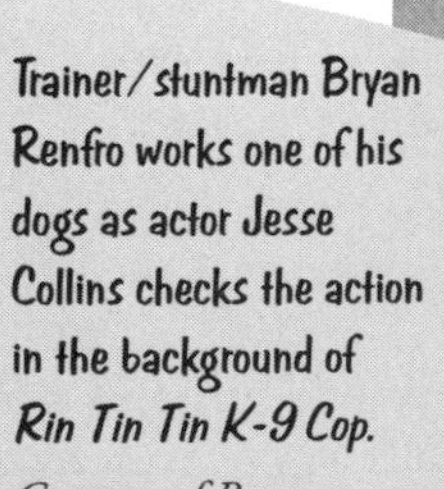

Trainer/stuntman Bryan Renfro works one of his dogs as actor Jesse Collins checks the action in the background of *Rin Tin Tin K-9 Cop.*

Courtesy of Bryan Renfro.

We could have done the entire series with just Ike. Ike was one in a million. He was just great with people and everything.

"Luke was the best-looking dog of the whole bunch, but he wasn't very good at training. His forte was running and jumping over things. I could be anywhere, and he'd try to jump across a lake to get to me. We had him go almost ten feet across from building to building. (There were safety nets below.)

"And X was our biting dog who did all our attacks. He was really good. He would come in and jump off tables and hit Bryan [the stuntman], stuff like that."

Renfro says the dog work was all the easier because of the way series star Jesse Collins related to the canines. "Jesse was just great. The dog has to work with a particular actor all the time. If the actor doesn't like the dog or the dog doesn't like the actor, your job is ten times as hard. It is so much easier if they get along, and Jesse was so good that he could work the dog himself."

Canadian actor Jesse Collins has marvelous memories of his canine costars on *Rin Tin Tin K-9 Cop*. "Rocky was great. He was the first relationship I had with the dog that was Rinty. He was a beautiful working dog who just did everything well. Rocky was this old stalwart. I enjoyed working with him," Collins says of the first season's star dog.

But he also has fond memories of Ike, the pup being groomed to take over as the main Rin Tin Tin. "Roger and Bryan had a big gangly pup named Ike who would eventually become the lead dog. I refer to Ike as one hundred percent dog. Dogs are a lot like

Ike and Jesse Collins became bosom companions as they partnered in the Canadian production of *Rin Tin Tin K-9 Cop*.
Courtesy of Jesse Collins.

people. They all have such different personalities. He was a bit of a goof when he was young, but he was a pretty exceptional dog in his ability in behavior and being able to put things together. Sure enough, by season two he was ready to step up.

"I had such a close relationship with Ike. We learned how to make an action-adventure show together. Roger said to me one day, 'One of the things you will see when working with an animal, if you have four different behaviors (or tricks), you'll notice the dog will start coming up with things on his own.' If we didn't get a scene after two or three takes, Ike started adding something. He would get to the second or third behavior and reach the conclusion that he was doing something wrong. He started improvising on his own. We knew he was a special one."

Collins grew up with a rural background

and was raised around many animals, as his father worked with horses. That made it easier for him when connecting with a half-dozen dogs or more during the course of the series.

"I had an affinity toward them," Collins says. "Roger and Bryan were kind of the costars as much as it was Ike. We three spent a lot of time together between takes and became fast friends. So I spent almost as much time with the dogs as I did the other actors."

Besides his two main doggy pals, there were the stunt dogs. Collins recalls, "X was our main attack dog, and we had a female attack dog named Cora, but X was our main guy. He was the go-to guy for the attacks. Luke was speedy. He could run like the wind. For one season, we had a dog named Jesse, which is my name, and that led to no end of confusion on the set."

The actor has one favorite memory of making the series. The moment occurred at the beginning of the show's third season. "We would shoot at an old converted helicopter airport in the southern part of Toronto. I remember going in, and I heard Bryan call, 'Hey, Jesse, Ike!' As soon as Ike heard me, he came running across that parking lot. It was the greatest sensation. We hadn't seen each other in several months. It's literally like working with another actor. He still knew who I was, and I certainly knew who he was."

Trainer/stuntman Renfro says that about five episodes of *Rin Tin Tin K-9 Cop* were shot in France. While there, he took the time to visit the grave of the original Rin Tin Tin, who is buried in Paris, the country of his birth.

Both Renfro and Schumacher had fathers who were Hollywood animal trainers. The late Lou Schumacher was a successful supplier and owner of animals that appeared in films and television shows of the 1960s through the 1980s. His forte was training chimpanzees.

Roger Schumacher, who has more than twenty-five years of experience, got into the business by watching his father's trainers at work and picked it up from them. His movie credits include *The Little Rascals, Homeward Bound II, 101 Dalmatians,* and *Dr. Seuss's How the Grinch Stole Christmas,* featuring his dog Kelly as Max.

The Roy Rogers Show

CBS, 1951–1957, 100 episodes.

Starring ***Trigger, Bullet, Buttermilk,*** *Roy Rogers, Dale Evans, Pat Brady, Harry Lauter as Mayor Ralph Cotton, and the Sons of the Pioneers (Bob Nolan, Karl Farr, Lloyd Perryman, and Hugh Farr).*

Set at the Double Bar R Ranch near Mineral City, *The Roy Rogers Show* traces the exploits of rancher and diner owner Roy Rogers and his wife, Dale Evans, as they maintain law and order in the modern West. Pat Brady and his Jeep with a mind of its own, Nellybelle, supply comic relief.

The show opened every Saturday morning with the announcer saying, "*The Roy Rogers Show*, starring Roy Rogers, King of the Cowboys; Trigger, his golden palomino; and Dale Evans, Queen of the West. With Pat Brady, his comical sidekick, and Roy's wonder dog, Bullet."

There was never any doubt who cowboy superstar Roy Rogers' favorite pet was: a golden palomino named Trigger. "Trigger did all the TV shows and all of the movies," recalls Roy's oldest child, Cheryl Rogers Barnett. "Dad got him in 1938 and used him in all the films. He first appeared in *Under Western Stars*. It was after the second or third film that he bought him for two thousand dollars. He was only making seventy-five dollars a week at the time, so he made payments on him."

Canine chef Bullet whips up a grainy concoction garnished with carrots for his favorite horse, Trigger.
Courtesy of Cheryl Rogers Barnett.

Trigger and his doubles were trained by two masters, Glenn Randall and Roy Rogers. Both spent long hours teaching the horses up to one hundred tricks.

Cheryl says, "Dad always credited the old horse for saving his career. When Gene Autry returned to the studio [Republic], they said they were going to put another actor on the horse. But then Dad told them they couldn't since they didn't own Trigger, he did. It's the old horse that you see with Dad bent down on his neck during the opening credits of the TV show. That's old Trigger. Everyone in the family referred to him as 'the old horse,' even trainer Glenn Randall, everybody."

Trigger's original name was Golden Cloud. He was foaled July 4, 1934, and his original owner was Roy Cloud Jr. of San Ysidro, California. The name change came about after a conversation Roy had with longtime sidekick Smiley Burnett. "Smiley said something like, 'Gee, you should name him Trigger 'cause he's quick as a trigger,'" says Cheryl.

One of the steed's other film credits from 1938 is *The Adventures of Robin Hood,* in which he was ridden by Olivia de Havilland. Not long after that film, Rogers bought him from Clyde Hudkins. The bill of sale states he was a four-year-old.

Cheryl recalls, "Trigger was seven-eighths thoroughbred. Daddy said 'cold blood,' meaning a mixed breed. He really didn't do many tricks. He threw kisses. He would rear."

And how. A *Life* magazine cover from 1943 depicts Roy astride a gorgeous, practically upright Trigger. "He would almost go straight up and down in those scenes," says Cheryl. "Dad says a couple of times he was sort of afraid that he would go over, but Trigger's balance was wonderful. Trigger was just a really great athlete."

Whoa! Trigger rears straight up as Roy Rogers waves for the camera.

Cheryl adds, "He loved to be petted and talked to. Dad had me on Trigger in a baby blanket, long before I could crawl or walk. When I was older, I used to ride him across the Van Nuys Wash. I would ride across the very middle of the San Fernando Valley. He knew that when we headed across that way, he was going to get a Coca-Cola. There was a little store there that sold treats. He'd even put his head in the door because he knew what was coming.

"Old Trigger liked people food a lot. He'd eat anything I ate. He liked mayonnaise sandwiches, and he drank Coca-Cola right out of the bottle. Dad just loved that horse. He had the greatest disposition."

Bill Catching, who was the stunt double for Roy in just about every episode of the TV series, recalls, "There's never been a western star that had a relationship with a horse like Roy had with Trigger. Trigger was so smart that he was a person."

Catching says, "A busload of fans drove out once to where they were filming an episode and somebody asked Roy, 'To what do you attribute your success?'

"Roy walked over to Trigger, and he took Glenn Randall's hand, and he said, 'These two right here.' He attributed his success to Trigger and Glenn Randall Sr."

Randall stabled Trigger at his house in North Hollywood for many years. He told author David Rothel, during an interview for his 1980 book *The Great Show Business Animals*, that Trigger "was a very exceptional horse. The title he had of 'The Smartest Horse in the Movies' absolutely fit. He was almost like a human; you could talk to him. He could do forty things by word cue. You'd just tell him and he would do it. But a lot of that comes from developing his intelligence through training and living with him."

Randall told Rothel that Trigger was especially adept at mouth work: "You could send him over to untie a horse or untie a hobble off himself, or he could go retrieve an article—like a retriever dog. He could take a pistol out of your holster. He could take the rope off the saddle. He could hold a rope in his mouth and you could swing one and children or Roy could jump the rope."

Glenn Randall was one of the greatest horse trainers in Hollywood history, and son Corky Randall followed in his tracks. Corky was the trainer behind Cass Olé, the star of two *Black Stallion* feature films, and he remembers his father working with Roy's Triggers. Randall says, "If my Dad were alive, he'd tell you his claim to fame was Trigger. We were working with horses that were exceptionally brilliant. They liked it. Any trained animal in movies where you see them alert and their ears up—those are animals that love what they are doing."

When Roy Rogers went to Grauman's Chinese theater in 1949 to leave his boot prints in cement, Trigger's hoof prints went in as well. Trigger died on July 3, 1965. Since Roy couldn't bear the thought of burying him, he had his pet mounted and placed in his museum, where he remains to this day.

"Dad would go and take people through

The King of the Cowboys sits at ease on Trigger.

the museum, and he'd get over to the old horse and stand there and get tears in his eyes. He just loved that horse," says Cheryl. "He never asked Trigger to do anything that he would refuse. I think they just totally trusted each other."

Roy Rogers said about his saddle pal, in his book *Roy Rogers: King of the Cowboys:* "Horses are like people. Everybody's got a different personality. Trigger had a different personality. He was a stallion, but you'd never know it, he was just so gentle and kind. And he had great rein on him as a cowpony. I've had several of my kids on him at one time, from his ears back to his tail and he would just . . . aw, he was a fabulous horse. Trigger made every picture. He was four and I was twenty-six when we made our first picture. And Trigger lived to be thirty-three. He was something. I think it was eighty-six features plus one hundred TV shows. Trigger made them all."

The cowboy king described him like this in *Happy Trails, Our Life Story*: "His mane and tail were full, flaxen white, and his palomino coat shone like a newly minted gold coin. He was 15.3 hands tall, which is about average height, but he was extremely strong and could turn on a dime and give you nine cents change. How that boy loved to run. All I had to do was shift my weight forward and he was off like a streak of lightning. There never was another horse like him. I insisted he get star billing in all my pictures. After all, what's a cowboy without a horse?

"They threw away the pattern when they made Trigger. He was the greatest horse, without a doubt, that ever came along. If there's a heaven for horses, that's where he is."

But while there was only one old Trigger, there were two other younger versions, Trigger Jr. and Little Trigger. "Trigger Jr., a Tennessee walking horse, did the rodeos, the state fairs, and public appearances," says Cheryl, about the horse which was purchased in the late 1940s out of Pennsylvania. Trigger Jr. was born May 11, 1941, and his birth name was Allen's Golden Zephyr.

"Trigger Jr. loved to dance," recalls Cheryl. "That was his specialty. He could do almost every stunt that those white stallions, the Lippizaners do, and he loved it. He did not make the movies, just the public appearances."

Trigger Jr., like his predecessor, stands today in the Roy Rogers and Dale Evans Museum. The horse actually lived in the museum for a few years, until his death in 1969.

"Trigger Jr. and Buttermilk had stalls in the first museum (it opened in 1966 in Apple Valley, California), and people that came to the museum the first three or four years saw Trigger Jr. and Buttermilk in the flesh," says Cheryl.

And then there was Little Trigger, a quarter horse, that was practically never acknowledged publicly. This was the horse that performed the movie stunts and who went with Roy into hospitals. Cheryl says, "He was housebroken. They'd put rubber shoes on him and take him into hospitals. He was almost like a dog. You could train him to do anything. He said his prayers. He did the counting. They could train him to do the funny stuff, like push Dad with his nose.

"He was the one in *Son of Paleface* [the 1952 film in which Trigger pulls the covers off of Bob Hope while sharing a bed; the film earned Trigger a PATSY]. He was extremely smart but also really ornery and very mischievous. The little horse took the pressure off the big horse because he did the touring throughout the 1940s before the arrival of Trigger Jr.

"Little Trigger hated women, and he didn't much care for little kids except for when Dad had him under saddle and bridle. He wasn't one you would let out in the paddock for little kids to go in and pat. He was not a pattable horse, but real temperamental."

Corky Randall says of Little Trigger, "That horse probably had more tricks on him than any other horse in the world."

As for the Queen of the West, Dale Evans had her good times and bad with Buttermilk, who was born in 1941. Cheryl remembers how the horse came into the Rogers family fold: "Buttermilk was Glenn Randall's cutting and roping horse. His name was Soda. Mom had just started riding the horse, and one of the wranglers who did a few stunts, Buddy Sherwood, says, 'Oh, look at that sky. Doesn't that look like a buttermilk sky. Why, that would be a good name for that horse.'" Dale Evans agreed.

"Buttermilk was a quarter horse and a gelding," says Cheryl. "Glenn had been offered tons of money from rodeo cowboys who wanted to use him because he was a great roping horse. He was just quick as a cat, really quick. Mom had a bit of a problem with him because he was so quick. He was trained for one thing, and she used him for something totally different. He knew the signal when you came out of there full speed after that calf. And then he learned what the clacker meant [scene four, take five]. He knew everything was starting, and he would take off like a shot, and Mom could hardly hold him back."

Buttermilk was so quick, in fact, that there were times when he would embarrass Trigger and Roy. Cheryl recalls, "Right out of the gate and into the first five or six strides, Buttermilk would leave Trigger in the dust. Dad would get so mad and tell Mom, 'That looks bad. People just don't understand.'"

Cheryl adds, "Buttermilk looked great

Dale Evans, Queen of the West, prepares to tie Buttermilk up to the hitching post.

Courtesy of Cheryl Rogers Barnett.

If Roy Rogers ever ran out of ammunition, he still had his favorite German shepherd, Bullet, at his side. A number of different dogs played Bullet over the years.

alongside Trigger with that black mane and tail. They had tried a bunch of different horses for Mom. None just really looked good with Trigger, but as soon as they saw these together, they said, 'Oh, this is the horse.' They bought him right away—around 1950.

"He was very short coupled. He had a short body and ran really choppy. For him to match strides with Trigger, he had to do lots of trotting. Buttermilk wasn't in the movies, and he didn't do tricks or stunts. He died in 1972." Buttermilk now has his permanent place in the Rogers Museum as well.

Next came Roy's dog, Bullet. A number of different German shepherds were used over the years. Bullet made his initial appearance in the Republic Pictures film *Spoilers of the Plains* in 1951.

"The first one, whose name was originally Ace, didn't live that long. He made a couple of movies and went on tour, and he had an accident and was killed," says Cheryl. "Bullet was always a German shepherd. They tried to get ones that looked as much alike as possible.

"There were stunt dogs that were used in attacking the bad guys and all. That wasn't Bullet. They used maybe three or four dogs for that. There were four or five dogs that played Bullet for film and television. They stayed at the trainers'. They could do all kinds of tricks: they could crawl; they could sit up. They had them jump through windows, open doors. They chewed the ropes off of Mom's hands. They'd bark on command. They'd limp.

"We always had German shepherds as pets at home, and we always had one named Bullet, but they were not the Bullets that were used on the shows or on tour."

However, Roy explained to an audience in 1977, "We made all of the TV pictures with the one dog, Bullet. As you probably know, though, it's necessary to use attack dogs for some action scenes, and you can't very well use a specially trained attack dog as the lovable dog that has to play with the kids in other scenes. It doesn't work very well. You're liable to give the dog the wrong cue and he'll chew someone's leg off. We sent to Germany at the beginning of our TV series and bought an attack dog to be used only for special action scenes where Bullet, who was a most gentle animal, would not work so well."

Frank Inn came in on the tail end of *The Roy Rogers Show* to work with Bullet. He said that Earl Johnson was the man who started with Ace as Bullet. After Johnson's death, Bill Koehler took over and trained a dog that looked like Ace. Then Inn worked the last Bullet of the series.

The Roy Rogers and Dale Evans Museum in Victorville, California, is filled with memorabilia from the careers of the two western singing stars. Western fans can still see Trigger, Buttermilk, and Bullet, who Roy and Dale have preserved at the museum.

Run, Joe, Run

NBC, 1974–1976, 26 episodes

Starring ***Heinrich as Joe,*** *Arch Whiting as Sgt. William Corey, and Chad States as Josh McCoy. Narration by Paul Frees.*

Run, Joe, Run is about an army-trained German shepherd, a member of the K-9 corps, falsely accused of attacking his master (à la David Janssen in *The Fugitive*). He flees before he can be put down and then crosses the country, aiding folks in need even though there is a bounty on his head. Meanwhile his best friend, Sgt. Corey, tries to track him down and clear his name. In the second season, Joe joins forces with a backpacker and encounters more adventures on the open road.

One of the more unusual aspects of this series is that Joe would experience a flashback to earlier, happier times in just about every episode. The network promoted the show saying, "Joe, a dog on the run—wanted for something he didn't do." The German shepherd star of *Run, Joe, Run* was just a regular Joe, only his name was Heinrich.

When producer William D'Angelo began to look for the right star, animal handler Lou Schumacher showed him lots of German shepherds, but not one caught his fancy. "None of them pleased him with their looks, attitude, or training," says Karl Lewis Miller, who trained Heinrich. "D'Angelo looked at each one of them and would say, 'Nope, that's not the dog.' After we had brought in shepherds from all over California, D'Angelo told us, 'You know, I got a dog at home that could do this part. He's not a movie dog, but he's the kind of dog I want. He's just a house pet.'

"Lou says, 'If that's the kind of dog you want, let the trainer take a good look at him, and we can tell you if he will work.'

"So we got the dog and I brought him to my house for a couple of weeks. A couple of weeks later, D'Angelo was amazed at what he saw, and he says, 'Yep, that's the dog for *Run, Joe, Run*.'"

Arch Whiting finally catches up to Heinrich, the German shepherd star of *Run, Joe, Run.*

So, forget the nepotism, but the star of the show was the producer's own dog. But using a regular mutt as compared to those canines who are trained for the business can really throw a monkey wrench into the works of professional trainers. Karl Lewis Miller shares a few secrets on some of the dos and don'ts that make a professional animal tick just right for the cameras: "First of all, in this business, our animals never go to work. We go to work; they go to play. The reason for this is that we want them to come back tomorrow and do it some more. If they think it's work, then pretty soon their ears are bent down and their tails are tucked down, and they don't want to work.

"It's got to be done with understanding. It's done with obedience training and with discipline, but the idea is the dog goes to make the movie, and he's got to go in there very confident, very comfortable and capable.

"We took this dog [Heinrich] through the training with the attitude and the approach, but we don't break bad habits. Our specialty is training dogs to look untrained. You can break your dog of digging holes, but if we get a script which calls for a dog to dig a hole . . ."

Miller gives a great example to fully illustrate his point. "In one episode this fugitive dog is on the run, and his handler is out there searching for him. The dog comes to a railroad yard and comes upon a hobo camp, and they had just stolen some chickens. They're barbecuing the chicken, and the dog is sneaking up, smelling that chicken cooking, and he's hungry. When the hobos turn their backs, he grabs the chicken off the fire and runs off with it.

"We had to train him not to be afraid of the smoke and the fire, which we accomplish very nicely. Now we go on hiatus, and we send Heinrich home to Bill D'Angelo for a little R&R. A couple of weeks later, D'Angelo says, 'Hey, can't you train this dog? What a nuisance. He jumps on people.' (He's simply doing all the things we trained him to do for the various scripts.) 'And,' D'Angelo says, 'the other day I had this big get-together with barbecue, and we go inside for a little while and when we came outside, the meat is off the spit, and the dog is over in the corner licking his chops.'

"Heinrich was a nice dog, and like most German shepherds he had the courage and strength of heart to do physical feats. Heinrich was also typical of your neighbor's untrained poodle, but with the proper training, he became a TV star and a celebrity. You've got to understand, your neighbor's dalmatian could have been Lassie if they [the producers] had wanted a dalmatian and Rudd Weatherwax got his hands on him. The dog is only as good as the trainer, and these are great dogs, but everything those animals do, I (and other trainers in the business) train them to do."

After the first season of *Run, Joe, Run,* Miller went on to another job, and Robert Weatherwax took over the training of D'Angelo's dog.

There were other Joes at work both seasons. "Heinrich had the look, the expression, the personality that D'Angelo wanted," says Miller, "but we worked on several more in preparation. We carried two extra dogs all the time. One dog predominantly plays the part, but there are understudies in training.

"We had one dog named Gus who was the understudy and a photo double for Heinrich. When we work animals for pictures and action, we cut down hazards to a minimum, so Gus would do the physical feats occasionally, saving Heinrich for a common shot.

"During hiatus, they cast Gus to star in the film *Won Ton Ton, the Dog That Saved Hollywood.* That meant Gus would not be available for another season of *Run, Joe, Run,* as he had gotten a starring role."

Miller says that D'Angelo then pulled a class act and took out ads in the Hollywood trade magazines announcing how wonderful it was in this day and age that even an understudy stunt dog could get a major role and become a celebrity.

As for Heinrich, he starred in a TV movie, *Kavic, the Wolf Dog,* and paired with Joe Don Baker in the feature film *The Pack.* And then he retired back to William D'Angelo's backyard where he could keep a well-trained eye on any neighborhood barbecuing that might be going on.

Sabrina, the Teenage Witch

ABC, 1996–present
(still in production)

Starring ***Elvis as warlock-turned-feline Salem Saberhagan,*** *Melissa Joan Hart as Sabrina Spellman, Caroline Rhea as Hildegard "Hilda" Antoinette Spellman, Beth Broderick as Zelda Spellman, Nate Richert as Harvey Kinkle, Jenna Leigh Green as Libby Chessler, Michelle Beaudoin as Jennifer Kelley, Soleil Moon Frey as Roxie, Elisa Donovan as Morgan Cavanaugh, Lindsay Sloane as Valerie Birckhead, Paul Feig as Eugene Pool, and Nick Bakay as the voice of Salem the cat.*

Sabrina, the Teenage Witch is about a teenage girl who discovers she is a witch with magical powers. Her best friend is her pet cat, Salem, a warlock who has had a curse put on him.

One of television's top cat stars of the

1990s has got to be Salem, Sabrina, the teenage witch's roommate. The character first appeared in the *Archie* comic books of the 1960s in which Sabrina had a tabby named Salem. When the TV show came to life in 1996, the story line had evolved so that Salem, a black cat, was actually a warlock who had been sentenced to one hundred years of life as a cat by the witches' council because of a failed attempt to take over the world.

Completely stripped of his powers, Salem still has his pride, plus a superiority complex that just won't quit. And he does possess a few of his human skills: Salem can read, as in poking through Sabrina's diary, and he is computer literate and enjoys going online.

Since the super-successful series began in 1996, a number of cats have worn Salem's hat, including Warlock, Witch, Lucy (who died in 1998), Salem, and Halloween, but Elvis has been the main cool cat to play the role.

Warlock is the action cat on the *Sabrina* set and the one who does the driving.
Courtesy of Cathy Pittman / Performing Animal Troupe.

Salem has proven so unique a teen pal that he was named Fave Animal/Fantasy Star by *Teen Beat*'s fourteenth annual Teen Star Awards in 1997, and he was selected Favorite Animal Star of the Year in 1998 by Nickelodeon's eleventh annual Kids' Choice Awards.

Writer, coproducer, and actor Nick Bakay provides the voice of the chatty cat. "There's just something fun about playing a cat. It's never been done like this before," Bakay said in an online cat chat several years ago. "I love portraying a cat."

And the writer and human in Bakay says, "Salem is my favorite character to write for because he seems to be a special voice. He's also a great vehicle for jokes."

Of the real-life cats to play Salem, Bakay is partial to "the big E." "My favorite is Elvis. He's mellow. He has the sweetest disposition. We all love Elvis," Bakay says.

All of the Salem players have been owned and trained by Hollywood veteran animal trainer Cathy Pittman, who with her husband, Gregg, operates Performing Animal Troupe, a menagerie of about 150 actor animals.

Pittman says of TV's most talkative feline: "There are three main cats that play Salem. Elvis is the lead cat. I tell him to talk, and he moves his mouth. I don't know of another cat in Hollywood that can do that right now."

Pittman found Elvis, "a pound kitty," twelve years ago at the Agoura Animal Shelter. "We want to see the ones that are calling to you from the cage, that are putting their paws out and trying to make contact," Pittman says. "Elvis was stable. Nothing bothered him, and most important, he's a real ham.

"He's very focused. His main thing is being aware of what's going on. When he's sitting there, and actors enter the room, he'll turn and look at them. He's very natural, and he really is a star, but because he's a star, he doesn't like to do his stunts. He only moves at one speed: the Elvis speed.

"He has a very commanding personality. He's the king. We hear all the time [from cast and crew], 'Elvis has left the building.'"

Indeed, Pittman named her feline thespian after the king of rock 'n' roll. "He has this little belly flap. He's Elvis in the later years, the Las Vegas years," says his owner with a laugh.

Elvis is a cat who wears many hats. "He drives all the vehicles on the show. This week we're prepping him to drive a forklift," Pittman said during a recent interview. "He wears a lot of costumes, and he waves and sits and comes, talks, lies down, and hits his marks. Elvis loves everybody on the set, but he doesn't like to be upstaged.

"He's been all over the world. He went to Romania for a horror movie about black cats, and he has been on *Buffy the Vampire Slayer* and in the movies *Till There Was You* and *Being John Malkovich.*"

Elvis is not a cat to sit still. "We use Witch for all the cuddling and caring. That's not Elvis's thing. He doesn't want to be slung around and carried around," Pittman says.

Witch is the calm cat that all the girls love to hold and stroke on *Sabrina,* but she also likes to ride elephants.

Courtesy of Cathy Pittman / Performing Animal Troupe.

As for tastes, Elvis goes for cooked chicken or baby food. "Elvis likes any kind of fresh meat, cooked chicken, pizza. He eats his kibbles in the morning, and during the day we take canned cat food and mix it with baby food."

Pittman's action cat for Salem is named Warlock. "Warlock does all the retrieving, jumping through things, clawing things. He had to leap onto a movie screen and start clawing for one scene. He's very agile. One

Cathy Pittman pets Elvis, the star feline who plays Salem on *Sabrina*. And yes, he was named after the king of rock 'n' roll.

Courtesy of Cathy Pittman / Performing Animal Troupe.

time Warlock had to drive a fire truck, back the truck up to a table, turn, and climb up the ladder rungs onto the kitchen table that was on fire. He did this all in a full fireman's outfit," Pittman says.

The trainer found Warlock in 1997 at the Lancaster Animal Shelter and put him to work during the second season of *Sabrina.* He's truly a stunt cat. "He has high energy. He's very, very fast and he can learn about anything. He's a brilliant, brilliant cat—the border collie of the cat world. Warlock's a little dictator. Elvis rules the roost, but Warlock rules everything else. When he's ready to work, don't get in his way."

Pittman says that she and her husband, Gregg, sleep in Elvis's bedroom, which they also share with Warlock and their dogs. "We have five dogs that sleep in here with us, but Warlock is a tough cat. He makes sure the dogs all stay in their particular sleeping spots. He doesn't take slack from anybody, and nothing scares him. However, he worships the ground I walk on."

As for his appetite, Warlock is anything but a finicky eater. "He'll eat anything," Pittman says.

The third and the charm of the Salem actors is wee Witch. "Witch is petite and very sweet," Pittman says. "Nothing bothers her. She's the smallest of the cats, so the girls like to hold her the best, and she likes to be held.

"You can put her anywhere. She'll fall asleep on the set. Once in a scene where the fire tower collapses and the whole building is shaking and the actors are screaming and the furniture is moving, Witch was sitting on a desk with snow blowing through the window, and she couldn't care less."

Witch is also a professional elephant driver. "The writers of the show wanted to put Salem on an elephant and wanted to know if the cats would be all right riding one," says Pittman. "I brought Witch over to our friend Susie the African elephant, and lo and behold, up on Susie's head she went."

Pittman discovered Witch, who is now nine, when she was a year old and nearly a goner. She says, "I went out to feed my horses and heard this little timid meow, and here was this cat, thin as could be and no hair, and its throat was slit from ear to ear. I think she must have gotten into a fight with a possum. I took her in, mended her up, and made her into a little movie star. She officially did the first scene of *Sabrina.*

"She is sweet and just wants to be held. You can usually find her on the producer's lap, while they are watching and taping."

Pittman says there is one more cat, named Halloween, that does a few stunts from time to time.

When the cats have their makeup on, it's difficult to tell which one is which. "Everybody that works on the show has to ask who's who. They're pretty good at telling who is Elvis. He is the only one with white whiskers," Pittman says. "Warlock has a little bit of white on his chest, and Witch has a spot on her chest, so if they are not in makeup, they can tell the difference."

And last and least is the puppet cat that is used to do the majority of the talking.

For Pittman, who started her company fifteen years ago, animals have been a lifelong passion. She supplies all the animals that have appeared on *Sabrina.* After more than one hundred episodes, that includes a tiger, lion,

Salem the cat, Sabrina's pet.
Courtesy of Cathy Pittman / Performing Animal Troupe.

leopard, cockroaches, elephants, yaks, a zebra, penguins, chickens, cows, chimps, pigs, sheep, goats, monkeys, alligators, turtles, flamingos, pigeons, and parrots. Pittman and company have also aided filmmakers with trained horses, rats, wolves, spiders, insects, exotic birds, maggots, snakes, and dogs.

She has also furnished creatures for *Buffy the Vampire Slayer, Angel, The Practice, Profiler, Roseanne, Picket Fences, JAG, NYPD Blue,* and lots of feature films, such as *Primary Colors, Bowfinger, Thick as Thieves,* and *Bedazzled,* as well as dozens of commercials.

Salty

Syndicated, 1974, 26 episodes

*Starring **Salty**, Mark Slade as Taylor Reed, Johnny Doran as Tim Reed, Julius Harris as Clancy Ames, and Vincent Dale as Rod Porterfield.*

When Taylor and Tim Reed lose their parents (and almost their own lives) in a hurricane, they learn to survive on their own and soon are pursuing adventures with their pet sea lion.

What in the undersea world was the inspiration for the unusual selection of a sea

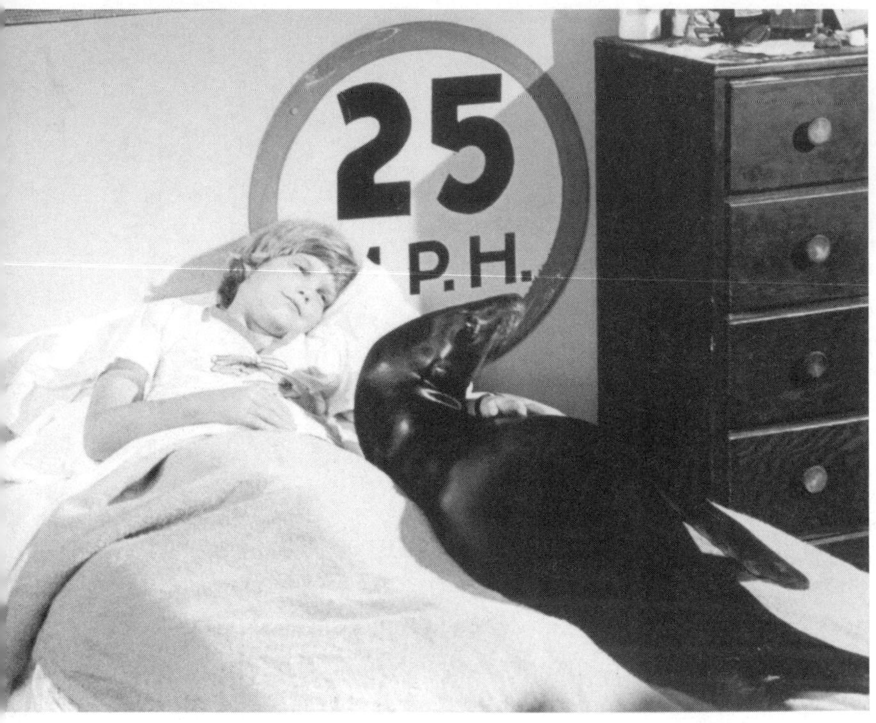

Salty, the only sea lion to star in his own TV series, visits his young friend in his bedroom.
Photo copyright 2001 Vincent Vaughan.

lion for the title role in a TV series? Creator Ricou Browning, also the driving force behind *Flipper*, explains simply, "Well, I wanted to do another animal show."

He elaborates, "Over a period of time, I decided that a sea lion would be a good animal to do a show around, and so I bought a sea lion from a company in California. It was four months old, and I took it home and I had to bottle-feed it. I raised it for about three years at my home. It was a female.

"I trained her the same way we trained Flipper. I found out later that a lot of it was not the way they trained sea lions, which wasn't really a mistake. But as far as things like balancing a ball, I had a difficult time teaching her that, which is the simplest trick you can teach one. I taught her everything. She could do more than fifty behaviors, both by voice command and hand command, and was friendly—that is, tame enough to do anything with.

"So I decided, 'Well, it's time to write a show.' So [brother-in-law] Jack and I got together and wrote a show. It took me a couple of years to raise the money from a group out of New York. We made the first *Salty* feature and then we made three years of television after that.

"When we got ready to do the feature, I got two more animals, which we trained as well, and at that time I hired my daughter Renée, who was a trainer, and my son Ricky, who was also a trainer, and I hired a regular sea lion trainer. His name was Adolph Frohn. He was excellent. He happened to be the first man who trained a dolphin at Marineland Studios. As far as I know, he's the first man that ever trained a dolphin. A real nice man."

Salty was filmed in the Bahamas, and although the show never found a network port, it stayed afloat for a while in syndication with the seal (aar-aar-aar!) of approval from viewers.

Sam

CBS, 1978, 7 episodes

Starring ***Sam*** *as* ***Sam,*** *Mark Harmon as Officer Mike Breen, and Len Wayland as Captain Tom Clagett.*

Sam was a short-lived police series about a Los Angeles cop and his partner, a dog, who work their beat in a patrol car.

Carl Spitz Jr., the trainer who worked with the canine star of *Sam*, says he cannot recall the original name of the yellow Labrador retriever who partnered with Mark Harmon. "We changed his name to Sam when the show started," says Spitz, and the name stuck for good.

Spitz was a part of the group, Frank Inn Incorporated, that owned the dog, whom he found south of Sun Valley, Idaho, near Ketchum.

"Sam was about four or five when we did the show," Spitz says. "He loved to work. He was a good dog and picked up on things pretty rapidly, a fast study."

And only one other factor seems to stand out about Sam: "He loved hot dogs, little pieces of hot dog," says the trainer.

The dog did have an excellent working relationship with his human costar Mark Harmon, about whom Spitz recalls a funny incident. "Mark is a real handy guy who likes to fix up things. We were doing a drive-by scene, where the car rolls along, and the camera is stationary. We were driving through the neighborhood, the camera is rolling, and the dog's head is out the window. Alongside the street, somebody had thrown away an old rocking chair. It's out there waiting to be picked up by the trash man. Mark slams on the breaks, opens up the trunk, grabs the chair and sticks it in the back and then drives on."

Spitz also recollects that working the cop series with producer Jack Webb was a good setup. "We were working in a warehouse in downtown Los Angeles on the pilot. Most directors are unrealistic about what animals

Mark Harmon starred as a Los Angeles policeman who had an unusual partner in a specially trained Labrador retriever in the 1978 CBS series *Sam*.

can do and can't do and how quickly you can get them to do it, but Jack Webb was not like that," says Spitz. "As a director or person to work for, I list him at the very top, an absolute jewel when it came to working around people and animals."

He adds, "One day about an hour before lunch break, Webb took me aside and said, 'I got an idea that differs from what the script calls for, so I know you're not prepared. If I give you a couple of hours, could you possibly try this?'

"I told him I could try but I didn't know, so he told me what he wanted, and he called for a lunch break. He let it run a little long, and told me to let him know if we would be able to do it or not. After an hour or so, I told him 'I think we can do it.'

"The bad guys were supposed to be hiding in a warehouse, and Mark Harmon was going in looking for them with the dog. A bad guy comes in behind Mark and gets the drop on him, and the dog has worked his way to the top of this stack of bags and gets behind the bad guy, and the dog barks and menaces the bad guy so that Mark gets him.

"Webb set it up after lunch. We shot it and we got it," says Spitz. "It wasn't exactly what Webb had pictured, but it was close enough that he said, 'That will work great.'"

Spitz worked with animals in movies and television for about eighteen years, following in the shoes of his father, Carl Spitz Sr., who owned and trained Terry, the dog who starred as Toto in *The Wizard of Oz*, and Buck, the big dog who starred in 1935's *Call of the Wild* with Clark Gable.

"I took over my dad's kennel in 1962, and my wife and I ran it until 1978," says Spitz. "My dad tried to keep me out of pictures. He said, 'Concentrate on the kennel,' but I got pulled into it.

"The first thing I did was the TV series *The Long Hot Summer* with a beagle. Then I did a couple of *Ironsides*, where we used several dogs. I did a lot of commercials, and I did *The Monroes* TV series with some Great Pyrenees."

Among Spitz's other credits were the rottweiler who belonged to Gregory Peck in the western *The Stalking Moon* and the animals in the TV movie *All the Kind Strangers*, and just like his father had done in the original, he worked sled dogs in a 1976 TV movie remake of *Call of the Wild*.

Sergeant Preston of the Yukon

CBS, 1955–1958, 78 episodes

Starring ***Yukon King, Rex,*** *and Richard (Dick) Simmons as Sgt. William Preston.*

Sergeant Preston of the Mounties patrolled the Yukon Territory of the 1890s, the days of the Gold Rush. Preston passed through towns such as Dawson, Yellowknife, and Whitehorse but most of his time was spent on the trail with his team of dogs, led by Yukon King, a giant malamute husky, and his horse Rex.

The show opened with the same introduction each week: "Sergeant Preston of the Northwest Mounted Police, with Yukon King, swiftest and strongest lead dog, breaking the trail in the relentless pursuit of lawbreakers in the wild days of the Yukon."

The television series had it origins in the radio show *The Challenge of the Yukon*, which aired from 1947 to 1955. It was created by George W. Trendle and Fran Striker, the two men who also created *The Lone Ranger* and *The Green Hornet.* After its original run in the 1950s, *Sergeant Preston of the Yukon* aired on Saturday morning TV in the early 1960s.

College graduate William Preston joins the Mounties so he can avenge the death of his father. In that initial episode, the Mountie stops a lynx attack and saves the life of a husky pup that has been raised by a female wolf. He names the dog Yukon King and raises it to be his partner in tracking down criminals.

Later in the first episode, King is blamed for a man's death, but Sergeant Preston clears his canine of the charge. In the course of the series, the Mountie and his dog maintain law and order in the Yukon as they face a wide array of obstacles: Eskimo uprisings, greedy miners, thieves after gold dust and furs, bank robbers, renegade Indians, evil whalers, and cantankerous trappers, not to mention the blizzards and snowstorms of the Arctic winter. Sergeant Preston uses skis, snowshoes, dogsleds, and his horse Rex to traverse the beautiful country that at times proves unmerciful.

Sergeant Preston's familiar cry of "On King! On you Huskies!" meant the chase was on. Once he had nabbed the bad guys, the Mountie would say, "I arrest you in the name of the Crown." As each episode wound down, he would turn to his dog and say, "Well, King, this case is closed."

When *Sergeant Preston of the Yukon* leapt from radio to television, King and Richard Simmons were ready to fit the bill as Yukon King and Sergeant Preston. "On King. On you huskies!"

Dick Simmons, star of the series, remembers well working with the dog that he came to love and admire. "His actual name was King. There's no animal capable of doing everything you want it to do [on a television series]. We mainly used one dog, King. The lead dog is the dog that the other dogs believe in and will follow. He's the dog that gets most of the attention.

"These dogs don't bark. They howl and sound much like a wolf. They have to be taught to bark. The dog was always beside me and had taken an exceptional liking to me. He would follow me wherever I would go. If he moved away from me, out of camera range, I would say, 'Come back, King, and sit down,' and he would.

"He was very fond of me. I always got along with him very well and never made any exceptions. I didn't treat him any differently than I would any other dog. I would take him on the airplane with me when I traveled to do shows. During the off-season, when we traveled doing rodeos and promotional tours, he generally stayed in the hotel with me. For all intents and purposes, I was the owner. He was owned by the company, but the dog was always with me. There was no way I was going to put this dog in a crate and put him in the hold of the airplane."

So King flew on the plane beside Simmons, just like a human passenger. "There were times when he walked up and down the aisle. Everybody would pet him. He was a very friendly animal."

King's trainer, Beverly Allen, agrees. "King had a lovely personality," says Allen. "He was nice with children. He was not a dog that would snap—he was very gentle, and got along well with Dick."

"The dog was bought from a kennel in Colorado," Allen adds. "He was about five when I started training on him. He was the first Malamute trained for motion pictures. They are pretty hard to train."

Allen, who was one of the first African Americans to train dogs in Hollywood, worked with the legendary Carl Spitz Sr. from 1937 to 1941 and then again after World War II ended. He assisted Spitz in the training of the dogs that played Toto in *The Wizard of Oz* and Buck in *Call of the Wild*.

Allen was personally hired by the show's owner, George Trendle. In training Yukon King, Allen first taught him small obedience and then proceeded to companionship. He then trained the dog to work through remote control or silent cues so that he could work the dog in a scene where there was dialogue and not interfere with the scene.

Allen recalls, "King was always a happy-go-lucky worker. When he had a pretty tough day, we fed him fried steaks. And we always kept him indoors with us."

And Allen remembers an accident the first day of shooting: "Our first shot, when we went up to shoot, the dog had to leap out of the window to follow the horse. He leaped out the window and injured his right leg. We had to just about stop shooting, take off, and go to Denver to get a doctor to patch him up. So I found a double, named Kim, and he was trained right on the set. Both dogs looked just alike. Kim was used for long shots."

Star Simmons says that the series was shot near Aspen, Colorado, at picturesque Ashcroft, where the altitude was 11,400 feet.

"You could take King out on the trail with the team, and he didn't run well hitched to the team," says Simmons. "The others dogs would snap at him. We had a dog that was the lead dog that looked just like King, but he was a real lead dog. We had eight dogs hitched up, and on rare occasion had fourteen dogs hitched up.

"We had fifty-two dogs that we used because we made up other teams. These dogs were all marked, beautiful dogs, every one of them. When they became unusually tired or if we had wrecks, they would fight. Then it was Katie bar the door. One dog would blame the other dog for the wreck.

"King was a working dog, and he was treated as that. He didn't do tricks, he didn't sit up, he didn't play dead or things like that for the most part. When the show ended, they wanted to know if I wanted the dog. I would have loved to have had the dog, but it would have been unfair to bring him in and keep him in a house. He weighed about 160 pounds; he was a big, big dog. In the summertime, he would shed something awful. Underneath that dog's coating is fine hair that grows in the wintertime. In the spring, when it gets warm, he'd lose so much hair it looked like the dog was underfed. We'd have to brush up the hair because he looked so skinny.

"We stopped shooting around 1958 or so. I believe the dog was five or six years old then. One fellow took him down to East Texas. Later I heard from him. He said, 'I've got a problem. King's sick—sick because he can't find you. He walks around here, and I know he's looking for you.' I told him that I missed King too. I could talk to him just like I was talking to a human. I honestly believe the dog understood what I was saying."

Simmons, a veteran horseman, relates that finding the right animal to be Rex was quite an ordeal. "The show's owner, George

Richard Simmons rides as Rex splashes through the Roaring Fork River on *Sergeant Preston of the Yukon*.
Courtesy of Richard Simmons.

Trendle, bought a real show horse out of New York. I believe he paid $17,000 for it. It was a beautiful animal, but he didn't belong in the woods. They brought the horse back to California, so trainer Glenn Randall called me because they were stabling the horse at his place.

"'You want to come out and see your horse? I must warn you—I don't think you're going to like him,' was what Glenn told me. So I went out to see him, and Glenn had the horse saddled and all shined up. We took the horse out into a ring, and I got on, and why I didn't break my neck, I'll never know. This horse would shy at everything it saw. It had never been out of the show ring in New York. Whenever cars would go by, the traffic noise would cause the horse to try to get back in the barn. I rode the horse for a couple of days, but it didn't do any good.

"I went to the producer, Chuck Skinner, and said, 'Chuck, I think we got a bad deal on this horse. He's not used to what you would call normalcy.' We entertained quite an argument about it. So I told him to write a note to himself that reads: 'This horse is gonna cost me money—plenty of it.'"

The tale continues in the mountains of Colorado. "All the first shows were done with the horse, not the dog team," says Simmons. "We got up there at 11,000 feet, and the horse didn't like that altitude. It made him a little woozy. I tried walking him across a shallow part of a river and thought, no way, this is ridiculous. Then I got him to running on a trail so we could shoot the first shot. Afterward the horse was so tired that he was leaning against the cabin.

"Skinner said, 'See, he's gonna be all right.' I said, 'Yeah, if you can hire somebody to run him, we'll have a nice looking tired horse.'

"Then I rode him alongside the Roaring Fork River, and the horse wheeled around and started up a bank. At that moment, a marmot, a rodent animal, came down the hill toward us, and that horse went absolutely bananas. He stood up on his back feet and went over backwards. We both fell, and I broke my left wrist. I got him back up on his feet and rode him back and told them, 'You're gonna have to get a new guy to play the part and you better get yourself a new horse.'"

Simmons did stick around to play Sergeant Preston, but the horse had to go.

Then Simmons and his actor friend Richard Arlen went looking for a new Rex. "Dick and I found the horse, an American saddle bred," Simmons says. "It belonged to a little girl and proved to be the handiest animal I had ever seen and looked great. A very handy animal.

"Everybody on the crew loved the horse. It was a kind of a nut in a way. He'd get so excited when he saw me coming that he'd just jump all over the place. I rode him throughout the series. He was a beautiful horse, even prettier than the one we spent all the dough for. I was always afraid the horse would step on the dog, but King was aware of that, and he stayed out of the way.

"The horse was young. I swam him across the Kern River in California one day. We had to do a pickup shot, and I told them, 'He'll do anything I make him do.' I slid him down a bank and into the river.

"After the show ended, it may be that he went back to the little girl that owned him. He would slide down hills. I was at the top of a hill on flat ground, and the director and camera were down below me. 'How you gonna get down the hill?' they asked. I said, 'I'll show you.' I got the horse up to full gait. We got to the edge, and he slid all the way down. 'How'd you know the horse would do that?' 'I just had a feeling he would.'" Simmons, the Mountie who always got his man with the good help of King and Rex, knew he could rely on his trusty steed.

Dog trainer Beverly Allen recalls that King and Rex were great pals. "When we first put them together, they didn't do anything but play," he says.

Bobby Lee "Beverly" Allen opened his own dog training school in Royal Oak, Michigan, in the 1950s. Now retired in the Detroit area, Allen has an illustrious history.

"I'm the first African American that ever trained dogs for motion pictures and the military," he says. "I trained dogs for the U.S. Army, Navy, and Marines at the Hollywood Dog Training School in World War II."

But he was not allowed to train dogs as a member of the armed forces because all of the other trainers in uniform were white.

Carl Spitz Jr. says, "Beverly Allen came to my father's business looking for a job. He walked into the office and had such a deep Southern accent. His real name was Bobby Lee Allen, but with his Southern accent, and my aunt's German mentality, she understood him as saying Beverly Allen. So for the rest of his life, he was known as Beverly Allen."

But by any name, Allen, like members of the Spitz family, was a superb trainer.

Sheena, Queen of the Jungle

Syndicated, 1955–1956, 26 episodes

*Starring **Neal as Chim the chimpanzee,** Irish McCalla as Sheena, and Christian Drake as Bob.*

Sheena, Queen of the Jungle is set in Kenya where the statuesque Sheena holds forth as a white goddess and guardian of the creatures and natives who live nearby.

Sheena's favorite ape is a four- or five-year-old chimpanzee named Neal. "He was a great little guy to work with. He never caused any trouble," says Christian Drake, who played Bob, Sheena's friend. "Neal was maybe two-and-a-half-feet tall. There was not anything he did exceptional except be a good guy. Everybody loved him. I never saw him get mad."

As Chim the chimp, Neal never really had to perform any stunts. Sheena would hold him in her arms in some of the non-action scenes. Otherwise, he would simply tag along behind her on the jungle trail (the series was filmed in Mexico). "It was mostly a following type of thing," Drake says. "He would follow her whenever she would be running and make noise. I don't remember any swinging scenes where he was on a vine. Sometimes he would raise both his hands above his head and yell at you like he was trying to tell you something,"

Irish McCalla's *Sheena* has got the monkey on her back. In this case, it's her friend Neal the chimpanzee.

But the little chimp had a foot fetish. Drake recalls, "He had a habit of pulling at her feet. She wore moccasins, and sometimes when they were going along, he'd trip her trying to grab her shoes. As a rule, he was a very, very tame chimp. He had a few moments where he would get upset and go up in a tree. The trainer could get him to work doggone good, and he took very good care of him.

"He had quite a large cage, and he was treated with all the respect you could give an animal. Neal was extremely afraid of gunshots. The trainer has a pistol with blanks, and if Chim got out of whack, the trainer would fire, and he would go screaming and running to his cage."

Drake even filled in one time as chimp handler for a few scenes. "The trainer had to go back to the States, and I had a scene where I tried to work him. I could hold his hand and he would work with me," says the actor who played Sheena's best friend.

Skippy (the Bush Kangaroo) / The New Adventures of Skippy

Skippy (the Bush Kangaroo): Syndicated, 1968–1969, 91 episodes

*Starring **Josephine as Skippy,** Ed Devereaux as Matt Hammond, Garry Pankhurst as Sonny Hammond, Ken James as Mark Hammond, Tony Bonner as Jerry King, Liza Goddard as Clarissa (Clancy) Merrick, and Elke Neidhardt as Dr. Anna Steiner.*

Set in the bushland of Waratah National Park in Australia, *Skippy* is about an injured and orphaned kangaroo who becomes best mate with the young son of the chief park ranger.

The New Adventures of Skippy: Syndicated, 1992–1993, 39 episodes

*Starring **Skippy,** Andrew Clarke as Sonny Hammond, Kate McNeil as Jerry Hammond, Simon James as Lou Hammond, Moya O'Sullivan as Thelma Woods, and Fiona Shannon as Kate Burgess.*

Set in Australia's tropical north, the twelve-year-old Sonny Hammond of the 1967 series is now a thirty-seven-year-old widower and the father of ten-year-old non-identical twins. Sonny co-owns Habitat, an animal theme park in the tropical Gold Coast hinterland. Here Skippy and his young friends find various exciting adventures.

Skippy has been one of Australia's greatest TV exports. Less than two years after the debut of the original series, it was airing in thirty-five languages and eighty-four countries across the globe. The family series has been dubbed in Spanish, Japanese, French, German, and Portuguese. Shot in color, it was originally shown in black and white, but now airs on cable TV in color. The

Garry Pankhurst cuddles up to Skippy.
Courtesy of Lee Robinson.

series spawned a 1969 feature film, *The Intruders.*

The show has a banjo-plucked theme, and the lyrics are simple enough: "Skippy, Skippy, Skippy, the bush kangaroo, Skippy, Skippy, Skippy, a friend ever true," sung by a group of children. Skippy was created as a bright kangaroo who sort of communicated with his best boy, Sonny, with a series of clicking sounds ("tch, tch, tch").

Lee Robinson, producer of the original *Skippy* series, said that the lead kangaroo who played Skippy had been brought to them by a woman who had a small kangaroo wrapped in pajamas. "It was a pet, and it was exactly what we were looking for. It was about the right height and a female. So we took that as the main Skippy, because it could be handled and treated like an intelligent animal," Robinson told Andrew Heasley of Australian newspaper *The Age* in the spring of 2000.

Dennis Hill, who created and coproduced *Skippy* with Robinson, says of the first Skip, "Our original Skippy and the one that went on promotional tours was, to the best of my memory, called Josephine. The original owner, a woman, told us Josephine lived in a sack or bag hanging from a nail on a wall. It knew no tricks, and like all kangaroos, when it became nervous, it licked its paws, so it left the set and crawled into its sack.

"When on location, waiting to film, kangaroos like to climb into a sack, which I guess is like a pouch. As Frank Thring, an Australian actor said, as he watched Skippy climb into the sack, 'If that's what they give the star as a dressing room, what can I expect?'"

Kangaroos have tiny brains and are not

Huddled around Skippy are (from left) Ken James, Tony Bonner, Ed Devereaux, and Garry Pankhurst in Australia's answer to Lassie.
Courtesy of Lee Robinson.

Kate McNeil and Simon James, right, have a great playmate in Skippy, the star of the second *Skippy* series in 1992–1993.

Courtesy of David Field.

noted for high IQ's, as Hill explains. "I think it is wonderful how some animals such as chimpanzees, dogs, and horses can be trained, but I can assure you that kangaroos and cows can't be taught. They are both beautiful but dumb.

"Mostly it seemed that when the kangaroo performed, responding to a spoken instruction such as 'stop, Skippy,' 'go left,' or 'go right,' we already had stock shots of these actions to cut into the film.

"Our second unit spent most of its time with Skippy. Noel Menzies, one of the second-unit animal handlers, told me that if the script called for Skippy to run toward and into a doorway, there were hidden animal handlers on either side of the proposed movement, progressively all making a noise so that Skippy stayed on course to the door."

And speaking of Skippy and noise . . . "The 'tch, tch, tch' [Skippy's verbalizing] was recorded by yours truly after I heard the sound uttered by a 'roo in a zoo," says Hill. "Bill Grimmond, our second-unit cameraman, achieved some visual effects of mouth movements from the 'roo by placing a light elastic band around its jaw."

And as for shots of Skippy's pouch, well, those were the real deal, but the kangaroo claw, shown reaching in and out (for letters, gloves, and so on), was a fake supplied by a taxidermist.

The crew discovered early on that kangaroos are easily agitated, so they wound up using more than a dozen look-alike 'roos to portray Skippy throughout the three years of production.

Robinson recalled that one of the kangaroos "loved chocolate. We worked out the way to get it to come to the little boy or anyone else was to crinkle silver paper. It knew the sound of the silver paper around chocolate."

But for the most part, the mob of Skippys dined daily on fresh veggies. "As vegetarians, they eat grass and any vegetables that were brought by our animal trainer, retired police officer Scotty Denham," Hill says.

As for the site, Hill says they found the suitable greenery fairly close to studio headquarters on the edge of a northern suburb of Sydney called Duffy's Forest, which was surrounded on three sides by Ku-ring-gai Chase National Park. "I gained approval from the state government for use of a big slice of bushland and for building our ranger headquarters, heliport and hangar, and animal pens," says Hill.

The location was registered as a zoo with pens for the animals, which included koalas, emus, and other fauna.

When the series ended, the star Skippy,

Josephine, was used for promotional appearances at shopping centers, where she often sported a diamond necklace.

"As I understand it, Skippy died from natural causes. It's a sort of reverse Parkinson's—you don't hop anymore," says Hill.

"When the original Skippy died, we buried her (in a national park)," Robinson said.

In 1992, *The New Adventures of Skippy* was born. Thirty-nine episodes were shot in 1992 and 1993 at the Warner Studios on Australia's Gold Coast.

German-born Robert Weber was hired to train the new Skippy. He started the task with sixteen kangaroos trying out, and gradually narrowed them down. "I have to admit I thought at first they were very dumb. The slightest disturbance would make them freak out or freeze up," Weber told Greg Roberts of the *Sydney Morning Herald* in early 1991.

"Each has its own personality. Some are cuddly, some are aggressive, some are dopey. I talk to them as if they are people and they are responding. We're making progress," he said, referring to three 'roos that had learned to jump onto boxes and two that were close to being able to shake hands.

A few facts are known about the star Skippy of series number two.

"He had originally been raised as a pet. He loved tea bags and would do anything for one. So if you wanted Skippy to come to you, you offered Skip a tea bag and he would hop over to you," says David Field, one of the executive directors of the new series.

"Skippy is alive and well although near the end of his life. Kangaroos only have a life span of ten years or so, and he lives with his trainer, Ron Roman, at Grantham in Queensland," Field reported in the fall of 2000.

In 1998 Skippy reappeared in a second reincarnation, as a cartoon character in *Skippy's Adventures in Bushtown.* Thus, it appears you cannot tie me kangaroo down, sport.

Spin City

ABC, 1996–present (still in production)

*Starring **Uncle Wesley as Rags,** Michael J. Fox as Deputy Mayor Michael Flaherty, Barry Bostwick as Mayor Randall Winston, Alan Ruck as Stuart Bondek, Richard Kind as Paul Lassiter, Michael Boatman as Carter Heywood, Heather Locklear as Caitlin, Charlie Sheen as Charlie Owen, and Lana Parrilla as Angie Ordonez.*

This sitcom follows the interpersonal lives and intraoffice antics of the New York City mayor's office.

He's old. He's suicidal. And when audiences are allowed to hear him thinking to himself, his voice sounds a lot like either David Letterman or Tim Allen. His name is Rags, Carter Heywood's scene-stealing pet Brussells Griffon, who constantly wants to be put out of his misery on *Spin City.*

His real name is Uncle Wesley. He was

born some time ago (but not as long ago as Rags, who was supposedly born in the 1940s). Uncle Wesley was rescued and raised in Manhattan, where he is owned by a nice lady named Ruth Powell. He received his formal training under Robert DeFranco, an applied animal behaviorist, and others at the Animal Behavior Center of New York (a division of the nonprofit American Foundation for Animal Rescue).

"I think Ruth was actually showing Uncle Wesley's photo around to some agencies or such, and somebody at Fox saw the dog and said, 'That's the perfect look,'" says Bob DeFranco. "They wanted to design a dog whose character would be this old, dying eccentric dog who wants to commit suicide all the time. When Ruth brought the dog here, he couldn't do anything except close his eyes and kind of go to sleep. We were trying to work with him to do some different things, like stay. But he would never stay. I think he's so attached to Ruth that we couldn't even really work with him when Ruth was on the set because all he would want to do is be with her. So we did some socialization work with him, and we had him following basic obedience commands and this and that. I don't know if any of those things were ever used because he did have someone else who was working with him on the set, too.

"Uncle Wesley was interesting because when you would work with him, he would just sit there and kind of close his eyes and fall asleep, so he was just like a little old man. If you want to train a dog for television, Uncle Wesley is not the best candidate. We worked with him because they [the producers] liked the look, but the fact is you want to take a dog that's got energy all over the place and loves food and then just hone that and shape that into something that's working for you. When a dog just sits there and falls asleep, it's kind of hard, and we had a lot of problems with that. We tried to motivate him, but he wouldn't accept food. He wasn't very big on food, and he just wasn't an overly active animal. All he liked to do was be held and follow Ruth around all the time. So even getting him to sit and stay in a room and having her leave the room was an accomplishment that took weeks and weeks."

DeFranco continues his sleepy tale: "He had just started the *Spin City*

Uncle Wesley is the distinctive dog who brings both some new and some old (very old) comedic wrinkles to Spin City.

Courtesy of Robert DeFranco.

job when they brought him to us. I think they had done some rehearsals. They'd put him on the couch, and he'd just jump off the couch, and so I think they kind of built his role around what he was capable of doing. When he left us, he was doing a lot more, but he certainly wasn't Lassie." At the same time, DeFranco points out, "Any dog that can do things can really pick up even a dull show. All of a sudden, you add a dog, and you give him a voice and stuff, and it's like everybody wants to see the show."

Uncle Wesley was made up (but not all that much) to look older for the role of Rags, the dog who desperately licks hot electrical outlets in hopes of achieving sufficient charge to send himself to the Great Doggie Bed in the Sky. Uncle Wesley was introduced in the juicy role in the third season of *Spin City* in 1998. The estimate is that he was about nine years old at the time, but nobody really knows.

When *Spin City* moved production from New York City to Los Angeles at the beginning of the 2000–2001 season, Uncle Wesley consented to make the commute to the West Coast to give the relocated show a valuable infusion of his canine star power. But one trip was enough for Uncle Wesley. New York is where he'd rather stay. (A reasonable supposition is that potential earthquakes might interfere with Wesley's desired sleeping habits.) Since then, several other dogs have been used to play the part of Rags—perhaps because no one dog could ever replace Uncle Wesley. Whatever the case, Uncle Wesley clearly doesn't care whether he goes on from Rags to riches. He just wants to sleep and occasionally to be held.

Ahhh, a dog's life indeed!

Spuds MacKenzie

One of the top spokesanimals of all time was Spuds MacKenzie, the bull terrier billed as the "original party animal" by Anheuser-Busch. Spuds, who was born in 1983, made his debut in TV ads for Bud Light beer during the 1987 Super Bowl.

Spuds quickly became the centerpiece of an ad campaign that featured him doing a variety of really hip sports and having exciting adventures while being admired by bikini-clad women. The likeness of Spuds was soon plastered on every imaginable type of merchandise and promotional item.

Honey Tree Evil Eye turned party animal when she became Spuds MacKenzie for Bud Light ads.

Though Anheuser-Busch tried to hide the fact, word finally got out that Spuds was no stud. He was in fact a female bull terrier named Honey Tree Evil Eye. But even such a revelation didn't dampen the high-living dog's popularity. Spuds continued to party with ever-greater gusto.

What finally ended the suds career of Spuds was the backlash of civic-minded folks who thought that he was a bad role model for young children and especially teenagers. When Mothers Against Drunk Driving voiced its concerns about his driving influence, Spuds was commercially neutered in 1989. When Spuds died in 1993, the news made headlines worldwide. His work lives on in the memories of millions and in the collectible merchandise in their bars and basements.

Star Trek: The Next Generation

Syndicated, 1987-1994, 178 episodes

Starring ***Brandy, Monster, and Tyler as Spot;*** *Patrick Stewart as Capt. Jean-Luc Picard; Jonathan Frakes as Cmdr. William Riker; LeVar Burton as Lt. Geordi La Forge; Denise Crosby as Lt. Tasha Yar; Michael Dorn as Lt. Worf; Gates McFadden as Dr. Beverly Crusher; Marina Sirtis as Counselor Deanna Troi; Brent Spiner as Lt. Cmdr. Data; Colin Meaney as Transporter Chief Miles O'Brien; and Whoopi Goldberg as Guinan.*

A new *Enterprise* takes up where the original one left off, give or take a century later, as the twenty-fourth-century crew, led by Captain Picard, continues space exploration.

The most famous TV cat in outer space has got to be Data's Spot. The cool cat was played by numerous felines over the years, but for the last four seasons, the work fell mainly to Brandy, Monster, and Tyler, three cats belonging to Rob Bloch of Critters of the Cinema, which employs about 150 dogs and cats.

"The main cat that did the lying around and sleeping was Brandy. He is a very loving, laid-back, mellow cat, and always has been," says Bloch of the survivor of the litter that Brandy came in. "They were all sweet and all different colors. He is a good cat for walking slowly. You have to work them within their personalities.

"Brandy doesn't play. He's never been an active cat. He lies in bed, then walks around, then goes back to sleep. Some cats are active and some are not. For just having the cat there, he was fine."

However, some of the spacey characters in their space makeup threw Brandy for a loop in the beginning. Bloch recalls, "The first time he saw Data, who has yellow eyes, he kind of stared at him. Then Data has to go away, and Worf [Michael Dorn] has to watch the cat. Worf asks, 'What do I do to take care of Spot?'

"'Clean and feed him,' says Data.

"Worf picks him way up at arm's length and looks at Data and says, 'I will feed him,' and the cat just stares at [the made-up] Michael Dorn like, 'What the hell is that?'"

The orange tabby, who was born in November 1988, was also in the seventh *Star Trek* feature film, *Star Trek Generations*, with one of his doubles. "The cats are in two scenes," says Bloch. "The one where Jordy and Data are sitting and talking, and Spot kept jumping up. That was Monster. Later on, when the ship crashed and they found Spot alive, that was Brandy."

Brandy has guested on *Melrose Place*; *Honey, I Shrunk the Kids*; *America's Funniest Home Videos*; and *The Man Show*; he was also in the *Hart to Hart* reunion TV movie. His commercial credits are legion: Tavist 1 allergy medicine, Honda, Diet Coke, Fresh Step cat litter, CompuServe, Sears, Kodak, Bell and Howell, Chef-Boy-Ardee, McDonald's, Scope mouthwash, Mattel games, and Cheez-Its, plus he's on the Friskies Web site and has appeared in a Brian Setzer music video.

"Brandy's a good kid and lives with one of my trainers. He's semi-retired," says Bloch. "The action cat was Monster, who came from an animal shelter. Monster died young at eight or nine in 1996. His first job was on *Murder, She Wrote*. He was just the opposite of Brandy. He had a tremendous food drive, and if you're holding him and he wants to go because of food at the other end of the room, he would not be averse to nipping you.

"Monster was into food and toys, and he tended not to relate to people. He would rather be going or doing things like a hyper kid."

Monster's various credits include a Tom Jones music video, the Janet Jackson feature film *Poetic Justice*, and Century 21 and Diet Coke commercials.

The most modern cat from outer space is Brandy, who starred as Spot, pet of Lt. Cmdr. Data, on *Star Trek: The Next Generation*.
Courtesy of Rob Bloch / Critters of the Cinema.

Completing the triumvirate of Bloch's Spots was Tyler, who did the running around. Tyler and the late Monster worked as part of the Friskies cat team and have been pictured on Friskies cat food bags. Tyler is the one shown playing the piano.

It's Friskies that keeps Tyler hopping these days as he tours the U.S. with a traveling Friskies show. But in the meantime he tackles commercials like the Arizona state lottery, Old Navy, Folgers coffee, and the Discovery Channel. He is also seen on the cover of the video game Tomba. Tyler also starred with Dennis Rodman in a Kodak commercial in which the basketball player rescues him from a tree.

Bloch gives credit to the cats that portrayed Spot during the first two seasons of *The Next Generation* as belonging to trainer Scott Hart.

Taco Bell Chihuahua

Gidget is the name of the female who played the nameless male Mexican-food-loving Chihuahua in TV and print ads for Taco Bell that began in 1997. With Carlos Alazraqui giving voice to memorable catch phrases such as "*¡Yo quiero Taco Bell!*" "Here, leezard, leezard, leezard" (in ads tying in with 1998's *Godzilla* remake), and "Drop the chalupa," the canine campaign created by the TBWA\Chiat\Day agency quickly stirred a frenzy of excitement and identity (and with it some ethnic controversy) for Taco Bell.

The eight-pound (that is, before eating a chalupa) Gidget was born in 1995 and is trained by Sue Chipperton and Deborah Dellosso. (Gidget is owned by Paul Calabria and Karen McGelhab of Studio Animal Service.) But the close-ups featuring those famous eyebrow movements were, alas, created digitally with a computer. And the talking was accomplished by superimposing a man-made jaw. *(¡Ay caramba!)* But the ears—those beautiful, giant ears—are all Gidget's, no gadgets.

Of course, it is not unusual for a big Hollywood starlet to get a little help with her appearance from modern science and technology. And there's no doubt that Gidget was indeed just such a megastar for three years (a virtual generation in dog years), until her Taco Bell campaign was abruptly dropped in 2000 when company sales drooped.

But while it lasted, this "extraordinary actress," as she was once described by a Taco Bell executive, was surrounded by all of the limousines and lawsuits befitting a cultural icon. And that's not to mention the tens of millions of plush toys, T-shirts, and refrigerator magnets emblazoned with her likeness.

At least Gidget had a movie career to fall back on. Before her Taco Bell work, she appeared in the movie *The Fan*. And later she was fea-

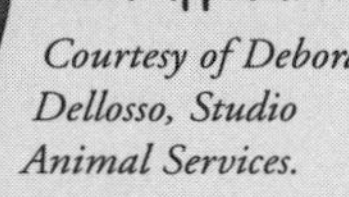

Even though Taco Bell dropped its Chihuahua ad campaign like a hot chalupa, Gidget is still "all ears" for offers for her to continue acting and to make promotional appearances.
Courtesy of Deborah Dellosso, Studio Animal Services.

tured in *Crazy in Alabama* with Melanie Griffith and Antonio Banderas. Like most big stars, Gidget has a stand-in. In her case, it's a male Chihuahua named Taco, who was rescued from an animal shelter in Florida. He's not to be confused with Dinkie, a female Chihuahua who sometimes played the supposedly male Taco Bell dog's possible love interest. (Of course, the Taco Bell dog's only true love interest was Taco Bell delicacies.)

Another planned double for Gidget was Moonie, but he never grew to be big enough. Moonie, also owned by Calabria and McGelhab, did get to appear with Gidget in the 2001 film *Legally Blonde,* in which Moonie starred as Bruiser opposite Reese Witherspoon. In one of the movie's more memorable gags, Moonie's Bruiser shows keen interest while watching a Taco Bell commercial featuring Gidget.

At one point, there was also a plan to make a movie based on Gidget's life story, but that too got morphed into a spicy legal salsa with some of Gidget's human handlers and so far has fizzled like so many fajitas.

One more twist to Gidget's charming story is this: Her trademark line "*¡Yo quiero Taco Bell!*" is no longer her only trademark. Now her name is trademarked as well. She's no longer known as Gidget. Her name is now officially and legally registered as Gidgey™.

It all sounds loco, but through it all, Gidget, or rather, Gidgey™, can still proudly hold her head eleven inches high and say, "*¡Vamanos, no nachos!*"

Tales of the Gold Monkey

ABC, 1982–1983, 21 episodes

*Starring **Leo as Jack,** Stephen Collins as Jake Cutter, Jeff MacKay as Corky, Caitlin O'Heaney as Sarah Stickney White, Roddy McDowell as Bon Chance Louis, John Calvin as Rev. Willie Tenboom, Marta DuBois as Princess Kaji, and John Fujioka as Todo.*

Tales of the Gold Monkey is set in the Marivella Islands of the South Pacific in 1938 at the port of Boragora and the bar known as the Monkey Bar. Jake Cutter is a pilot, an adventurer, and an ex-member of the Flying Tigers who has a Grumman Goose seaplane. With his sidekick Corky, an ace mechanic with a tendency to over-imbibe, and Jack, a terrier with one eye who wore an eye patch because Jake had lost the dog's glass eye (an opal with a sapphire center) while playing poker, Jake finds adventures aplenty as he searches for treasure and battles Japanese and German spies.

When Jack barked once, it meant no; two barks meant yes. And he understood English, Japanese, and Spanish (hey, it's a TV series).

Jack was played by Leo, a Jack Russell terrier mix owned by Hollywood veteran Karl Lewis Miller, who got the dog by happenstance. "He came to me through another trainer who was in transit from Florida and couldn't keep all his animals at the time. So he just gave me Leo," Miller says.

Miller suspects that Leo got the gig, his first starring role, because not many shows, if any, were using the Jack Russell look in the early 1980s. "Donald Belisarius [the show's producer-creator] looked at a lot of dogs, and I think he picked Leo because he was a different-looking kind of dog. Everyone was showing golden retrievers, etc., and he had this unusual brindle color, a kind of brown with black stripes. Leo was a terrier, just a mischievous, snotty but little, lovable, cuddly dog. He wants to be with you and all that, but, boy, they can sure get in trouble."

Leo starred as one-eyed Jack, while Stephen Collins was Jake Cutter and Caitlin O'Heaney played Sarah Stickney White in the wonderful, short-lived series *Tales of the Gold Monkey.*

The eye patch Leo had to wear for the cameras as Jack caused an unusual evolution in the dog's appearance. "When we did the pilot, both of his ears were flopped down," Miller says, "but now we started into the show. The dog used to strain one ear as a radar to compensate for his eye not being able to see. By the end of shooting, that ear was straight up as opposed to the pilot where it was down.

"We take time to train our dogs and position them like an athlete or a stunt person. We train them to tolerate their equipment, whether it be collars or a harness or whatever, so we had trained him to leave the patch alone and tolerate it, but almost weekly we could see the ear coming up higher and higher and higher. He didn't wear the patch all the time, just when they rolled the camera. It might just be twenty minutes some days and two hours the next, but every time we put that patch on to work him, you could tell he was constantly trying to figure out what was going on on that side, and that ear started working like radar."

The one-eyed role on *Tales of the Gold Monkey* was the first to let viewers put a name on a dog most had seen in the background of many movies and TV episodes. "Before the *Gold Monkey*, that dog was like [character actor greats] Jack Elam or Dub Taylor of the movies. He was a character dog that you saw in every project, but you didn't know his name. In *The Blue Knight* [1975 on CBS], he was a regular street dog that always pestered George Kennedy's character, Bumper Morgan. This dog would turn up in the darnedest places at the right time to break the monotony or the silence of the scene."

Miller adds, "His first project was in the Warren Beatty movie *Shampoo*, where he was just a street dog. He did several appearances on *M*A*S*H* as a Vietnam camp dog, and he was on *Punky Brewster*. He used to run the streets of the western town on *Kung Fu*.

"At one time or another that dog appeared in just about every TV show, but in a bit part or in the background action. I think I watched TV one night and saw him on four different shows. He made a good bouncy, barky, stray dog."

Little Leo died peacefully of old age.

"All my dogs grow old gracefully like actors," says Miller. "And when they get old, they just get older parts."

Tarzan

Tarzan: NBC, 1966–1968, 57 episodes

*Starring **Vicky as Cheetah, Major the lion, Modoc and Margie the elephants,** Ron Ely as Tarzan, Manuel Padilla Jr. as Jai, Alan Caillou as Jason Flood, Rockne Tarkington as Rao, and Stewart Rafill as Tall Boy.*

The original TV series version of Edgar Rice Burroughs' *Tarzan* was set in the jungles of Africa, where the lord of the jungle got into all sorts of adventures with his chimp, Cheetah, and an orphan boy, Jai.

Tarzan: Syndicated, 1991–1994, 75 episodes

*Starring **Archie as Cheetah, Numa the lion, Tantor the elephant,** Wolf Larson as Tarzan, Lydie Denier as Jane Porter, Sean Roberge as Roger Taft Jr., and Malick Bowens as Simon.*

TV's second *Tarzan* series has the lord of the jungle aiding Jane, a French environmental scientist working at an African wildlife

Tarzan, played by Ron Ely, plays ball with Cheetah (Vicky the chimp) and Margie, a young elephant, in the 1960s TV series *Tarzan.*

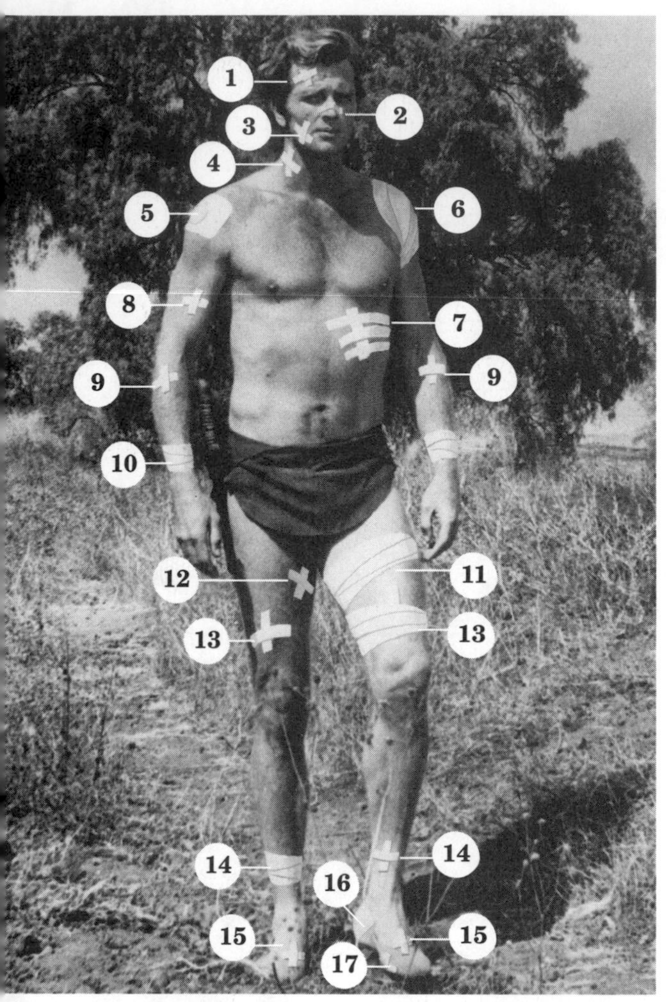

Ron Ely insisted on doing his own stunts and animal fights while making the *Tarzan* TV series and limped away with a few injuries after practically every episode. The numbers indicate his injuries: (1) stitches from a lion bite, (2) broken nose, (3) jaw dislocated in a fight, (4) wrenched neck and disc from a vine-swinging mishap, (5) shoulder separation from vine swinging, (6) shoulder broken when a vine broke in mid-swing, (7) ribs broken in the same accident, (8) muscle torn fighting a lion, (9) claw cuts from a puma fight, (10) wrist sprains from an action scene, (11) pulled muscle running from a lion, (12) pulled thigh muscle, (13) bites and claw marks from various beasts, (14) ankle sprain from hard landings, (15) feet lacerated in a fall down a hill, (16) cracked left heel bone, and (17) foot injury from walking barefoot where shoes were required.

institute, where they face a multitude of troubles.

The 1960s saw the first TV version of the story of Lord Greystoke, the jungle lad raised by great apes who grew into the jungle lord. The production of this show was no stroll through the Serengeti.

Ron Ely's simian costar was supposed to be a male chimp named Dinky, who had done a couple of *Tarzan* feature films with movie star Tarzan Mike Henry (*Tarzan and the Valley of Gold, Tarzan and the Great River*, and *Tarzan and the Jungle Boy*). Early into the filming of the second *Tarzan* feature in Brazil, Dinky bit Henry in the jaw so badly that the production shut down. The actor needed twenty stitches to close the wound and spent three weeks recuperating.

Fernando Celis, trainer of the chimps for the *Tarzan* series and the Henry *Tarzan* flicks, was run ragged, as at one point the TV series and a feature film were being shot simultaneously near Rio de Janeiro, Brazil, and he was running animals back and forth from both locations on the same day.

After Dinky showed his fangs, Celis had to switch to another chimp, a little female named Vicky, who worked the entire TV series as Cheetah. Celis found Vicky in Redondo Beach, California, when she was about two-and-a-half-years old. "We paid five hundred dollars for her from a place that looked almost like a body shop. They had her just running around on a small skateboard. She was getting big, and they didn't know what to do with her," says Celis.

The trainer says Vicky was one smart chimp, almost too smart, because she learned movie commands. "Ron Ely got along very well with her. Many times I would just sit down and she would take the command from him. He would say, 'Cheetah, come here,' and instead of waiting for me to say, 'Go to him,' she would look at me and just go. She got to the point where she would start on the director's word 'Action!' She wouldn't wait for me to say, 'All right, go.' If the director said 'Cut!' she would stop.

"Vicky had to work with a young boy on *Tarzan*, and it is very difficult to have any kind of animal with a kid because animals don't like them. The animals want to show the kids that the kids are not their boss, but one of Vicky's great qualities was that she never attempted to bite anybody.

"She was very smart and had many behaviors that most chimps don't get into. She was very original. You could point your finger like a gun and make a noise, and she would fall dead as if you had shot her. It all came natural to her, just like playing games. She was very good with my lions. It was very cool to have the little boy and the chimp riding on the lion."

Celis, a native of Mexico, had a small zoo in Acapulco when he went into show biz with some of his animals in TV commercials. His first film was the 1964 Mike Henry *Tarzan* film. It was there that his lion Major made his movie debut. Major was in three *Tarzan* films and the Ely *Tarzan* TV shows.

Ely, a bronze, muscle-bound giant from Texas, enjoyed doing practically all his own stunts and, as a result, took a few bad spills as well as cat nips and scratches in the course of the series, which was filmed in Brazil, Mexico, and Acapulco, among other locations.

Trainer Fernando Celis and his chimp Vicky meet three silver screen Tarzans (left to right): Jock Mahoney, Johnny Weissmuller, and James Pierce.

Courtesy of Fernando Celis.

He found there was no end to the hazards of a role where all he wore was a loincloth. As Tarzan, Ely was bitten repeatedly by cats, he had his jaw dislocated and nose broken in fights, he broke his left shoulder and three ribs in a fall from a vine, and sprained his wrist and leg muscles.

"If you have pride in the business and are hammering out a product frequently from your own blood, sometimes it is very satisfying," Ely told a network publicist in 1967.

He definitely had the scars and bruises to prove his manifesto. And he learned to respect the big cats. "They can kill me and I know it," he said.

Celis witnessed just about all of Ely's misfortunes, including a nasty spill during a swinging incident. "Before the new TV season began, we did some second-unit shooting, like stock footage, of Tarzan swinging left to right, things we would need to use through all the series," Celis says. "For one scene the director wanted Vicky sitting on Ron's shoulder as he was swinging and doing a return from one vine to another. He was about thirty to forty feet high in the trees, and somehow during the transfer, he lost it and fell to the ground, but Vicky managed to grab the vine with one hand and she was OK." Ely wasn't quite so lucky. He broke his shoulder.

Vicky also made one other narrow escape from danger. "I remember one time there

Fernando Celis poses with his leopard Rajah and his lion Major in 1963.
Courtesy of Fernando Celis.

was a chase with the natives chasing the white doctor, and the chimp and boy were in a Jeep and it crashed. It was a bad wreck, but Vicky wound up on a tree branch," Celis says. "Somehow she jumped two seconds before the impact and landed in the tree."

Vicky also had her own stunt chimp, one that Celis calls "real gutsy." He recalls, "Elmer was just fantastic. He would not get into doing tricks. He was more like a fun-loving chimp, very athletic, and had incredible behavior. One time he saved my life after a lion got me in the compound. He crawled under the cage, skinned his whole back, and came running to help me, and the lion went after him and that gave me the chance to break."

Rockne Tarkington worked as an actor and animal trainer on *Tarzan* and recalls one wild ride that Ely made on the back of Major: "He was supposed to jump on the lion and wrestle it, but the lion took off running through the jungle in Brazil. Finally Ron rolled off, and he was all marked up with the briars and tree limbs that had scratched him."

Tarkington also had his own close encounter with Ralph Helfer's big elephant Modoc. He recalls, "Modoc took off one time, and Ralph yelled at me, 'Rockne, get in front of him and wave your arms.' I said, 'Are you crazy?!' He was in the trot mode, but I got in front and waved my arms. He just took his trunk and wrapped around me and threw me about forty feet in the air, and I landed on top of some straw fifty feet from where he tossed me. We laughed about it later, but that was the last time I stood in front of old Modoc."

After two seasons, *Tarzan* was canceled, and Celis went to work on *Daktari* and *Cowboy in Africa*. He brought Vicky and Major the lion, along with a leopard. Major did some double work for Clarence, the star lion of *Daktari*. Major lived to be twenty-three and spent his last few years at Magic Mountain in Saugus, California, where an average of 120 children a day had their photos taken on his back.

After *Daktari* stopped production, Celis sent Vicky and Elmer to a chimp sanctuary, and he became stunt coordinator on *The Life and Times of Grizzly Adams*. Sometime later he learned that both of his chimps had been destroyed, a setback that made him decide he no longer wanted to own animals himself.

"You can't have chimps with people after they get to be about eight," Celis says. "Dinky was so good we thought he would be good forever—until he bit Mike [Henry]. I think Dinky ended up somewhere in the space program."

Celis, coincidentally, makes his home today in Tarzana (near Los Angeles), where Edgar Rice Burroughs, the creator of *Tarzan*, once lived.

Television's second *Tarzan* series, set in a modern wildlife institute in Africa, aired in 1991. Portraying Cheetah, Tarzan's best beast, was a chimpanzee named Archie.

Star Wolf Larson recollected his simian sidekick during an interview with Bill Groves for *TV Chronicles* in 1997: "Archie was terrific. The brighter the chimp—and I guess there's as much of a range of intelligence in chimps within the chimp community as there is in people—is what gives them their personality. Chimps in a lot of ways are like little kid bullies who will do whatever they can and see what they can get away with. If they have respect for you, then you're the greatest person on the planet. If they don't, they will do anything in their power to get you, which is scary."

He added, "What I used to do with Archie was play with him. I played with him all the time on set, and I would play with him in a very physical fashion, much like you would play with your little brother. . . . He loved playing with me. The only other person that could do anything to that degree was the trainer who had raised him. . . . So I actually looked forward to working with him. Unfortunately, if the series would have gone another two, three years, they probably would have had to retire him, because as they get older and stronger, then no matter how much they liked you when they're younger, they're going to be starting to finally look at you, going, 'I think I can take him now.'"

Larson also recalled a vine-swinging accident that nearly cost his little friend his life. The two were swinging from a platform to a rocky shelf when the vine (actually a disguised cable) stretched and dropped them below their intended target.

"We were going along at a fair clip, because it was a very fast swing across this ravine. I started noticing the chimp, Archie, on my back," Larson said in his interview with Bill Groves. "He was going from one side to the other because he was seeing what I was seeing, and realizing that we were not going to make it. And he bailed, probably a second before I hit the wall, and I had to hit with my legs, then spun off around it and had to hang on, because I would have hit the rocks down below. He actually jumped and fell into an area. I guess he must have timed it fairly well, and dropped about forty feet. Didn't hurt himself at all. Amazing, those little animals. Amazing."

Tequila & Bonetti

CBS, 1992, 12 episodes

*Starring **Foster as Tequila,** Jack Scalia as Det. Nick Bonetti, Brad Sanders as the voice of Tequila, Mariska Hargitay as Angela Garcia, Charles Rocket as Capt. Midian Knight, Terry Funk as Sgt. Nuzo, W. K. Stratton as Det. Lee, and Joe Vita as Officer Vita.*

As kind of a *McCloud* in reverse, New York cop Nico Bonetti gets temporary duty in Southern California, where his partner is a French mastiff named Tequila. The dog has an appetite like Frank Cannon and a James Bond–like taste for everything else. Tequila also shares his thoughts with the audience in very good English.

"We had a team of three or four dogs that played Tequila," says trainer Mathilde de Cagny, "but Foster was the main one. It was a brand-new dog that we had just finished training for this show.

"Foster was born in France. We went and picked him in France. I don't know the date he was born, but he was about a year old when we started to shoot *Tequila & Bonetti.* He went on to work on *General Hospital* for several years, but I didn't work with him on that; another trainer did." (De Cagny's next big job after *Tequila & Bonetti* was working with Moose for the role of Eddie on *Frasier.*)

Jack Scalia was Bonetti and Foster was his French mastiff, Tequila, in the short-lived police comedy/drama *Tequila & Bonetti,* in which the the dog provided running commentary, voice courtesy of Brad Sanders. A newer version of the series, with Scalia still in the lead human role, has proved a bona fide hit across Europe in the past few years.

De Cagny continues, "It was a hard show to do because the type of dog they're cast to be is not the kind of dog they are. They're not really warriors. The types of behaviors they wanted the dogs to do on the show were not really in their personality. They are gentle dogs. So the show was challenging in regards to teaching the stunts and making sure they weren't afraid of anything because they really are scaredy-cats. The challenging part was making them look fearless.

"On one of the very first shows we did, the dog had to do an arm attack. We had a toy that we hid in the stuntman's sleeve. So the dog knew to go get his toy, and he did that just fine. So then we film the scene and the dog goes for the actor's arm and the actor's character screams, which of course makes sense. The dog got so scared that he let go of the arm like, 'Oh my gosh! What have I done?' So we had to dub in the screaming."

Though *Tequila & Bonetti* was a relatively short-lived show, de Cagny says, "It was a great show to be on and a very good learning experience for me as it was somewhat early in my career." She adds that Foster died around 1999.

An interesting side note is that *Tequila & Bonetti* has now become an Italian television series starring Jack Scalia. It is a huge hit in Europe.

Thunder

NBC, 1977–1978, 13 episodes

*Starring **Ott as Thunder, Cupcake as Cupcake the mule,** Clint Ritchie as Bill Prescott, Melissa Converse as Ann Prescott, Melora Hardin as Cindy Prescott, and Justin Randi as Willie Williams.*

Thunder was a Saturday morning TV series about a half-wild black stallion who comes under the care of a young girl who lives on a ranch in the Southwest. Shot in Bishop, California, the series was created by the original writers and producers of *Fury.*

Ott, a straight thoroughbred and the star of *Thunder,* was one of Hollywood's top horses from the 1960s through the 1980s. Owner-trainer Bobby J. Davenport got him in the early 1960s near Lone Pine, California.

"He was an awful good, sound horse," says Davenport. "I could turn him right and left without anything on him. He was good-tempered and could tolerate anything. We did shots as many as twenty or thirty times, and he never would fail. Ott was perfect with children. They could ride him without anything on him.

"We were working on *Thunder* one time and had a mountain lion that he was supposed to fight. They had the mountain lion staked with cable, and I sent Ott in to rear him and the mountain lion lunged and broke the cable, and when they both came down, they just stared straight at each other.

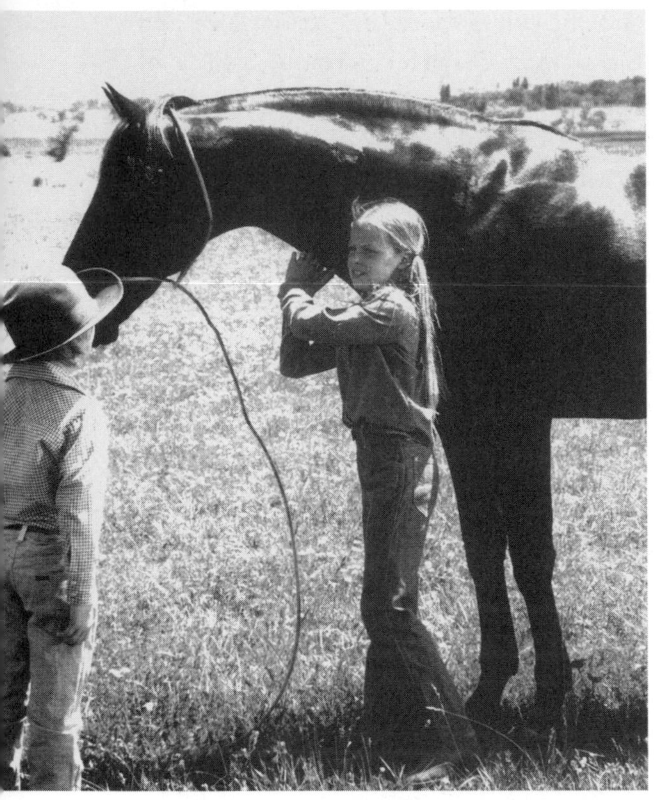

Justin Randi and Melora Hardin spend time in the pasture with their favorite horse, Thunder.
Courtesy of Melora Hardin.

Ott never moved or the cat would have grabbed him.

"Ott was best horse in the business at that time in the 1970s and 1980s. I won three PATSY Awards [for work on *Bonanza*, *Lassie*, and *Run, Joe, Run*] with him," Davenport says of his horse that also worked many episodes of *Little House on the Prairie* and was in the 1971 feature film *Black Beauty*. Ott lived to age twenty-one.

Ott's double on *Thunder* also worked under the tutelage of Davenport. Mostly quarter horse, Rex, now thirty-two, came into the trainer's hands out of Saugus, California. "He's an awful good horse, too," says Davenport. "I still have him. I got him retired."

Ott's animal costar on *Thunder* was a cookie-eating mule named Cupcake. Cupcake's double was a mule named Jake that also belonged to Davenport. "Jake is still alive," Davenport says. "He was the star of *Gus* [the Disney movie about a football-kicking mule]. He did a little of all of it. But I had a double mule trained to kick the ball."

Davenport, who originally hailed from Uvalde, Texas, started in the business with a trained horse that he showed at rodeos and fairs. He had a liberty horse, one that worked without halter or bridle as it obeyed his commands.

His talents took him to Hollywood where, beginning in 1955, he worked out of the stables of Glenn Randall for about five years and made a name for himself as one who truly knew the ropes of equine education.

Eventually Davenport worked horses in practically all of the late 1950s and 1960s TV westerns. He also worked the horses in *The Mickey Mouse Club* miniseries *Corky and White Shadow*, and he worked his star horse on five episodes of *Lassie*.

Actress Melora Hardin recalls her days of *Thunder* quite glad-heartedly. "A week before the audition, I told my Mom that I wanted to do a TV series with a horse. It was a wish come true. I loved horses," says Hardin, whose grandfather had a ranch in Mesquite, Texas.

"I had been riding since I was about five," Hardin continues. "When I went for the final audition with Bobby Davenport (the horse trainer on the series), it was to see if I could ride.

I got on the horse, and we sort of rode around cones and went around a simple course. Bobby was pretty excited that I could actually ride, but he taught me how to ride better. He had me doing a little barrel racing. I had a stunt double, a boy, who did the dangerous stuff. I did all the easy trots and walking. Whenever it was saddled, I was allowed to do more.

"The horses were incredible. Both were very tall, at least sixteen hands, and one was particularly good at all the tricks. He did all the standing and whinnying and smiling. I think it was Ott. He was an amazing horse.

"Ott was a little star. He knew he was very well taken care of, very loved. He was so brushed and so shiny, so perfect all the time. He had more makeup and hair handlers than I did. He was so beautifully groomed."

Hardin also says that she and Justin Randi really enjoyed the mule. "The mule didn't have a name, so they started calling him Cupcake. The mules were funny, sweet little animals, but they were really stubborn, and there were plenty of times we had to wait.

Justin Randi and Melora Hardin pose with Thunder's pal, Cupcake the mule.
Courtesy of Melora Hardin.

"Bobby [Davenport] let us pet the horses, and we played with the animals as much as we could. In one episode there was a pot-bellied pig, and the trainer let the pig go down by the stream, and he would sit down and roll in the mud. He was adorable."

The Today Show

NBC, 1952–present (still in production)

*Starring **J. Fred Muggs, Phoebe B. Beebe, Kokomo Jr.,** Dave Garroway (1950s host), Jack Lescoulie (sidekick), and Frank Blair (newsman).*

Television's first major animal celebrity hit the air in February 1953 as J. Fred Muggs joined NBC's early morning news-information show, *Today.*

The effect was stupendous, as Mr. Muggs kept *Today* from going down the tube. The National Broadcasting Company made a boatload of bananas, and the show continues to roll along nearly fifty years later. All because America went nuts over a charming chimpanzee.

J. Fred Muggs and sweetheart Phoebe B. Beebe pose with a grinning Dave Garroway on the *Today* set.

Richard A. R. Pinkham, director and vice-chairman of Ted Bates Advertising Company, Inc., in New York and former vice chairman of the board of NBC, told *Advertising Age* in a May 14, 1979, article: "J. Fred Muggs saved the *Today* show when it was about to go under in 1953. I was the executive producer, and nobody was looking at television at 7 A.M. We were producing a serious news program, which nobody knew they needed. Muggs became our comic strip, designed to attract the kids, who would expose their parents to the early television news. It worked. Had it not, I suspect *Today* would have been canceled. So I figure he made a $100 million difference to NBC."

Television historian Wesley Hyatt agrees. In his book *The Encyclopedia of Daytime Television*, Hyatt wrote about *Today* and its animal star, "The element most responsible for making thc show a hot ticket with the public was a chimpanzee dubbed J. Fred Muggs, whose mischievous antics tickled kids and forced their parents to watch the show.

"In fact, when the program scored an early major exclusive on June 29, 1953, as ex-President Harry Truman visited outside the big street window where the camera occasionally ventured to get shots of New Yorkers, Truman mistook J. Fred Muggs for a human infant."

So who was Muggs?

Muggs was a magnificent chimp with a marvelous intellect, an amazing array of talents, and the desire to please people. And when the new millennium officially began on January 1, 2001, Muggs was still around to celebrate it!

Born March 14, 1952, in the French Cameroons of Africa, Muggs is owned by Buddy Mennella and Roy Waldron. They bought him at thirteen weeks of age for six hundred dollars from animal supplier Henry Trefflich. The little simian weighed three-and-a-half pounds.

Mennella and Waldron were best of friends as both worked as pages at NBC in New York City, but they were also partners in the Glen Rock Pet Shop in Glen Rock, New Jersey.

They purchased the chimp to help publicize the pet shop. One of their first ideas was to hold a contest in the local newspaper to name the chimp. Young Ron Pardie submitted the name of Muggs, thinking that the chimp's face reminded him of a mug. For his efforts, he won a bird, a bird cage, and some birdseed, but Muggs and company were on the brink of coast-to-coast stardom.

Muggs's first TV appearance, even before he became J. Fred Muggs, was on *The Perry Como Show*. The singer was a friend of Mennella and Waldron. The pair, along with Muggs, went to visit him on the set. Someone suggested Muggs be added to the show that day, so Como held the little guy in his arms and crooned "Jambalaya."

Not long afterward, Mennella was visiting his dad in the hospital in New York City. "Now, wherever Buddy and Roy went, Muggs went with them. So they stopped by to see Uncle Jim Harkins, Fred Allen's manager," says Jerry Preis, who has been handling business affairs for Muggs for nearly forty years.

"After their visit, they went down to the coffee shop in the RCA Building to have coffee. Some people from the NBC *Today* show had seen them in the building. The *Today* show was suffering. Ratings were bad, and they needed a gimmick to promote the show. So they were sitting there having coffee. Muggs was dunking a doughnut, and a young man staring at Muggs said to Buddy, 'Do you mind if I sit here and watch him?'" (The curious onlooker was an unknown actor named James Dean, says Preis.)

"In the process, the NBC people came and grabbed the three of them from the coffee shop and brought them to the *Today* show office and booked them for one show," Preis continues. "This was in the winter, and they were to appear at 7:00 A.M., but the night before they had a terrible winter storm with a foot of snow. They woke up late and got there late, so NBC told them forget it. 'If we need you again, we'll call.' As they were on their way out, NBC brought them back and signed them to a five-year contract."

The trio began a five-year run on *Today* from 1953 to 1957 at a fee of two hundred dollars a week. And the young simian had his name changed to J. Fred Muggs to give it "an air of distinction."

The early morning gig was not an easy one as it required an early wake-up call. Mennella, Waldron, and Muggs awoke each weekday morning at 4:00, arrived at the studio at 6:00, and at 7:00 the show began its two-hour live broadcast.

Besides his pure cuteness, Muggs became renowned for his skill as a celebrity impersonator. Among those he aped were Jimmy Durante, Bob Hope, Jackie Gleason, Popeye, Jack Benny, Ed Sullivan, and Groucho Marx.

"He would do Gleason's 'away we go!' and for Durante he wore a hat and a false nose. For Popeye, he put his bottom lip over his top lip and wore a pipe and sailor hat. He did Jack Benny by folding his arms and directing his eyes upward as he kind of moved back and forth," Preis says. "It wasn't hard to teach Muggs. We just told him what to do, like, 'take the hat and put it on.' He was brought up like a child to understand words."

One of the most outlandish stunts that occurred daily on *Today* was a portion of the show referred to as "The Chase." Most of the time, Muggs sat with Dave Garroway on his lap or with his owners on a staircase of the set waiting to be called. When "Chase" time came, Muggs's owners worried.

"That was something we didn't like at all," says Preis. "Dave Garroway wanted that to happen. 'The Chase' was where they would let Muggs loose on the set and run around and have Garroway chase him and pan to wherever Muggs wound up on the set. They thought it was funny, but Buddy didn't like it.

"The audience liked it as he would run around the desk and go up into the lights. Muggs's popularity had become a nightmare to Garroway. Muggs got more fan mail than he did, so it got to the point where he resented Muggs.

"A stagehand approached Buddy one time and said, 'He [Garroway] wants him to go up in the lights and have him electrocuted, so that we can air one of the largest funerals ever in New York City.'"

While there were some reports that Muggs bit some people on the set, Preis says, "Muggs never bit anyone on the show or anywhere else, even though it was reported as such. My true opinion of those episodes is that Muggs should have bit some of the folks on the show, given the circumstances he was put into, and what Garroway tried to do to him.

"In one instance, Garroway kept candy in a trick drawer at his desk. Muggs knew it was there. The drawer was out of camera's eye and it took two knocks on the desk to open the drawer. So of course, Muggs, as smart as he was, would knock all the time. One time Garroway purposely closed Muggs's hand in the drawer—purposely. For that, Muggs should have bit him."

Garroway may not have cared much for the little scene stealer, but NBC took pretty good care of its star simian. During the course of his run, Muggs had more than four hundred outfits made by designer Paul DuPont. "Muggs didn't like long sleeves; he liked only short sleeves," Preis says. "I think the long hairs stuck through the fabric."

And for footwear, Muggs has always worn U.S. Keds. "Keds made all his shoes throughout his lifetime. They specially designed a shoe for Muggs. We took him to the factory to be measured for his feet, or we would trace his feet and mail them the tracing. Keds would make his shoes all different colors to match his wardrobe."

One of the biggest splashes Muggs made on *Today* was when he went around the world on a forty-two country tour in 1954. Sponsored by American Express, Muggs and the *Today* show became goodwill ambassadors as they did "live" remotes. "It was filmed, and the film was flown back to New York and shown the next day," Preis says. Muggs built up thirty thousand frequent-flier miles in thirty days.

Globetrotter Muggs also had an eye for beautiful ladies. "Muggs loved women," Preis says. "In fact, *Life* magazine once did a story about Muggs's ten loves, as they named ten of the most famous women that Muggs had appeared with. Anita Ekberg was one of them. She was on the *Today* show, and it was live on the set. Muggs was hugging her, and in

Dave Garroway watches as J. Fred Muggs digs into a cake celebrating the fifth anniversary of *Today*.

the process he knocked one of her earrings off, and it went down the front of her dress. His reaction was to take one hand and put it down the front of her dress to get her earring."

Then there was his "soul kiss" with Kim Novak. "She was on the *Today* show promoting her movie *Picnic*," Preis says. "They wanted to do a publicity shot, so they said to her, 'Strike a sexy pose,' and she opened her mouth and Muggs stuck his tongue in her mouth. She said, 'All right, which one of you guys taught him that?'"

The ten loves of Muggs, by the way, were Ekberg, Novak, Ava Gardner, Jayne Mansfield, Debbie Reynolds, Terry Moore, Martha Raye, Marilyn Monroe, Judy Garland, Jo Stafford, and Betty White.

But Muggs really has only one true lady love: Phoebe B. Beebe. The producers of *Today* wanted the ape to have a girlfriend, so the question was asked, "What was Muggs's huggry muggry?"

"Viewers had to guess, and of course, it was Phoebe," says Preis. "We introduced her on the *Today* show, probably in 1953. She was presented inside a TV without a screen. Her face was the screen. She was announced to the press and notables at New York's Hampshire House, which was noted as her 'coming out' party."

Muggs left *Today* in March 1957, and it happened unexpectedly. "Muggs's abrupt ending on the *Today* show came by surprise, while he was at home recuperating from pneumonia," says Preis. "It was announced in the newspapers before it was ever told to us."

A lawsuit was brought by Mennella and Waldron against the network, and it was settled for an undisclosed amount.

But the overall *Today* experience had been a marvelous one for Muggs. He'd met kings and queens and three U.S. presidents (Truman, Eisenhower, and Kennedy), and through the years he made the acquaintance of dozens of movie stars. One was Bob Hope, whom he visited on the set of the movie *The Seven Little Foys*. J. Fred and Bob were photographed on the set, and the picture hit all the newspapers. Intrigued by Muggs, Hope later tabbed Muggs to join him in a six-city college tour for ROTC in the early 1960s.

Muggs made his own way in the 1960s. He played five European countries while touring army and air force bases. He performed in a vaudeville stage show with Milton Berle and Tiny Tim, did an East Coast state fair tour, and toured Canada with a variety show. By the early 1970s, he was playing assorted venues.

"We were appearing in the Hamptons along with Georgie Jessel in a vaudeville-type show," says Preis. "After the show, Robert Bean, general manager of Busch Gardens, came backstage and said, 'We want you to open the new Stanleyville Theater at Busch Gardens in the African Village for six weeks.'"

That was in 1972. The show proved a smash, so Busch Gardens continued to renew his contract for three-and-a-half years in the Tampa, Florida, tourist attraction. Among other talents, Muggs would fence, and for a grand finale he played "The Bells of St. Mary's" on a set of octave bells.

Muggs kept busy in other media. He was the cover chimp of *TV Guide* for ten years from 1978 to 1985, as J. Fred was used as spokesperson to knock TV personalities in an annual article known as the J. Fred Muggs Annual Blooper Awards.

He starred in numerous commercials for such companies as Levis, Baker's Coconut, U.S. Rubber, American Express, and Milton Bradley. And Muggs cashed in on plenty of merchandising on his own with such J. Fred Muggs items as dolls, games, ashtrays, puppets, his own Little Golden Book, chimp piggy banks, pull toys, and a collector series of NBC star cards.

Muggs not only made national magazine covers, but he even illustrated national magazine covers. The chimpanzee has painted more than ten thousand paintings, including the March 1958 cover of *Mad* magazine.

"Every show he ever did, he did finger painting live on stage. Those paintings are now on sale at eBay, all signed by him and dated," says Preis. "Buddy takes Muggs's hand and helps him autograph. It is his legal signature."

As for the chimp's personality, Preis says, "Muggs wears a button that says 'be kind to people.' Muggs is a people lover. He just loved people, and he could tell when people loved animals. He would run up to them and hug them. He trusted people.

"Today he is 49 years old, weighs 245 pounds, and he still comes in the house, and we have him at the table and he still likes to dunk his doughnuts in coffee at the table."

And Muggs and his sweetheart, Phoebe B. Beebe, still share companionship today and are inseparable.

What's a day in the life of Muggs like today? Preis describes it very nicely: "He gets breakfast between seven and eight—usually oatmeal, coffee, orange juice, and chewable vitamins. Sometimes after breakfast, about three times a week, he gets a bath and shave and manicure, and rubbed down with Ledosane, a skin moisturizer.

"On very nice days, he is outside frolicking with Phoebe and basking in the Florida sun. He lolls around. He and Phoebe have all kinds of apparatuses in their cage to swing on and interact with each other. We have a special building the chimps are housed in. He has his own television and radio.

"His main meal consists of a wide variety of fresh fruits and vegetables, such as bananas, apples, oranges, heads of lettuce, celery, cucumbers, raw onions, carrots, cabbage, wheat, bread, corn on the cob, and whatever fruits may be in season, like watermelon, peaches, plums, mangoes, or grapefruit. Three times a week, he gets some kind of soup, and he loves pasta e fagoli, spaghetti with meatballs, or hot dogs and beans.

"Occasionally, he comes in the house and sits down with us. He will have coffee and doughnuts, and of course, he loves to dunk his doughnut into the coffee. We also interact with him at the swimming pool, which he loves to dunk his feet into. Chimps do not usually like water. He loves to watch television, especially cowboy movies. He watches with intensity, gets real excited when there is real action. I sense with the cowboy movies that he has a lot of interest in the horses."

"His health is fabulous," adds Preis, who besides managing Muggs's career has coordinated his wardrobe and the music behind his acts.

As for the simian star's relationship with Buddy Mennella, Preis says, "Muggs is the love of Buddy's life. He was brought up like a child, living in the house, interacting with him 24/7. They truly know what each of them thinks. Muggs hugs Buddy with a passion, and it is very different than a hug which Muggs gives to anyone else.

"Buddy has been and still is Muggs's mother, father, and best friend. Buddy taught Muggs to understand words, which proved to be a godsend, as it is not too difficult to get him to do almost anything—like 'Muggs, turn on the lights, change the TV channel, wash your hands, flush the john, don't do that, sit down, go do this or that.' He truly understands words, and he will also tell you if anything is wrong with him. He will show you a boo-boo, scratch, or bruise, wanting to be treated with a first-aid cream and Band-Aid, or Muggs will tell you he wants something. He will knock on something to get your attention and then point to what he wants. Best described, Muggs is like Buddy's favorite son.

J. Fred Muggs and Dave Garroway mug for the camera.

"Buddy says that Muggs is a part of him, like his right arm or leg. The look in Muggs's eyes when he looks at Buddy is truly one of love and respect. It is awesome to see." Such is the bond between man and chimp that has been growing strong for forty-eight years.

And so it is that J. Fred Muggs is a chimp who has thrived by always truly living for today.

After a fabulous five years of J. Fred Muggs on the *Today* show, a new chimpanzee was brought in to share the spotlight with host Dave Garroway.

The new second banana, young Kokomo Jr., was about a year-and-a-half old when he joined the early morning news/entertainment program. Born in the Belgian Congo of Africa around November 17, 1955, Kokomo made his way to the Chase Wild Animal Farm on Cape Cod, Massachusetts. It was there that entertainer Nick Carrado discovered him in 1956.

Kokomo Jr. seems to enjoy listening to Jack Benny play the violin on the *Today* show.

Courtesy of Nick Carrado.

Though out of the spotlight for many years, Kokomo Jr., like his predecessor J. Fred Muggs, was still hale and hearty as of January 1, 2001.

Koko's favorite human, Carrado, recalls how the two met and how he named the chimpanzee, who stands about three-and-a-half feet tall, weighs ninety pounds, and is believed to be a "pygmy chimp." "I was doing a nightclub act on the weekends in Boston, and I would go visit zoos. I loved animals. So I saw him and bought him from the animal farm. It was love at first sight," says Carrado, who was a magician at the time.

"I named him after two buddies of mine, Coco and Moe, that were killed in Korea. We were friends in the marines together. We all used to say how we would name our children after each other. I added the Jr. from my name, thus coming up with Cocomo Jr.

"When I got on the *Today* show, I changed the "C" to "K" for promotional purposes. The "K" was more eye-catching. They had wanted to run a contest like 'name the chimp,' but I told them, 'No, we can't do that. His name is there for a purpose.' I told them the story behind the name and they said 'OK.'"

From the beginning, Carrado raised Kokomo Jr. like a son. "I raised him as close to the way you would raise a human being as possible. I tried teaching him words rather than teaching him to be an act. Years later we did perform as an act, but in the beginning, it was teaching him more and more words for television," says the man behind the chimp.

In the early days, Carrado and his star simian toured elementary schools in upstate New York. He tailored their performance for individual classrooms. But stardom was beckoning from around the corner.

The partners found themselves in Miami, Florida, on WCK-TV working on morning shows, first *The Bob Clayton Show* and then *Major Bandwagon.* Kokomo was used heavily in station breaks promoting the station. "Miami took Koko to heart," Carrado says.

Back in the Big Apple, the *Today* show folks discovered that an NBC affiliate in the South had a great chimpanzee on their hands, and since they had a void to fill after Muggs's departure, they came calling.

When the *Today* staff came to Miami, the local station programmed that specific show around Kokomo. "We had him doing a lot of different things. He took all kinds of hand signals from me and eventually became known as 'one-take Kokomo,'" recalls Carrado. "*Today* loved him and hired us on the spot. We began in February or March of 1957 and worked for about two years, five days a week.

"They used him intermittently for the three hours on the show. Sometimes Garroway would be writing something, and he would break his pencil. He would say, 'Hey, Kokomo,' and Koko would take the pencil over to the pencil sharpener and sharpen it and bring it back to him.

"Kokomo would hold up signs in the window like 'Hello, Oshkosh,' and he might walk back and forth with the sign. He had a desk that he used to sit in, but he spent a lot of time on the desk with Garroway because Garroway would talk to him a lot and ask him to do things. He would call him from his desk and say, 'Come on over here.' And he'd get up on the desk, and Garroway would say, 'I understand today you're going to show us a magic trick?' Koko would nod his head yes. Garroway would say, 'Are you gonna show us how?' Koko would shake his head no."

Kokomo, like Muggs, had a customized wardrobe while on *Today.* "He's got fifty suits," Carrado says. "Brooks Brothers made him a tuxedo. Once we did a live remote in Oklahoma. They made him a little Indian outfit for that, and one time we shot a film for the navy and they made him a little miniature outfit. It was a five-minute film about a day in the life of navy recruits. They had Kokomo with a regular platoon of recruits and showed him swabbing the deck and eating in the mess."

The *Today* show wasn't Kokomo's only TV exposure. He was on *The Howdy Doody Show* for about a year in 1957, and he guested on all the hot network game shows of the day, including *The Price Is Right, I've Got a Secret, Candid Camera,* and *What's My Line?*

Besides his *Today* show gig, Kokomo Jr.'s biggest claim to fame was that he was the world's first and only talking chimp. "To my knowledge, that is the truth," Carrado says. "I taught him to say 'mama.' That's the closest to talking like a human being, and one of the first words a baby can speak. I probably could have taught him a lot more words if I had had the time."

How did Carrado and Kokomo do it? "First I had to break the movements down and teach him to vocalize before the word can come out. I taught him how to shape his mouth and his tongue," says Carrado.

Unfortunately, Kokomo Jr.'s "mama" wasn't uttered on live national television. "He said 'mama' after we left the *Today* show. Phil Santora, a writer for the *New York Daily News*, didn't believe he could talk, so I brought Kokomo up to the *News* office. I sat him down and I showed them. Santora was so surprised—they gave the story a whole page. Kokomo understood words. Once they understand, then they're just like a person."

Carrado poses a riddle. "How do you make a chimp chew gum without swallowing it?"

And he answers his own question. "You take a little piece of gum and give it to him and ask for it back. When he gives it back to you, you make a big fuss, pet him, and dance around and celebrate the fact that he gave it back. Then give a bigger piece and keep repeating. Finally you make a wad so big that it's impossible for him to swallow it."

Carrado confesses to keeping two Kokomos around the house. He added a second chimpanzee after he left the *Today* show. He calls the second chimp simply "Kok" or "Hey you."

"They know who I'm talking to," he says. "I had to get another one so they don't get tired or cranky."

Kokomo Jr. is the first chimp; that is, he is a chimp of many famous firsts. Carrado claims his chimp was the first to perform such feats as skiing down a mountain, opening his own checking account, and writing a syndicated newspaper column. The column, "Kokomo Jr. Says," ran once a week for several years in the *Moore County News* in Carthage, North Carolina. In it Koko gave his opinion on all sorts of topics.

Over the years, the chimp met many celebrities, including Julie Newmar, Buddy Hackett, and Jack Paar. Carrado says that Jack Paar "loved Koko the most of all, and Koko really took a shine to him."

Koko has boosted many human charities over the years, ranging from the Leukemia Society to the Cancer Fund and the American Heart Association.

As for hobbies, Koko has turned his love of painting into a vocation. He's been painting since 1957, and today has his own greeting card line, available via the Internet.

Both Kokomo (Koko) and Kok (Hey You) live with Carrado and his wife in North Carolina. "They live in the house with us and have their own room, twenty-four by twenty-four," says Carrado. "They have a refrigerator and washing machine, a TV set and radio, paint and paint brushes, and toys. They like Big Wheels and ride them like a tricycle. They like to tip the bike over and spin the wheel a lot, and they enjoy playing with a basketball and football."

And like many civilized chimps, the pair enjoys watching television, especially programs featuring other animals.

And Kokomo Jr.'s favorite pastime? Would you believe perusing the pages of the

National Geographic? "Big Kok loves it. He'll see a native woman or a baby and kiss them," says Carrado. "The magazine features a lot of animals that are colorful, and they like that."

As for the chimps' diet, their father figure says it changes daily: "One day they may be crazy about apples, the next day maybe pineapple. They love spaghetti and meatballs. Koko eats with a fork and twirls it. He likes minestrone soup and loves romaine lettuce."

Yes, you read that right, Kokomo Jr. uses a knife and fork when dining. "That's how we live at home. He goes to the refrigerator and helps himself."

At one time, Carrado had Kokomo performing magic tricks. But that was in the good ole days. "I taught him to do box magic, easy stuff. He could do maybe ten or fifteen tricks," Carrado says.

"When we retired, I told Kokomo that was it. 'You don't have to do anything anymore.' We do what we want to do."

Thus, Kokomo Jr. and his protégé and Carrado retired in 1983 from show biz. They formed Monkey Packaging Tape, a business that sells shipping-room supplies. Carrado runs the company, and Kokomo is mascot, a job he can handle like a ripe banana.

So how does the famous ape relax? "He loves to sleep in late," says Carrado. "Then he has breakfast, watches a little TV, and looks at the *Geographic.* He may go for a little walk on the property, then come back in and do a little painting, or he'll watch me on the computer."

Sounds like the life of Riley, but no, that's just the life of Kokomo Jr., a little chimp who's got it made.

Topper

CBS, ABC, and NBC, 1953–1956, 78 episodes

*Starring **Neal and Cappy as Neil,** Anne Jeffreys as Marian Kirby, Robert Sterling as George Kirby, Leo G. Carroll as Cosmo Topper, Lee Patrick as Henrietta Topper, Kathleen Freeman as Katie, Thurston Hall as Mr. Schuyler, and Edna Skinner as Maggie.*

Topper is a comedy about a pair of ghosts who returns to haunt their old house, which is now the residence of a stuffy banker and his wife. The young couple was killed in an avalanche while on a skiing vacation, and a third victim was the St. Bernard who tried to rescue them. The ghostly trio can be seen only by the banker.

The TV series was based on the characters in a book by Thorne Smith, which had earlier been made into a couple of feature films, the original starring Cary Grant. The dog was not part of Smith's story but was simply added to the TV series.

One other interesting fact about the character Neil is that the St. Bernard was an alcoholic and almost always would be seen with a small brandy keg snuggled beneath his chin.

Carl Spitz visits with Cappy, one of his big St. Bernards that starred in the 1950s series *Topper.*
Courtesy of Carl Spitz Jr.

The dual St. Bernard stars of *Topper* were 140-pound giants named Cappy and Neal, the property and pets of famed Hollywood trainer Carl Spitz Sr.

Spitz was the man behind Dorothy's Toto, a cairn terrier named Terry, in *The Wizard of Oz*, and a St. Bernard named Buck in 1935's *Call of the Wild.*

Neal and Cappy, both males, were no relation to either movie star dog, but Spitz treated them like stars and almost like sons. "My dad always believed that any of the dogs he worked with in the movies should live with him as part of the family. He felt that was the best way to get to know the personality of the dog," says the trainer's son, Carl Spitz Jr. "The dogs stayed at our home. We had a kennel, and we lived at the kennel. My dad did boarding for people's pets and he did obedience training, so we were living right there on the kennel premises."

Spitz says the pair came from Sanctuary Wood Kennels in Oregon, where they had been raised by breeder Beatrice Knight. He estimated that the dogs were about three to five years old during the show's run.

While Spitz Sr. trained and worked the dogs on *Topper*, Carl Jr. visited the set from time to time. "I would act as stand-in for the actors when they were training the dogs on the set," Spitz Jr. says. "When my dad trained, he worked primarily with Neal, but he always rehearsed them and always worked with both of them on everything. Both dogs were capable of doing whatever the script called for, but he concentrated on Neal as the number one dog.

"They were pretty much similar in personality. Neal was a tad more willing to please. He worked at it a little harder than Cappy. Cappy always lacked concentration."

As for training, "Papa" Spitz was pretty close to a perfectionist. "My dad did not deal in terms of tricks," Spitz Jr. recalls. "Dad believed in good old basics and just rehearsal, and he always wanted the dog to look like he was working with the actor—that there was not a trainer somewhere in the background.

"He went through great pains to teach a dog to be head straight. Ninety percent of the time, you are behind or off to the side someplace [working the animal]. My dad always had a hand signal and a verbal command for head straight, so the dog would turn his head away from my dad and look at the actor. So if he was working from behind, the dog could face the actor. If he wanted the dog's attention to give him another command, he carried a choke chain in his back pocket, and he would rattle it just a little bit. Then the dog knew to turn to look for another signal."

Spitz Jr. says the two *Topper* behemoths pretty much ate normal dog food. "Dad would use some treats and stuff at times when he was working them, but he was very sparing in that. He really believed a dog should work for praise, and he felt a dog was much more dependable if he worked for praise rather than goodies."

And it is a good thing there were few goodies around on the *Topper* set, as Neal and Cappy had a nasty habit that is common to St. Bernards. "St. Bernards have the problem of slobbering. They drool pretty heavy," Spitz Jr. says. "I recall on several occasions, Anne Jeffreys was pretty put off by the dogs' slobbering. They slobber when it's hot and have a tendency to shake their heads and kind of sling it. My dad constantly had a towel in his pocket and had to run in there and swab the dog's mouth."

Although the dogs lived near Spitz Jr. when he was a teenager, he didn't get to play with them often. However, there were still some special times. "I did exercise them some and roughhouse with them a little bit," Spitz Jr. recalls. "They worked five days a week, and Dad worked nights with them on the next script. They were working dogs. Afterwards, when the series was closed, we had a pretty good-sized grassy area out back of the kennel. When things were closed up at night and the other dogs were in the kennels, we let them go out and cavort there and have a ball."

After *Topper*, the duo did very few other jobs. Says Spitz Jr., "Frank Inn used them a little bit after the series closed here and there. They guested once on *Let's Make a Deal.* The contestant, a lady, was offered the dog or what was behind a door. She asked for the dog. Well, Monty Hall had to do some real fast talking to get the woman to go for the door, and she finally did."

Neal and Cappy died in the mid-1960s.

"Dogs live very closely with each other," says Spitz Jr. "When they died, they died within a couple of days of each other. It was a very spooky feeling, like they had a pact: when one goes, the other is gonna go. They were cremated. Dad kept the ashes with him, I think."

Carl Spitz Sr. came to Hollywood from halfway around the world. He began by training dogs in Germany as a hobby and immigrated to America in 1924 by way of Chicago. One of his first jobs was working as a hod carrier, a chore he didn't much like. One day he spotted a help-wanted ad in a newspaper, which led to a job working in a kennel and training dogs.

After several years, he had family back in Europe ship him a female German shepherd named Asta, and he drove himself and his dog to California. He opened a small kennel in La Habra and went door to door offering his services to people as a dog trainer.

"After he got enough money, he moved to

Studio City and started a kennel there, and then later moved to a larger facility on Riverside Drive," says Spitz Jr. "He got to know trainers doing studio work, like Rennie Renfro, Henry East, the Weatherwaxes, and Lee Duncan.

"Lee Duncan rented some space from my dad and built a section of kennels. We called it the Lee Duncan Kennels. Those people kind of got him into the studios, and then he did *Call of the Wild* with his St. Bernard Buck. Clark Gable really liked Buck, and he and my father became friends. My dad talked about how they got snowed in on location at Mount Baker, Washington, to such a great degree that they were going out the second-story window because snow was so high. Clark would spend time with my dad in his room and share drinks."

"Papa" Spitz and his dogs worked many other films in the 1930s through the 1950s, including *Little Lord Fauntleroy, Trigger Trio, Melody Trail,* and *Call of the Yukon,* but it's *Oz* and *Call of the Wild* that stand out. "Toto and Buck are his two greatest accomplishments," says his son.

The Waltons

CBS, 1972–1981, 221 episodes, 7 TV movies

Starring ***Reckless the dog, Old Blue the white mule, Chance the Cow, Calico the cat, Myrtle the goat,*** *Ralph Waite as John Walton, Michael Learned as Olivia Walton, Will Geer as Zeb (Grandpa) Walton, Ellen Corby as Esther (Grandma) Walton, Richard Thomas as John-Boy Walton, Judy Norton-Taylor as Mary Ellen Walton, David W. Harper as Jim-Bob Walton, Kami Cotler as Elizabeth Walton, Jon Walmsley as Jason Walton, Mary Elizabeth McDonough as Erin Walton, Eric Scott as Ben Walton, Joe Conley as Ike Godsey, Ronnie Claire Edwards as Corabeth Godsey, Helen Kleeb as Mamie Baldwin, Mary Jackson as Emily Baldwin, Robert Donner as Yancy Tucker, and Merle Earle as Maude Gormsley.*

Set in the Blue Ridge Mountains of Virginia during the Great Depression, *The Waltons* is about a family with seven children growing up when times were hard but love and caring relationships were strong. The stories center on the joys and trials of the parents, the grandparents, and their kids as the events of everyday life unfold on Walton's Mountain.

Because the series was set in the country and because there were seven children in the family, animals abound in the story lines. Main creatures, great and small, that appeared in the course of the show included Reckless the family dog; Chance the cow; Myrtle the goat; Old Blue the white mule, who was John-Boy's choice of transportation; Rover the peacock; Lancelot the fawn; Calico the mama cat; Pete the raccoon; Porthos the guinea pig; Jabez the 4-H pig;

Little Boy Gull the seagull; Rover the pig; and Jim-Bob Jr. the baby mallard duck.

Earl Hamner Jr., the creator of the series and the man upon whose life the show was based, recalls that his real-life family had many animals, especially dogs. "We treated Reckless pretty much as a farm dog, so he was never cute in the sense of television pets. He was a working dog, sensible, no frills," says Hamner of the TV hound. "Reckless was given that name by John McGreevey, the writer of the episode. I thought the dog played rather well, a good actor."

Actor Jon Walmsley, who played Jason Walton, recalls that they used several dogs as Reckless over the course of the series. "The dogs were always good, well trained, very friendly, and easy to work with," he says. "The animals on our show were not required to do a lot of tricks."

Genny Kerns was one trainer who worked with Reckless. "The dog belonged to Hal Driscoll and Bill Koehler, and he was a redbone hound named Prince," she says. "He didn't have to do anything special, just stay with the family and hang out."

Although he may have looked lazy, Reckless was protective of his family. When strangers came too close to the Walton house, he would bark a warning. And he was also kind of a hunting dog, as he would track game up on the mountain.

Sadly, the family dog himself gets shot and dies on the mountain during the eighth season of the show.

Several of *The Waltons* episodes with animals were taken from incidents that took place on the Hamner family farm in Schuyler, Virginia, the town which is home of The Waltons Museum today.

Six of *The Waltons* children pose with the series creator, Earl Hamner Jr., and the family dog, Reckless. The actors are (from bottom left) Judy Norton-Taylor, Eric Scott, Jon Walmsley, Mary Elizabeth McDonough, David W. Harper, and Kami Cotler.

"Those animals in the show were really composites," Hamner says. "My brother, Jim, did find a peacock. He had a Volkswagen with a sunroof, and he showed up one day with a peacock with its head sticking out of the sunroof. Someone had injured it on the road, and he brought it home and nursed it back to health." (Rover the peacock first appears in "The Baptism" episode.)

Hamner adds, "There was one episode with a carnival breaking down on Walton's Mountain. The way that started, a carnival really did break down in my hometown when I was a boy, and one of the animals was injured, a camel, but we didn't put the animal in the story.

"As for Chance, my father bought that cow from a woman named Mrs. Frank Hall, and she said, 'I'll sell her to you, but she likes her name and you have to let her keep it, which is Chance.' He asked her 'How does a cow get a name like that?' She answered, 'Well, she gives a good chance of butter.'

"If you know 'chance' in old Elizabethan English, it has the meaning of 'a goodly amount.'"

He also recalls a sticky shooting sequence that was finally solved. "It was not a pet, but in one of the episodes there was a horse that had to pull a wagon through the Baldwin ladies' gate. It was important to see the wagon go through the gate. The horse was afraid of the gate and wouldn't pull the wagon through in any way. So the animal trainer said, 'I've got a camel back at the ranch. If I bring the camel on the set, the horse will run away from it.'

"He went to his ranch and brought back the camel and unloaded it, and when the horse saw it, it took off and not only went through the gate, but knocked it down."

Actor Walmsley remembers another camel story on the set, when John-Boy enters a horse race on Old Blue. "Now we had never put a saddle on her, but for the race John-Boy had to use a saddle. They wrote the scene where John-Boy tries to put a saddle on the mule for the first time, and she was the sweetest, tamest animal in the world. You can do anything to it. So the problem was how can we get this mule to act like it's afraid of a saddle? They tried all kinds of stuff but could not get the mule to act like it was afraid.

"Somebody heard that mules and horses were afraid of camels. They hired this camel, and the trainer starts bringing the camel around from the other side of the house, off camera, just to make the mule afraid, and it worked the first and second time, but the third time was not so good, and by the fourth time the mule is not giving any reaction. They tried everything. So there we are with this rented camel and suddenly it's not working.

"So the craft serviceman, who cleans up and serves coffee, said, 'Why don't we bang some trash can lids together?' So we did, and the mule just takes off running. So I guess the moral is, why rent a camel when you can bang trash can lids."

Walmsley recollects that riding Old Blue without a saddle was no simple feat. "The mule was a lot of fun. None of us were great riders, but we all rode the mule at one time or another, and we probably all fell off because we never used a saddle. I would hold on to the mane and hope that I would not fall off, but I know I fell off a couple of times.

"We actually used that mule at a show at the Hollywood Bowl for a benefit for a Shakespeare theater company. There were all these well-known actors, Shakespearean and otherwise, at the benefit and some were performing songs and skits, and Alice Cooper did a song from *West Side Story*, and Will Geer [Grandpa on *The Waltons*] was a big Shakespearean actor. He put together a skit, 'As You All Like It,' and we [*The Waltons* children] came out on stage riding the mule at the Hollywood Bowl."

Walmsley says that it became a standing joke on the set that if Elizabeth got a new pet, then it was going to die. "We had so many animal deaths and animal funerals. I remember one scene where we stood around in the rain burying this raccoon and I was playing the harmonica."

Creator Hamner remembers the incident. "There was an episode about a raccoon [Pete]. Now actors will put up with almost anything to make a scene play well. When we were shooting that episode, the raccoon died, and one of the children [Elizabeth] wanted to have a funeral service for it. While they were trying to hold the funeral, it began to rain, but the director thought rain would make a wonderful, gloomy setting for a funeral, so they got carried away and rain was pouring down, and Ralph Waite finally said, 'To heck with it. I'm not standing in this drenching rain to bury a raccoon.'"

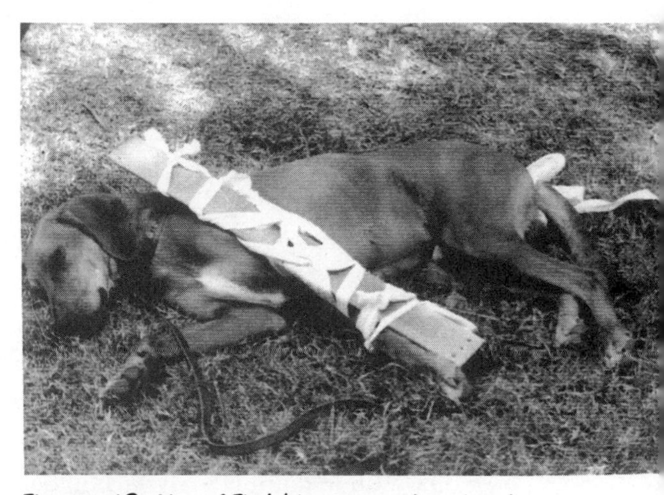

The original Reckless of *The Waltons* was a redbone hound named Prince. This shot is from an episode where he was supposed to be injured.
Courtesy of Genny Kerns.

Master trainer Frank Inn worked with a variety of the animals that appeared on *The Waltons*. "I had Old Blue the white mule, and the cat and goat were mine," Inn says. "I remember working a wolf in it once. I remember the goat because I had given it to Ricky Nelson. Later the goat had babies, and stray dogs came in and killed them. So Ricky and his wife and kids brought the goat back to me."

The Waltons' animals played integral parts in plenty of episodes, and peripheral roles in others. Chance the calf was just like a part of the family. In a first-season episode, "The Calf," John Walton is forced to sell off some stock, and Jim-Bob and Elizabeth hide the calf to protect it. About one year later, when John-Boy is graduating from high school, he comes home and hears a little whimper in the yard. He finds Elizabeth crying up in the tree house because Chance has died. When John-Boy enters the house, he discovers the rest of the family sitting around the table, depressed because Chance has passed away.

John-Boy's mule, Old Blue, was a gift to him from Granny Ketchum. The idea to add the mule was actor Richard Thomas's notion.

Other plot lines involved Myrtle the goat, who belonged to Maude Gormsley. She gave her goat to the Waltons because the goat was always running over to their house anyway. Grandma Walton didn't like Myrtle but took care of her.

Then there was Calico the mama cat, who died after giving birth to kittens, and Erin's deer Lancelot. She placed a bell around its neck. It was later taken to a game preserve.

Jabez the pig was a 4-H project that Elizabeth once sneaked into the house in a bag. And there was Porthos the guinea pig, the class mascot, that belonged to Jim-Bob.

Another animal lover on *The Waltons* was friendly but irascible Yancy Tucker, who had a dog named Tiger and a rooster named Earl. Tiger was a lazy dog, but Yancy wanted folks to think he was vicious. Many of Yancy's critters lived in the house with him.

One other pet was Rover the pig, a gift from Yancy to Ben. They entered the porker in the greased-pig contest at the county fair only to find out that Rover belonged to another man. Yancy liked animals too well, it seems.

Kami Cotler, who portrayed Elizabeth Walton, worked with another animal before *The Waltons* became a series. She costarred with a chimpanzee named Jackie in *Me and the Chimp* for one season. After the first season of *The Waltons* and two straight years of spending lots of time on sets filled with animals, she discovered she was allergic to them. "My sinuses were swollen shut, but I was only six and not aware of the fact that people were supposed to breathe through their nose," Cotler told an interviewer in 1989.

Allergy shots solved the dilemma, and Elizabeth could breathe freely again the wonderful air of Walton's Mountain.

And that's the story of the animals who had many good days and, of course, good nights on *The Waltons.*

The Westerner

NBC, 1960, 13 episodes

*Starring **Spike as Brown,** Brian Keith as Dave Blassingame, and John Dehner as Burgundy Smith.*

Dave Blassingame is an adventurer who wanders the Old West of the 1890s along the Mexican border with his big mongrel, Brown. He calls his dog Brown "'cause he's a big brown dog." Blassingame hopes to settle down on a ranch of his own, but he moseys from place to place making friends and enemies. Burgundy Smith is a conman that Blassingame keeps crossing paths with during his meandering ways.

Before signing a TV contract to partner with Brian Keith in 1960, Spike had already tasted the heady success of the silver screen. His first and most famous role was as the canine hero of Walt Disney's *Old Yeller*.

Spike, a large, yellow, flop-eared pup with extra large feet, was discovered in an animal shelter in Van Nuys, California, in 1953. He had been a resident of the shelter for one month when veteran Hollywood dog trainer Frank Weatherwax spotted him.

"He was all head and feet, but he looked smart," said Frank Weatherwax, brother to Lassie's owner Rudd Weatherwax. "I thought he might make an actor, so I bailed him out for three dollars."

Frank's son, Richard Weatherwax, remembers the dog. "When my dad got him, he was big and clumsy, and he had a bark that still sounded like a puppy. I didn't think the dog would amount to anything. I liked him, and he was one of my favorites. My dad liked him because he was always eager to try to please my dad."

Frank spent four years and twenty thousand dollars worth of training time on Spike before the dog got his big break as Yeller in 1957. He had made two appearances on *Lassie* and was in a low-budget flick, *The She Creature,* when he got the role of a lifetime. His roughneck appearance and heavyweight build were just what Disney was looking for. The 115-pound dog with a Mixmaster pedigree nabbed the title role, even though a dozen other dogs had auditioned for the juicy position. His biggest problem was that he didn't know how to act vicious.

Brian Keith played a cowpoke with a dog named Brown in the Sam Peckinpah TV series *The Westerner.* Spike, the star of Disney's *Old Yeller,* played Brown.

Old Yeller was based on Fred Gipson's novel of the same title. Gipson collaborated on the movie screenplay and described *Yeller* as fiction based on fact. "My grandfather owned a big yellow stray dog who could throw wild range cattle and who once rescued him from a meat-eating hog. Out of these and true incidents, I wrote the story of *Old Yeller,*" Gipson told Disney publicists.

Spike fit the bill to a T. "He was just a great dog," recalls Spike's *Old Yeller* costar

Kevin Corcoran, who played young Arliss Coates. "The Weatherwax family had a hard time doubling him [finding stunt dogs for the dangerous scenes] when they had to do certain things like fight the bears and wild pigs. They had a heck of a time matching it. He was a deep red dog and huge.

"I played with him a lot in between. He was very friendly. He could pretend like he was hurt and crawl along the ground and whimper. He could do just about anything. I'm sure that's why they used him again in *The Westerner*. He was an unusually smart dog."

In fact, Spike was so smart and his acting was so good that he took home the PATSY award in 1958 for his work as Yeller. That same year, Spike was put under contract for *26 Men*, a TV western series about the Texas Rangers. He appeared in only three episodes. Then in 1959, he returned to the big screen to star in *A Dog of Flanders* with David Ladd, son of Alan Ladd.

Larry Weatherwax, another son of Frank Weatherwax, worked with his father on Spike. Larry recalls, "He was a big dog, and he was an independent dog. He just loved to work. He and Brian Keith were good friends. I remember that in one of the bar fights, the dog had to take his rival outside to fight. He grabbed him by the arm and just dragged him outside the saloon."

Robert Weatherwax, son of Rudd and nephew of Frank, comments briefly about Spike. "We got him at the dog pound. I remember that we taught him to pull a cart in *A Dog of Flanders*. They're actors, not trick dogs. We taught them to do their parts naturally and to do them at the right time. Later we had a Spike Junior, and he may have also been in *A Dog of Flanders*. Frank trained Spike, but my father [Rudd] also helped on *Old Yeller*. It was a family affair."

Spike Junior appeared as Rontu in the 1964 film *Island of the Blue Dolphins* and was in the first two episodes of the TV series *Hondo*. Spike's grandson worked in the Steve McQueen movie *Junior Bonner*.

Wishbone

PBS, 1995–1998, 49 episodes

*Starring **Soccer as Wishbone,** Larry Brantley as the voice of Wishbone, Jordan Wall as Joe Talbot, Christie Abbott as Samantha Kepler, Adam Springfield as David Barnes, Mary Chris Wall as Ellen Talbot, and Angee Hughes as Wanda Gilmore.*

Wishbone is an educational and entertaining series about a Jack Russell terrier who, with his human comrades, brings classic books to life. Blessed with an incredible imagination, the dog, his young owner, and two other juvenile friends find themselves in story lines parallel to those of literary classics.

Soccer is one of the superstar canines of the 1990s. He's filled more classic roles than even Charlton Heston. Among the leading characters he has taken on are Dr. Frankenstein, Hercules, Robin Hood, Mark Twain, Sherlock Holmes, Oliver Twist, Tom Sawyer, Ivanhoe, Jim Hawkins, Romeo, Ali Baba, Quasimodo, Ichabod Crane, David, King Midas, and Cyrano de Bergerac.

Behind every great dog there is a human, and in Soccer's case it is his owner and trainer, Jackie Martin Kaptan. "You can raise and train a dog and never get a break. There have been a lot of great dogs in this industry that never get a break," says Kaptan. "Previously he had done a Mighty Dog commercial and been a day player in episodes, but nothing you'd ever notice. I always had a feeling that someone would see this little dog some day, realize that he is unique, and would run with it."

Soccer, the star of *Wishbone,* holds a toy soccer ball. He got his name because he resembled a small soccer ball as a pup. *Courtesy of Jackie Martin Kaptan.*

Kaptan's premonitions were right on. The *Wishbone* producers had looked at more than one hundred canine actors, but when they saw Soccer, the search was over.

"Trainers and animal stars do showings," says Kaptan. "It's like a casting call. At the time I was working on the movie *River Wild* in Montana. Trainer Steve Martin called me and said, 'I've shown a lot of dogs and they've not seen anything that has moved them. Can you send any of your dogs?'

"I sent Soccer and couple of others down with a friend of mine. The producer really liked him. He says, 'Yeah, that's my dog.'

"Soccer was just a day player. People would say he was too pretty or too typecast or they really liked him. What really got him the *Wishbone* role was a unique trick that he and I spent a lot of time on. He did a back flip, which I don't think at that time other dogs were doing. The director really liked this behavior.

"On the show *Wishbone,* the dog walks through classic literature. You really have to have the dog express emotions, feelings, or reactions with his body. Soccer was good at that. He could back up, crawl, or flip for 'yippee,' and he had all these things that could show feelings."

Kaptan has been working with animals professionally for twenty-five years. She had her eye out for a special Jack Russell terrier. She wanted one with extraordinary markings. Then came a fateful phone call from a friend in Connecticut, and she took the dog sight unseen.

"I bought him when he was eight weeks

Soccer stars as Wishbone/Romeo in "Rosie, Oh, Rosie, Oh!"

old," Kaptan says. "I had alerted a couple of Jack Russell breeders that I was looking for a specific look—an eye patch—that real unique type. Luckily a friend of mine called and says, 'Guess what? I just had one born that is the cutest puppy I have ever seen.'

"I said, 'I'll take him.' When I picked him up, he had a patch on his eye and his ear and his back, and he looked like a little tiny soccer ball. He was so cute." So Soccer he became.

"I felt if I could be blessed with three dogs like him in my career, I am really lucky," says Kaptan. "A lot of dogs will go through the motions but not give you their heart. Soccer may not be the brightest dog, but he is so devoted to working for me and wants to please me so that I get a better product from him. He likes his work. He loves being out in front of the camera. I can teach animals to go through the motions, but I can't teach animals to enjoy it.

"Soccer has favorites on the crew, mostly because they brought him toys. He's a toyaholic. He runs in there and looks for his favorite people, and says, 'You want to play?' He always wanted to go to work a lot more than I did."

Kaptan confesses that Soccer has been pampered, especially when it comes to travel. "He always flew first class. Lyric Corporation [the production company behind *Wishbone*] would buy him a first-class seat next to me. We were never separated on a flight. I buckled his cage down. I never travel without my dogs in a crate, which is like a car seat for a child. The crate is his home away from home on the set. He has a little cord on the inside of the door, and he will go in and shut it as his way of saying, 'I'm tired' and he goes to sleep."

As for Soccer's favorite eats, Kaptan says, "I feed Iams and Eukanuba to all forty of my dogs. I'll measure out his kibbles—he eats about a cup and a half a day. He also gets cooked chicken and cooked beef, little chunks that I bag and freeze. He gets a balanced diet, but he really enjoys chicken. I take the skin off and barbecue it with a little garlic powder."

And as for the good times, "He's very much toy-oriented. I balance training through praise, food, and toys. That keeps it from getting boring. He really likes to hear my approval."

His favorite toy is a little soccer ball, a squeak toy a little bigger than a golf ball.

Soccer not only has played more diverse roles than any other pooch, but has also been adorned in the most incredible costumes. "He has played so many great characters that he has two hundred costumes. Sometimes there were three to four changes in a show. Stephen Chudej designed the costumes, and two stitchers sewed them. It took about a week to make a costume, and we had an on-set dresser," Kaptan says.

She was partial to Soccer in the guise of Robin Hood. "He looks really buff in Robin Hood. That was probably the hardest part of the show for him. Wearing the costume was not hard, because he had worn sweaters in the winter, but he had never worn a hat. Some of them were pretty big. The Three Musketeers hat was big, and he had to do a back flip in a full costume with feather and hat, and that's really a feat for a fifteen-pound dog. All the costumes have Velcro down the back so we can just jump him in or out."

The *Wishbone* series was shot on film, not videotape, near Dallas, Texas, on a fifty-thousand-square-foot sound stage. In 1998 Soccer made his first and only TV movie for Showtime, a western called *Wishbone's Dog Days of the West.*

The little guy really did work like a dog during his *Wishbone* days. "I worked with two trainers, Nancy Withrow and Brian Turi (the second-unit trainer), and we did an episode every five days," Kaptan recalls. "Every four weeks we got a week off. We did two seasons of *Wishbone*, and in almost every scene you see Soccer. We did have one stunt double named Shiner and another dog that was a stand-in and did still photography, Bear."

Kaptan says that thirteen-year-old Soccer

is now retired and fairly well spoiled. "Between the two trainers and the crew, they spoiled this little dog so bad. He goes home with one of the trainers on the weekend. He has a lot of friends. Everybody is always calling and asking, 'Can I have Soccer for the weekend?'"

Kaptan has another Jack Russell ready to step into Soccer shoes should *Wishbone* go back in front of the cameras. "Popeye, my younger dog, has taken over. He is two."

With his acting days behind him, Soccer has socked away some great memories. Those include the many public appearances he made when his TV show shut down for hiatus. Kaptan says, "We went to New York, Philadelphia, Washington, Oregon, St. Louis, Sea World of Florida. We did Mall of America, where seven thousand people were screaming for Wishbone, and his reaction was like, 'Gee, how come they're all so happy to see me?'

"We've done lots of school appearances. They have contests and win 'Wishbone comes to your school.' He likes kids. People would stand in line for two-and-a-half hours to meet this little dog."

Kaptan grew up training dogs with her father, who did it for a hobby. Then she raised and trained wild animals for Steve Martin. She also learned under the expert eyes of Frank Inn. And as for her dream of having three great dogs, it came true. Kaptan taught Buffy, the yellow Labrador retriever who played Maggie on *River Wild*, and she had a silky terrier mix named Patch, whom she calls "the smartest little dog I ever trained, but she never got a break."

Bibliography

Books

Amaral, Anthony. *The Fascinating Techniques of Training Movie Horses.* North Hollywood, Calif.: Wilshire Book Company, 1967.

Autry, Gene, and Mickey Herskowitz. *Back in the Saddle Again.* Garden City, N.J.: Doubleday & Company, 1978.

Bartel, Pauline. *Amazing Animal Actors.* Dallas: Taylor Publishing Company, 1997.

Beebe, Lloyd. *Wilderness Trails and a Dream: The Story Behind the Olympic Game Farm.* Sequim, Wash., 1995.

Besser, Joe. *Not Just a Stooge.* Orange, Calif.: Excelsior Books, 1984.

Bond, Tommy "Butch," with Ron Genini. *Darn Right, It's Butch: Memories of Our Gang.* Wayne, Pa.: Morgin Press, 1994.

Brooks, Tim, and Earle Marsh. *The Complete Directory to Prime Time Network and Cable TV Shows.* New York: Ballantine Books, 1999.

Collins, Ace. *Lassie: A Dog's Life.* New York: Penguin Books, 1993

Cotter, Bill. *The Wonderful World of Disney Television.* New York: Hyperion, 1997.

Cox, Stephen. *The Beverly Hillbillies.* New York: HarperPerennial, 1993.

Cox, Stephen. *The Hooterville Handbook: A Viewer's Guide to* Green Acres. New York: St. Martin's Press, 1993.

Daniels, Stephen. *Famous Animal Stars of Movies and TV.* Mahwah, N.J.: Watermill Press, 1980.

Edelson, Edward. *Great Animals of the Movies.* New York: Doubleday, 1980.

Grossman, H. Gary. *Saturday Morning TV.* New York: Dell Publishing, 1981.

Hargrove, Brian. *My Life as a Dog by Moose.* New York: Harper Entertainment, 2000.

Helfer, Ralph. *The Beauty of the Beasts: Tales of Hollywood's Wild Animal Stars.* Los Angeles: Jeremy P. Tarcher, Inc., 1990.

Hyatt, Wesley. *The Encyclopedia of Daytime Television.* New York: Billboard Books, 1997.

Koehler, William R. *The Wonderful World of Disney Animals.* New York: Howell Book House, Inc., 1979.

Maltin, Leonard. *Leonard Maltin's Movie and Video Guide.* New York: Signet Books, 2000.

McCrohan, Donna. *The Life and Times of Maxwell Smart.* New York: St. Martin's Press, 1988.

Moore, Clayton, and Frank Thompson. *I Was That Masked Man.* Dallas: Taylor Publishing Company, 1996.

Nalven, Nancy. *The Famous Mister Ed.* New York: Warner Books, 1991.

Rogers, Roy, and Dale Evans, with Jane Stern and Michael Stern. *Happy Trails: Our Life Story.* New York: Simon & Schuster, 1994.

Rogers, Roy, with Georgia Morris and Mark Pollard. *Roy Rogers: King of the Cowboys.* San Francisco, Calif.: Collins Publishers, 1994.

Rothel, David. *The Great Show Business Animals.* La Jolla, Calif.: A. S. Barnes & Company, Inc., 1980.

Smith, Dave. *Disney A to Z: The Official Encylopedia.* New York: Hyperion, 1996.

Terrace, Vincent. *Complete Encyclopedia of Television Programs.* Cranbury, N.J.: A. S. Barnes & Company, Inc., 1979.

Tors, Ivan. *My Life in the Wild.* Boston: Houghton Mifflin, 1979.

Williams, Barry, with Chris Kreski. *Growing Up Brady.* New York: HarperPerennial, 1992.

Young, Alan, with Bill Burt. *Mister Ed and Me.* New York: St. Martin's Press, 1994.

Magazines and Other Publications

Famous Westerns, issue no. 3, 1981.

Television Chronicles, issue nos. 2, 6, 8.

Under Western Skies, issue no. 51, 1998.

Various publicity releases from ABC, CBS, and NBC television networks

Various articles from *The Tennessean* and *The Nashville Banner* newspapers

Index

The Abbott and Costello Show, 1
Ace Ventura II (motion picture), 46, 58, 100
Acting Dogs, 193
Adamson, George, 34, 36
Adamson, Joy, 34, 36
Addicted to Love (motion picture), 100
The Adventures of Annie Oakley, 179
The Adventures of Brisco County, Jr., 2–4
The Adventures of Champion, 108–113, 179
The Adventures of Rin Tin Tin, 4–7, 112
Africa, on-location filming, 34–38
Africa USA, 50, 59, 94, 115
    Daktari filmed at, 58
    film site, 56
Africa-Texas Style (motion picture), 94
Agee, Johnny, 110, 111
Aines, Janine, 73–74, 230–231
Airhead (motion picture), 191
Alex, the Stroh's Beer Dog, 7–9
Alex Mack, 46
ALF, 10–11
All Acting Animals, Karl Mitchell's company, 22
All the Kind Strangers (TV movie), 274
All My Children, 58
All the Pretty Horses (motion picture), 31
All That Glitters (motion picture), 78
Allen, Bobby Lee "Beverly," 276, 278–279
Allen, Dayton, 152–153
Allied Movie Dogs, 251
American Beauty (motion picture), 204
American Humane Society, PATSY Awards given by, 235–242
America's Funniest Home Videos, 287
Anatomy of a Murder (motion picture), 145–146
The Andy Griffith Show, 11–13
Angel, 271
Animal Actors Hall of Fame, 121
Animal Actors of Hollywood, 73, 102, 201, 230
Animal trainers
    Agee, Johnny, 110, 111
    Aines, Janine, 73–74, 230–231
    Allen, Bobby Lee "Beverly," 276, 278–279
    Baccari, Rick, 134
    Barnes, Frank, 5, 6
    Bayliss, Doree Sitterly, 201–204
    Beebe, Ken, 168
    Beebe, Lloyd, 168–170
    Benedon, Susan, 71
    Berwick, Ray, 20–22, 53, 89, 136, 137, 171, 172
    Blair, Bob, 112, 126, 145, 146
    Bloch, Robert, 113–115, 126, 286–288
    Browning, Ricou, 90–94, 272
    Burke, Betty, 154
    Calkins, Richard, 166
    Camp, Joe, 67
    Casey, Bill, 83–86
    Celis, Fernando, 292–295
    Chipperton, Sue, 288
    Coulter, Sam, 10–11
    Cox, Monty, 117
    Davenport, Bobby J., 297–299
    de Cagny, Mathilde, 95–98, 296–297
    DeBor, Vern, 117
    DeFranco, Robert, 284–285
    Dellosso, Deborah, 288
    Denham, Scotty, 282
    Derby, Ted, 60, 63
    Di Sesso, Moe, 26–28, 124–125, 150
    Downey, Marvin, 15
    Driscoll, Hal, 141, 250, 251, 252, 253, 313
    Duncan, Lee, 5–6
    Dunn, Bob, 99
    East, Henry, 140, 242
    Eisenmann, Charles P., 175–178
    Forbes, Mark, 86, 88, 89
    Garner, Glen, 123–124, 141, 254–255
    Gero, Gary, 86, 88, 89, 98, 256
    Green, Joy, 73
    Grisco, Dennis, 74–75
    Haggis, Ted, 76
    Hart, Scott, 191–193
    Helfer, Ralph, 56, 58–67, 94, 100, 115–117, 121, 138–139, 197–198, 201, 217–219

Animal trainers *(continued)*
Hilton, Les, 205–214, 220, 222, 223
Hornok, Joe, 40
Hudkins, Ace, 112–113, 223
Hudson, Bryan, 147
Inn, Frank, 12, 24, 25, 33, 39, 112, 120, 122, 124, 141, 146, 147, 151–152, 223, 226, 242–244, 244–250, 265, 315
James, Cindy, 139–141
Johnson, Earl, 55, 140, 265
Kaptan, Jackie Martin, 319–322
Keener, Darrell, 151, 152
Kelly, Tracy, 70–71
Kemsley, John, 205
Kemsley, Loretta, 205, 206, 207, 208, 211, 212, 213
Kerns, Genny, 120, 171, 225, 245–247, 252–253, 313
Koehler, Bill, 141, 251, 265, 313
Koontz, Melvin, 48, 50
Lamping, Frank, 66
Lee, Kenny, 179, 184, 228–229
Levy, Laura, 147–148
Lindell, Jack, 205, 223
Linn, Betty, 188–191
McCutcheon, Ralph, 103–105, 107, 223, 243
Maples, Tammy, 44–45
Martin, Steve, 57–58, 78, 319
Martwick, Robert, 214–216
Mears, Alvin, 7, 9, 79–82
Melcher, April, 71
Miele, Cristie, 102–103, 202, 233–234
Miller, Karl Lewis, 39–40, 74, 118, 120, 121, 153–155, 186–187, 246–247, 250, 254–255, 265–267, 289–291
Mitchell, Karl, 20–23, 53, 137
Morris, Mike, 99
Moss, Steve, 15
Nimeth, Mike, 142–144
O'Feldman, Ric, 94
Oxley, Ron, 57
Parker, Gail, 76
Parker, Rick, 76, 77, 78
Perry, Ralph, 57, 65
Perry, Virginia Lee, 182
Peterson, Rex, 29–31
Pittman, Cathy, 268–271
Politzer, Merissa, 99
Pope, Bud, 179
Randall, Glenn, 29–31, 223, 259–261
Renfro, Bryan, 20–21, 137, 138, 172, 256–258
Renfro, Rennie, 33, 159, 242
Riedell, Bob, 50, 66, 199, 200, 201
Ritt, Steven, 193–196
Ross, Wally, 50, 152
Roth, Louis, 49
Rowe, Clint, 72, 73
Sanders, Denise, 46, 99
Schumacher, Roger, 87, 256–258
Scott, Eugene, 48
Shannon, Henry, 39, 126, 146, 147, 226
Smith, Mark, 14
Spencer, Gordon, 2–4
Spitz, Carl Jr., 141, 273–274, 279, 310–312
Spitz, Carl Sr., 274, 276, 310–312
Stark, Mabel, 50
Sylvester, Julian, 15–17
Turi, Brian, 321
Twiford, Curly, 27, 150
Tyndell, "Chief" Henry, 48, 50
Weatherwax, Bill, 19
Weatherwax, Frank, 32
Weatherwax, Larry, son of Frank, 32
Weatherwax, Richard, son of Frank, 19
Weatherwax, Robert, son of Rudd, 157, 158, 163–165, 267
Weatherwax, Rudd, 18–19, 33, 120, 157–161, 163, 165, 242, 243, 267
Weber, Robert, 283
Wells, Hubert, 36, 37, 38, 151
Williamson, Bill, 135
Withrow, Nancy, 321
Woodley, Steve, 41–44
Woods, Sammy, 127
Anne of Green Gables (TV miniseries), 177
Annie (motion picture), 28
Annie Oakley, 14–15
Apollo, 191–193
Armed and Dangerous (motion picture), 193
Arngrim, Stefan, 154–155

Arnold, the semi-wonder dog, 166–167
Arnold Ziffel, vii, 122–125, 141
Asta, 158
Autry, Gene, 14, 108–113

Babe (motion picture), 58
Baccari, Rick, 134
Bachelor Father, 18–19
Back in the Saddle Again (Autry), 111
Back to the Future (motion picture), 89
Baker, Cathy, 135
Ball, Lucille, 200
The Ballad of a Gunfighter (motion picture), 184, 185, 186
Bandit, 172
The Barefoot Executive (motion picture), 200
Baretta, 20–23
Barkley, 201–204
Barnaby Jones, 120
Barnes, Frank, 5, 6, 112
Barnett, Cheryl Rogers, daughter of Roy Rogers, 259–264
Barney Miller, 28
Baron of Arizona (motion picture), 180
Batman, 28
Batman Returns (motion picture), 89
Bayliss, Doree Sitterly, 201–204
Bear (chimpanzee), 15–17
Bears, vii
  Ben, 167–170
  Ben, Gentle, 115–117
  Bozo, 57
Beatty, Clyde, 51
Beauregard (*Hee Haw*), 130–135
Beauregard (*In the Heat of the Night*), 147–148
Beauregard Jr. (*Hee Haw*), 130–135
The Beauty of the Beasts (Helfer), 59, 217
Bedazzled (motion picture), 271
Beebe, Ken, 168
Beebe, Lloyd, 168–170
Beethoven (motion picture), 121, 255
Beethoven II (motion picture), 255
Being John Malkovich (motion picture), 269
Bellamy, Earl, 126, 149, 150, 181–182
Bells of Capistrano (motion picture), 109
Ben, the bear, 167–170
Ben, Gentle, 115–117
Ben (motion picture), 27
Benedon, Susan, 71
Benji, vii, 82, 245
Benji Christmas (TV special), 227
Benji the Hunted (motion picture), 249
Benji (motion picture), 227
Berwick, Ray, 20–22, 53, 89, 136, 137, 171, 172
Besser, Joe, 1
Bessie, 23
Best, James, 79–82
The Better Dog, The Educated Dog (Eisenmann), 178
Betty White's Pet Set, 177
The Beverly Hillbillies, 12, 23–25, 120, 141, 151, 245, 246
Bewitched, 39
Bif, 46
Big Cat Encounters, 22
Big Red (motion picture), 141, 251
Bijou, 139–141
Bimbo, the elephant, 47–49
Bingo, the chimp, 1
The Bionic Woman, 26–29, 120
The Bird Man of Alcatraz (motion picture), 20
Birds, 11, 78
  Caw-Caw, 150
  Fred, 20–23
  Guapo, 28
  Herman the Pigeon, 27
  Jimmy the Raven, 27
  Rover the peacock, 312
  Sigmund the duck, 114–115
Birds & Animals Unlimited, 86, 88, 89, 95, 98, 256
The Birds (motion picture), 20
B. J. and the Bear, 15–17
Black Beauty (motion picture), 103, 298
The Black Stallion, 29–32
The Black Stallion (motion picture), 29, 31
The Black Stallion Returns (motion picture), 29
Blair, Bob, 112, 126, 145, 146
Blake, Robert, 20–22
Bloch, Rob, 113–115, 126, 286–288
Blondie, 32–34, 159
Blue Rodeo (motion picture), 102
Bo Jangles (motion picture), 78
Bob Dunn's Animal Services, 46, 99

The Bodyguard (motion picture), 87
Bomba the Jungle Boy, 148–150
Bonanza, 12, 28, 298
Bond, Tommy "Butch," 174
Bonzo Goes to College (motion picture), 149
Boomer, 136–138
Boone's Animals for Hollywood, 70
Born Free, 34–38, 151
Bowfinger (motion picture), 271
"Boy," 244–250
A Boy and His Dog (motion picture), 40
Boyd, Grace Bradley, 142
Boyd, William, 141–144
Bozo, 57
Braddock, Mickey *see* Dolenz, Mickey
The Brady Bunch, 39–40, 120
Brandon, 254–255
Bring 'Em Back Alive, 38, 151
Bristle Face (TV movie), 141
Brock Hammond, 46
Brooks, Rand, 5–7, 144
Brown, 316–318
Browning, Ricou, 90–94, 272
Bruce the ocelot, 138–139
Buck, 41–44, 276, 310, 312
Buck (*Married . . . With Children*), 193–196
Buddy (motion picture), 46
Buffalo Bill Jr., 179
Buffy the Vampire Slayer, 269, 271
Buford, 130–135
Bullet, 55, 258, 264–265
Burke, Betty, 154
Burke, Chris, 166
Burton, Richard, 78
Buttermilk, 258, 263–264, 265
Buttons, 199–201

Cabot, Roy, 50
Cagney and Lacey, 114
Calico the cat, 312, 316
Calkins, Richard, 166
Call of the Klondike (motion picture), 55
Call of the Wild, 41–44, 276, 310, 312
Call of the Wild (motion picture), 274
Call of the Yukon (motion picture), 312
Camp, Joe, 67, 247, 248, 249
Campanero, Tony, 174
Campbell, Bruce, 2–4
Canadian Wrangler Motion Picture Animals Limited, 77
Candid Camera, 307
Candy, 46
Canfield, Mary Grace, 128–129
Captive Girl (motion picture), 149
Carl the Cat, 83–86
Caroline in the City, 44–46, 46, 202
Carrado, Nick, 306–309
Casey, Bill, 83–86
Cat People (motion picture), 58
Catchings, Bill, stuntman-wrangler, 107, 111, 260
Cats, 78
  Bruce the ocelot, 138–139
  Calico the cat, 312, 316
  Carl the Cat, 83–86
  Clarence the cross-eyed lion, vii, 58–67
  Elsa, 34–38
  Fluffy, 39
  Hubie, 28
  Lucky, 10–11
  Morris the cat, vii, 214–216
  Nuba, 47
  Salem Saberhagan, 267–271
  Salty, 44–46
  Spot, 286–288
  Sultan, 47
Caw-Caw, 150
Celis, Fernando, chimp trainer, 292–295
Centennial (TV miniseries), 31
Cha Cha, 216–219
Champion, 108–113
Chance the cow, 312, 314, 315, 316
Charlie, 127–130
Cheers, 89
Cheetah, vii, 291–293
Chim, 279–280
The Chimp Channel, 46–47
Chimpanzees
  Bear, 15–17
  Bessie, 23
  Bif, 46
  Bingo, 1
  Brock Hammond, 46

Chimpanzees (*continued*)
Buttons, 199–201
Candy, 46
Charlie, 127–130
Cheetah, vii, 291–293
Chim, 279–280
Enoch, 127–130
Ford Carter, 46
Ham, 46
Harry Waller, 46
J. Fred Muggs, 299–309
Judy the chimp, 58, 65–67, 217
Kokomo Jr., 299, 306–309
Lancelot Link, 23, 130, 150–153
Marina, 46
Mata Hairi, 150
Maybelle, 23
Phoebe B. Beebe, 299, 300, 303
Skipper, 23
Stan, 46
Tamba, 148–150
Timmy Briar, 46
Chipper, 153–155
Chipperton, Sue, 288
CHiPs, 120
Cimarron (motion picture), 222
Circus animals, 121
Circus Boy, 47–52
The Cisco Kid, 186
Clan of the Cave Bear (motion picture), 58
Clarence the cross-eyed lion, vii, 58–67, 217, 295
Clarence, the Cross-Eyed Lion (motion picture), 59, 60, 62, 94
Clark, Roy, 130, 133
Clean Slate (motion picture), 203
Cleo, 242–244, 249
Cletis Tout (motion picture), 78
Clio Award, 114
Coach, 52–53, 100
Cockatoo, 20
Cole Brothers Circus, 142
Collins, Ace, 165
Collins, Gary, 34–37
Collins, Jesse, 257, 258
Columbo, 53–54
Comet, 2–4, 73, 101–103, 234
Commander Darwin, 150
Connors, Chuck, 57, 91
Cooper, Gary, 222
Cooper, Jackie, 243, 244
Corky and the White Shadow (Mickey Mouse Club serial), 54–56, 298
Costello, Lou, 1
Coulter, Sam, 10–11
Cowboy in Africa, 56–58, 60, 94, 295
Cows, 11
Chance the cow, 312, 314, 315, 316
Cowtown (motion picture), 109
Cox, Monty, 117
Craven Award, about, 235
Crawford, Joan, 103
Crawford, Johnny, 107
Crazy in Alabama (motion picture), 289
Creative Animal Talent, 41, 42
Creature from the Black Lagoon (motion picture), 90
Crider, Dorothy, 54–55
Critters of the Cinema, owned by Rob Bloch, 115, 286
The Crow (motion picture), 89
Crowell, Henry, 111
Crowley, Patricia, 253
Cujo (motion picture), 28, 121, 255
Curtis, Joann, 166, 167

Daisy, 32–34, 159
Daktari, 50, 56, 58–67, 94, 101, 201, 295
Dances with Wolves (motion picture), 58
D'Angelo, William, 265–267
The Danny Thomas Show, 12
Dante's Peak (motion picture), 89
Darn Right, It's Butch: Memoirs of Our Gang (Bond), 174
Davenport, Bobby J., 297–299
Dave's World, 67–69
Davis, Gail, 14, 15
de Cagny, Mathilde, 95–98, 296–297
Dead Man's Gun, 42
Death Becomes Her (motion picture), 89
Death Valley Days, 39
Debbie, 121
DeBor, Vern, 117
The Deerhunter (motion picture), 58

DeFranco, Robert, 284–285
Dellosso, Deborah, 288
Denham, Scotty, 282
Dennis the Menace, 145–147
Derby, Ted, 60, 63
Detroy, Gene, 127–128, 130
Dharma & Greg, 69–71, 100
Di Sesso, Moe, 26–28, 124–125, 150
Diamond, Bobby, 104, 105, 106
The Dick Van Dyke Show, 12
Diefenbaker, 76–79
The Doberman Gang (motion picture), 141, 255
"Dog," 53
A Dog of Flanders (motion picture), 318
Dogs
- Alex, the Stroh's Beer Dog, 7–9
- Apollo, 191–193
- Arnold, the semi-wonder dog, 166–167
- Asta, 158
- Bandit, 172
- Barkley, 201–204
- Beauregard (*Hee Haw*), 130–135
- Beauregard (*In the Heat of the Night*), 147–148
- Beauregard Jr. (*Hee Haw*), 130–135
- Benji, vii, 82, 245
- Bijou, 139–141
- Boomer, 136–138
- "Boy," 244–250
- Brandon, 254–255
- Brown, 316–318
- Buck, 41–44, 276, 310, 312
- Buck (*Married . . . With Children*), 193–196
- Buford, 130–135
- Bullet, 55, 258, 264–265
- Chipper, 153–155
- Cleo, 242–244
- Comet, 2–4, 73, 101–103, 234
- Cujo, 28
- Daisy, 32–34, 159
- Diefenbaker, 76–79
- Dog, 53
- Dreyfuss, 86–89
- Duke, 23–25
- Eddie, vii, 95–98, 254
- Eddie McDowd, 233–234
- Fang, 18–19
- Flash, 79–82
- Fred, 144–146
- Freeway, 126–127
- Fremont, 145–147
- Friday, 113–114
- Get Off the Couch, 57
- Higgins, vii, 120, 141, 244–250
- Jack, 171
- Jack, one-eyed, 289–291
- Jasper, 18–19
- Joe, 265–267
- Kingfish, 130–135
- Klaus von Puppy, 28
- Ladadog, 250–253
- Lassie, vii, 12, 90, 98, 156–165, 167, 174
- London, 174–178
- Lucky (*Married . . . With Children*), 196
- Matisse, 71–73
- Maximillian, 26–29
- Murray, 188–191
- Neil, 309–311
- Nelson, 250–253
- Nunzio, 69–71
- Pax, 186–187
- Quincy, 52–53
- Rags, 283–285
- Rebel, 108, 112
- Reckless, 312, 313
- Rin Tin Tin, vii, 4–7, 27
- Sam, 273–274
- Scruffy, 118–121
- Skipper, 150
- Smiley, 12
- Speedy, 73–74
- Spike the seeing-eye dog, 83–86
- Spuds MacKenzie, Anheuser-Busch dog, 7, 285–286
- Stinky, 69–71
- Taco Bell Chihuahua, 288–289
- Tequila, 296–297
- Tiger, 39–40
- Toto, 159, 274, 276, 310
- Tramp, 141, 223–226
- Waldo, 141, 226–227
- White Shadow, 54–56

Dogs *(continued)*
Wiener Dog, 230–231
Wishbone, vii, 318–322
Wolf, 74–75
You Too, 57
Yukon King, 274–278
Zeus, 191–193
A Dog's Day in Court (Eisenmann), 178
Dolenz, Mickey, 47–49
Dolphins, Flipper, 60, 90–94
Don't Tell Her It's Me (motion picture), 203
The Doris Day Show, 250–253
Douglass, Donna, 23, 25
Down and Out in Beverly Hills, 71–73
Down and Out in Beverly Hills (motion picture), 71, 72
Downey, Marvin, 15
Downs, Hugh, 91
Dr. Doolittle (motion picture), 89, 152
Dr. Kildare, 250
Dr. Quinn, Medicine Woman, 74–75
Dr. Seuss's How the Grinch Stole Christmas (motion picture), 258
Dragnet, 28
The Drew Carey Show, 73–74, 102, 202, 230
Dreyfuss, 86–89
Driscoll, Hal, 141, 250, 251, 252, 253, 313
Ducks, Sigmund the duck, 114–115
Due South, 76–79
Duke, 23–25
The Dukes of Hazzard, 79–82
Duncan, Lee, 5–6
Duncan, Mrs. Lee, owned rights to Rin Tin Tin, 27
Dunn, Bob, 99
Dunston Checks In (motion picture), 46

Early Edition, 83–86
Earthman, Douglas, 132–134
East, Henry, 140, 242
East of Kilimanjaro (motion picture), 59
The Ed Sullivan Show, 127, 128
Eddie, vii, 95–98, 254
Eddie McDowd, 233–234
Eisenmann, Charles P., 175–178
Eldrenkamp, Marilyn, horse enthusiast, 108–110, 112
The Electric Horseman (motion picture), 31
Elephants, 25
Bimbo, 47–49
Debbie, 121
Margie, 67
Maya, 196–199
Modoc, 100–101, 121, 198, 217, 291, 294, 295
Elk, 78
Elsa, 34–38
Ely, Ron, 292–294
Emergency!, 54
Empty Nest, 86–89
The Encyclopedia of Daytime Television (Hyatt), 300
Enoch, 127–130
Entertainment Tonight, 72
Equus (motion picture), 78
ER, 234
Ernest the bloodhound, 67–69
Ernest Goes to Jail (motion picture), 203
Ernest Saves Christmas (motion picture), 58
Ernest Scared Stupid (motion picture), 203
Escape from Fort Bravo (motion picture), 107
Ethel, 67
Etude in Black (motion picture), 53
Evans, Dale, 258–259, 263–264
Evigan, Greg, 16

Falk, Peter, 53–54
Family Law, 203
The Fan (motion picture), 288
Fang, 18–19
Fangs of the Arctic (motion picture), 56
Fantasy Island, 22, 58
Far and Away (motion picture), 31
Fat Jones Stables, 222, 223
Father Murphy, 86
Feldon, Barbara, 19
Field, Sally, 255
Fish, 11
Fithian, Joe, 251, 252
Flash, 79–82
Flicka, 219–223
Flintstones II (motion picture), 100
Flipper, 60, 90–94
Flipper (motion picture), 94

Flipper, 90–94
Flipper: The New Adventures, 90, 94
Flipper's New Adventures (motion picture), 94
Flowers for Algernon (motion picture), 78
Fluffy, 39
Fluffy (motion picture), 66
Fluke (motion picture), 74, 87
The Flying Nun, 255
Foghorn, water buffalo, 67
For the Love of Benji (motion picture), 227
Forbes, Mark, 86, 88, 89
Ford Carter, 46
Ford, Tennessee Ernie, 24
Forest, 14
Francis, Anne, 138
Francis the Talking Mule, 205, 235
Frank Inn Animals, 141
Frasier, 95–98, 254
Fred (cockatoo), 20–23
Fred (dog), 144–146
Freeway, 126–127
Fremont, 145–147
Friday, 113–114
Friends, 98–100, 202, 204
Frontier Circus, 100–101
Frye, Soleil Moon, 254
Full House, 73, 74, 101–103, 202, 204, 234
Funicello, Annette, 66
Fury, vii, 103–107, 297
Fury, 103–107

Gable, Clark, 103, 107, 312
Gabor, Eva, 125
Garner, Glen, 123–124, 141, 254–255
Garrett, Patsy, 227
Garroway, Dave, 299, 300, 302–303, 305, 306–307
The Gazebo (motion picture), 27
The Gene Autry Show, 108–113
General Hospital, 113–115
Gentle Ben, vii, 57, 94, 115–117
Gentle Giant (motion picture), 94, 115
George of the Jungle, 46
George of the Jungle (motion picture), 100
Gero, Barbara, 98
Gero, Gary, 86, 88, 89, 98, 256
Get Off the Couch, 57
Get Smart, 18–19
Ghost Dog (motion picture), 74
The Ghost and Mrs. Muir, 118–121
The Ghost and Mrs. Muir (motion picture), 118
Giant (motion picture), 103, 243
Gilbert, Melissa, 171
Gilligan's Island, 28
Gipson, Fred, 317
Goats, 11
    Myrtle, 312
Goebel, Kathleen, 51
Goebel, Louis, started World Jungle Compound in twenties, 49, 50
Gomer Pyle, U.S.M.C., 255
Gone with the Wind (motion picture), 5
Good Morning America, 72
Goodbye, My Lady (motion picture), 140
Gordon, Gale, 200
Grant, Kirby, 55–56
Graves, Peter, 104, 105, 106, 107
The Great Outdoors, 58
The Great Show Business Animals (Rothel), 21, 260
The Greatest Show on Earth, 121
The Greatest Show on Earth (motion picture), 101
Green Acres, 120, 122–125, 141
Green Grass of Wyoming (motion picture), 219
Green, Joy, 73
Grisco, Dennis, 74–75
Gropp, Bobby, 131, 132
Guapo, 28
Gunsmoke, 28
Gypsy Colt (motion picture), 103

Haggerty, Dan, 169
Haggis, Paul, 76
Haggis, Ted, 76
Halpin, Luke, 91, 92, 94
Ham, chimp in space, 46
Hammer, Earl Jr., 313–315
Happy Days, 120
Happy Trails, Our Life Story (Rogers), 262
Harmon, Mark, 273–274
Harry and the Hendersons (motion picture), 140
Harry Waller, 46
Hart, John, 181, 182
Hart, Scott, 191–193

Hart to Hart, 126–127, 287
Hart, William S., 222
Hasan, 47
The Hathaways, 127–130
Hawkins, Jimmy, 14, 15
Hazel, 12, 245
Hee Haw, 130–135
Helfer, Ralph, 56, 58–67, 94, 100, 115–117, 121, 138–139, 197–198, 201, 217–219
Henning, Paul, 245, 246
Henry, Mike, 292, 293
Here's Boomer, 136–138
Here's Lucy, 127
Herron, Bobby, stuntman, 181
Higgins, vii, 120, 141
High Anxiety (motion picture), 22
High Noon (motion picture), 179
Hill Street Blues, 58
The Hills Have Eyes (motion picture), 27
Hilton, Les, 205–214, 220, 222, 223
Hippopotamus, 25
    Ethel, 67
Hogan's Heroes, 120
Holden, Bill, 107
Hollywood Dog Training School, 279
Home Improvement, 58
Homeward Bound (motion picture), 45
Homeward Bound II (motion picture), 87, 89, 258
Hondo, 318
Hondo (motion picture), 159
Honey, I Shrunk the Kids (motion picture), 287
Honey West, 138–139
Hooker, Hugh, horse supplier, 179
Hooperman, 139–141
Hopalong Cassidy, 141–144
Hope, Bob, 303
Horne, Trader, 49, 51, 148
Hornok, Joe, 40
The Horse Whisperer (motion picture), 31
Horses, 11
    Buttermilk, 258, 263–264, 265
    Champion, 108–113
    Comet, 2–4
    Flicka, 219–223
    Forest, 14
    Fury, vii, 103–107
    Hasan, 47
    King, 228–229
    Lucky, 10–11, 103
    Mr. Ed, vii, 3, 204–214, 222, 226
    Pixie, 14, 15
    Rex, 274–275, 277–278
    Silver, vii, 178–186
    Target, 14
    Thunder, 297–299
    Topper, 141–144
    Trigger, vii, 55, 258–265
Hostettler, Anita, 134, 135
Hostettler, Joe, 134, 135
Hound of Hell (motion picture), 27
Howard, Clint, 116
The Howdy Doody Show, 307
Hubie, 28
Hudkins, Ace, 112–113, 223
Hudson, Bryan, 147
Hunter, 68
Hutchins, Will, 33
Hyatt, Wesley, 300

I Dream of Jeannie, 39
I Love Lucy, 144–146
I Was That Masked Man (Moore), 180
In the Heat of the Night, 147–148
The Incredible Journey (motion picture), 141, 251
Inn, Frank, 12, 24, 25, 33, 39, 112, 120, 122, 124, 141, 146, 147, 151–152, 223, 226, 242–244, 244–250, 265, 315
Instinct (motion picture), 100
Ironsides, 274
Island of the Blue Dolphins (motion picture), 318
I've Got a Secret, 307

J. Fred Muggs, 299–309
Jabez the pig, 312, 316
Jack, 171
Jack, one–eyed, 289–291
JAG, 271
James, Cindy, 139–141
Jasper, 18–19
Jeff's Collie, 165
Jerri, 46
Jimmy the Raven, 27

Joe, 265–267
Johnny Guitar (motion picture), 103
Johnson, Earl, 55, 140, 265
Jonathan Livingston Seagull (motion picture), 20
Jones, Fat, 179
    movie horses, 222, 223
Judy the chimp, 58, 65–67, 217
The Jungle Book, 100
The Jungle Book (motion picture), 58
Jungle Book II (motion picture), 46
Jungle Exotics, 44
Jungle Jim, 148–150
Jungle Jim (motion picture), 50
Jungleland, 50, 51
    bankruptcy of, 52
Junior Bonner (motion picture), 318
Just Shoot Me, 46

K-9 (motion picture), 121
Kangaroo, Skippy, 280–283
Kaptan, Jackie Martin, 319–322
Kavic, the Wolf Dog (motion picture), 267
Kaye, Danny, 127
KeeKaWa Kennels, 79
Keener, Darrell, 151, 152
Keith, Brian, 317, 318
Kelly, Tracy, 70–71
Kemsley, John, 205
Kemsley, Loretta, 205, 206, 207, 208, 211, 212, 213
Kerns, Genny, 120, 171, 225, 245–247, 251–253, 313
King, 228–229
King of the Grizzlies (motion picture), 170
King of the Wild Stallions (motion picture), 103
Kingfish, 130–135
Klaus von Puppy, 28
Knight, Eric, writer of Lassie stories, 157
Koehler, Bill, 141, 251, 265, 313
Kokomo Jr., 299, 306–309
Koontz, Melvin, 48, 50
Kung Fu, 120

L.A. Law, 202
Lad, a Dog (Terhune), 251
Ladadog, 250–253
Lamping, Frank, 66
Lancelot the fawn, 312
Lancelot Link, 23, 130, 150–153, 201
Lancelot Link, Secret Chimp, 150–153
Land of the Giants, 120, 153–155
Lando, Joe, 74, 75
Landon, Michael, 172
Lassie, vii, 12, 90, 98, 156–165, 167, 174, 298
Lassie, 120, 125, 156–165
Lassie: Animal Planet, 157
Lassie Come Home (motion picture), 158
Lassie: A Dog's Life (Collins), 165
Lassie and the Forest Rangers, 156
Lassie on the Ranch, 156
Lassie the Wanderer, 156
Last of the Pony Riders (motion picture), 110
Late Night with David Letterman, 72
Lee, Kenny, 179, 184, 228–229
Legally Blonde (motion picture), 289
The Legend of the Lone Ranger (motion picture), 184
Leonard, Sheldon, 12
Lester, Tome, 125
Let's Make a Deal, 311
Levy, Laura, 147–148
Life Goes On, 166–167
The Life and Times of Grizzly Adams, vii, 57, 167–170, 295
The Life and Times of Maxwell Smart (McCrohan), 19
Lindell, Jack, 205, 223
Lindsey, George, 13
Linn, Betty, 188–191
Lions, 34–38, 100
    Clarence the cross-eyed lion, vii, 58–67, 217, 295
    Major, 291, 294, 295
    Nuba, 47
    Zamba the lion, 217, 218
    see also cats
Little House on the Prairie, 28, 171–172, 298
Little Jerry Seinfeld, 23
Little Lord Fauntleroy (motion picture), 312
The Little Rascals, 173–174, 258
The Littlest Hobo, 174–178
The Littlest Hobo (motion picture), 175–176
Living Free (motion picture), 38
Livingston, Stanley, 223–224, 226
London, 174–178

The Lone Ranger, 178–186
The Lone Ranger and the Lost City of Gold (motion picture), 181
Lone Star (motion picture), 103, 107
The Long Hot Summer (motion picture), 274
Longstreet, 120, 186–187
Lost Boys (motion picture), 75
Lost in Space, 23, 151
Love Boat: The Next Wave, 202
Love Stinks (motion picture), 74
Lovullo, Sam, 134, 135
Lubin, Arthur, 205
Lucan, 151
Lucky, 10–11, 103
Lucky (*Married . . . With Children*), 196
The Lucy Show, 28, 200

*M*A*S*H*, 291
McCrea, Joel, 222
McCutcheon, Ralph, 103–105, 107, 223, 243
McFarland, George "Spanky," 174
MacMurray, Fred, 223
Mad About You, 188–191
Magic of Lassie (motion picture), 163
Magnum, P.I., 191–193
Major, 291, 294, 295
Malcolm in the Middle, 202
The Man from U.N.C.L.E., 250
The Man Show, 287
Mannix, 28, 120
Mantooth, Randolph, 54
Maples, Tammy, 44–45
Marcel, 98–100
Margie, 67
Marina, 46
Mark of the Gorilla (motion picture), 149
Marquis Chimps, 127, 128
Married . . . With Children, 193–196
Martin, Steve (animal trainer), 57–58, 78, 319
Martwick, Robert, 214–216
Mata Hairi, 150
Matisse, 71–73
Maximillian the bionic dog, 26–29
Maya, 196–199
Maybelle, 23
Mayberry R.F.D., 39
Maynard, Ken, 222
Mazursky, Paul, 72
Me and the Chimp, 199–201, 316
Mears, Alvin, 7, 9, 79–82
Meego, 201–204
Meier, Shane, 43
Melcher, April, 71
Melody Trail (motion picture), 312
Melrose Place, 287
Men in Black (motion picture), 234
Menzies, Noel, 282
Meredith, Don, 126
The Merry Widow (motion picture), 184, 186
Mice, 78
The Mickey Mouse Club, 298
Miele, Cristie, 102–103, 202, 233–234
The Mike Douglas Show, 177
Miller, Cheryl, 62–63
Miller, Karl Lewis, 39–40, 74, 118, 120, 121, 153–155, 186–187, 246–247, 250, 254–255, 265–267, 289–291
Mister Ed, vii, 3, 204–214, 222, 226
Mitchell, Karl, 20–23, 53, 137
Mix, Tom, 222
Modoc the elephant, 100–101, 121, 198, 217, 291, 294, 295
Monkee Movies, 47
Monkeys
- Marcel, 98–100
- *see also* Chimpanzees

The Monkey's Uncle (motion picture), 66
The Monroes, 274
Monte Walsh (motion picture), 28
Moore, Clayton, 179, 180, 182, 183
Moose, Morty the moose, 232–233
Morris the cat, vii, 214–216
Morris, Mike, 99
Morty the moose, 232–233
Moss, Steve, 15
Mr. Smith, 130
Mr. Smith, 216–219
Mules
- Francis the Talking Mule, 205, 235
- Old Blue, 312, 314, 315, 316

Mulligan, Richard, 88
Murder, She Wrote, 287

Murphy Brown, 28
Murray, 188–191
Murray, Bill, 194
Murray Price, 46
My Friend Flicka, 219–223
My Life in the Wild (Tors), 60
My Sister Eileen, 129
My Stepmother Is an Alien (motion picture), 28
My Three Sons, 141, 223–226
Myrtle the goat, 312, 316

Namu the Killer Whale (motion picture), 94
Nanny and the Professor, 141, 226–227
Nash Bridges, 58
National Velvet, 228–229
Neil, 309–311
Nelson, 250–253
The New Adventures of Skippy, 280–283
The New Lassie, 156, 163
Night of the Grizzly (motion picture), 170
Nimeth, Mike, 142–144
Nine Lives commercial, 215–216
No Time for Sergeants (motion picture), 24
Nolte, Nick, 72
The Norm Show, 230–231
North, Jay, 146, 197, 198
Northern Exposure, 58, 232–233
Northern Patrol (motion picture), 56
Northwest Territory (motion picture), 56
Not Just a Scrooge (Besser), 1
Nothing Too Good for a Cowboy, 42
Nuba, 47
Nunzio, 69–71
NYPD Blue, 271

O'Connor, Carroll, 148
O'Feldman, Ric, 94
Oklahoma (motion picture), 103–104
Old Blue, 312, 314, 315, 316
Old Yeller (motion picture), 159, 317, 318
100 Deeds for Eddie McDowd, 78, 233–234
101 Dalmatians (motion picture), 89, 258
102 Dalmatians (motion picture), 89
O'Neill, Ed, 194
Orangutans
    Cha Cha, 216–219
    Commander Darwin, 150
    Murray Price, 46
Our Gang, 173–174
Outbreak (motion picture), 100
Outlaw Stallion (motion picture), 103
Owens, Buck, 130, 133
Oxley, Ron, 57

The Pack (motion picture), 267
Pajama Tops (zebra), 56
Pal Joey (motion picture), 147
Palance, Jack, 121
Parker, Gail, 76
Parker, Rick, 76, 77, 78
Patriot Games (motion picture), 31
PATSY Award, 21, 27, 55, 62, 73, 82, 122, 149, 219, 223, 244, 253, 263, 298, 318
    about, 235
    list of winners, 235–242
Pax, 186–187
Peaceable Kingdom, 38
Pee–Wee's Big Adventure (motion picture), 58
Peeli Peeli, 57
The People's Choice, 242–244, 249
Perfect Strangers, 114
Performing Animal Troupe, 268
The Perry Como Show, 301
Perry, Ralph, 57, 65
Perry, Virginia Lee, 182
Pete the pup, 173–174
Pete the raccoon, 312, 315
Peterson, Rex, 29–31
Petticoat Junction, vii, 120, 141, 244–250
Phantom Empire (movie serial), 109
Phoebe B. Beebe, 299, 300, 303
Picket Fences, 271
Picture Animals Top Star of the Year *see* PATSY Awards
Pig in the City (motion picture), 58
Pigs
    Arnold Ziffel, vii, 122–125, 141
    Jabez the pig, 312, 316
Pinson, Allen, stuntman, 180
Pittman, Cathy, 268–271
Pittman, Gregg, 268, 270
Pixie, 14, 15

Please Don't Eat the Daisies, 250–253
Please Don't Eat the Daisies (motion picture), 141, 225, 251
Poetic Justice (motion picture), 287
Politzer, Merissa, 99
Pope, Bud, 179
Port Charles, 115
Porthos the guinea pig, 312
Powell, Ruth, 284
The Practice, 271
Preminger, Otto, 146
The Pretender, 202
The Price Is Right, 307
Primary Colors (motion picture), 271
Problem Child 2 (motion picture), 204
Profiler, 271
Project X (motion picture), 152
Provost, Jon, 160, 161, 162
Punky Brewster, 120, 254–255, 291

Quincy, 52–53

Race to Space (motion picture), 46
Rags, 283–285
Randall, Glenn, 29–31, 223, 259–261
Randall, Tony, 66
Range Rider, 179
Rats, 78
The Raven (motion picture), 27
Raymond, Bill, 57, 101
    animal handler, 50
Real Kids, Real Adventures, 78
Rebel, 108, 112
Reckless the dog, 312, 313
The Red Hand Gang, 136
Renfro, Bryan, 20–21, 137, 138, 172, 256–258
Renfro, Rennie, 33, 159, 242
Resident Evil (motion picture), 89
Rettig, Tommy, 160, 162
Rex, 274–275, 277–278
Reynolds, Gene, 118, 119
Richards, Billy, 49, 51
Riedell, Bob, 50, 66, 199, 200, 201
The Rifleman, 107
Rin Tin Tin, vii, 4–7, 27
    "the dog that saved Hollywood," 5
Rin Tin Tin K-9 Cop, 256–258
Ringling Brothers and Barnum & Bailey Circus, 121
Ripcord, 94
Ritt, Steven, 193–196
Ritter, John, 139, 140
River Wild (motion picture), 322
Robbins, Charlie, 232–233
The Rockford Files, 120
Rogers, Roy, 7, 55, 107, 111, 258–265
Rogers, Will, 205
Romancing the Stone (motion picture), 28
Rooney, Mickey, 29, 30
Rooster, 23
    Little Jerry Seinfeld, 28
Roseanne, 271
The Rosie O'Donnell Show, 202
Ross, Wally, 50, 152
Roth, Louis, 49
Rover the peacock, 312, 313
Rowe, Clint, 72, 73
Roy Rogers and Dale Evans Museum, 262, 265
Roy Rogers: King of the Cowboys (Rogers, Morris & Pollard), 261
The Roy Rogers Show, 258–265
Run, Joe, Run, 120, 265–267, 298
Runaway Bride (motion picture), 31

Sabrina, the Teenage Witch, 267–271
Salem Saberhagan, 267–271
Salty, 271–272
Salty (cat), 44–46
Salty (sea lion), 271–272
Sam, 273–274
Sam, 273–274
Sanders, Denise, 46, 99
The Santa Clause (motion picture), 58
Santini, Milton, 92
Saturday Night Live, 72
Saukko, Pat, 185, 186
Saukko, Richard, 185, 186
Savage Sam (motion picture), 141
Saved by the Bell, 46
Scarborough, Tex, 50
Schumacher, Lou, 258
    animal supplier, 39, 120, 186–187, 199, 201
Schumacher, Roger, 87, 256–258

Schwartz, Sherwood, 40
Scott, Eugene, 48
Scott, Randolph, 222
Scrooged (motion picture), 194
Scruffy, 118–121
Sea Hunt, 91, 94
Sea lion, Salty, 271–272
Search and Rescue, 58, 78
Secret Chimp, 23, 130
Seinfeld, 28
Seinfeld, Jerry, 1
Sergeant Preston of the Yukon, 274–279
Seven Brides for Seven Brothers (motion picture), 28
The Seven Little Foys (motion picture), 303
Sgt. Bilko (motion picture), 31
The Shaggy Dog, 46
The Shaggy Dog (motion picture), 141
Shampoo (motion picture), 291
Shamus (motion picture), 216
Shannon, Henry, 39, 126, 146, 147, 226
The She Creature (motion picture), 317
Sheena, Queen of the Jungle, 279–280
Sheffield, Johnny, 148, 150
Sigmund the duck, 114–115
Silver, vii, 178–186
Silverman, Joel, 87, 88, 89
Simmons, Richard (actor), 275–278
A Simple Plan (motion picture), 87
Sinbad (camel), 47
Sioux City Sue (motion picture), 109
Skinner, Chuck, 277–278
Skipper (chimp), 23
Skipper (dog), 150
Skippy, 280–283
Skippy (the Bush Kangaroo), 280–283
Skippy's Adventures in Bushtown, 283
Sky King, 56, 179
Sleepwalker (motion picture), 42
Smiley, 12
Smith, Mark, 14
Snow Dog (motion picture), 55
Snowfire (motion picture), 184
Son of Flicka (motion picture), 219
Son of Paleface (motion picture), 262
Speedy, 73–74
Spike the seeing-eye dog, 83–86
Spin City, 283–285
Spitz, Carl Jr., 141, 273–274, 279, 310–312
Spitz, Carl Sr., 274, 276, 310–312
Spoilers of the Plain (motion picture), 264
Spot, 286–288
Spot Marks the X (TV movie), 73
Spuds MacKenzie, 7
    Anheuser-Busch dog, 285–286
The Stalking Moon (motion picture), 274
Stan, 46
Star Trek: The Next Generation, 114, 286–288
Stargate (motion picture), 42
Stark, Mabel, lion tamer, 50
Steel Magnolias (motion picture), 87, 256
Stephen King's Sleepwalkers (motion picture), 11
Stephens, John, 224
The Steve Allen Show, 101
The Steve Harvey Show, 100
Stinky, 69–71
Stop, Sit, and Think (Eisenmann), 178
Storm of the Century (motion picture), 78
The Strawberry Roan (motion picture), 109, 111
The Streets of San Francisco, 120
Striker, Fran, 275
Stroh's Beer Dog (Alex), 7–9
Studio Stables, horses from, 179
Sultan, 47
Summer Rental (motion picture), 87
Swiss Family Robinson (motion picture), 46, 141
Sylvester (motion picture), 31
Sylvester, Julian, 15–17
    herpetologist, 36

Taco Bell Chihuahua, 288–289
Tale of a Dog (motion picture), 173
Tales from the Crypt, 202
Tales of the Gold Monkey, 289–291
Tamba the chimp, 148–150
Target, 14
Tarzan, 291–296
Tarzan (motion picture), 50, 130, 218, 292
Taylor, Elizabeth, 103
Taylor, Ken, 179
Tequila, 296–297
Tequila & Bonetti, 296–297
Terhune, Albert Payson, 251

That Darn Cat (motion picture), 251
Thibodeaux, Keith, 145
Thick as Thieves (motion picture), 271
The Thin Man (motion picture), 120, 158
Third Rock from the Sun, 28, 46
This Boy's Life (motion picture), 204
Thompson, Marshall, 59–67
Thunder, 297–299
Thunder, 297–299
Thunderhead (motion picture), 219
Tiger (dog), 39–40
Tigers, 100
    Sultan, 47
Till There Was You (motion picture), 269
Timmy Briar, 46
Timmy and Lassie, 156
To Kill a Mockingbird (motion picture), 141
To Tell the Truth, 246
Toby Tyler (motion picture), 141, 201
The Today Show, 177, 299–309
Tomboy (motion picture), 114
Tommy Boy (motion picture), 78
The Tonight Show, 125, 177
The Tonight Show with Jay Leno, 100
Topper, 309–312
Topper (horse), 141–144
Tors, Ivan, 59, 60, 61, 91, 94
Toto, 159, 274, 276, 310
Touched by an Angel, 74
Trader Horne's World Jungle Compound, 49
Trail of the Yukon (motion picture), 55
Trainers *see* Animal trainers
Tramp, 141, 223–226
Trendle, George, 182, 275, 276
The Trial of Old Drum (TV movie), 74
Trigger, vii, 55, 258–265
Trigger Trio (motion picture), 312
Tucker's Witch, 28
Turi, Brian, 321
Twiford, Curly, 27, 150
Tyndell, "Chief" Henry, 48, 50

The Ugly Dachshund (motion picture), 141, 251
Under Western Stars (motion picture), 259
USA High, 46

Van Dyke, Charles, 182
Van Dyke, Jerry, 52
Vance, Jerry, 184
Volcano (motion picture), 204

Waldo, 141, 226–227
The Waltons, 28, 125, 312–316
Ward, Bill, horse supplier, 179, 180, 183, 184, 185
Ward, Carl, 206
Warlock, Dick, stuntman, 185
Washbrook, Johnny, 219–221
Watchers (motion picture), 255
Watchers IV (motion picture), 74
Wayne, John, 222
Weatherwax, Bill, 19
Weatherwax, Frank, 32, 317
Weatherwax, Jack, 120
Weatherwax, Larry, son of Frank, 32
Weatherwax, Richard, son of Frank, 19, 317
Weatherwax, Robert, son of Rudd, 157, 158, 163–165, 267
Weatherwax, Rudd, 18–19, 33, 120, 157–161, 163, 165, 242, 243, 267, 317
Webb, Jack, 273–274
Weber, Robert, 283
Weissmuller, Johnny, 50, 51, 130, 148–149
Wells, Hubert, 151
    lion trainer, 36, 37, 38
The Westerner, 316–318
Westfall, Dan, 127
What Lies Beneath (motion picture), 87
What's My Line?, 125, 307
Where the North Begins (motion picture), 5
The White Dog (motion picture), 255
White Shadow, 54–56
Who's Who in Western Stars, 110
Wiener Dog, 230–231
Wild Is the Wind (motion picture), 103
Will and Grace, 28
Willard (motion picture), 27
Williams, Barry, 40
Williamson, Bill, 135
Wishbone, vii, 318–322
Wishbone, 318–322
Wishbone's Dog Days of the West (motion picture), 321
The Witching Hour (motion picture), 87

Withrow, Nancy, 321
The Wizard of Oz (motion picture), 27, 274, 276, 310
Wolf, 74–75
The Wolf Hunters (motion picture), 55
Wolves, 41–42
Wonderboys (motion picture), 89
Woodley, Steve, 41–44
Woods, Sammy, 127
    see also Detroy, Gene
Working, 46
World Jungle Compound, home base for movie animal stars, 49–52
Wrather, Jack, 182, 183
W. W. and the Dixie Dance Kings (motion picture), 132

The X-Files, 102

A Yank in Vietnam (motion picture), 59
Yodelin' Kid from Pine Ridge (motion picture), 112
You Too, 57
Young, Alan, 206, 208, 209, 210, 211, 212, 213
Yukon Gold (motion picture), 56
Yukon King, 274–278
Yukon Manhunt (motion picture), 56
Yukon Vengeance (motion picture), 56

The Zack Files, 76
Zamba the lion, 217, 218
Zebra, Pajama Tops, 56
Zebra in the Kitchen (motion picture), 94, 197, 201
Zeus, 191–193